DELINQUENT
VIOLENT YOUTH

ADVANCES IN ADOLESCENT DEVELOPMENT

AN ANNUAL BOOK SERIES

Series Editors:
Gerald R. Adams, *University of Guelph, Ontario, Canada*
Raymond Montemayor, *Ohio State University*
Thomas P. Gullotta, *Child and Family Agency, Connecticut*

Advances in Adolescent Development is an annual book series designed to analyze, integrate, and critique an abundance of new research and literature in the field of adolescent development. Contributors are selected from numerous disciplines based on their creative, analytic, and influential scholarship in order to provide information pertinent to professionals as well as upper-division and graduate students. The Series Editors' goals are to evaluate the current empirical and theoretical knowledge about adolescence, and to encourage the formulation (or expansion) of new directions in research and theory development.

Volumes in This Series

DELINQUENT VIOLENT YOUTH
Theory and Interventions

Edited by

Thomas P. Gullotta
Gerald R. Adams
Raymond Montemayor

ADVANCES IN ADOLESCENT DEVELOPMENT

An Annual Book Series Volume 9

SAGE Publications
International Educational and Professional Publisher
Thousand Oaks London New Delhi

For information:

SAGE Publications, Inc.
2455 Teller Road
Thousand Oaks, California 91320
E-mail: order@sagepub.com

SAGE Publications Ltd.
6 Bonhill Street
London EC2A 4PU
United Kingdom

SAGE Publications India Pvt. Ltd.
M-32 Market
Greater Kailash I
New Delhi 110 048 India

Printed in the United States of America

Library of Congress: 90-657291

ISSN 1050-8589

ISBN 0-7619-1334-3 (cl.)

ISBN 0-7619-1335-1 (pbk.)

This book is printed on acid-free paper.

99 00 01 02 03 04 10 9 8 7 6 5 4 3 2

Acquiring Editor:	C. Deborah Laughton
Editorial Assistant:	Eileen Carr
Production Editor:	Astrid Virding
Production Assistant:	Lynn Miyata
Typesetter/Designer:	Marion Warren
Print Buyer:	Anna Chin

Contents

Introduction

In this volume of **Advances in Adolescent Development,** we examine selected aspects of criminal and violent behavior among young people. In keeping with the mission of this book series, we have invited a distinguished group of scholars from different disciplines and different perspectives to examine this topic. Our intention is to provide the reader with the views of different disciplines on this issue of concern.

The issue of criminal behavior among our youth is deeply troubling to Americans. It does not fit our desired understanding of adolescence. Is not adolescence an awkward retrospectively humorous time of growth? Is not adolescence an introspective attempt to define oneself in the context of time, place, and others? Is not adolescence a time of innocent blunders and foolish escapades? For some young people, the answer to these questions is yes—sometimes. But there are other times that adolescence does not follow the script of the television situation comedy. There is crushing poverty that makes black market activities such as drugs and prostitution appealing. There is the absence of the one meaningful, lasting adult friendship that all youth need to grow up successfully. There is a profound depression among growing numbers of youth that life—any life—has value.

In the first chapter, Robert Googins contrasts the writings of Charles Dickens's urban environment with those of Mark Twain's rural settings and the social conditions of the late 1800s that led to the development of the juvenile justice system. Mark Eddy and Laurie Swanson Gribskov continue this discussion in the second chapter, introducing the reader to the theoretical and social policy thinking that helped shape society's responses to youth in trouble. In the next chapter, Ruth Seydlitz and Pam Jenkins examine the vast literature concerning how families, peers, schools, and the community influence delinquent behavior. This is followed by Carl Leukefeld and his associates' investigation of the role that substances play in delinquent behavior. In the fifth chapter, Robert Sege discusses the influ-ence that television has on violent behavior in childhood and adoles-cence.

The remainder of the book focuses attention on treatment and prevention interventions for youth involved in or at risk for involve-ment with the criminal justice system. For example, in Chapter 6, Charles Borduin and Cindy Schaeffer examine conceptual issues and research findings pertaining to the nature and treatment of violent criminal behavior in adolescents and the implications these have for treatment. In Chapter 7, Daniel Flannery, Ronald Huff, and Michael Manos provide a developmental perspective of youth gangs. In this chapter, these scholars define gangs, gang activity, and the role of gang activity in adolescent life. They conclude this chapter with a discussion of those interventions that have shown promise and those that have failed in modifying gang activity. Next, Cassandra Stanton and Aleta Meyer survey the literature to identify effective commu-nity-based approaches for treating juvenile offenders. This is fol-lowed in Chapter 9 with an examination of effective interventions for incarcerated youth by Evvie Becker and Annette Rickel. The volume concludes with a provocative chapter by Martin Bloom on the pro-motion of juvenile rightency. In that chapter, Martin appropriately challenges us to consider the potential of youth rather than their all-too-numerous (perceived) deficiencies.

To the graduate student, program director, or clinician who wants to increase her or his knowledge of violent delinquent behavior, this volume offers a solid overview. It reviews the current knowledge and provides clear direction to services that appear promising. To the policymaker interested in establishing sound approaches to dealing with violent delinquent youth, this volume provides guidance in choosing those approaches that work and those that do not. It is our hope that the reader will take this knowledge and apply it to the promotion of juvenile rightency.

—THOMAS P. GULLOTTA
Child and Family Agency
of Southeastern Connecticut

1. Reflections on Delinquency, Dickens, and Twain

Robert Googins

Victorian literature enthusiasts, and particularly students of Dickens and Twain, are aware that the social issues addressed by novelists of that era are virtually the same as those we confront today. In looking back at the amazing technological advances achieved by humans in the past 200 years, it is disheartening to view the relative stagnation in progress concerning our ability to resolve social conflicts. It seems incongruous that we can put people on the moon and scientifically explore our universe yet remain unable to maintain peace and civility on earth—as the strife and atrocities in the former Yugoslavia and in too many of the developing countries painfully remind us.

Needless to say, man's inhumanity to man is not limited to under-developed countries or totalitarian regimes, because both Great Britain and the United States—each a bastion of democracy and haven of human rights—deal with intolerance and incivility in our cities, streets, and homes as poverty, drugs, and crime take their toll.

One troubling aspect of crime and social disorder relates to how society deals with youthful offenders and those in need of special care to avoid delinquency and a subsequent life of crime. Particularly bothersome is the apparent increase in violent juvenile crime and the age at which serious crime is being committed. Several highly publicized serious incidents involving young children in the United States and England have focused attention on the different issues such occurrences raise. Indeed, the media are replete with appalling stories of juvenile misconduct on a regular basis.

In just the past few years, headlines have reported

- that a 9-year-old was named as the suspect in the stabbing of a 12-year-old during an argument (Halloran, 1996)
- that an 11-year-old murderer was killed by his own gang, which feared that he might confess (Grace, 1994)

1

- that a 14-year-old girl was being held in the stabbing death of a cab driver, a crime that was committed while she was a runaway from a youthful offender program (Kauffman, 1996b)
- that a 13-year-old rapist would be the first youthful offender to be tried as an adult under a new North Carolina law (Lacayo, 1994)
- that a 17-year-old slaughters four people (Leukhardt, 1996)
- that a 1-month-old baby was savagely beaten by a 6-year-old, who is believed to be the youngest person ever charged with attempted murder in the United States ("From the Fists of Babes," 1996; Jacobs, 1996)

Yet as the chapters in this volume suggest, greater progress has been made over the past 100 years in how we deal with juveniles than in other aspects of dealing with social problems. Recently, however, calls are increasing to return to older times and treat juveniles as adults for serious offenses committed by those approaching adult status ("Dole Gets Tough," 1996; Jacobs, 1996). As attention is drawn to violent crime committed by juveniles, the public has called for tougher sanctions. In response, a number of states have enacted laws giving government officials greater latitude in prosecuting minor criminals as adults. This is particularly the case where the minor has a prior history of egregious conduct (Brown, 1993; "Juvenile Justice Under Fire," 1986; Nethaway, 1996).

This trend is not limited to the United States; leaders here and in Great Britain have called for treating certain youthful offenders as adults. At the outset of his second term, President Clinton has joined the chorus calling for such treatment. Consistent with this tougher stance, a number of leaders have also called for the public release of the names of juveniles responsible for serious crimes or those involving gangs, drugs, or guns, and that their criminal record should stay with them as a permanent blot ("Dole Gets Tough," 1996; Hall, 1997; Hayward, 1995; Jacobs, 1996; Wintour, 1993).

Another popular trend in attempting to deal with the problem of juvenile delinquency and crime is to place greater legal responsibility on the parents. In the United States, recent attention was given to a Michigan couple who were fined for the criminal conduct of their son, based upon a recently enacted city ordinance. Although another parent of a teenage truant escaped a fine in Great Britain (angering education officials), the parent was expected to improve her escorting of her child to and from school each day (Goodman, 1996; Kauffman, 1996a; Smolowe, 1996).

The news coverage associated with the 14-year-old girl held in the stabbing death of the cab driver cited at least 10 states that had passed laws making parents responsible for the acts of their children with the possibility of imprisonment for up to 6 months for the "improper supervision of a minor." Other proposals to keep pressure on parents involve fines or the reduction of welfare payments, assessing parents the costs of keeping children in juvenile detention centers, and the requirement that parents undergo mandatory counseling (Kauffman, 1996b).

In reviewing the development of the law's treatment of juveniles, it occurred to me that this progress could be related in terms of the lives and characters of the two novelists who were the first to make children the central characters of many of their works and who lived in England and the United States during a period of major change in the laws dealing with crime—Charles Dickens (1812-1870) and Mark Twain (1835-1910). This chapter examines these authors in that light.

PRE-DICKENS DEVELOPMENT

There is little doubt that deviant behavior in children is as old as humankind and that parents were looked to as responsible for their discipline. The stern Puritan code of the Bay Colony in America held parents accountable for the acts of their children—accountability that has just received new attention in the United States. Unruly children could be taken from their parents after appropriate warning, and magistrates could order them to be whipped. The laws of 1668 allowed for the commitment of stubborn children to a House of Correction (Lerman, 1970).

With respect to criminal conduct, the English common law developed to treat children younger than age 7 as being incapable of a crime; from ages 7 to 14, children were presumed incapable of criminal design, but this presumption could be rebutted; and children older than age 14 were presumed responsible for their acts (Parsloe, 1978). English law also developed the concept of *parens patriae*, whereby the sovereign assumed responsibility for children in need of protection— a function assumed by the Court of Chancery, that institution so roundly criticized in Dickens's (1853/1894) *Bleak House*.

American colonists established their system of law based on the common law of England and on aspects of the Poor Laws, which placed control of vagrants and support of the infirm, young, and the poor in the hands of local guardians (Parsloe, 1978). Notwithstanding this concern for children in need, when it came to dealing with children accused of a crime, the early American practice provided no haven for children, who were often punished more severely than adults. Similarly, at the end of the 1700s in Britain, the criminal law (the "bloody code") was probably at its most severe, with more than 200 offenses carrying the death penalty—a counterproductive harshness that often caused some offenders to be overlooked. Yet even into the early 1800s, children were still being imprisoned or transported for what would now be viewed as trivial offenses (Collins, 1964; Parsloe, 1978).

Both in England and America, children were subject to the death penalty. The Gordon Riots—the subject of Dickens's (1841/1894) *Barnaby Rudge*—reflect death sentences carried out on children. In Chapter 74, Denis, the hangman, recalls

> the great estimation in which his office was held, and the constant demand for his services; when he bethought himself, how the Statute Book regarded him as a kind of Universal Medicine applicable to men, women, and children, of every age and variety of criminal constitution. (p. 103)

In America, young females, one as young as 12 in 1786, have been executed for crimes. Even as late as 1912, a 16-year-old was executed in Virginia for murder (Streib & Sametz, 1989).

CHANGES IN THE 19TH CENTURY

Whereas the 1700s produced some evidence of the need for treating children differently from adults, the 19th century resulted in substantial change both in England and the United States as the change to an industrial society unfolded. It is in this period that the young heroes and heroines of Dickens and Twain lived, although in dramatically different circumstances that often contrasted the city streets of London with the pastoral setting of Hannibal, Missouri.

When the infant Dickens saw the first light of day in 1812, no separate system of justice for children existed. Youthful offenders were subject to the same courts, punishment, and prison as adults, and the Old Bailey witnessed the execution of a 13-year-old in 1831. However, in the early part of the century, English magistrates were searching for better ways to deal with children, and the practice of releasing youthful offenders to their parents or masters developed (Parsloe, 1978).

In 1823, a separate hulk, like the ones observed by Pip in *Great Expectations* (Dickens, 1861/1894), was set aside for children, and 15 years later, a separate facility was established on the Isle of Wight for boys awaiting transportation—the fate that awaited Kit, wrongfully convicted of the theft of a five pound note in the *Old Curiosity Shop* (Dickens, 1841/1894). In 1839, England developed a special institution for juvenile offenders, and a year later, a bill was introduced into Parliament that, if passed, would have established a separate juvenile court system (Parsloe, 1978).

Across the Atlantic, civic-minded citizens concerned with children in New York established a House of Refuge in Madison Square in 1825, and the following year, public funds were allocated to its support. The city of Boston opened a House of Reformation to take youths convicted of a crime and, by the time of Dickens's visit to Boston in 1842, had established its Boylston School for potential delinquents (Lerman, 1970; Parsloe, 1978).

By the middle part of the century, the reform school movement replaced the Houses of Refuge. Following the establishment of the first public juvenile institution in New Orleans in 1845, New York established its state agricultural and industrial school. On the West Coast, in California, an industrial school for boys and girls was founded in 1859 and a reform school was opened in 1861. However, immediately prior to that, boys as young as 12 were imprisoned in the state prisons at San Quentin and Folsom (Fact Sheet, n.d.; Parsloe, 1978).

In 1869, Indiana had set up a reformatory institution for women and girls, and by the following year, a number of states had separate institutions or training schools for delinquents. In 1876, the first major correctional institution for juveniles was established—the New York Reformatory at Elmira. With the growth of the reformatory movement, other juvenile institutions were relieved of older and more troublesome inhabitants (Lerman, 1970; Parsloe, 1978).

Back in England, similar developments were taking place. Under the Larceny Act of 1847, magistrates were empowered to deal with children younger than 14 in a summary fashion, and later magistrates were able to send children to workhouses to await trial rather than to jail—formalizing a practice already employed by some magistrates. The Youthful Offender Act enacted by Parliament in 1854 gave the courts power to commit children to reformatories, although a compromise in the tension between the "punishment" and "welfare" approaches required that offenders spend the first 14 days in prison (Parsloe, 1978).

The Youthful Offender Act created a three-part system of local courts, the central government, and voluntary bodies (schools and reformatories). The Industrial School Act of 1857 provided for juvenile nonoffenders in need of care. The predecessor of these institutions were the "ragged schools," which were outside the system of justice and offered poor children at risk an opportunity for education and guidance. Dickens was a great supporter of the need to provide children at risk with an education and often visited the ragged schools (Ackroyd, 1990).

The first part of the century was dominated by voluntary efforts to aid children and the recognition of the need to separate youthful offenders from adults; the century ended with a major event that would shape the reform in the 1900s—the establishment of the first official juvenile court in Cook County, Illinois, and the passage of the Juvenile Court Act by the Illinois legislature. This Act provided for the decriminalization of offenses committed by children and was a major innovation and shifted the balance in the new Juvenile Courts toward a "welfare" approach in dealing with juvenile offenders (Lerman, 1970; Parsloe, 1978).

THE 20TH CENTURY

Led by the Indiana inaugural of a separate juvenile court system, other states followed suit, and in 1923, the National Probation Association proposed a Standard Juvenile Court Act at its annual conference. By 1925, all but two states had juvenile courts, and by the mid-century mark, Maine and Wyoming had joined the movement (Parsloe, 1978).

However, despite the development of a Standard Juvenile Court Act, there was still a wide disparity between states as to the jurisdiction of such courts and the handling of juveniles—although the trend for separating juveniles from adults continued. Furthermore, the financial turmoil produced by the Depression in the early 1930s, with the attendant governmental budget problems, stemmed the progress of the development of a full-fledged juvenile justice system.

Although the 1940s and 1950s saw the increase in intervention strategies involving intensive counseling and training, this period also saw the development of large detention facilities. Moreover, the decriminalized and less formal proceeding founded on the *parens patriae* approach had deprived juveniles of many of the legal rights afforded adults, which would become the focus of later attention (Lerman, 1970; Parsloe, 1978).

In England, the turn of the century also saw renewed attention to the youthful offender with the passage of the Probation of Offenders Act in 1907, and the following year saw the adoption of the Children Act of 1908, which required the establishment of juvenile courts as well as the codification of a number of acts and practices dealing with juveniles. However, unlike their companions in the United States, the English juvenile courts took the form of special sittings of magistrate courts with both criminal and civil jurisdiction. As a result of the retention of the criminal jurisdiction in the English juvenile courts, the traditional legal rights afforded adults generally applied, in contrast to the early development of such courts in the United States (Parsloe, 1978).

Later, hanging as a punishment was eliminated for those younger than age 18; whipping was ended in 1948, and prison assignments were effected. Further emphasis on prevention and the welfare of the child came about under the 1969 Children and Young Persons Act (Parsloe, 1978).

THE DICKENS INVOLVEMENT

As Philip Collins (1964) noted, Dickens's lifetime coincided with one of the greatest periods of legal and penal reform in English history. In her first speech to Parliament, Queen Victoria noted the changes regarding capital punishment, and by the middle of her reign, almost every aspect of the social treatment of crime had been overhauled.

Moreover, Dickens was a part of this change because he continually confronted the public with the system's failings—particularly where children were concerned. He was appalled by a system that could witness the hanging of a 9-year-old in 1831 for setting fire to a home, or the whipping of hungry children caught stealing bread. His weekly journalistic efforts often cited the sad record of unjust punishment inflicted on children who could know no better. The preface to *Barnaby Rudge* cites the notorious case of Mary Jones, who was hung in 1771 for shoplifting to help her starving children. This event was also incorporated in Chapter 37 of the novel as the hangman recalls "a young woman of nineteen who came up to Tyburn with an infant at her breast, and [was] worked off for taking a piece of cloth off the counter of a shop" (Dickens, 1841/1894, p. 300). The plight of the weak, women, children, and the powerless was a continuous focus of his writings from his early stories in *Sketches by Boz* (Dickens, 1837/1894) to his last novels and journalism.

His writings reflect a fascination with crime, penal institutions, the police detective, workhouses, schools, and social institutions that aided or abused the downtrodden. They also reflect his belief that if children were provided with a proper education, they would acquire the moral character and work skills that would enable them to make an honest living and shun a life of crime. Dickens was a prominent supporter of poor children's education. He closely followed the Ragged School movement of the 1840s (where he supposedly met the children Ignorance and Want made famous in *A Christmas Carol*) and played a lead role in establishing refuges for fallen women roaming the streets of London (Ackroyd, 1990). In "The Prisoners Van" in *Sketches by Boz* (Dickens, 1837/1894), the author bemoans the plight of a 14-year-old girl thrown on the London streets by a rapacious mother.

Dickens also understood the need to keep juvenile offenders away from hardened criminals, as Rose Maylie urged that young Oliver Twist (Dickens, 1838/1894) not be sent to prison, where he would have no hope for "amendment." Subsequently, Dickens was encouraged by improvements in the English prison system as control shifted away from local government and greater attention was given to instruction, probation, and, it is hoped, redemption.

MARK TWAIN

Although both Dickens and Twain had similar backgrounds and common influences (journalism, keen observation, great insight about the human character), the youths that they portrayed in their works often had disparate backgrounds. Despite occasional forays into the countryside, Dickens's adolescents were products of the city, whereas Twain's were products of his childhood days in St. Petersburg (Hannibal, Missouri). The resulting differences were stark.

Aside from childish pranks, the occasional purloined river raft, a modicum of truancy, and the proverbial missing pie once cooling on the windowsill, Huck and Tom were products of an agrarian community where street crime was not a common ingredient of daily living. There was not a major gulf between the "model boy" Willie Mufferson and Tom Sawyer—or even Huck, for that matter.

Although Injun Joe, the Duke, and Dauphin were often just two steps ahead of "the law", Dickens's children were often caught up in it, from the Artful Dodger and the rest of Fagin's boys to Barnaby Rudge and his companions and poor Kit, wrongfully imprisoned and sentenced to transportation for the alleged theft of a five-pound note. Tom Sawyer never had to meet Mr. Fang, the police magistrate confronted by Oliver Twist, nor were any of Twain's children denizens of prison, "born and bred in neglect and vice, who have never known what childhood is," as the young girl encountered in Dickens's "A Visit to Newgate" in *Sketches by Boz* (Dickens, 1837/1894, p. 190).

Indeed, one can surmise that Hannibal, Missouri and environs was just the kind of setting that young boys, uncared for in New York City, were being sent to by the New York House of Refuge and the Children's Aid Society. Moreover, although it would be difficult to classify Huck as other than poor and neglected, one never gets the sense of his living in miserable squalor, subject to the dangers of a big city such as the fate of Jo and the Neckett children of *Bleak House's* Tom-all-Alones (Dickens, 1853/1894).

CONCLUSION

From time to time, the literary children of both Dickens and Twain ran afoul of the law or were in need of the intervention of social service agencies that exist today but that were few and far between in their literary lifetimes. Both in terms of the application of criminal codes and the availability of services for children in need of protection, we have made progress. But those forward strides are tenuous at best, as the morning newspaper and the evening television broadcasts detailing juvenile crime and returns to harsher sentencing painfully remind us. The remaining chapters of this volume show how little progress has been made in some areas (e.g., in Chapter 5 on the continuing negative influence television exerts on behavior) and greater progress in others (e.g., in Chapter 8 on community treatment interventions). Clearly, we have a long way to go to ensure that youth are treated with the forgiving firmness found in the fictional stories of Twain and in the pleas of Dickens.

REFERENCES

Brown, C. (1993, October 19). Minister attacks child criminals. *The Independent*, Home News section, p. 9.

Collins, P. (1964). *Dickens and crime* (2nd ed.), London: Macmillan.

Dickens, C. (1894). *Sketches by Boz*. New York: Houghton Mifflin. (Originally published in 1837)

Dickens, C. (1894). *Oliver Twist*. New York: Houghton Mifflin. (Originally published in 1838)

Dickens, C. (1894). *Barnaby Rudge*. New York: Houghton Mifflin. (Originally published in 1841)

Dickens, C. (1894). *The old curiosity shop*. New York: Houghton Mifflin. (Originally published in 1841)

Dickens, C. (1894). *Bleak House*. New York: Houghton Mifflin. (Originally published in 1853)

Dickens, C. (1894). *Great expectations*. New York: Houghton Mifflin. (Originally published in 1861)

Dole gets tough on juvenile criminals. (1996, July 7). *The Hartford Courant*, p. A7.

Fact Sheet. (n.d.). U.S. Attorneys Office, San Diego. Unpublished.

From the fists of babes. (1996, May 6). *Time*, p. 38.

Goodman, E. (1996, May 22). The sins of the son. *The Atlanta Journal and Constitution*, p. 15A.

Grace, J. (1994, September 12). There are no children here. *Time*.

Hall, M. (1997, February 20). Clinton pushes juvenile crime plan: $495 million is requested for initiative. *USA Today*, p. 4A.

Halloran, L. (1996, November 10). Boy, 12, stabbed: 9 year old is suspect. *The Hartford Courant*, p. B1.

Hayward, M. (1995, June 4). Reform would put delinquents in spotlight. *The Union Leader*, p. B1.

Jacobs, J. (1996, May 22). Candidates peddling baloney: Juvenile crime problems must be solved locally [Editorial]. *The Atlanta Journal and Constitution*, p. 14A.

Juvenile justice under fire: Status offenders and those who commit serious crimes. (1986, November 3). *Scholastic Update*, p. 3.

Kauffman, M. (1996a, June 2). Holding parents responsible, liable. *The Hartford Courant*, p. 1.

Kauffman, M. (1996b, October 11). Girl, 14, rejects plea in killing city cabdriver. *The Hartford Courant*, p. A3.

Lacayo, R. (1994, October 19). When kids go bad. *Time*, p. 60.

Lerman, P. (1970). *Delinquency and social policy*. New York: Praeger.

Leukhardt, B. (1996, October 2). Teen suspect in Southington killings arrested. *The Hartford Courant*, p. A3.

Nethaway, R. (1996, May 22). Americans are confused: Government should do what it can to encourage parental responsibility [Editorial]. *The Atlanta Journal and Constitution*, p. 15A.

Parsloe, P. (1978). *Juvenile justice in Britain and the United States*. New York: Routledge.

Smolowe, J. (1996, May 20). Parenting on trial. *Time*, p. 50.

Streib, V., & Sametz, L. (1989). 22 *Connecticut Law Review*.

Wintour, P. (1993, March 1). Youth reoffences should count. *The Guardian*, Home Section, p. 2.

2. Juvenile Justice and Delinquency Prevention in the United States: The Influence of Theories and Traditions on Policies and Practices

J. Mark Eddy
Laurie Swanson Gribskov

During the past decade, official reports of escalating youth gang activity, drug use, and violence (Klein, 1995; Snyder & Sickmund, 1995) in the United States have been highly publicized. Such trends support the common perception that this generation is more out of control than youth of previous generations. Interestingly, this same perception of the increasing danger of youth has been held by American adults at least since delinquency first became a significant social problem (Bernard, 1993; Krisberg & Austin, 1993; Mennell, 1973).

Delinquency ascended to social-problem status during the Industrial Revolution. In one of the largest U.S. population centers at the time, New York City, the first institution of juvenile justice was created soon after this ascent. At the time, the most frequently cited causes for the initiation and maintenance of delinquent behavior were inadequate and criminal parents and association with criminal youth and adults. City leaders decided that removing delinquents and potential delinquents from their parents and from their associates on the city streets was the best solution to the problem. A "refuge

AUTHORS' NOTE: This project was supported by grant MH-37940 from the National Institute of Mental Health to John B. Reid, Ph.D. We express our deep appreciation to librarian Sue Boyd, reporter Joe Kidd, and the reporters for the *Register-Guard* during the past 50 years; Linda Wagner of the Lane County Department of Youth Services; Barbara Seligen of Oregon Juvenile Court Directors Association; Tom English of the Oregon Council on Crime and Delinquency; Craig Campbell, formerly with the Oregon Attorney General's Office; and numerous others for their helpful assistance on the Oregon aspects of this project. Correspondence regarding this chapter may be addressed to J. Mark Eddy, Oregon Social Learning Center (www.oslc.org), 207 E. Fifth Ave., Suite 202, Eugene, OR 97401; (541) 485-2711; FAX (541) 485-7087; marke@oslc.org.

house" was built on the outskirts of town to house troubled youth and to provide occupational, moral, and religious training. The solutions applied by policymakers in subsequent generations have been similarly linked to popular perceptions of the causes of delinquency.

Beginning with the New York City refuge house, in this chapter we provide a historical overview of juvenile justice and delinquency prevention in the United States. We divide the past 200 years into three phases: the creation of the juvenile justice system, the rise of Federalism, and Federalism in action. Within each phase, we first discuss the prevailing theories of delinquency at that time and then highlight the significant policies and practices that were in use. We then provide a description of the modern public policy process and illustrate how theories of delinquency are shaping policy decisions in the present. Finally, we speculate about how decisions in the present might influence future juvenile justice and delinquency prevention policies.

THE PAST

Phase 1: The Creation of the Juvenile Justice System

The primary institutions of juvenile justice in the United States, the juvenile court and the reform school, were created during the 19th century. Although the theories and practices that led to the formation of these institutions were not new, the catalyst that brought them together was: industrialization. As people left the countryside to work in the new factories, city populations began to increase dramatically.

The poor were particularly vulnerable within these new urban areas. The traditional family structures and extended family networks that had socialized and supervised lower-class children were disrupted, and the number of impoverished, unsupervised, and homeless children on city streets swelled. Many of these disenfranchised children simply had no way to survive except through stealing, and juvenile property crimes quickly became the dominant form of crime in urban areas (Bernard, 1993).

Once delinquency was a significant problem, the first systems of juvenile justice were created. As urbanization spread to new locations and delinquency appeared, so did juvenile justice. New justice systems were modeled on the existing systems until jurisdictions throughout the country shared a similar framework.

The Refuge House and Probation

In New York City, one of the first American cities to experience a juvenile crime wave, the process that led to the development of the first system of juvenile justice was initiated by two Protestant (Quaker) prison reformers, Thomas Eddy and John Griscom (Bernard, 1993). Eddy, the first warden of the first adult penitentiary in New York, and Griscom, a professor of philosophy and chemistry, brought together a group of community leaders to discuss the problem of delinquency and to generate solutions.

Influencing Theories

Original sin. Christianity, specifically Protestantism, was the dominant religion in the United States (Martin, 1985). U.S. Protestants of the 19th century believed that since creation, humans tended to behave in ways that separated them from the goodness of God (i.e., to sin). A variety of behaviors were considered sinful, including the stealing of property. If a sin was committed, a person was considered to be separated from God until forgiveness was sought. People unrepentant for their sins were thought to be doomed to unhappiness not only in this life but in "life" after death.

Members of the upper classes commonly believed that many of the poor were poor because they had unrepentantly sinned against God (Bernard, 1993). The term "pauper" was used to describe these "evil" poor. Paupers were blamed for numerous urban problems, including the existence of large numbers of potential paupers: their unsupervised, delinquent children. It was believed that the best counter to future pauperism was to provide proper religious and practical training early in life to potential paupers. Because paupers were seen as "lost" to evil, they were not considered appropriate individuals to provide such training for their children. Thus, within this belief system, an alternative "parent" was needed for delinquent youth.

Classical theory. In concert with the idea of original sin, the dominant philosophy of the 18th century viewed humans as self-centered creatures who were motivated by the pursuit of pleasure and the avoidance of pain (Leahey, 1980). Philosophers believed that the impact of consequences (i.e., pleasure or pain) following a behavior influenced whether or not a behavior would occur again (Gottfredson & Hirschi, 1990). Jeremy Bentham extended this framework to criminal behavior, writing about how consequences intentionally applied by the state could have an optimal impact on the criminal behavior of individuals (Bentham, 1789/1970). Classical theory thus supported the idea that in the case of delinquent youth, the state could successfully assume the role of "parent."

Policies and Practices

The Refuge House. Both the tradition of original sin and classical theory supported a system that offered delinquent and predelinquent youth new "parents" to train them how to function in society. Within the next 50 years, two variations on this general theme arose: the institution as parent (i.e., the refuge house) and the court as parent (i.e., the probation officer). The New York City group of community leaders, christened the Society for the Prevention of Pauperism, studied the problem of youth crime and concluded that many delinquents did indeed have parents who had failed in their duties (Bernard, 1993). Compounding this problem, youth who were convicted of crimes at that time were placed into adult penitentiaries, and the Society was concerned that this practice gave delinquents new "parents" who simply exacerbated the initial problem: "The penitentiary cannot but be a fruitful source of pauperism, a nursery of new vices and crimes, a college for the perfection of adepts in guilt" (Pierce, 1869/1969, p. 40).

With these two ideas in mind, the Society changed its name to the Society for the Reformation of Juvenile Delinquents and dedicated itself to the construction of a youth "house of refuge" on farmland outside the city. The refuge house was intended to provide rehabilitation and training not only for "true" delinquents (generally, someone who stole property) but also for children judged to be at risk for delinquency and adult pauperism. Once committed, a youth remained at the house until adulthood (i.e., age 21).

Although seemingly a "new" idea, the refuge house was the 19th-century version of a 17th-century English institution, the poorhouse (Bernard, 1993). Impoverished urban youth were placed in poorhouses and eventually apprenticed out to work in rural areas (Trattner, 1974). Poorhouses were used in the American colonies but had fallen out of vogue by the turn of the 19th century. The refuge houses rejuvenated many poorhouse practices, including placing youth out into farming apprenticeships. By the turn of the 20th century, many localities had refuge houses, which by that point had been renamed "industrial," "trade," "training," or "reform" schools (The President's Commission, 1967).

The probation officer. Whereas some children were apprenticed into rural foster homes from the refuge houses, other children were placed directly from the streets into foster families. Once again, this was the revival of an earlier practice. During the 1700s, it was common in small towns to bind problematic children to families assumed to be more suitable child rearers than their biological families (Mennell, 1973). In the 1840s, a Boston shoemaker named John Augustus renewed this practice by bailing out both adults and boys and bringing them into his home in an attempt to "reform" them (Moreland, 1941).

Court officials apparently thought that Augustus was quite successful in his attempts, and in 1869, his work led to the employment of agents in Massachusetts courts charged with protecting the best interests of youth during court proceedings. The tasks of court agents included investigating the background of the accused youth, monitoring the legal process, and supervising the youth after his disposition. In 1878, these practices were formalized further through a Massachusetts state law requiring paid probation officers in all courts (Schultz, 1973). Within 25 years, similar laws were passed in various states throughout the country.

The Juvenile Court

By the mid-19th century, 40,000 youth were held in more than 20 refuge houses throughout the United States (Pierce, 1869/1969). As resident populations in the houses increased, problems arose, including increasing levels of youth violence within the houses (Bernard, 1993). Gradually, the principle of committing children who had not committed any crime (i.e., potential paupers) to the houses began to be challenged.

One of the most significant challenges occurred in Illinois. In the late 1860s, the Illinois State Supreme Court accepted the case of

Daniel O'Connell, a poor boy with no criminal record who had been committed to the new Chicago Reform School (Pickett, 1969). O'Connell's parents protested his placement, and eventually, the case reached the high court. The court ruled that O'Connell be released, commenting, "Why should minors be imprisoned for misfortune? Destitution of proper parental care, ignorance, idleness and vice, are misfortunes, not crimes" (Mennell, 1973, p. 125).

Following the O'Connell ruling, "preventive" institutionalization of presumed predelinquents decreased. By the turn of the century, the ruling was cited as the cause of the collapse of the reform schools in Illinois (Mennell, 1973). This collapse was felt most acutely in the metropolis of Chicago, which had grown from a population of 5,000 people in 1840 to a population of 1,500,000 people in 1900 (Finestone, 1976). Juvenile crime was viewed as a major problem within the city, and there was widespread agreement that a new approach was needed to control the problem. This new approach was influenced both by English and American legal traditions and by social interpretations of Darwin's theory of evolution.

Influencing Theories

Legal traditions. Since feudal times, the English chancery court had asserted protective jurisdiction over children on behalf of the king in cases where the property rights of a child were jeopardized (i.e., a practice referred to as *parens patriae,* or parent of the country). When the English system was brought to North America, the chancery court's protection was extended to children at risk for personal injury (The President's Commission, 1967). While chancery court protection was restricted to dependent and neglected children, English common law specifically addressed delinquent children. Under common law, children younger than age 7 were presumed to be incapable of criminal intent, and children between the ages of 7 and 14 years were presumed incapable unless proven otherwise (Glueck & Glueck, 1934). These assumptions supported the extension of court protection to the delinquent and predelinquent children who had traditionally populated the refuge houses and reform schools but who were now roaming the streets of Chicago.

Social Darwinism and atavism. From the beginning, not only had most children committed to the refuge houses been poor, but their ethnicity had reflected the prejudices of governing leaders. For example, not long after the influx of large numbers of Irish Catholics into Protestant-controlled New York City, Irish Catholic children comprised most of the population of the New York City refuge house (Finestone, 1976). Following the publication of Charles Darwin's extension of evolution theory to humans (Darwin, 1871), "Social Darwinism" became quite popular in the United States (Leahey, 1980) and was used to justify discriminatory actions against ethnic groups.

Social Darwinists posited that some racial groups were more highly evolved than others. White Anglo-Saxon Protestants, who dominated the political and economic power structures of the 19th-century United States, were considered the most highly evolved group. The presumably less evolved groups (i.e., non-White Anglo-Saxon Protestants) were seen as the source of social problems because of their inferior genetic constitution.

While Social Darwinism was being embraced by the American public, an Italian prison doctor named Cesare Lombroso applied Darwinian ideas to crime. Based on his work with hundreds of prisoners, Lombroso hypothesized that criminals possessed evolutionarily inferior (i.e., atavistic) physical and cognitive traits (Lotz, Poole, & Regoli, 1985). Although his research methods were flawed, Lombroso was the first criminological theorist to base his theory at least partially on actual field observations rather than on purely philosophical arguments (Wolfgang, 1961).

Lombroso's ideas about the evolutionary inferiority of criminals fit well with the American ideas about the evolutionary superiority of the leading Whites. Within the United States, not only were Social Darwinism and atavism used to justify the institutionalization of immigrant (and impoverished) delinquents (Empey, 1985), they were also used to justify the forced sterilization of adults thought to possess heritable antisocial traits (Leahey, 1980). In some states, sterilization practices continued until the 1960s.

Policies and Practices

The juvenile court. As the Illinois system for handling delinquents was collapsing, support for developing a new legal solution for delinquency was growing, particularly within the influential Illinois Board of Public Charities and the Chicago Bar Association (Platt, 1977). Following the advocacy work of several elite social reformers such as Julia Lathrop (Carson, 1990), a committee appointed by the Chicago Bar drafted legislation creating a separate court for children (Hawes, 1971; Platt, 1977). The legislation transferred jurisdiction over children from the traditional courts (e.g., criminal court) to a new court dedicated to broadly and exclusively serving the "best interests" of children. Under pressure from members of the Chicago Bar, the Illinois legislature passed the Juvenile Court Act of 1899 (Platt, 1977).

By the time of the Great Depression, almost every state in the union had passed a similar act (Platt, 1977). Under these acts, the juvenile court was established as a county or circuit-level (i.e., a geographic region of a state) court. The jurisdiction of the court included neglected, dependent, and "problem" children, including delinquents. For example, court jurisdiction in Illinois extended from "any child who for any reason is destitute or homeless or abandoned" to "[any child] who is found living in any house of ill fame or with any vicious or disreputable person" to "any child under the age of 8 years who is found peddling or selling any article or singing or playing any musical instrument upon the street or giving any public entertainment" (Mennell, 1973, p. 131). Thus, a child could be brought under the jurisdiction of the court for numerous reasons, including noncriminal offenses that were only a violation of law if committed by children or youth (i.e., "status" offenses).

The new juvenile courts shared several other characteristics as well. Court hearings were designated as nonpublic and informal, and records were confidential. Youth held in jail prior to receiving a disposition were to be detained separately from adults. Probation staff were appointed to supervise progress during and following the "treatment" prescribed by the court. Most importantly, the court was given the broad and undefined task of serving the best interests of the child. Under the "best interests" banner, the court could use a variety of extremely intrusive practices if these were deemed necessary, including the placement of children who had committed relatively trivial offenses into reform schools for lengthy periods of time (The President's Commission, 1967).

The Rise of Clinical and Research Institutions

Although juvenile court legislation in most states was modeled on the Illinois act, there was great variability in the actual practices of the new juvenile courts. By 1920, only 16% of juvenile courts actually conducted separate hearings for children or had official juvenile probation services (Tappan, 1949). Even as late as the 1960s, federal government surveys revealed that there was "nothing uniform" across the country in terms of juvenile court procedures and operations (The President's Commission, 1967). Although the practices of juvenile justice varied immensely, the idealized version of the court as set out in the original legislation changed little during the first half of the century. During this period, the most significant advances relevant to juvenile justice and delinquency prevention were the rise and proliferation of institutions related in some way to the juvenile court system, including child guidance clinics and university social work, sociology, and psychology departments.

Influencing Theories

Psychodynamics. Founding theorist Sigmund Freud and his followers viewed the maladaptive behaviors of youth and adults as manifestations of unconscious mental conflict (Leahey, 1980). This conflict was hypothesized to develop from parent-child interactions during early and middle childhood. Because mental conflict was not directly observable, Freud advocated the observation of the behavior of an individual patient within the context of a doctor-patient relationship. All behaviors within this relationship context, no matter how trivial, were seen as clues to the patient's mental conflict. Through observation over time, it was believed that patterns eventually could be found in the behavior of the patient, and that knowledge of these patterns would lead to a cure.

These ideas were congruent with the philosophy of the new court. For example, children could become eligible for entry into the juvenile justice system for relatively minor offenses or even noncriminal offenses. Once in the system, the courts focused on the individualized assessment and treatment of children brought under their jurisdiction. Furthermore, the confinement of children to institutions for long periods of time facilitated the use of such procedures.

Positivism. Rather than a theory on the cause of delinquency, positivism is a philosophy of science (Leahey, 1980). Positivism was formalized by Auguste Comte in the early and mid-19th century and became the dominant philosophy of scientific researchers during the 20th century. Positivism rejected speculation about unobservable philosophical entities and focused instead on the prediction and control of observable phenomena.

In the study of crime and delinquency, Lombroso was the first to work within the positivist framework. Although Lombroso's ideas about evolution are seen as erroneous today, his emphasis on studying identified "criminals" and his attempt to compare criminals to noncriminals influenced later research on crime and delinquency (Wolfgang, 1961). In contrast, although psychodynamic thought had a significant impact on the treatment practices supported by the juvenile court, psychodynamic theory was rejected even by early academic researchers as nonpositivistic (Leahey, 1980). Thus, Freud and his followers had little influence on later studies of juvenile delinquency.

Social control theory. Comte viewed sociology as the most "comprehensive" and least developed of the sciences (Leahey, 1980). Sociological research did not start in earnest in the United States until the establishment of the first sociology department at the University of Chicago during the early 20th century. With the guidance of Robert Park and George Herbert Mead, the department pioneered the study of social change (Faris, 1967). In the study of juvenile delinquency, the two most prominent figures from the University of Chicago were Clifford Shaw, a former juvenile court probation officer, and Henry McKay.

Shaw and McKay mapped rates of delinquency within several American cities and found support for a "zonal" hypothesis (Burgess, 1929): Delinquency rates peaked in the "transition" and "working-class" neighborhoods (or zones) around the inner business district and declined with increasing distance from these zones (Shaw & McKay, 1942). Within the high delinquency zones, the researchers found numerous problems, including high rates of poverty and adult criminality. Furthermore, they found that delinquency rates tended to be stable across time despite marked shifts in the composition of the population. Shaw and McKay hypothesized that this stability was due to the collapse of traditional social control mechanisms within these zones. Delinquency was thus viewed as one symptom of social disorganization among the lower-income people living within such areas (Shaw & McKay, 1942).

Shaw and McKay hypothesized that the delinquent behavior of youth living in disorganized areas developed in stages. Such behaviors were hypothesized to first occur within the context of the neigh-

borhood peer group. If the local peer culture supported the continuation of such behaviors, a youth would move from experimenting to
systematically committing a variety of antisocial behaviors. As these
behaviors increased in severity, a youth would label himself as a
"deviant" relative to the norms of society. In the final stage of development, the now-deviant youth would eventually become a "professional" criminal. Since their original writings, Shaw and McKay's
ideas on the importance of social context on development, the influence of the peer group, and the movement of youth through stages
have been recycled and refined within numerous theoretical frame-
works relevant to juvenile justice and delinquency prevention.

Policies and Practices

Child guidance clinics. The creation of the formal juvenile court,
the continued lobbying of social reformers, and the rise of formal
psychology and sociology departments in universities all contributed to the development of a new class of government-supported
"experts" on the treatment of delinquency. The first group of
experts to arise were social workers. While social reformers such
as Julia Lathrop and Jane Addams were advocating for a new
juvenile court in Chicago, they were also establishing the first
social work movement (Mennell, 1973; Trattner, 1974). Originally,
the social work movement emphasized true reform: Social workers directly lobbied government and business leaders in an attempt to change economic conditions and social opportunities.
However, while the movement was still in its infancy, it turned
away from this approach and adopted a different strategy: individual casework with the poor (Bernard, 1993).

The interest of Lathrop and Addams in individual casework and
the juvenile court eventually led to the creation of a formal institution
dedicated to casework with delinquents. In 1909, the Juvenile Psychopathic Institute was established to study the backgrounds of
delinquents who went through the Chicago juvenile court. The first
director of the Institute, physician William A. Healy, had studied
in Europe and was familiar with the work of Freud (Krisberg &
Austin, 1993). In concert with psychodynamic practitioners, Healy
believed strongly in the study and treatment of the individual. He
also believed in empirical observation, and he employed some of

Lombroso's anthropometric measurement techniques in his research (Mennell, 1973).

Under the guidance of the first board of directors, which included Julia Lathrop, Healy emphasized the comprehensive evaluation of the youth brought before the court, including their mental and physical "defects," their home and neighborhood environments, and the mental and physical histories of their ancestors (Hawes, 1971). In their new role as caseworkers, social workers had already begun to do similar kinds of evaluations, and thus the institute served as an ideal vehicle for the growth of the profession. In 1911, the tie between social work and the court in Illinois was strengthened even further through the passage of an amendment that granted judges the discretion to distribute government financial aid to poor children (Bernard, 1993).

The "child guidance clinic" model developed at the Juvenile Psychopathic Institute soon spread throughout the United States. Healy was invited to Boston to develop a court-related child guidance clinic at the Judge Harvey Baker Foundation. While in Boston, Healy assisted in the establishment of numerous clinics throughout the United States, each operating in tandem with a local juvenile court. By 1931 alone, more than 232 child guidance clinics were in operation (Krisberg & Austin, 1993).

Effectiveness research. Several years after Healy opened the child guidance clinic at the Judge Harvey Baker Foundation, Sheldon and Eleanor Glueck studied the effectiveness of the treatment methods that Healy and others were advocating. The Gluecks examined the outcome of approximately 1,000 delinquent children who had come through the Boston juvenile court. They found that 88% of these children had committed further offenses within 5 years after the termination of their involvement with the court (Glueck & Glueck, 1934). Even more disconcerting, the Gluecks found that in cases where the treatment recommendations of the child guidance clinic were actually followed by the court, recidivism was still very high. After this initial study, the Gluecks went on to conduct a series of groundbreaking longitudinal studies on delinquency (Glueck & Glueck, 1972; Sampson & Laub, 1994).

Prevention research. Richard Cabot, Sheldon Glueck's former professor and a cousin of the judge who invited William Healy to open a child guidance clinic in Boston, believed the Glueck's findings indicated a lack of knowledge of the causes of delinquency (McCord, 1992). Although he thought that the expansion of such knowledge would improve the efficiency of rehabilitative efforts, Cabot believed he already knew a solution that would decrease delinquency: mentoring. He hypothesized that children could be diverted from committing delinquent behaviors through a long-term relationship with a devoted, non-family-member adult.

Cabot combined a search for knowledge with a test of the effectiveness of mentoring in his Cambridge-Somerville Youth Study, the first large-scale attempt in the United States to systematically study the long-term impact of a preventive intervention for delinquency (McCord, 1992). Participants in the Youth Study were boys under the age of 12 who lived in impoverished areas of eastern Massachusetts. Participants did not have to exhibit deliquent behavior to participate (McCord, 1990).

Using data collected from teachers, physicians, families, neighbors, and the courts, boys were matched on age, intelligence, physique, social environment, "delinquency proneness," and family environment and history (Powers & Witmer, 1951). One boy in the matched pair was randomly assigned to the treatment group, and the other was placed in a control group that received no systematic intervention. Treatment group members were assigned a professional social worker whose tasks were to build a strong personal relationship with the boy and to help the boy and his family in any way possible.

By the time the program ended in 1945, boys in the treatment group had been visited by their mentors an average of twice monthly for more than 5 years. During the course of treatment, most treatment boys had participated in numerous recreational activities, more than 50% had received academic tutoring, and more than 50% had attended summer camps (McCord, 1992). Treatment families received help with a variety of problems, including unemployment and physical illness. In contrast, boys in the control group received no systematic intervention and were excluded from any activities designed especially for the treatment group.

Unfortunately, the results of the Cambridge-Somerville study were as discouraging as those of the Gluecks. By 1948, boys in the treatment group had appeared before the juvenile court as frequently as boys in the control group (Powers & Witmer, 1951). Even more disconcerting, the average number of referrals to the court was the same for both groups. Subsequent follow-ups revealed either no difference between the groups (McCord & McCord, 1959) or a negative impact of treatment relative to control (McCord, 1978, 1981, 1992), including an *increased* likelihood of repeat arrests.

Community research. The findings of the Gluecks did not alter the rehabilitation methods recommended by the child guidance clinics, and the findings of the Cambridge-Somerville group did not dampen the popularity and growth of mentoring programs throughout the country. However, a project that began in Chicago during the same era as the Cambridge-Somerville study—Henry Shaw's Chicago Area Project (CAP)—had great influence on subsequent delinquency prevention efforts. Grounded in Shaw and McKay's social control theory, the CAP pioneered the use of self-governing neighborhood committees to develop and implement preventive interventions (Sechrest, 1970).

An innovative strategy was used to seed these committees: A leader within each of the neighborhoods targeted by the project was recruited by project staff, and these leaders formed committees within their own neighborhoods. This strategy was used to ensure that the resulting committee would be an indigenous enterprise with strong links to the institutions most important to the functioning of the neighborhood (Bursik & Grasmick, 1993). Once established, the new committees were assisted in their work by the CAP board of directors, which was responsible for raising and distributing funds.

Most neighborhood committees initiated activities within three general domains: youth recreation, community improvement, and community resource development (Kobrin, 1970). Youth recreation programs often promoted the involvement of neighborhood adults with the hope of fostering a sense of community responsibility for youth (Schlossman & Sedlak, 1983). Community improvement programs tended to focus on changing the physical appearance of neighborhoods, including garbage removal and house maintenance. Community development programs usually included attempts to bring more financial resources into a neighborhood, improve the relationships between residents and local government institutions (e.g., the juvenile court, police), or seed other community organizations, such as parent-teacher associations (Bursik & Grasmick, 1993).

It is unclear whether the Chicago Area Project as a whole decreased delinquency rates (Witmer & Tufts, 1954). There is no doubt that it did not work in the most disorganized neighborhoods (DuBow,

McCabe, & Kaplan, 1979). Whether or not the program was effective, the CAP did develop a model of intervention that has become the staple of community delinquency prevention interventions in the United States: Influential community leaders are brought together to plan and manage local delinquency intervention or prevention efforts with the guidance of professional "experts."

Phase 2: The Rise of Federalism

During World War II, "precipitous" increases in official reports of juvenile crime were observed throughout the United States (Edson, 1960). This trend continued into the 1950s. As public concern over delinquency mounted, states began once again to change their juvenile justice systems. Several states followed the early lead (i.e., prior to World War II) of California and created state "youth authorities," responsible for the administration of all aspects of juvenile corrections, including placement, programs, and parole. The centralized bureaucracies of the youth authorities enabled the rapid spread of new treatment and rehabilitation techniques throughout the country, including behavior modification, group therapy, psychopharmacological therapy, group homes, and halfway houses.

The creation of youth authorities was promoted throughout the United States by the American Law Institute, which lobbied state legislatures for more "efficiency, rationality, and effectiveness" in the legal system at large (Krisberg & Austin, 1993). As the attention of lobbyists and state policymakers on delinquency increased, for the first time in U.S. history, federal policymakers began to consider intensively the problem of juvenile delinquency. In the mid-1950s, a U.S. Senate subcommittee initiated a long-term study of juvenile justice and delinquency (Hurst, 1990). The recommendations of this subcommittee, which were quite critical of juvenile justice, created a foundation for further legislative and executive action during the end of the Eisenhower administration and the beginning of the Kennedy administration.

Influencing Theories

Strain theory. Kennedy created the President's Commission on Juvenile Delinquency and Youth Crime and appointed Attorney General Robert F. Kennedy as chair. The President's Commission was strongly influenced by sociologists advocating *strain theory* (Cloward & Ohlin, 1960) as an explanation for youth crime. Cloward and Ohlin, sociologists at Columbia University in New York City, hypothesized that delinquency was a function of the great disparity between what the members of the lower class wanted and what they could actually obtain. Because few legitimate opportunities were available to rise out of poverty, impoverished youth were thought to turn to crime as the only available means to achieve wealth.

This same basic philosophy had been proposed earlier by sociologists such as Merton (1938) and Cohen (1955). What was relatively novel in Cloward and Ohlin's thinking was their hypotheses about criminal subcultures. Differences in the availability of even illegitimate opportunities were thought to lead to different criminal paths. For example, in communities with cohesive adult gangs and official corruption, impoverished youth were thought to be most at risk to become career criminals working within an institutionalized criminal subculture. In more stressed communities where even criminal activities had failed to organize, youth were thought to be most at risk for involvement in a violent criminal subculture characterized by ongoing conflict between youth-dominated gangs. Poor youth unable to succeed within either of these subcultures were thought to be most likely to retreat into an isolated world of drug abuse.

Labeling theory. Like Kennedy, President Johnson also appointed a commission on delinquency. Johnson's commission was influenced by yet another sociological theory of crime, *labeling theory*. The labeling of children as delinquent had been raised as a potential problem during the 19th century (Mennell, 1973) but was not incorporated into a formal theory of delinquency until Tannenbaum (1938).

Tannenbaum rejected the idea that delinquents and nondelinquents were fundamentally different types of people as some biological theorists had proposed (e.g., Lombroso). Like Shaw and McKay, he argued that many youth labeled delinquent by society had started their criminal behaviors within groups of children who "playfully" experimented with low-level delinquent acts. Some peer groups never progress beyond this experimentation stage, but others become criminal gangs. Tannenbaum thought that one of the forces that pushes a group from the experimental to the criminal stage was the labeling of the group as criminal by the community at large. Similarly, labeling a child delinquent was thought to increase the likelihood that a child would label himself as such, affiliate with other children who had the same label, and display further and increasingly problematic antisocial behaviors.

Lemert (1951), another labeling theorist, was particularly concerned with the way that the juvenile court itself created and solidified the definition of the delinquent. Lemert hypothesized that having a juvenile court record and spending time in jail with others who had court records established a stigma for the child: "Such stigma, represented in modern society as a 'record,' gets translated into effective handicaps by heightened police surveillance, neighborhood isolation, lowered receptivity and tolerance by school officials, and rejections of youth by prospective employers" (Lemert, 1967, p. 92).

Policies and Practices

Juvenile Delinquency and Youth Offenses Control Act. The first major federal act targeting delinquency was the Juvenile Delinquency and Youth Offenses Control Act of 1961. Following strain theory, the act made competitive funds available for community efforts to increase legitimate opportunities for youth to succeed in conventional society. Programs intended to ameliorate family problems, prevent school dropout, or assist youth in preparing for and finding employment were particularly encouraged (McGarrell, 1988).

The Mobilization for Youth project. One of the first and most extensively funded programs under the 1961 act was the Mobilization for Youth project (MFY). The MFY began before the 1961 act was passed and actually served as a model for projects funded under the act (Krisberg & Austin, 1993). During the late 1950s, the MFY was initiated in a lower-income neighborhood in New York City by a committee similar to those seeded by the Chicago Area Project. Unlike the Chicago committees, the New York neighborhood committee did not have direct access to supportive funding. Obtaining such funds independently turned out to be quite difficult. To improve access to funding, the committee requested assistance from the Columbia University School of Social Work, and strain theorists Cloward and Ohlin became consultants on the project. The reconstituted MFY committee, now a mix of neighborhood residents and School of Social Work faculty and staff, was able to garner a significant amount of financial support from a variety of public and private funding sources (Helfgot, 1981).

The MFY attempted to increase legitimate opportunities for youth by empowering local adults. Project organizers hypothesized that if neighborhood residents themselves controlled the political and economic structure of the neighborhood, the delinquent behavior of neighborhood youth would decrease (Helfgot, 1981; Weissman, 1969). Initially, the MFY attempted to increase local control through the provision of supportive services, including youth recreation programs, mental health services, vocational programs, and resident-led gang interventions. However, as it became increasingly clear that these types of programs had little impact on the desired outcome, the project began to support activities designed to alter more directly the power structure of the neighborhood. Strikes, boycotts, and protests were held, and soon the MFY was accused of being a "communist" organization (Weissman, 1969). Several investigations by the city, state, and federal governments followed. Eventually, administration of the project was taken over by the city government (Moynihan, 1969). Under city administration, the MFY returned to more traditional and conservative interventions, such as job training and counseling (Weissman, 1969).

Similar to the Chicago Area Project, the overall impact of the MFY on neighborhood delinquency was unclear (Miller & Ohlin, 1985). It is also unclear whether the MFY made an impact on the primary target of the project: increasing legitimate opportunities for success for adults and youth. Unfortunately, the assessment of intervention effectiveness was not a central concern of either the MFY or the Chicago Area Project, and thus neither project provided clear information on the usefulness of neighborhood councils in reducing the prevalence of neighborhood delinquency.

Commission on Law Enforcement and Administration of Justice. As funding for the 1961 act waned, President Johnson appointed his own commission to examine the continuing problems of crime and delinquency. Prominent sociologists served as consultants to the Commission, including labeling theorist Lemert and social control theorist McKay. In 1967, the Commission produced a landmark report on youth crime. Rather than individual psychopathology, the report highlighted the importance of the structure of society as the primary cause of delinquency. Echoing the conclusions of the 1950s Senate subcommittee, the report also cited numerous problems within the current system of juvenile justice, including the ineffectiveness of rehabilitative efforts and the lasting stigma of the "delinquent" label (Fabricant, 1983).

The Commission recommended four major types of reforms: *decriminalization* (i.e., the removal of noncriminal status offenders from juvenile court jurisdiction); *diversion* (i.e., moving first-time and small-time offenders into community-based systems); *due process* (i.e., formalizing court procedures to better protect the constitutional rights of accused children); and *deinstitutionalization* (i.e., moving offenders out of traditional locked, out-of-community institutions and into open community settings; Empey, 1978). Some of these reforms were congruent with changes occurring elsewhere in the world. For example, several years earlier, the Second United Nations Congress on Prevention of Crime and Treatment of Offenders had recommended that the term "juvenile delinquency" refer only to criminal law violations (United Nations, 1961).

In 1968, an attempt was made to encourage these reforms throughout the United States by the passage of the Juvenile Delinquency Prevention and Control Act by the U.S. Congress. The goal of the act was twofold: to provide financial assistance to juvenile justice systems for the development of local diversion programs (Kobrin & Klein, 1983), and to provide technical assistance to promote increased cooperation among the justice system, social agencies, and community members (Krisberg & Austin, 1993). To aid in the accomplishment of these goals, the act specified the establishment of local Youth Service Bureaus. Ideally, these bureaus were to bring together community members and representatives of key public agencies to make decisions jointly about program content and program funding (Norman, 1972).

Unfortunately, the Youth Service Bureaus did not prove to be very successful (U.S. Department of Health, Education, and Welfare [HEW], 1973). Congress attributed at least part of this failure to inept administration within the branch of HEW created to administer the bureaus, the Youth Development and Delinquency Prevention Administration (YDDPA; Hurst, 1990; Krisberg & Austin, 1993). As a result, the YDDPA was gradually phased out of delinquency prevention programming, and juvenile justice concerns were shifted out of HEW and into the Department of Justice (Law Enforcement Assistance Administration, 1974).

U.S. Supreme Court rulings. Concurrent to this activity within the legislative and executive branches of the federal government, the U.S. Supreme Court made a series of decisions that strongly affected the juvenile justice system. The first case from the juvenile court ever to rise to the level of the U.S. Supreme Court was *Kent v. The United States* (1966). In *Kent*, the court ruled that the juvenile courts must provide the essentials of due process when transferring juveniles up to the adult criminal court system. In *In re Gault* (1967), the judges ruled that juveniles have four basic rights during hearings that could result in commitment to an institution: the right to counsel, the right to be notified of charges, the right to question witnesses, and the right to be protected against self-incrimination. These cases and those that followed (see Snyder & Sickmund, 1995) have made it clear that the contemporary U.S. Supreme Court's interpretation of the U.S. Constitution is that juvenile proceedings must be carried out in a court of law and must be subject to many of the same standards applied to adult criminal cases.

The Juvenile Justice and Delinquency Prevention Act. During President Nixon's administration, yet another commission, the National Advisory Committee on Criminal Justice Standards and Goals, reiterated the recommendations of the 1967 Task Force (National Advisory Committee, 1976). The committee cited state reform schools, whose populations were rising at the time, as particularly ineffective methods of rehabilitation. Local juvenile justice systems also were criticized for failing to reintegrate youth into the community upon release from reform schools.

The committee's recommendations, the failure of the YDDPA, and the rulings of the U.S. Supreme Court all contributed to a new round of legislative activity. One year later, Congress passed the Juvenile Justice and Delinquency Prevention (JJDP) Act of 1974. The Act created a new program of formula grants designed to encourage deinstitutionalization and to discourage the detention of youth in adult jails. To receive federal funds under the Act, a state was required to submit plans specifying how progress would be made on these two fronts within a limited period of time. The Office of Juvenile Justice and Delinquency Prevention (OJJDP) was created within the Department of Justice to administer the Act.

Phase 3: Federalism in Action

Since the passage of the original JJDP Act, the federal government has played a prominent role in shaping the juvenile justice policies of the states. Most states have participated in the Act, and state participation has led to changes in local juvenile justice systems. Amendments to the JJDP Act have either expanded or enlarged the original mandates: The 1980 amendment required participating states to completely remove juveniles from adult jails within a 5-year period, and the 1992 amendment required participating states to ensure that minority youth are not detained or institutionalized at proportionally higher rates than nonminority youth. Whereas federal involvement in juvenile justice has had a significant impact on systems, federal involvement in delinquency prevention has had a significant impact on research activity. Since the original act, research on the prevention and treatment of juvenile delinquency has increased in sophistication, and OJJDP and other federal agencies that fund preventive efforts throughout the country (see Mrazek & Haggerty, 1994) have strongly supported the use of scientifically sound strategies and adequate program evaluation.

Influencing Theories

Classical theory. As the federal government was advocating reforms that decreased the level of state control over juvenile offenders in general (e.g., deinstitutionalization, diversion), a movement influenced by sociological theory began to expand state control over juvenile offenders who had committed serious crimes. A group of sociologists known as the "neoclassicalists" (e.g., Fogel, 1975; Fox, 1974; Morris, 1974) revitalized a philosophical theory that influenced the original juvenile justice system, 18th-century classical theory. The neoclassicalists rejected the notion that society is responsible for individual behavior and began once again to frame criminal behavior as a function of individual propensities. If individuals are responsible for their own behavior, the theorists reasoned that "desserts"-based sanctions (i.e., let the punishment fit the crime) were the fairest response to crime and delinquency. Thus, a number of juvenile justice system changes were advocated by neoclassicalists, including a lower age of accountability for criminal behavior, uniform sentences, and harsher penalties (McGarrell, 1988).

Social development theory. At the same time that the neoclassicalists were gaining influence with U.S. voters and policymakers, social developmental theories of juvenile delinquency were gaining influence with academic researchers. Social developmentalists

(Dishion, French, & Patterson, 1995) posit that delinquent behaviors are generated, nurtured, and maintained within social relationships. As a child moves through the key social settings (i.e., home, school, peer group, neighborhood) of childhood, the reinforcements and punishments that he receives within these settings are hypothesized to shape him to behave in certain ways.

According to social development theorists, children who receive inconsistent discipline when they are young are inadvertently reinforced for oppositional and defiant behaviors (Patterson, 1982). A child who tends to be oppositional and defiant is likely to have difficulty completing academic work upon entry into school and is likely to get into conflictual situations with teachers, schoolmates, and neighborhood peers. Repeated conflict within these settings is likely to lead to social rejection. As the child matures, repeated negative outcomes such as rejection decrease the opportunities that the child has for competency-building situations that are crucial for gaining the skills needed for success in conventional society (Patterson, Reid, & Dishion, 1992).

Whereas some social developmentalists theorize that it is behavioral reinforcement patterns alone that ultimately lead a child to commit delinquent behaviors (Patterson et al., 1992), others emphasize the joint importance of maladaptive thought processes (Dodge, 1991) or emotional "bonds" (Greenberg, Speltz, & DeKlyen, 1993; Hirschi, 1969). The social developmentalists who have been most influential in juvenile justice favor the idea of bonding as the major determinant of future behavior (Catalano & Hawkins, 1996). These theorists hypothesize that youth behaviors are most influenced by the bonds youth have developed with the social groups that are most prominent in their lives (e.g., family, peers).

A bond is defined as the commitment of an individual to the fundamental beliefs shared by members of the influencing social group. Bonds are thought to be created by three factors: opportunities, skills, and reinforcements. If a group provides a youth with opportunities for social involvement, skills and consistent rewards for successful involvement, and consistent punishments for unsuccessful involvement, a bond between the child and group will form. If bonds are formed to prosocial groups that advocate against delinquent behaviors, youth are hypothesized to be less likely to commit crimes.

Policies and Practices

The juvenile justice system. Several years after the reemergence of classical theory, three high-profile advisory commissions—the National Advisory Committee on Criminal Justice Standards and Goals, the Juvenile Justice Standards Project, and the Twentieth Century Fund Task Force on Sentencing Policy Toward Young Offenders—supported desserts-based sentencing (Flicker, 1977; Mahoney, 1987; National Advisory Committee, 1976; Twentieth Century Fund Task Force, 1978). During President Reagan's administration, juvenile justice systems throughout the country increased their focus on repeat, violent offenders (Krisberg & Austin, 1993). The federal government supported this trend. For example, in 1986, U.S. Attorney General Edwin Meese announced the creation of a model juvenile code that emphasized many of the recommendations of the neoclassicalists and the advisory committees, including mandatory sentences based on the seriousness of the offense and prior criminal record (McGarrell, 1988).

Juvenile delinquency prevention. While many states began instituting "get tough" measures for juvenile criminal offenders, support for early interventions intended to prevent entry into the juvenile justice system was growing (see Mrazek & Haggerty, 1994). This growth was due to several interrelated factors. The accumulating body of scientific knowledge about the causes and course of delinquency was being translated into more sophisticated developmental models. In turn, these models served as clear guides for intervention efforts. Finally, the establishment of the OJJDP as well as prevention branches within existing research funding institutes (e.g., the prevention branches at the National Institute of Drug Abuse, the National Institute of Mental Health, and the National Institute on Alcohol Abuse and Alcoholism) created a federal support structure dedicated to funding these preventive intervention efforts.

The continuation of this new structure was supported by increased advocacy efforts specifically targeting prevention (e.g., the work of the National Mental Health Association). These efforts were boosted by prevention work in other areas of health. For example, the positive attention that federally funded preventive efforts were receiving in heart disease further increased pressure on the federal and state governments to fund preventive attempts.

The 1992 amendment of the JJDP Act reflected the growing national interest in prevention. Through Title V of the Act, support was earmarked for community-based delinquency prevention efforts. The Act emphasized the importance of using coalitions of community leaders to direct preventive efforts, developing comprehensive community plans to reduce delinquency, employing prevention programs that have demonstrated efficacy, and monitoring the impact of programs on the risk and protective factors that are relevant to delinquent behavior within a given community (Steiner, 1994).

The strong emphasis on these program components reflected the influence of the Hawkins and Catalano social development model on the 1992 Act. Specifically, Hawkins and Catalano developed a community prevention intervention strategy, Communities that Care (CTC), that embodies these components (Hawkins, Arthur, & Olson, in press), and the CTC strategy has been held up as a model by OJJDP in federal publications created under the Act. Rather than solely targeting delinquency, the CTC strategy focuses on reducing risk and enhancing protective factors conducive to the general mental, emotional, and physical health of children and adolescents within a given community. This broad focus on general health is supported by numerous studies demonstrating strong correlations between many youth problem behaviors, including delinquency, risky sexual behavior, academic failure, and substance use (e.g., Donovan, Jessor, & Costa, 1988; Metzler, Noell, Biglan, Ary, & Smolkowski, 1994).

The CTC uses aspects of early community programs such as the Mobilization for Youth and the Chicago Area Project. However, the CTC improves upon these earlier efforts by providing community leaders with a scientifically based framework to guide delinquency prevention efforts. During the first phase of the CTC program, key community leaders (i.e., mayor, school superintendent, police chief, public agency directors, private agency directors, business leaders) are briefed on the Catalano and Hawkins social development model and the risk and protective factors strategy. If these leaders decide that they would like to participate further, a board of directors is created comprising the community leaders and representatives of important community constituencies (e.g., minority group representatives, church leaders). The board then undertakes a survey of community risk and protective factors relevant to youth problem behavior. Once the survey is completed, the factors are prioritized, and an intervention strategy is developed to address the highest priority risk factors and to enhance the highest priority protective factors. The intervention strategy is guided by a menu of promising prevention programs for which efficacy has been demonstrated under controlled conditions. The strategy is then implemented through task forces with vested interests in the targeted outcomes. As intervention programs are completed, current levels of community risk and protective factors are assessed and compared to baseline levels, and outcomes are used to guide further planning.

THE PRESENT

Despite the increased influence of the federal government over the past 30 years, the *systems* of juvenile justice in the United States continue to be created and administered by state and county governments. The future of juvenile justice thus depends on how policymakers at these local levels coordinate the costs and consequences of the new "get tough" policies for serious offenders with the promise of preventive interventions (Rubin, 1997). To illustrate the public policy decision-making process and how it interfaces with theories of delinquency, we next describe a popular model for this process, the Advocacy Coalition Framework, and then illustrate this model within a local system of juvenile justice.

The Advocacy Coalition Framework

Sabatier and Jenkins-Smith (1993) hypothesize that public policy on a given issue is driven by the interactions between competing advocacy coalitions and policy brokers (see Figure 2.1). Advocacy coalitions comprise public and private individuals who share a set of policy goals and agree on methods to achieve those goals. A coalition is usually brought together because of change in the steady state of a prominent external factor or factors (e.g., economics, technologies, related policies, or governing coalitions) that threatens the self-interests of coalition members.

Usually, stable and dominant advocacy coalitions exist for most issues, and thus public policies also tend to be stable. However, this stability is upset when a high level of dissatisfaction is present with the current state of affairs, especially when it is commonly thought that an important issue is being neglected by the current administrative bodies or when external events undermine the status quo. A

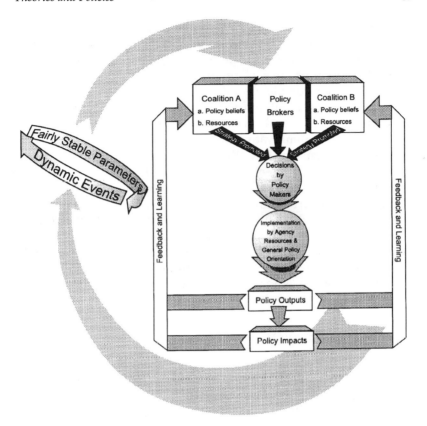

Figure 2.1. The Advocacy Coalition Model

SOURCE: Adapted from Sabatier and Jenkins-Smith (1993).

common result of either situation is that several opposing coalitions emerge to compete for the forefront of influence on the neglected issues or undermined policies.

Mediating between these competing coalitions are policy brokers (e.g., elected politicians, appointed officials, administrators) who attempt to minimize conflict among competitors and find compromise solutions. How straightforward this compromise process is depends on the stability of external factors relevant to the issue at hand. Some external factors, such as the constitutional structure of government, are difficult to change. These factors limit the extent to which new policies can differ from current policies. Other external factors, such as economic downturns or highly publicized crimes, are less predictable. The occurrence of one of these events may have upset the status quo in the first place, and the occurrence of further events might create new pressures for change. Such events may result in the formation of other competing coalitions or might drive an existing coalition completely out of the process.

The process of competition and compromise may be quite lengthy, but ultimately, policy brokers side with one of the coalitions. Through legislative and administrative decisions, brokers enact a policy and set the parameters for how the policy will affect the day-to-day functioning of government. These policy parameters frame the nature of the debate in the next round of compromise. For example, if a policy is endorsed but funds are not mandated, the policy may have little meaning, and competing coalitions may decide that further work on the issue is moot unless major changes occur in the balance of power (e.g., conservative majority versus liberal majority). On the other hand, if policies do receive full funding and competing coalitions are still viable, pressure will be stronger to push the issue back into public debate.

Competing Advocacy Coalitions: An Illustrative Example

At present, we posit that two "advocacy coalitions" are competing on the issues of juvenile justice and delinquency prevention in the United States. Each is aligned with a theory of delinquency: the first, the Get Tough coalition, is aligned with neoclassical theory; the second, the Prevention coalition, is aligned with social development theory. Because juvenile justice ultimately is a local issue, these coalitions are competing for positions within local levels of government. To illustrate this competition, we discuss changes in juvenile justice over the past 20 years within a U.S. state (Oregon) and county (Lane County, Oregon).

The Get Tough coalition. By the mid 1980s, the Oregon system had made a series of rapid policy changes that had significantly changed the population of youth in the juvenile justice system. Since the beginning of the juvenile court in Oregon in 1905, the Oregon juvenile justice system had dealt with a rather broad population of at-risk children, many of whom had committed status rather than criminal offenses. However, beginning in the 1960s, federal pressure exerted through both legislative acts (e.g., the JJDP Act) and judicial rulings (e.g., U.S. Supreme Court, local

U.S. District Court) resulted in a series of laws that narrowed the focus of the Oregon system to repeat, serious criminal offenders.

Despite this limit in focus, the absolute number of offenders in the already overcrowded system increased dramatically during the 1970s. Between 1975 and 1978, when the population of incarcerated youth throughout the United States decreased 8%, the number of youth in the Oregon state training schools increased 64% (Oregon Governor's Task Force on Juvenile Corrections, 1978). Several system changes were made in an attempt to reduce these commitments. In 1979, a bill was passed that mandated the development of local services as alternatives to state institutions and penalized counties for sending youth to the state training schools. Nevertheless, overcrowding in the schools continued, and in 1985, commitments to the schools were capped. Despite these attempts to quell the flow of youth into state institutions, by 1986, Oregon numbered among the top 10 states in terms of the number of delinquent youth committed into secure custody (Oregon Children's Services Division, 1986).

Between 1988 and 1992, as the state continued to grapple with overcrowding, official reports of violent offenses by youth increased 80% (Oregon Governor's Juvenile Crime Prevention Task Force, 1996). During this same period, for the first time, urban-style youth gang activity became visible in numerous locales across the state. By the mid-1990s, concern was mounting over youth violent crime. State voters responded by passing a citizen's initiative, Measure 11.

Measure 11 mandated state legislators to pass a law requiring that juveniles between the ages of 15 to 17 years charged with certain serious crimes be prosecuted as adults. The measure further prescribed the minimum length of prison sentences for youth convicted of those crimes. Subsequent legislation instituted these mandates as well as a variety of other "get tough" measures supported by the Office of the State Attorney General (Oregon Governor's Task Force on Juvenile Justice, 1994), including waivers to adult court for 12- to 14-year-olds charged with certain violent felonies, the fingerprinting and photographing of juveniles involved in delinquency cases, and the registration of juvenile sex offenders. The legislation also mandated the development of a new multi-tier juvenile corrections system (i.e., regionally based secure facilities, boot camps, and residential academies) to handle the increasing population of juvenile offenders.

Clearly, Measure 11 and its implementation legislation represented the ascendance of the Get Tough coalition in Oregon. The rise of this coalition was fueled by an undermined status quo (e.g., overcrowded institutions, inability to respond to only the most severe offenders, rising rates of violence) and accompanying high levels of public dissatisfaction. The rise of this coalition was punctuated by an additional aspect of the implementation legislation, the transfer of juvenile corrections out of the state child welfare division and into its own division, the Oregon Youth Authority (OYA). Thus, not only did the coalition succeed in creating a more severe response system, but it also succeeded in creating a separate administrative structure to maintain the new system. The large number of capital construction projects mandated within the OYA (i.e., the multitier corrections system) ensured a large and continuing flow of state dollars to support the new administrative structure in the future.

The Prevention coalition. While the social changes were occurring that led to the ascendence of the Get Tough coalition, a second advocacy coalition with direct implications for juvenile justice was forming, the Prevention coalition. Beginning in the late 1960s and early 1970s, pieces of the framework that ultimately would become a part of social development prevention models were growing in popularity throughout the state of Oregon. Counseling services with preventive implications (e.g., youth substance abuse, parenting skills) were added to many county juvenile justice systems. Child development specialists were hired in various public schools to assist at-risk children and families in receiving the services they needed before child behavior problems became extreme. Within the nonprofit sector, numerous agencies with a commitment to providing mental health treatment or preventive services were formed.

On the crest of this expansion of services, landmark state reports in 1978 (Oregon Governor's Task Force on Juvenile Corrections, 1978) and 1986 (Oregon Children's Services Division, 1986) recommended that Oregon focus both on the development of primary prevention programs for childhood problems (including juvenile delinquency) and the continued improvement of services for children already exhibiting problems. In 1989, a bill was passed declaring that nothing was more important to Oregon than children and families. The bill ordered state agencies serving children and families to coordinate their efforts to provide a "balanced and comprehensive range" of services to those in need.

Several attempts at coordination followed, culminating in a 1993 act creating the Oregon Commission on Children and Families. With the support of this state body, each county was to have its own commission charged with developing and implementing a "seamless web" of mental health services to meet the needs of children and youth and to prevent the occurrence of expensive outcomes to society, such as delinquency and teen pregnancy. In 1995, county-based public safety coordinating councils were created to confront justice-related issues specifically, including prevention, on an interagency and multijurisdictional level.

With the establishment of these two policy-making bodies in each Oregon county, an infrastructure was created across the state that was responsible for planning and implementing prevention programs, including programs targeting juvenile delinquency. Concurrent to these state events, social development models of juvenile delinquency rose to prominence at the federal level, most notably through Title V of the 1992 amendment of the JJDP Act. These models fit well with the notions of prevention that had been developing within the state, and local social developmental researchers such as Hill Walker (Walker, Colvin, & Ramsey, 1995) began to increase their communications with various local and state policy brokers. Walker subsequently served on a state task force on the prevention of juvenile delinquency that strongly emphasized social development models of prevention in its final report (Oregon Governor's Juvenile Crime Prevention Task Force, 1996).

Thus, a second coalition has formed around the issue of juvenile justice in Oregon. Unlike the Get Tough coalition, which was brought to power by a citizen-driven initiative, the Prevention coalition has been dominated by professionals (i.e., mental health professionals, researchers, agency administrators, juvenile court judges, advocates) and has yet to gain the same level of public fervor. Furthermore, the first coalition has established itself through legislation dictating specific state actions, whereas the second coalition has established itself through more diffuse legislation creating committees charged with deciding which further actions need to be taken.

Conceivably, these two coalitions could work in concert rather than in competition. However, it is highly unlikely that the policy goals of each can be met simultaneously. This improbability is due to the major external event that has limited prevention throughout its tenure in Oregon: a lack of money.[1]

Competing coalitions and money. The impact of money on the functioning of juvenile justice is best illustrated at the primary unit of the system, the county level. During the 1970s, a "web" of prevention and treatment programs had been developed in the Lane County, Oregon[2] juvenile services department that was in marked contrast to the options available during the rest of the century (i.e., detention or being sent home after a lecture; Baker, 1979). Unfortunately, this web was soon broken. As the U.S. economy went into a recession, the timber-dependent economy of Lane County dove into a depression, and county government lost a significant chunk of its funding (i.e., federal funds tied to the production of wood products). Soon after, a variety of county services were cut sharply.

Within the county juvenile justice system, by 1983, the juvenile services division had been reduced to 44 people from a high of 90 in 1978 (The Register-Guard Staff, 1983). This reduced level was the same as in 1966, when the department received approximately 4,000 referrals. Unfortunately, in 1983, the department received 6,000 referrals. The loss of personnel meant drastic reductions in a variety of programs, including staff training, data management, data analysis, and counseling and prevention programs. While these cuts were occurring at the county level, city governments were also cutting back. For example, the juvenile department of the police force of the largest city in the county, Eugene, was declared inactive.

During this period of time, official reports of juvenile crime decreased, but so did the total number of officers on the street. Over the next 8 years, the county slowly rose out of this budget crisis, but in 1991, a new budget crisis was created. A citizen-sponsored property tax limitation initiative, state Measure 5, was passed by voters. Deep cuts in juvenile corrections followed (Neville, 1991).

In 1996, the juvenile justice system was hampered further by the passage of Measure 47, another citizen-sponsored property tax initiative that severely curtailed the financial resources available to local governments and schools. Measure 47 also specified that additional taxes could not be levied to make up for these losses without the approval of more than 50% of all registered voters (rather than slightly more than 50% of those who vote). In 1997, a revised version of Measure 47, Measure 50, was passed by voters, affirming once again the desire of voters for decreased taxes.

At the time of this writing, county school districts are considering the closure of schools and the increase of class sizes in the remaining schools to offset budget shortfalls. The city of Eugene, having just failed to pass a levy to make up for lost revenues, is considering cutting $2.4 million from recreation programs, $400,000 from policing, $140,000 from social services, and $130,000 from library operations (Kidd, 1997). The county, having also just failed to pass a supportive levy, is considering cutting 70 full-time jobs in areas such as public safety, youth services, and public health (Mosely, 1997). Thus, with government-sponsored programs relevant to youth under strong pressure to cut services, few funds are available for even the basic functions of juvenile justice (e.g., juvenile justice intake and probation), let alone expanded functions (e.g., juvenile delinquency prevention programs).

THE FUTURE

Back to the Future?

Juvenile delinquency first appeared in the United States at the beginning of the Industrial Revolution. Industrialization led to urbanization and increases in family disruption. Family disruption led to increases in child neglect and abuse, decreases in the supervision of youth, and the ascendance of juvenile delinquency to social-problem status. The first "system" of juvenile justice was created soon after this rise, yet delinquency remained a problem. Subsequent attempts to change the system to better address the problem also have been unable to solve the problem of delinquency.

A variety of theories (see Figure 2.2) have influenced the design of these subsequent attempts. However, despite the underlying theory in vogue at the time, policymakers have tended to cycle between two general approaches to youth crime: punishment and rehabilitation. Bernard (1993) labeled this tendency the "cycle of juvenile justice."

Bernard suggested that this cycle begins when public opinion and policymakers view juvenile crime as particularly high (see Figure 2.3). The response is to "get tough" by increasing harsh methods to

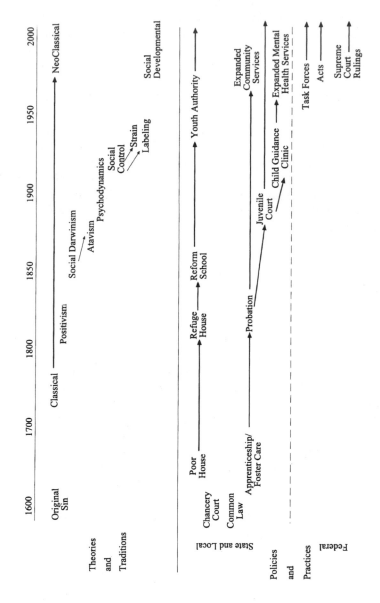

Figure 2.2. Theories and Traditions and the Policies and Practices of Juvenile Justice

punish juvenile offenders for their past behavior and decreasing programs intended to assist in the control of their future behavior. Over time, this response tends to result in a forced choice situation: juvenile justice officials must decide between applying extremely rough sentences or doing nothing at all. As a result, some minor offenders do not face any consequences for their behavior. Eventually, this situation becomes unacceptable to society, and a major reform is put forth to balance punishment and rehabilitation. Prevention programs are more likely in this type of climate. When this "middle-road" approach is perceived to be equally unsuccessful in eliminating juvenile crime, harsh measures are gradually reintroduced, and the system cycles back to a punishment phase.

Costs and Benefits: A New Future?

Many states today, including Oregon, clearly are in the midst of the punishment phase of Bernard's cycle. The high costs of this phase, compounded with the decreasing funds available to all levels of government, leave little, if any, funds remaining for juvenile justice programs with a preventive focus. Fortunately, the increasing focus on cost effectiveness within government may be the external force necessary to end Bernard's cycle and move juvenile justice to a new level of functioning. At this new level, the juvenile justice system would no longer vacillate between approaches but would balance prevention, rehabilitation, and sanctions in a way that maximized the safety and well-being of the public at large while minimizing costs.

Recent work by Peter Greenwood and colleagues (Greenwood, Model, Rydell, & Chiesa, 1996) illustrates how a cost-effectiveness approach to juvenile justice could significantly change the nature of the policy debate. Rather than evaluate responses to crime on philosophical or emotional grounds, Greenwood et al. (1996) address the issues of fiscal responsibility, conservative usage of resources, and long-term planning. The researchers compared various preventive interventions to adult incarceration (specifically, California's Three Strikes policy) in terms of both their effectiveness in reducing serious crime and their financial costs.

Based on conservative estimates of the costs and benefits of each response, the Greenwood group estimated that adult incarceration under Three Strikes was a more expensive way to avert serious felonies ($16,000 per serious felony prevented) than were interven-

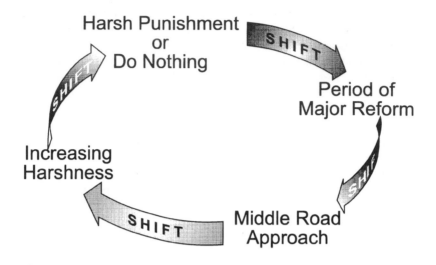

Figure 2.3. The Cycle of Juvenile Justice

SOURCE: Adapted from Bernard (1993).

tions such as parent training ($6,500 per felony) or delinquent supervision ($14,000 per felony). Greenwood calculated that early home visits and day care programs for high-risk infants (e.g., Olds, Henderson, Chamberlin, & Tatelbaum, 1986; Olds, Henderson, & Kitzman, 1994) were also effective but costly. However, recent work by Olds, Henderson, Phelps, Kitzman, and Hanks (1993) has demonstrated that these programs can pay for themselves within a few years by reducing social service and welfare costs. For example, such programs reduce child abuse by a factor of four and medical emergency room visits by nearly 50% (see Olds, 1997). Within a social developmental framework (Patterson et al., 1992), decreases in inappropriate discipline and child abuse during early childhood would be expected to lead to decreases in child problem behavior during middle childhood, which in turn would lead to decreases in the prevalence of delinquency during adolescence. Thus, over the long run, the benefits of even potentially expensive programs such as early home visitation could be quite significant indeed.

The accumulating knowledge base about the causes of delinquency (Peplar & Rubin, 1991) and the costs and benefits of interventions (Yates, 1996) places policymakers in increasingly advantageous decision-making positions in terms of juvenile justice and delinquency prevention. However, this knowledge is only useful in the context of a long-run approach to delinquency and crime. Reducing these problems will take the type of long-term commitment shown by automotive designers and pharmaceutical developers, who make investments of time and resources over decades to produce consistent, effective, and ultimately profitable products.

Without this same type of long-term vision for the prevention of human problems, it is unlikely that community programs can be created and maintained that will produce consistent and effective results in the prevention of delinquency or related youth problem behaviors (e.g., drug use and abuse, early sexual behavior). Given the relatively short tenure of most shapers of public policy, the demands for quick solutions by a nervous and angry citizenry, decreasing state and local budgets, and escalating juvenile corrections costs, it will take considerable resolve and ingenious budgeting to establish and maintain prevention as a function of government.

NOTES

1. The prominence of this external factor is well described by Susan Dey, manager of the Lane County Oregon Children Services Division office:

> In my 26 years of experience in social work, lack of prevention has always been a lack of money. It's true, if you do more prevention, ultimately you won't have to do as much intervention. But I wonder how that can happen when there's not enough money even to do intervention—you can't just take it out of one pocket and put it in the other. (Bjornstad, 1993, p. 4A)

2. Lane County has a population of approximately 300,000 and is about the size of the state of Connecticut. The county has one major urban area, Eugene-Springfield.

REFERENCES

Baker, A. (1979, June 24). Counseling for families may be cut. *The Register-Guard,* p. 1C.

Bentham, J. (1970). *An introduction to the principles of morals and legislation.* London: Athlone Press. (Originally published in 1789)

Bernard, T. J. (1993). *The cycle of juvenile justice.* New York: Oxford University Press.

Bjornstad, R. (1993, August 3). Legislature passes child services bill. *The Register-Guard*, pp. 1A, 4A.

Burgess, E. W. (1929). Urban areas in Chicago. In T. V. Smith & L. D. White (Eds.), *Chicago: An experiment in social science research* (pp. 45-69). Chicago: University of Chicago Press.

Bursik, R. J., & Grasmick, H. G. (1993). *Neighborhoods and crime: The dimensions of effective community control.* New York: Lexington Books.

Carson, M. (1990). *Settlement folk, social thought, and the American settlement movement, 1885-1930.* Chicago: University of Chicago Press.

Catalano, R. F., & Hawkins, J. D. (1996). The social development model: A theory of antisocial behavior. In J. D. Hawkins (Ed.), *Delinquency and crime: Current theories* (pp. 149-197). New York: Cambridge University Press.

Cloward, R., & Ohlin, L. E. (1960). *Delinquency and opportunity.* New York: Free Press.

Cohen, A. K. (1955). *Delinquent boys: The culture of the gang.* New York: Free Press.

Darwin, C. (1871). *Descent of man.* London: John Murray.

Dishion, T. J., French, D. C., & Patterson, G. R. (1995). The development and ecology of antisocial behavior. In D. Cicchetti & D. J. Cohen (Eds.), *Developmental psychopathology, Vol. 2: Risk, disorder, and adaptation* (pp. 421-471). New York: John Wiley.

Dodge, K. A. (1991). The structure and function of proactive and reactive aggression. In D. J. Pepler & K. H. Rubin (Eds.), *The development and treatment of childhood aggression* (pp. 201-218). Hillsdale, NJ: Lawrence Erlbaum.

Donovan, J. E., Jessor, R., & Costa, F. M. (1988). Syndrome of problem behavior in adolescence: A replication. *Journal of Consulting and Clinical Psychology, 56,* 762-765.

DuBow, F., McCabe, E., & Kaplan, G. (1979). *Reactions to crime: A critical review of the literature.* Washington, DC: U.S. Department of Justice, Law Enforcement Assistance Administration.

Edson, P. (1960, September 19). Crime data adds to grim total. *The Register-Guard*, p. 12A.

Empey, L. T. (1978). *Juvenile justice: Legacy and current reforms.* Charlottesville: University of Virginia Press.

Empey, L. T. (1985). The family and delinquency. *Today's Delinquent, 4,* 5-46.

Fabricant, M. (1983). *Juveniles in the family courts.* Lexington, MA: Lexington Books.

Faris, R. E. (1967). *Chicago sociology, 1920-1932.* Chicago: University of Chicago Press.

Finestone, H. (1976). *Victims of change: Juvenile delinquents in American society.* Westport, CT: Greenwood.

Flicker, B. (1977). *Standards for juvenile justice: A summary and analysis.* Cambridge, MA: Ballinger.

Fogel, D. (1975). *We are the living proof: The justice model for corrections.* Cincinnati, OH: Anderson.

Fox, S. (1974). The reform of juvenile justice: The child's right to punishment. *Juvenile Justice, 25,* 2-9.

Glueck, S., & Glueck, E. (1934). *One thousand juvenile delinquents: Their treatment by court and clinic.* Cambridge, MA: Harvard University Press.

Glueck, S., & Glueck, E. (Eds.). (1972). *Identification of predelinquents.* New York: International Medical Books.

Gottfredson, M. R., & Hirschi, T. (1990). *A general theory of crime.* Stanford, CA: Stanford University Press.

Greenberg, M. T., Speltz, M. L., & DeKlyen, M. (1993). The role of attachment in early development of disruptive behavior problems. *Development and Psychopathology, 5,* 191-213.

Greenwood, P. W., Model, K. E., Rydell, C. P., & Chiesa, J. (1996, April). Diverting children from a life of crime: Measuring costs and benefits. *RAND Corporation Bulletin,* MR-699.0-UBC/RC/IF.

Hawes, J. M. (1971). *Children in urban society: Juvenile delinquency in nineteenth-century America.* New York: Oxford University Press.

Hawkins, J. D., Arthur, M. W., & Olson, J. J. (in press). Community interventions to reduce risks and enhance protection against antisocial behavior. In D. M. Stoff, J. Breiling, & J. D. Maser (Eds.), *The handbook of antisocial behavior.* New York: John Wiley.

Helfgot, J. H. (1981). *Professional reforming: Mobilization for Youth and the failure of social science.* Lexington, MA: Lexington Books.

Hirschi, T. (1969). *Causes of delinquency.* Berkeley: University of California Press.

Hurst, H. (1990). Juvenile probation in retrospect. *Perspectives, 5*(1), 16-19.

In re Gault. (1967). 387 U.S. 1, 87 S.Ct. 1428.

Kent v. The United States. (1966). 383 U.S. 541, 86 S.Ct. 1045.

Kidd, J. (1997, May 22). Eugene levy gets majority of votes not of voters. *The Register-Guard,* pp. 1A, 6A.

Klein, M. W. (1995). *The American street gang: Its nature, prevalence, and control.* New York: Oxford University Press.

Kobrin, S. (1970). The Chicago Area Project: A twenty-five year assessment. In N. Johnson (Ed.), *The sociology of crime and delinquency* (pp. 81-104). New York: John Wiley.

Kobrin, S., & Klein, M. W. (1983). *Community treatment of offenders: The DSO experiments.* Beverly Hills, CA: Sage.

Krisberg, B., & Austin, J. F. (1993). *Reinventing juvenile justice.* Newbury Park, CA: Sage.

Law Enforcement Assistance Administration. (1974). *Indexed legislative history of the Juvenile Justice and Delinquency Prevention Act of 1974.* Washington, DC: U.S. Government Printing Office.

Leahey, T. H. (1980). *A history of psychology: Main currents in psychological thought.* Englewood Cliffs, NJ: Prentice Hall.

Lemert, E. M. (1951). *Social pathology.* New York: McGraw-Hill.

Lemert, E. M. (1967). The juvenile court—Quest and realities. In The President's Commission on Law Enforcement and Administration of Justice (Ed.), *Task force report: Juvenile delinquency and youth crime* (pp. 91-106). Washington, DC: U.S. Government Printing Office.

Lotz, R., Poole, E. D., & Regoli, R. M. (1985). *Juvenile delinquency and juvenile justice.* New York: Random House.

Mahoney, A. R. (1987). *Juvenile justice in context.* Boston: Northeastern University Press.

Martin, M. (1985). *Pilgrims in their own land: 500 years of religion in America.* New York: Penguin.

McCord, J. (1978). A thirty-year follow-up of treatment effect. *American Psychologist, 33,* 284-289.

McCord, J. (1981). A longitudinal perspective on patterns of crime. *Criminology, 19,* 211-218.

McCord, J. (1990). Crime in moral and social contexts—The American Society of Criminology 1989 Presidential Address. *Criminology, 28*(1), 1-16.

McCord, J. (1992). The Cambridge-Somerville Study: A pioneering longitudinal experimental study of delinquency prevention. In J. McCord & R. E. Tremblay (Eds.), *Preventing antisocial behavior: Interventions from birth through adolescence* (pp. 196-206). New York: Guilford.

McCord, W., & McCord, J. (1959). *Origins of crime.* New York: Columbia University Press.

McGarrell, E. F. (1988). *Juvenile correctional reform: Two decades of policy and procedural change.* Albany: State University of New York Press.

Mennell, R. M. (1973). *Thorns and thistles: Juvenile delinquents in the United States, 1825-1940.* Hanover, NH: University Press of New England.

Merton, R. K. (1938). Social structure and "anomie." *American Sociological Review, 3,* 672-682.

Metzler, C. W., Noell, J., Biglan, A., Ary, D., & Smolkowski, K. (1994). The social context for risky sexual behavior among adolescents. *Journal of Behavioral Medicine, 17,* 419-438.

Miller, A. D., & Ohlin, L. E. (1985). *Delinquency and community: Creating opportunities and controls.* Beverly Hills, CA: Sage.

Moreland, D. W. (1941). History and prophecy: John Augustus and his successors. *National Probation Association Yearbook, 12,* 5-10.

Morris, N. (1974). *The future of imprisonment.* Chicago: University of Chicago Press.

Mosely, J. (1997, May 22). County using soft numbers to form budget. *The Register-Guard,* pp. 1C, 2C.

Moynihan, D. (1969). *Maximum feasible misunderstanding.* New York: Free Press.

Mrazek, P. J., & Haggerty, R. J. (Eds.). (1994). *Reducing risks for mental disorders: Frontiers for preventive intervention research.* Washington, DC: National Academy Press.

National Advisory Committee on Criminal Justice Standards and Goals. (1976). *Juvenile justice and delinquency prevention.* Washington, DC: U.S. Government Printing Office.

Neville, P. (1991, December 6). Cutbacks at CSD could hamstring juvenile services. *The Register-Guard,* pp. 1E, 4E.

Norman, S. (1972). *The Youth Service Bureau: A key to delinquency prevention.* Hackensack, NJ: National Council on Crime and Delinquency.

Olds, D. L. (1997). The prenatal/early infancy project: 15 years later. In G. W. Albee & T. P. Gullotta (Eds.), *Primary prevention works* (pp. 41-67). Thousand Oaks, CA: Sage.

Olds, D. L., Henderson, C., Chamberlin, R., & Tatelbaum, R. (1986). Preventing child abuse and neglect: A randomized trial of nurse home visitation. *Pediatrics, 78,* 65-78.

Olds, D. L., Henderson, C. R., & Kitzman, H. (1994). Does prenatal and infancy nurse home visitation have enduring effects on qualities of parental caregiving and child health and 25 to 50 months of life? *Pediatrics, 93,* 89-98.

Olds, D. L., Henderson, C. R., Phelps, C., Kitzman, H., & Hanks, C. (1993). Effects of prenatal and infancy nurse home visitation on government spending. *Medical Care, 3,* 1-20.

Oregon Children's Services Division. (1986). *Oregon's agenda for the 1990s: Children, youth, and families.* Salem: State of Oregon.

Oregon Governor's Juvenile Crime Prevention Task Force. (1996). *Final report.* Salem: State of Oregon.

Oregon Governor's Task Force on Juvenile Corrections. (1978). *Report of Governor's Task Force on Juvenile Corrections, Vol. I.* Salem: State of Oregon.

Oregon Governor's Task Force on Juvenile Justice. (1994). *Final report.* Salem: State of Oregon.

Patterson, G. R. (1982). *Coercive family process.* Eugene, OR: Castalia.

Patterson, G. R., Reid, J. B., & Dishion, T. J. (1992). *Antisocial boys.* Eugene, OR: Castalia.

Peplar, D. J., & Rubin, K. H. (Eds.). (1991). *The development and treatment of childhood aggression.* Hillsdale, NJ: Lawrence Erlbaum.

Pickett, R. S. (1969). *House of refuge.* Syracuse, NY: Syracuse University Press.

Pierce, B. K. (1969). *A half century with juvenile delinquents.* Montclair, NJ: Patterson Smith. (Originally published in 1869)

Platt, A. M. (1977). *The child savers: The invention of delinquency* (2nd ed.). Chicago: University of Chicago Press.

Powers, E., & Witmer, H. (1951). *An experiment in the prevention of delinquency: The Cambridge-Somerville Youth Study.* New York: Columbia University Press.

The President's Commission on Law Enforcement and Administration of Justice. (1967). *Task force report: Juvenile delinquency and youth crime.* Washington, DC: U.S. Government Printing Office.

The Register-Guard Staff. (1983, July 24). Staff level at lowest since 1967. *The Register-Guard,* p. 5B.

Rubin, E. L. (Ed.). (1997). *Minimizing harm as a goal for crime policy in California.* Berkeley: California Crime Policy Seminar.

Sabatier, P. A., & Jenkins-Smith, H. C. (Eds.). (1993). *Policy change and learning: An advocacy coalition approach.* Boulder, CO: Westview.

Sampson, R. J., & Laub, J. H. (1994). Urban poverty and the family context of delinquency: A new look at structures and processes in a classic study. *Child Development, 65,* 523-540.

Schlossman, S., & Sedlak, M. (1983). The Chicago Area Project revisited. *Crime & Delinquency, 29,* 398-462.

Schultz, L. (1973). The cycle of juvenile court history. *Crime & Delinquency, 19,* 457-475.

Sechrest, D. (1970). *The community approach.* Berkeley: University of California School of Criminology.

Shaw, C., & McKay, H. (1942). *Juvenile delinquency and urban areas.* Chicago: University of Chicago Press.

Snyder, H. N., & Sickmund, M. (1995). *Juvenile offenders and victims: A national report.* Washington, DC: Office of Juvenile Justice and Delinquency Prevention.

Steiner, P. (1994). Delinquency prevention [On-line]. Available: http://www.ncjrs.
    org/txtfiles/delp.txt.
Tannenbaum, R. (1938). *Crime and the community*. New York: Columbia University
    Press.
Tappan, P. W. (1949). *Juvenile delinquency*. New York: McGraw-Hill.
Trattner, W. I. (1974). *From poor law to welfare state*. New York: Free Press.
Twentieth Century Fund Task Force on Sentencing Policy Toward Young Of-
    fenders. (1978). *Confronting youth crime*. New York: Holmes and Meier.
United Nations. (1961). *Report prepared by the Secretariat*. New York: Author.
U.S. Department of Health, Education, and Welfare. (1973). *National study of youth
    service bureaus—Final report*. Washington, DC: HEW.
Walker, H. M., Colvin, G., & Ramsey, E. (1995). *Antisocial behavior in schools:
    Strategies and best practices*. Pacific Grove, CA: Brooks/Cole.
Weissman, H. (1969). *Community development in the Mobilization for Youth*. New
    York: Associated Press.
Witmer, H., & Tufts, E. (1954). *The effectiveness of delinquency prevention programs*.
    Washington, DC: U.S. Government Printing Office.
Wolfgang, M. (1961). Pioneers in criminology: Cesare Lombroso. *Journal of Criminal
    Law, Criminology, and Police Science, 52*, 361-369.
Yates, B. T. (1996). *Analyzing costs, procedures, processes, and outcomes in human
    services*. Thousand Oaks, CA: Sage.

3. The Influence of Families, Friends, Schools, and Community on Delinquent Behavior

Ruth Seydlitz
Pamela Jenkins

There is a perception in the United States that juvenile delinquency is increasing at an alarming rate, despite evidence to the contrary (Albanese, 1993; Cook & Laub, 1986; Empey & Stafford, 1991, pp. 82, 89; Osgood, O'Malley, Bachman, & Johnston, 1989; Sarri, 1983; Siegel & Senna, 1991, p. 37). This perception fuels the public outcry for someone to do something. This cry has caused many criminologists, public health and law enforcement officials, politicians, and social workers to view the current explanations, policies, and prevention efforts to curb juvenile delinquency as inadequate. In an effort to counteract the public's concern, policies in the late 1990s reverse many of those begun in the late 1890s. For example, at the end of the previous century, programs were initiated to separate juvenile offenders from adult criminals, whereas many current policies concern the treatment of young offenders as adults (Simonson, 1991).

This chapter reviews the existing research about causes of delinquency and places our understanding about this issue in the social context of the late 20th century. We examine the vast literature concerning how families, peers, schools, and the community affect delinquency in ways that both reduce and increase the commission of delinquent behaviors, including drug use and gang behavior. In summary, we draw on these results to make recommendations for prevention and intervention strategies.

Why focus on families, peers, schools, and the community? First, the literature demonstrates the powerful influence of families, peers, school, and the community on juvenile offending. Second, when incarcerated delinquents were questioned about the causes of delinquency, they mentioned family issues most frequently, followed by peer influences and drugs as well as schools and some community

53

issues, such as poverty (Goldstein, 1990). We begin our presentation of the literature by discussing the effects of families.

FAMILIES

Much has been written about the influence of the family on delinquency, and some researchers also examine the influence of delinquent acts on family ties. Delinquents identified some family factors as important: lack of parental love; parental rejection; discipline issues (e.g., harsh parental discipline and abuse, lax parental discipline, and lack of enforcement of disciplinary actions); learning from the family; family discord and family violence; and the quality of the relationship with a single parent (Goldstein, 1990). In this section, we discuss the following issues: relationship to the family, communication, discipline, family modeling, and family conflict and violence. Family structure, working mothers, and family size are also included because these topics are often referred to in the media and discussed in the juvenile court as causal factors in juvenile delinquency. As our review points out, family structure, working mothers, and family size are rarely significantly linked to juvenile delinquency.

Relationship to the Family

Focus on the family as a causal factor in juvenile delinquency has ebbed and flowed in the past century. The recent resurgence of interest in the family began in the late 1950s and accelerated after Hirschi first posited in 1969 that parents have a strong effect on delinquency. Until the 1980s, the spotlight was on the adolescents' attachment to parents, which was considered a unidimensional construct. In the 1980s, some researchers found that there are multiple, independent, yet interrelated family factors that influence delinquency. At the same time, experts realized that parental rejection was more than just the absence of attachment and began examining this construct carefully. More recently, investigators have demonstrated that there is greater complexity among these family variables and their effect on delinquency than previously thought. Others examined parents' behavior toward their children. We present these issues and then follow up with a discussion of how social status factors—

socioeconomic status, gender, age, and ethnicity—influence the relationships between family variables and delinquency.

As mentioned above, attachment to parents is an early concept in the area of the effect of the family on delinquency. Attachment to parents, defined as either the adolescents' feelings about the parents or the adolescents' perceptions of the parents' feelings, reduces delinquent behavior (Cernkovich & Giordano, 1987; Laub & Sampson, 1988; Liska & Reed, 1985; McCord, 1991; Messner & Krohn, 1990; Wiatrowski, Griswold, & Roberts, 1981; Wright & Wright, 1994).[1] Attachment to parents not only reduces general delinquency, it is also a powerful family-related predictor of persistent, serious delinquency (Gold, 1963; Laub & Sampson, 1988). Yet there is some question concerning whether the same-gender parent or the opposite-gender parent is more important (Hill & Atkinson, 1988; Krohn & Massey, 1980). In addition, researchers were unsure if attachment affected delinquency or delinquency affected attachment. The relationship between parental attachment and delinquency is the proverbial chicken-and-egg problem; in other words, which came first— low parental attachment or delinquency? Research has supported the idea that low parental attachment precedes delinquency (Liska & Reed, 1985).

Attachment to the family not only reduces delinquency directly, but it also can lessen exposure to delinquent peers and thus decrease delinquency. Adolescents who are attached to their parents, spend time with their parents, and are supported and supervised by their parents are less likely to have delinquent friends and are therefore less likely to commit delinquent acts (Dentler & Monroe, 1961; Hirschi, 1969; Jensen, 1972; Nye, 1958; Poole & Regoli, 1979; Warr, 1993b; West, 1973). In fact, some researchers suggest that the effects of parental attachment and delinquent peers on delinquency is more complex. These researchers have shown that the effect of delinquent peers on delinquency is enhanced if parental attachment is low (Agnew, 1991; Conger, 1976; Jensen, 1972; Poole & Regoli, 1979).

The findings concerning substance use are similar. Attachment to parents, closeness with parents, parental support, and family bonding inhibit adolescent drug use (Anderson & Henry, 1994; Kandel, 1980; Kandel & Adler, 1982). Moreover, family caring reduces associations with peers who use drugs, and, subsequently, reduces drug use (Hays & Revetto, 1990; Hundleby & Mercer, 1987).

In the 1980s, researchers examined the possibility that the influence of the family is multidimensional. Canter (1982a) found that a wide variety of family variables—family involvement, parental influence, family aspirations, family social isolation, and particularly family normlessness—are inversely related to delinquency, especially general delinquency and status offenses. This was one of the earliest studies to include family normlessness. Similarly, Fagan and Wexler (1987) showed that family normlessness increases delinquency. On the other hand, Hundleby and Mercer (1987) claimed that the most important family predictors of adolescent drug use are parental trust and concern.

In the 1980s, interest in parental rejection as a separate concept, not the opposite of parental attachment, became popular. This has proved to be one of the most, if not *the* most, powerful predictors of delinquency. Rejection of parents or perceived rejection by the parents has been found to be related to the commission of delinquency (Kaplan, Martin, & Robbins, 1982; Nye, 1958; Simons, Robertson, & Downs, 1989; Wright & Wright, 1994); it has also been found to decrease identification with the norms, increase associations with drug-using friends, and increase the adolescent's own drug use (Kaplan et al., 1982). Unilateral rejection—rejection of the adolescent by the parents or rejection of the parents by the adolescent—slightly increased delinquency, but mutual rejection was more important, regardless of the adolescent's gender (Nye, 1958). Again, researchers questioned the direction of the effect, but it has been demonstrated that parental rejection occurs prior to the onset of delinquency (Simons et al., 1989).

In the late 1980s and early 1990s, some experts questioned the assumption that family factors are independently, not multiplicatively, related to delinquency. They felt that particular combinations of these variables would be powerful inhibitors of delinquency, whereas other combinations could be conducive to delinquent acts. The research suggests that their concern was warranted. For example, the combination of weak parental affection and strong parental controls enhances delinquency (Agnew, 1991), especially among early adolescent females (Seydlitz, 1993a, 1993b). As Ellis (1986) points out, if parental control is viewed by the adolescent as legitimate and is carried out in an atmosphere of warmth and love, conformity is enhanced. Yet if such control is combined with less affection, delinquency may be enhanced. In fact, rigid parental control and low affection for parents may be an indication of dysfunctional families, and such families are likely to produce individuals with behavior problems (Beavers, 1982; Olson, Sprenkle, & Russell, 1979). Furthermore, McCord (1991) showed that competent mothers—mothers who were nonpunitive in their discipline and affectionate—and high family expectations reduced sons' delinquency.

The old adage that states "all things in moderation" applies to supervision, control, and discipline. Research suggests that the highest level of family factors, especially supervision, discipline, and control, may not be the optimal level for reducing delinquency (Nye, 1958; Seydlitz, 1993b; Wells & Rankin, 1988).

At the same time, a few researchers studied parental behavior—how parents treat their children and discipline them—not just adolescents' feelings and reports of parents' acts. A few of these studies show that parental behavior is important (Barnes, Farrell, & Banerjee, 1994; Conger, 1976; McCord, 1991; Peterson, Hawkins, Abbott, & Catalano, 1994; West, 1973), possibly even more important than attachment to parents for males (Conger, 1976; Dembo, Grandon, La Voie, Schmeidler, & Burgos, 1986). Poor parental behavior and low competence are conducive to delinquency (McCord, 1991; West, 1973), whereas good family management practices—monitoring, communicating clear expectations, and administering positive reinforcement—reduce alcohol use, substance use, and deviance for both African American and white adolescents (Barnes et al., 1994; Conger, 1976; Peterson et al., 1994).

There may be differences by gender, age, and ethnicity in the ability of family variables to reduce delinquency. Studies have found variations by gender. Many family variables, including parental attachment, parental controls, parental support, and parental rejection, are better predictors of delinquency for males than females (Canter, 1982a; Elliott & Voss, 1974; Johnson, Su, Gerstein, Shin, & Hoffman, 1995; Johnson, 1979; Krohn & Massey, 1980; Seydlitz, 1991), but one study showed that these variables were equally good predictors for males and females (Simons, Miller, & Aigner, 1980). Others have reported that different aspects of attachment to parents and measures of family interactions are important for males and females (Gove & Crutchfield, 1982; Johnson et al., 1995); in fact, the importance of these factors varies by gender, ethnicity, and the combination of gender and ethnicity (Cernkovich & Giordano, 1987). To further complicate matters, Hagan, Gillis, and Simpson (1990) reported that the gender difference in theft was greater in patriarchal families because in these families, mothers control daughters more than sons, and daughters develop less taste for risk. However, in less patriarchal families, commission of theft is more equal because sons and daughters are treated more equally and develop a more equal taste for risk.

A few investigations show the importance of age in examining the relationship between parental variables and delinquency. Attachment varies with age and parental control decreases as adolescents become older (Seydlitz, 1991). Age influences parental assessments of behavior and the intensity of child-parent conflicts (Gottlieb & Chafetz, 1977; Gottlieb & Heinsohn, 1973), and it affects the impacts of attachment to parents, parental supervision, and parental controls on delinquency (Hirschi, 1969; LaGrange & White, 1985; Matsueda & Heimer, 1987; Nye, 1958; Seydlitz, 1990, 1991; White, Pandina, & LaGrange, 1987). In fact, the effects of social bonds and parental controls on delinquency vary by gender, age, and the type of delinquency (Krohn & Massey, 1980; LaGrange & White, 1985; Seydlitz, 1990, 1991).

Some other researchers have shown that the effect of parental factors on delinquency varies by ethnicity. Rosen (1985) demonstrated that the interaction with the father was more important for African American males, possibly because of the lack of resources in their communities, such as weaker social institutions and more tolerance of deviance. However, Joseph (1995) found that attachment to parents was unrelated to delinquency for African American males and females, and Lauritsen (1994) reported that family attachment decreased sexual activities for white males, but not for white females or African Americans. Furthermore, Giordano, Cernokovich, and De Maris (1993) discovered that there is greater intimacy between African American youths and their families than among whites, whereas Cernkovich and Giordano (1987) reported that the importance of various aspects of family attachment depends on gender, ethnicity, and the combination of gender and ethnicity.

Communication

Good communication with parents has been shown to inhibit delinquency and substance use (Barnes et al., 1994; Cernkovich & Giordano, 1987; Conger, 1976; Dentler & Monroe, 1961; Denton & Kampfe, 1994; Gold, 1970; Hirschi, 1969; Kafka & London, 1991; Nye,

1958; Peterson et al., 1994). Parental counseling on dating, religion, schoolwork, and future careers reduces delinquency (Nye, 1958), as does talking with and confiding in parents (Dentler & Monroe, 1961; Gold, 1970). However, Conger (1976) pointed out that communication reduces delinquency for males only if the communication is positively reinforced. The importance of communication with parents as an inhibitor of delinquency may depend on socioeconomic status. Gold (1970) stated that talking with parents was a stronger predictor of delinquency in the lower class.

Discipline

Discipline is related to delinquency, both as a variable conducive to delinquency and as a factor that inhibits delinquency. The studies that demonstrate a delinquency-enhancing effect of discipline focus on poor or excessive parental discipline (Conger, 1976; Denton & Kampfe, 1994; Gold, 1970; McCord et al., 1959; Messner & Krohn, 1990; Sampson & Laub, 1994; Wells & Rankin, 1988; West, 1973). Punitiveness, strong parental control, and coercive control—the use of scolding, unfair rules, and punishments that restrict the adolescent—increase delinquency, especially for males (Conger, 1976; Denton & Kampfe, 1994; Messner & Krohn, 1990; Wells & Rankin, 1988). In addition, lax discipline, erratic discipline, and physical discipline increase the likelihood of delinquent behavior (Denton & Kampfe, 1994; Gold, 1970; McCord et al., 1959; Straus, 1991; West, 1973). Also, excessive psychological punishment may be damaging to adolescents, particularly if it becomes emotional and verbal abuse (Foucault, 1979; Loseke, 1991).

On the other hand, studies suggest that parental discipline may reduce delinquency, particularly supervision and appropriate, consistent punishment (Cernkovich & Giordano, 1987; Fagan & Wexler, 1987; Hirschi, 1969; Laub & Sampson, 1988; Messner & Krohn, 1990; Nye, 1958; Patterson & Dishion, 1985). Good supervision can inhibit delinquency even among the most serious, chronic, and violent offenders (Fagan & Wexler, 1987). However, as the findings in the above paragraph demonstrate, care must be used in advocating discipline because moderate supervision and normative control—parents explaining their rules and feelings—are best for reducing delinquency (Messner & Krohn, 1990; Nye, 1958; Wells & Rankin, 1988).

Family Modeling

Although Elliott and Voss (1974) reported that delinquent siblings and criminal parents are not related to delinquency, most of the studies concerning family modeling suggest that there is an indirect effect of deviant family members on delinquency (Laub & Sampson, 1988; Loeber & Dishion, 1983; McCord et al., 1959; Rosenbaum, 1989; Sampson & Laub, 1994; West, 1973). Parental deviance and parental instability contribute to deviance by adversely affecting attachment, discipline, and supervision and thus increasing delinquency (Laub & Sampson, 1988; Sampson & Laub, 1994; West, 1973).

Parents, modeling, and drugs. However, in the area of substance abuse, the results concerning family modeling consistently demonstrate that this aspect of the family is important. Parental use of alcohol and other legal drugs (including over-the-counter and prescriptions) predicts the youth's use of alcohol and other drugs (Bowker, 1978; Hundleby & Mercer, 1987; Johnson & Pandina, 1991; Kandel, 1980; Peterson et al., 1994). Moreover, family drug use, by both parents and other family members, increases juveniles' drug use (Anderson & Henry, 1994; Denton & Kampfe, 1994; Kandel, 1980). Adolescents who use drugs come from troubled environments, including low satisfaction with the family, poor quality of relationships, communication difficulties, and discipline problems (Denton & Kampfe, 1994).

In addition, parental drug use influences how the attachment to parents affects adolescents' drug use. If parents do not use drugs, then attachment to parents reduces the adolescent's likelihood of using alcohol or marijuana (Jensen & Brownfield, 1983). If parents use legal drugs, then attachment to parents significantly reduces the adolescent's use of alcohol and marijuana (Dembo et al., 1986), but this inverse relationship is not as strong as it is when parents do not use any drugs (Jensen & Brownfield, 1983). Yet if parents use illegal drugs, then attachment to parents does not influence the adolescent's use of alcohol and marijuana (Jensen & Brownfield, 1983).

Family Conflict and Violence

To many scholars, family conflict is at the heart of delinquency. Family conflict, parental hostility, lack of warmth, and neglect increase delinquency (Brown, 1984; Cernkovich & Giordano, 1987; Conger et al., 1991; Gold, 1970; Johnson & Pandina, 1991; McCord et al., 1959; Richards, 1979; Wright & Wright, 1994). Researchers wondered about two issues concerning this relationship: (a) the strength of the association; and (b) the direction of the association, that is, whether family conflict precedes involvement in delinquency or delinquency causes family conflict. Evidence suggests that the strength of the association is moderate (Wright & Wright, 1994) and that at least some of the hostility occurs before the delinquent behavior (Meadow, Abramowitz, de la Cruz, & Bay, 1981).

Family conflict may or may not directly involve the children and will affect them even if they are not directly involved. Child abuse directly involves the children and is related to the commission of delinquent behavior. Most of the research concerning the connection between abuse and delinquency reports that abuse increases the risk of delinquency. Cruelty, emotional abuse, sexual abuse, and neglect are conducive to engaging in delinquent acts (Brown, 1984; Chesney-Lind, 1989; Rosenbaum, 1989; Smith & Thornberry, 1995; West, 1973; Wright & Wright, 1994). Moreover, Brown (1984) stated that the evidence suggests that the abuse comes before the delinquency, not after it. Wright and Wright (1994) concluded that the literature demonstrates that violent offenders have higher rates of victimization; in fact, the existence of child abuse distinguishes violent and nonviolent offenders. Yet most of the children who are abused do not become abusive parents, delinquent, or violent criminals (Wright & Wright, 1994), possibly because these children have an enlightened witness who supports them and helps them deal with the abuse (Miller, 1993, 1994). Rickel and Becker-Lausen (1995) state that "children who appear to thrive despite the most difficult circumstances have an established bond with at least one caregiver" (p. 316).

Family Structure

Many studies suggest that living in a single-parent home either is not related to delinquency and drug use when other factors are considered or has a negligible effect (Barnes et al., 1994; Cernkovich & Giordano, 1987; Gold, 1970; Gove & Crutchfield, 1982; Hundleby & Mercer, 1987; Johnson & Pandina, 1991; Nye, 1958; Rankin, 1983; Rankin & Wells, 1987; Richards, 1979; Wells & Rankin, 1988; Wright & Wright, 1994). Most of these studies demonstrate that the quality of the home is more important than the structure (Barnes et al., 1994; Cernkovich & Giordano, 1987; Hundleby & Mercer, 1987; Johnson & Pandina, 1991; Nye, 1958). Wright and Wright (1994) concluded that there is a weak, positive association between living with a single parent and delinquency. However, they also declared that the delinquency-enhancing effect of marital discord is greater than that of living with a single parent, and there is no difference in delinquency between living in a broken home or living in an intact home that includes conflict, low parental esteem, parental alcoholism, and criminality (Wright & Wright, 1994). Rickel and Becker-Lausen (1995) found that intact, conflictual homes are worse for a child's well-being than are stable single-parent or stepparent homes.

However, other studies report some relationship between single-parent homes and delinquency (Datesman & Scarpitti, 1975; Denton & Kampfe, 1994; Gold, 1970; Jenkins, 1995; Johnson, 1986; Lauritsen, 1994; Rankin, 1983; Rosenbaum, 1989). Single-parent homes are related to the commission of status offenses (Datesman & Scarpitti, 1975; Rankin, 1983) and to the reaction to adolescents by the schools, police, and juvenile justice system (Datesman & Scarpitti, 1975; Johnson, 1986) but not to the actual commission of other offenses (Johnson, 1986).

The relationship between family structure and delinquency may be affected by gender and ethnicity. Austin (1978) discovered that the relationship between father absence before age 5 and the commission of offenses against people was greater for white females than for white males. Matsueda and Heimer (1987) found that the effect of broken homes on delinquency was greater for African American males than for white males. In contrast, Lauritsen (1994) found that white males and females who live with both biological parents are less likely to engage in sexual activities than are those from other family structures, but family structure had no effect on sexual activities for African Americans. Another related topic to family structure is the relationship between delinquency and working mothers.

Working Mothers

Some studies show that the mother's employment is unrelated to delinquency (Dentler & Monroe, 1961; Richards, 1979), particularly if confounding variables are controlled (Nye, 1958; Simons et al., 1989; Wells & Rankin, 1988). One study found a relationship in particular circumstances. Gold (1963) reported that white-collar families with a working mother were more likely to have sons who were repeat delinquents, whereas a working mother had no effect on delinquency in working-class families. Moreover, the mother's education has been found to be unrelated to delinquent behavior (Barnes et al., 1994).

Size of Families

A few studies discuss the size of the family and its relationship to delinquency. Some results suggest that larger families enhance delinquency (Jenkins, 1995; Rosenbaum, 1989; Tygart, 1991; Wells & Rankin, 1988; West, 1973). Rosenbaum (1989) reported that female adult offenders who had been incarcerated as adolescents tended to come from large families. Yet she noted that the association between the large size and delinquency was due to the dysfunction in the homes, including family conflict and violence, and family criminality. Analogously, West (1973) showed that a large family was associated with lax or careless discipline, which has been demonstrated to be associated with delinquency. Similarly, Wells and Rankin (1988) pointed out that larger family size may be associated with other variables related to delinquency, such as reduced supervision and discipline, economic problems, and delinquent siblings.

Summary

The weight of the evidence reported suggests the following. First, attachment to parents reduces delinquency. The more strongly the adolescent is attached to his or her parents, the less delinquent he or she is likely to be. The actual degree of reduction in delinquency may depend on social factors including gender, age, ethnicity, and socioeconomic status. Second, good communication with parents decreases delinquency. Third, parental supervision is important in controlling delinquency, more so than discipline. Yet consistent, appropriate, nonphysical punishment can reduce delinquency, whereas inconsistent, lax, harsh, and physical punishment increases delinquency. Fourth, family conflict, abuse, and neglect increase delinquency. Not many studies address these family problems, but of those that exist, the results show that these issues create conditions conducive to delinquency. Fifth, parents' use of drugs affects a youth's use of drugs, but the association depends on what drugs parents use and their amount of use. Sixth, several factors that appear crucial for controlling delinquency in popular literature are not demonstrably important when attachment; communication; supervision and discipline type and amount; and family conflict, abuse, and neglect are taken into account. These issues are parents' criminality, family structure, mothers' employment, and family size. The best conclusion for how the family affects delinquency comes from Rosen (1985). He suggested that it is irrelevant how the quality of the parent-adolescent relationship is measured; if the relationship is poor, the adolescent is more likely to be delinquent.

Despite the popularity of parental problems and dysfunctional homes in the mass media, a number of studies suggest that the parents and family are not the most powerful factors in affecting delinquency. In the next section, friends and gangs are shown to have a strong, possibly the strongest, influence on adolescents' behaviors, including delinquency.

FRIENDS

As feared by parents, teachers, counselors, and members of the juvenile and criminal justice systems, exposure to delinquent peers is strongly related to committing delinquency. In fact, when incarcerated delinquents were asked what they thought caused delinquency, the second most frequently mentioned cause was peers (Goldstein, 1990). Researchers claim that "association with delinquent peers is the best predictor of delinquency in current research" (Agnew & Huguley, 1989, p. 703). In this section, we will review the literature concerning the effect of delinquent friends on the commission of offenses, including drugs, and briefly discuss some of the studies concerning gangs.

Peers and Delinquency

There is a long history of research that examines the effect of peers on adolescents' engagement in delinquent deeds. These studies have shown that delinquent acts are often committed by adolescents in groups (Erickson & Jensen, 1977; Giordano, 1978; Giordano & Cernkovich, 1979; Gold, 1970; West, 1973), and that delinquents are more peer oriented than other adolescents (Agnew, 1985; Friday & Hage, 1976; Peterson, 1974; Polk & Burkett, 1972; Poole & Regoli, 1979; Wiatrowski et al., 1981). Youths behave in the same manner as their friends; if their friends are delinquent, they tend to be delinquent (Conger, 1976; Richards, 1979). Not surprisingly, adolescents, particularly males, with more delinquent friends are more likely to commit delinquency (Fagan & Wexler, 1987; Hindelang, 1973; Hirschi, 1969; Jensen, 1972; Johnson, 1979; Matsueda, 1982; Messner & Krohn, 1990; Patterson & Dishion, 1985; Poole & Regoli, 1979; White et al., 1987). Many researchers have concluded that delinquency is a direct result of having delinquent friends (Elliott, Huizinga, & Ageton, 1985; Erickson & Jensen, 1977; Messner & Krohn, 1990; Thompson, Mitchell, & Dodder, 1984). The effect of delinquent friends on commission of delinquency is enhanced if adolescents are attached to these friends, spend much time with these friends, feel that these friends approve of delinquency, and perceive pressure from these friends to engage in delinquent deeds (Agnew, 1991).

Around age 13, adolescents report knowing a peer who has committed a delinquent act, particularly less serious acts; adolescents know fewer peers who commit serious deeds (Warr, 1993a). In addition, peers are more important during midadolescence; their importance peaks at age 17 and declines rapidly thereafter (Warr, 1993a). Thus, the rapid onset of and rise in delinquency around ages 13 and 14 and the rapid decline in commission of delinquent behavior after age 17 follows the same pattern as knowing delinquent peers and the importance of peers.

Some authors have wondered whether it is delinquent friends' attitudes or behavior that encourages delinquency. The answer is both (Johnson, 1979; Matsueda & Heimer, 1987; Warr & Stafford, 1991; White et al. 1987). However, friends' behavior is more important than attitudes (Matsueda & Heimer, 1987; Warr & Stafford, 1991), particularly when friends commit delinquent acts but believe that such behavior is wrong (Warr & Stafford, 1991).

Adolescents' feelings about their delinquent friends are an unresolved issue. It is unknown whether or not adolescents care deeply about and are attached to their delinquent friends. Hirschi (1969) posited that attachment to peers would reduce delinquency because delinquents would not care about their friends as strongly or in the same manner as nondelinquents do. Results concerning attachment to friends and its influence on delinquency are inconsistent. Attachment to peers has been found to increase delinquency, to weakly decrease it, and to be unrelated to delinquency (Agnew, 1991; Colvin & Pauly, 1983; Conger, 1976; Elliott et al., 1985; Hindelang, 1973; Hirschi, 1969; Johnson, 1979; Matsueda, 1982).

Similarly, the quality of delinquents' relationships is unresolved. Some writers claim that such relationships are cohesive, emotionally close, and gratifying, whereas others argue that they are cold, brittle, and are maintained only because of rivalry with outsiders or the lack of other choices (Agnew, 1991). Results on this issue are mixed (Elliott et al., 1985; Giordano, Cernkovich, & Pugh, 1986; Hirschi, 1969; Patterson & Dishion, 1985), but some authors have suggested that there may be different types of delinquent groups that vary in degrees of closeness and cohesiveness (Colvin & Pauly, 1983; Giordano et al., 1986).

Peers and Drug Use

Substance abuse shows the most consistent and strongest effects of peers (Dinges & Oetting, 1993). As occurs with delinquency in general, adolescents who are more peer oriented and have drug-using friends are more likely to use drugs (Aseltine, 1995; Burkett & Jensen, 1975; Jaquith, 1981; Kandel, 1980; Kandel & Adler, 1982; Kandel & Davies, 1991; Kaplan et al., 1982; Meier, Burkett, & Hickman, 1984; Smith & Paternoster, 1987; White et al., 1987). Yet peer influence on drug use is more immediate and short-lived than are parent influences (Kandel, 1980). Whereas perceived rejection from the family and school and lowered self-esteem can lead to the establishment of friendships with drug-using peers and the use of drugs (Kaplan et al., 1982), rejection by drug-using peers inhibits drug use and enhances identification with conventional norms (Dinges & Oetting, 1993; Kaplan et al., 1982). Also, openness with a close friend and peer pressure are not related to substance abuse (Kafka & London, 1991), whereas belief about friends' use is positively correlated with adolescents' use (Hundleby & Mercer, 1987; Kafka & London, 1991).

Some adolescents may be more susceptible to peer pressure to become involved in delinquency and substance use. Ethnicity influences the effect of peers on the commission of offenses, but the research is not conclusive. For example, African American youths may be less attached to their peers than whites and thus less susceptible to peer pressure and less willing to lie to protect peers (Giordano et al., 1993). They might also be more likely to commit delinquent acts alone (Gold, 1970). Yet Lauritsen (1994) found that peer involvement increased sexual behavior for African American females and white males but not African American males and white females. Contrarily, Joseph (1995) found that associating with delinquent companions was significantly related to delinquency for African Americans, but the effect was greater for males.

Gender also affects the relationship between peers and delinquency. Some results suggest that delinquent companions have a greater effect on males' than females' delinquency (Jensen, 1972; Thompson et al., 1984), but also that white males might be more likely to commit delinquent deeds alone than white females (Gold, 1970). Some researchers have demonstrated that females, particularly white females, become involved in delinquency through their association with males (Bowker, 1978; Giordano, 1978), whereas males become involved through the influence of their male friends (Bowker, 1978). As a predictor of delinquency, peers are more important for males during early and late adolescence (LaGrange & White, 1985). Also, the effect of having friends with differing opinions on substance abuse varies by gender. Females with support for refraining from using marijuana will abstain, even if they have friends who want them to use marijuana, whereas males with support for using marijuana will use it even if they have friends who want them to abstain (Bowker, 1978). Also, females are more likely than males to have social support for not using alcohol and drugs (Bowker, 1978).

In addition, socioeconomic status is a variable in the relation between peers and delinquents. Delinquent peers are less important predictors of delinquent deeds for upper-status males than for lower- and middle-status males (Erickson & Empey, 1965; McGee, 1992). Furthermore, Biddle, Bank, and Marlin (1980) found that the effect of parent and peer norms and modeling on adolescents' drinking differed by age, ethnicity, gender, and socioeconomic status. White, middle-class, and midteen adolescents' drinking was influenced primarily by peers, whereas working-class, African American, and young adolescents' alcohol consumption was related more to parental norms.

Gangs

Gangs are of great concern to parents, school personnel, members of the juvenile and criminal justice systems, and the media; in short, they are viewed as a serious problem by everyone. A thorough review of all of the literature on gangs is beyond the scope of this chapter, but at least a brief discussion is warranted. It should be noted that although practically all adolescents have friends and many have been exposed to delinquent peers, few join delinquent gangs (Esbensen & Huizinga, 1993).

There is no established definition of a delinquent gang (Esbensen & Huizinga, 1993; Fagan, 1989). However, researchers interested in delinquent gangs have required that such groups have all the following characteristics: a name, colors, and some involvement in offending.

As expected, gang members, especially males, are more delinquent than adolescents not in gangs (Esbensen & Huizinga, 1993; Fagan, 1989). There is a great debate about the direction of influence: (a) Are gang members more delinquent before they join the gang ("birds of a feather flock together"), or (b) does joining the gang make the adolescents more delinquent, or (c) do both processes occur? The answer seems to differ by behavior: Both processes occur for the commission of crimes, whereas only the second process is involved in drug offenses. Specifically, Esbensen and Huizinga (1993) found that gang members committed more offenses than nongang members before they joined the gang, and that gang members engaged in even more crimes while they were gang members than they did either before or after they were in the gang. In contrast, gang members were more involved in drug crimes while they were in the gang, but their commission of drug offenses before and after they were in the gang was not significantly higher than those adolescents who were never in a gang.

Contrary to media portrayals, delinquent gangs are not all alike. Gangs vary by their popularity and, consequently, membership size (Fagan, 1989; Hagedorn, 1994). Furthermore, they vary in both the amount and types of offenses committed (Fagan, 1989; Hagedorn, 1994; Huff, 1989). Both Fagan (1989) and Hagedorn (1994) found that only 25% to 28% of all gang members belonged to the most deviant kinds of gangs. The most organized gangs commit a large amount of crime and substance offenses, including sales; in other words, the media stereotype. There were three other types of delinquent gangs (Fagan, 1989; Huff, 1989). One is the social gang, and its members mainly hang out together and use substances like alcohol and marijuana. The second is the party gang or hedonistic gang, and its members are highly involved in the use of all drugs and sales of these drugs but not other offenses like property or violent crimes. The third is the serious delinquent gang or instrumental gang; these adolescents commit a high number of property and violent offenses but are not highly involved with drugs other than alcohol and marijuana.

Contrary to popular beliefs, most of the gang members in all but the most serious types of gangs were interested in work and conventional lifestyles (Fagan, 1989; Hagedorn, 1994). Also, in opposition to media presentations, gang membership for most adolescents is transitory (Esbensen & Huizinga, 1993; Hagedorn, 1994). For example, 67% of gang members belonged to the gang for only 1 year, and only 3% belonged for 4 years (Esbensen & Huizinga, 1993).

Summary

As parents have always suspected, being a member of a delinquent group or gang is an excellent predictor of delinquency. Based on the evidence presented above, peers encourage delinquency by teaching how and why youths should do these acts and performing them together. There may be some effects of social statuses—gender, ethnicity, age, and socioeconomic status—on the strengths of the relationships between having delinquent friends, joining deviant gangs, and committing delinquency. However, having delinquent friends and joining delinquent gangs increases delinquency for *all* youth. Now we will examine how the third major socialization agent, the schools, influences delinquency.

SCHOOLS

Explanations of delinquency gain and lose favor. Although friends have always been a popular causal factor for research, other topics such as the family and schools have not continuously received research attention. Currently, families are in favor, and there is far less research about schools. Schools were a more common research interest in the late 1960s and the 1970s, although some experts still conduct research on this topic. Yet delinquents themselves mentioned schools:

Well, um, sometimes they help cause it. Like if a kid has a problem and some teachers say go to them and they'll help them out. But they don't do that. . . . Sometimes the teacher treats them like "Well, let me pass them so they don't have to be in my class." . . . They'll just give you somethin' to keep you out of their way, and things like that. (Goldstein, 1990, pp. 56-57)

Research concerning the influence of schools on delinquency demonstrates that the climate and structure of schools can reduce or enhance delinquency. For instance, academic achievement and adolescents' attitudes toward schools reduce delinquency. Yet some practices in schools are conducive to delinquency, including tracking, disciplinary activities, and the ways that schools influence dropping out or actually push adolescents out of school.

Schools Inhibit Delinquency

Academic achievement. Academic achievement consistently has been found to reduce delinquency. School achievement, IQ, grades, academic skills, and the perception of being a good student have been shown to be inversely related to delinquency and substance use (Agnew, 1985; Patterson & Dishion, 1985; White et al., 1987; Wiatrowski et al., 1981; Wiatrowski, Hernsell, Massey, & Wilson, 1982).[2] Students who are more intelligent and do better in school are less delinquent (Hagan, 1991; Hirschi & Hindelang, 1977; West, 1973). Academic pressure may provoke delinquent behavior (Denton & Kampfe, 1994; Gold, 1970). The relationship between school performance and delinquency exists regardless of race (Jensen, 1976), self-esteem (Mann, 1981), attitude toward school (Mann, 1981), and gender (Elliott & Voss, 1974; Rankin, 1980), although the delinquency-enhancing influence of academic failure is stronger for males (Elliott & Voss, 1974; Gold, 1970; Johnson, 1979; Peterson, 1974).

Schafer and Polk (1972b) state that several conditions in schools contribute to academic failure. First, school personnel believe that economically disadvantaged children have only limited potential; therefore, they do not help these students, as suggested in the quote above. Second, the school curriculum is irrelevant, particularly for economically disadvantaged students, and ignores the social problems that these children face. Third, the teaching methods are often inappropriate, and in addition, remedial education is inadequate.

Fourth, testing groups and tracking are biased by class; lower-class students are less likely to be college-prep tracked regardless of ability. Fifth, schools are economically and racially segregated to the detriment of educational attainment. Finally, there is a great distance between schools and the community most noticeably in the lower-class communities.

Academic failure has many negative consequences, particularly the development of a negative attitude toward school. Studies show that students who do poorly in school are shunned by teachers and other students, dislike school, view school as dull and boring, devalue themselves, develop a negative attitude toward schoolwork and school rules, perceive school as irrelevant, spend more time with friends, have more friends who are dropouts, and view peers as more salient (Frease, 1973; Polk & Richmond, 1972; Schafer & Polk, 1972a). In addition, Pink (1982) found that teachers' and administrators' middle-class assumptions about minorities and their attitudes toward school lead to poor school performance, which in turn induces antisocial student behaviors and attitudes.

Attitude toward school. Researchers who examine the association between attitude toward school and delinquency use two main concepts, commitment to school and attachment to school. Commitment refers to the adolescent's degree of belief in the goals of school, and attachment means the degree to which the adolescent likes school. Commitment will be discussed in this paragraph and attachment in the subsequent one. Students who are not committed to school are more delinquent than are students who are committed (Conger, 1976; Elliott & Voss, 1974; Hirschi, 1969; Jenkins, 1995; Krohn & Massey, 1980; Polk & Burkett, 1972; Polk & Halferty, 1966; Schafer & Polk, 1972a; Thomas & Hyman, 1978; White et al., 1987). In addition, higher educational and occupational aspirations and a strong future orientation reduce delinquency (Hirschi, 1969; Polk & Burkett, 1972; Polk & Pink, 1972; Stinchcombe, 1964; White et al., 1987). Educational disappointments, which occur when aspirations exceed expectations, enhance delinquency (Gold, 1970; Lauritsen, 1994; West, 1973). Adolescents who view the school as irrelevant and as lacking a connection to their futures are more rebellious and delinquent (Schafer & Polk, 1972a; Stinchcombe, 1964; West, 1973).

Students who are less attached to school and do not like school are more delinquent than are students who are attached and like school (Conger, 1976; Frease, 1973; Gold, 1963; Hindelang, 1973; Hirschi,

1969; Johnson, 1979; Joseph, 1995; Mann, 1981; Peterson, 1974; Polk & Burkett, 1972; Polk & Halferty, 1966; Rankin, 1980; Thomas & Hyman, 1978; Wiatrowski et al., 1981). Perceived rejection by the school and anger at school officials increase delinquency and substance use (Kaplan et al., 1982; Richards, 1979). However, the issue of causal order has not been resolved: Does attachment to school reduce delinquency, or does delinquency cause attachment to school to decrease? In a longitudinal study, Liska and Reed (1985) suggest that for white males, delinquency decreases attachment, but for African American males, attachment reduces delinquency. More studies concerning this relationship are necessary.

Parents, teachers, and employees in the juvenile justice system feel that recreation programs after school and in the summer inhibit delinquency. The results concerning involvement in extracurricular activities are mixed. According to some studies, involvement in school and extracurricular activities reduced delinquency (Hindelang, 1973; Peterson, 1974; Polk & Burkett, 1972; Polk & Halferty, 1966), whereas other studies showed no relationship between involvement and delinquency (Elliott & Voss, 1974; Rankin, 1980; Schafer, 1972b; Thomas & Hyman, 1978). The differences in the findings may be due to the measurement of involvement. Polk and Burkett (1972) measured involvement as time spent on homework, an indicator of commitment, and the students' perception of themselves as being close to the center of school activities, whereas Rankin (1980) and Schafer (1972b) measured involvement as participating in extracurricular activities such as clubs and sports.

The relationship between variables measuring adolescents' attitudes toward school may influence offending differently by gender, ethnicity, and socioeconomic status. Research has demonstrated that the delinquency-inhibiting effects of attachment, commitment, and perceptions of opportunities are greater for females than males (Datesman, Scarpitti, & Stephenson, 1975; Hindelang, 1973; Krohn & Massey, 1980; Rankin, 1980). In addition, school bonding has the same delinquency-inhibiting effect for African Americans and whites, and African Americans are as strongly bonded to the school as whites (Giordano et al., 1993), but perceived blocked opportunities are a better predictor of delinquency for whites than for African Americans (Cernkovich & Giordano, 1979). Moreover, McGee (1992) demonstrated that commitment and attachment to school are more important inhibitors of delinquency for lower- and middle-class adolescents than for upper-class youths.

The structure and practice of schools can cause students to have low commitment to school (Schafer & Polk, 1972b). This low commitment is created in the following ways: excluding students from serious educational planning and decisions, excluding students from authority, teaching in a manner that requires passive learning, and extreme individualism in success and failure. Schafer and Polk (1972b) also feel that the climate and discipline in the schools and the overall rigidity contribute to lack of respect for rules, police, and society. Yet interventions consciously undertaken by the schools can reduce delinquency. O'Donnell, Hawkins, Catalano, Abbott, and Day (1995) found that skills training for prosocial involvement, school bonding and achievement, norms against substance use, and avoidance of people involved in antisocial behavior consistently inhibited aggressive boys from involvement in serious delinquency and substance use in early adolescence.

Schools Induce Delinquency

Standard practices in the schools, unless consciously examined, can contribute to delinquency. Frease (1973) suggests that schools create a group of second-class students who earn poor grades, dislike school, find school boring and irrelevant, have low self-esteem, perceive themselves to be adversely labeled, and become delinquent. Schafer (1972a) states that schools generate delinquency by offering limited opportunities for success and judging students adversely on characteristics unrelated to their actions. In addition, violence and crime in the school increase delinquency among the most serious, chronic, and violent offenders (Fagan & Wexler, 1987). Studies suggest that the relationship between school conditions and delinquency is due to adolescents' attempts to resolve immediate failure and school problems through delinquency (Elliott & Voss, 1974; Polk, 1969, 1983; Rankin, 1980).

Tracking. Students who are placed in the non-college-bound track are more rebellious and more delinquent (Kelly, 1974; Kelly & Pink, 1982; Polk, 1969, 1983; Schafer et al., 1972); more likely to perceive school as irrelevant (Schafer & Polk, 1972a); less attached and committed to school (Polk, 1983; Schafer, Olexa, & Polk, 1972); more likely to drop out of school (Schafer et al., 1972); and less involved in extracurricular activities (Schafer et al., 1972). They also have lower self-esteem (Kelly & Pink, 1982; Polk, 1983, 1984) and receive lower grades (Polk, 1983). The perception that

school is irrelevant, as well as lowered attachment and commitment and lower grades, have been shown to increase delinquency
(see above). Kelly (1974) demonstrated that tracking was more
strongly related to delinquency than were socioeconomic status
and gender.

Schafer and Polk (1972b) and Pink (1982) claim that schools contribute to a perception of a lack of payoff for doing well in school
for non-college-bound students. There is no occupational preparation for non-college-bound students, and occupational guidance and
placement are inadequate for these students. There is no real work
experience in school for these students, and vocational programs and
industrial arts do not teach general skills that can be used in a variety
of jobs.

Discipline. According to Schafer and Polk (1972b), the schools'
responses to misbehavior heighten delinquency. This increase in
delinquency occurs for a number of reasons: school personnel
assume that students intend to misbehave because either they are
bad or they are from a dysfunctional family, school personnel label
students, school rules are often vague, and discipline procedures
result in labeling and bad feelings about the school (Schafer, 1972a;
Schafer & Polk, 1972a, 1972b). Schafer (1972a) claims that the poor
use of disciplinary procedures undermines students' motivation,
and Messner and Krohn (1990) report that males who perceive the
school as coercive are more likely to be delinquent.

Dropouts and pushouts. The relationship between dropping out
and delinquency is unknown. Some researchers have speculated
that adolescents will be less delinquent after leaving school because they are escaping a negative environment. Others believe
that adolescents who drop out of school will be more delinquent
because they are cutting their ties to a major socialization institution that attempts to enhance conformity. As will be shown, research supports both ideas. Escaping from school through either
graduation or dropping out decreases delinquency (Elliott & Voss,
1974; Glaser, 1978). Juveniles are less delinquent after they leave
school, including dropouts who were first arrested while in school
(Glaser, 1978), although high school dropouts are more delinquent
than are graduates (Elliott & Voss, 1974), and delinquency increases the likelihood of dropping out. Furthermore, Elliott and
Voss (1974) reported that dropping out of school is a group adaptation to school problems; entire groups of adolescents drop out
of school together.

In contrast, Thornberry, Moore, and Christenson (1985) reported that there was no immediate decrease in crime after dropping out of school. In fact, they found no immediate reduction for working-class or African American youths, and the delinquency-enhancing effect of dropping out remained even after controlling for marriage and unemployment. They showed that the convergence in arrest rates between dropouts and graduates did not occur until youths reached their mid-20s. Similarly, Krohn, Thornberry, Collins-Hall, and Lizotte (1995) found that problems such as delinquency and drug use that began while the youth was in school continued after the adolescent dropped out. Moreover, Jarjoura (1993) discovered that the reason for dropping out affected subsequent behavior. Dropouts committed more delinquent acts and used more substances, but the reason for leaving school influenced both the quantity and types of acts in which the youths engaged. More research is needed on this topic to determine if dropping out increases delinquency, decreases it, or has no effect either immediately after dropping out or in subsequent years.

Elliott and Voss (1974) also claim that one fifth of dropouts are not really dropouts but pushouts, because their early departures from school are not voluntary. Bowditch (1993) focuses on the process by which unwanted students are pushed out of school and asserts that as many as one fourth of all dropouts may really be pushouts. She found that schools use disciplinary procedures to get rid of students who are defined as troublemakers—low grades, poor attendance, prior disciplinary procedures, lower socioeconomic status, and older. Almost nothing is known about this group of adolescents and their behaviors both before and after being pushed out of school.

Summary

The research reviewed shows that schooling is an important predictor of delinquency. In fact, Cernkovich and Giordano (1992) claim that school factors are as important as friends and family. This literature demonstrates that academic achievement and a good attitude toward school reduce delinquency. Yet the evidence also demonstrates that schools contribute to delinquency through labeling some students as less important than others in the tracking system. In addition, schools enhance delinquent acts by creating conditions that alienate students and make them want to escape, including poor disciplinary practices. Just as parental use of poor disciplinary habits increases delinquency, so does school officials' use of these practices. In fact, Agnew (1992) claims that delinquency is one result of negative relationships, including associations with peers, families, and authority figures in the schools. Kelly and Pink (1982) conclude their article on school crime as follows:

> We would suggest that instead of looking rather exclusively within the individual to explain pathology, the search must be broadened to include an investigation of the structural origins of school crime. It is clear that, while beefing up the artillery may help (e.g., using more guards, monitors, or alarm devices), such a "solution" is only temporary at best, primarily because the "problem" has structural roots. Again, then, we urge a closer and more systematic examination of the short and long term consequences of commonplace educational practices that are (1) producing deviant career identities and (2) maintaining high rates of school crime. (p. 61)

COMMUNITY

The use of the concept of community in explaining delinquent behavior has many different meanings. The term is sometimes used to refer to the neighborhood and its compositional characteristics. Neighborhoods that experience compositional changes also undergo changes in their delinquency rates (Bursik & Webb, 1982). The word can also stand for the person's position in the community. Many researchers use social status variables—gender, ethnicity, socioeconomic status, and age—as proxies for this concept. Yet the community can influence individuals in another way, through value formation. Many studies in the field of delinquency examine how adolescents' moral and religious beliefs affect their commission of offenses. The literature concerning these three ways of capturing the community-delinquency connection will be reviewed below.

Neighborhood

One of the more interesting trends in understanding criminology is to focus on the neighborhood and societal level rather than just the individual level (Hagan, 1993). The orientation toward the larger community and society reframes the understanding of delinquency by widening the lens through which we frame the problem.

Bursik and Grasmick (1993, pp. 16-18) reframe the problems of crime and delinquency in terms of neighborhoods, not individuals. They examine the private level of social control (grounded in the intimate, informal primary groups in a neighborhood, such as families); the parochial level of social control (the broader interpersonal networks and local institutions, such as schools, churches, and voluntary organizations); and the public level of social control (the neighborhood's ability to secure public goods and services from governmental agencies not in the neighborhood). Delinquency and crime occur in neighborhoods where one or more of the three levels of social control are weak.

The significance of the degree of disorder in the neighborhood due to low levels of control has been demonstrated in the literature. Males who perceive more trouble in the neighborhood are more likely to commit delinquent acts (Jensen, 1972). For males, trouble in the neighborhood reduces parental supervision and increases the likelihood of having delinquent friends, thus elevating definitions in favor of delinquency, particularly for African American males (Matsueda & Heimer, 1987).

Poverty and racism are also important in understanding how neighborhoods affect delinquency. Massey (1990) claims that neighborhoods in which poverty and racism are combined have high crime rates, poor schools, and excessively high rates of mortality. In fact, Massey argues that the combination of poverty and racism is the defining characteristic of the underclass. Blackwell (1991) shows that ethnic inequality is a strong predictor of homicide rates. The effect on adolescents of living in neighborhoods in which homicides occur frequently is an important part of understanding juvenile violence. Yet there is no agreement about these influences; thus intervention is more difficult (Harer & Steffensmeier, 1992).

Sampson and Laub (1993) examine juvenile court proceedings to show how those defined as underclass black males are perceived as members of threatening populations that must be controlled. Although the authors do not diminish the offenses of these young perpetrators, they demonstrate that there is a link between poverty, racism, and the reactions of local systems of social control. These systems believe that poverty and racism are relevant to delinquency;

thus, they treat these adolescents by these characteristics as much as by their offenses.

The neighborhood remains a crucial element in understanding substance use as well as delinquency. Neighborhoods reflect the small primary group and effects of the larger social networks. Esbensen and Elliott (1994) found that individual socioeconomic status characteristics did not influence the discontinuity of illicit drugs. They found instead that life events that infer adult status, such as marriage and becoming a parent, increase the odds of discontinuing drug use. As discussed previously, drug use and delinquency are highly influenced by friendships that tend to be formed in neighborhoods; therefore, neighborhoods and the type of friends assume greater importance (Goldstein, 1990).

Yet the effect of neighborhoods on delinquency is not entirely captured by examining only the experiences available to young people within them. Youths' commitment to and involvement in the neighborhood is also relevant. Adolescents with greater involvement in the community, such as participation in the YMCA, greater commitment to the community, and intimate relationships with other people in the community are less delinquent (Friday & Hage, 1976). In fact, having a job reduces delinquency by making youths feel like they are a part of society and have a stake in it (Friday & Hage, 1976). Friday and Hage (1976) claim that delinquency was worse after World War II because there were fewer jobs for young people, a larger youth subculture, and greater family mobility. All three reduce commitment to and involvement in the community. The stopping of delinquency corresponds to the gaining of new adult roles such as a job or getting married.

Fagan and Wexler (1987) showed that positive work environments and opportunities lower violence, even among the most serious offenders. In addition, Sampson (1987) demonstrated that joblessness among African American males leads to family disruption and increases crime, especially delinquency. The influence of joblessness remained significant even when other relevant factors were taken into account, such as income, region of the country, ethnic and age composition of the area, population density, city size, and welfare benefits. He concluded that to control crime, it is necessary to address poverty and unemployment and to assist female-headed households instead of cutting welfare and incarcerating African Americans.

Some studies suggest that although the neighborhood may be important, its effect on delinquency is largely mediated by other factors such as the family, mobility, economic problems, and dependence (Conger et al., 1991; Laub & Sampson, 1988; Sampson & Laub, 1994; Sommers & Baskin, 1994). Sampson and Laub (1994) concluded that

apparently, the fundamental causes of delinquency are consistent across time and rooted not in race (e.g., black inner-city culture) but generic family processes—such as supervision, attachment and discipline—that are systematically influenced by family poverty and structural disadvantage. (p. 539)

Social Statuses

A person's position within the community and society is also meaningful in understanding delinquency. Although it is accepted that social status variables do not fully capture this concept, they are commonly used proxies largely because there is no other feasible method to measure an adolescent's standing in his or her neighborhood, peer group, school, and family. Therefore, the following discussion will summarize the influences of gender, socioeconomic status, ethnicity, and age on delinquency.

Gender. One of the most well-established facts about delinquency is that females commit less frequent and less serious delinquent acts than do males (e.g., Barnes et al., 1994; Canter, 1982b; Cullen, Golden, & Cullen, 1979; Dentler & Monroe, 1961; Elliott & Huizinga, 1983; Eve, 1982; Gold, 1970; Hindelang, 1971; Jensen & Eve, 1976; Johnson & Pandina, 1991; Kelly, 1974; Norland & Shover, 1977; Simons et al., 1980). Yet the pattern of offenses for males and females is similar (Canter, 1982b; Cernkovich & Giordano, 1979; Eve, 1982; Gold, 1970; Hindelang, 1971; Jensen & Eve, 1976; Regan & Vogt, 1983). In other words, those offenses committed most frequently by males are most commonly engaged in by females as well, and those rarely undertaken by males are rarely committed by females. In fact, Cernkovich and Giordano (1979) pointed out that delinquency patterns were more similar across gender than across race. However, the difference in delinquency by gender may be affected by other variables, such as social class.

Hagan, Gillis, and Simpson (1985) found that males were more delinquent than females, but the gender difference depended on social class. This difference was greatest in the highest class (employer class—people who employ others to work for them) and reduced to nonsignificance in the lowest class (unemployed, often referred to as the surplus class).

Socioeconomic status. The relationship between socioeconomic status and delinquency has been hotly debated (Hirschi, Hindelang, & Weis, 1982; Kleck, 1982; Tittle, Villemez, & Smith, 1982; Wellford, 1975). Some results suggest that socioeconomic status and delinquency are related (e.g., Cernkovich & Giordano, 1992; Clark & Wenninger, 1962; Elliott & Ageton, 1980; Elliott & Huizinga, 1983; Gold, 1970; Johnson et al., 1995; LaGrange & White, 1985; Polk, 1967; Reiss & Rhodes, 1961; Wiatrowski et al., 1981; Wolfgang, Figlio, & Sellin, 1972). Many researchers in the area of delinquency accept that lower-class adolescents are overrepresented in serious and repetitive delinquency. Yet it should be noted that contrary results do exist. LaGrange and White (1985) showed a significant positive effect of socioeconomic status and delinquency for males during late adolescence, and Barnes et al. (1994) demonstrated a positive effect between family income and deviance.

On the other hand, research using both official and self-reported delinquency has shown (a) no relationship between socioeconomic status and delinquency, (b) no relationship between these two variables when more important explanatory factors are considered, and (c) that socioeconomic status explains very little of the variance in delinquency (e.g., Jensen & Thompson, 1990; Joseph, 1995; Larzelere & Patterson, 1990; Tittle & Meier, 1990).[3] Even Marxian social class measures have not been significantly related to delinquency (Jensen & Thompson, 1990; Messner & Krohn, 1990). Although many researchers and practitioners believe that there is a negative relationship between delinquency and socioeconomic status, Tittle (1983) concluded that there is very little evidence to support this belief. Johnson (1979) agreed with Tittle's conclusion that socioeconomic status itself was not a good explanatory factor for delinquency, but he pointed out that it is related to conditions that are good factors—poverty, welfare, and unemployment.

Other research implies that the relationship depends on the seriousness of delinquency and gender. Johnstone (1978), in his study of the effects of peers, family integration, family socioeconomic status, and community poverty on delinquency, demonstrated that the family socioeconomic status and community poverty influenced the commission of more serious delinquent offenses, that family integration affected less serious offenses such as status offenses and substance abuse, and that peers were related to the commission of all behaviors but especially less serious ones. He concluded that dysfunctional families are more important in predicting delinquency in benign environments, and that negative environments overshadow home influences on delinquency. In addition, the relationship between socioeconomic status and delinquency may depend on gender. Two studies demonstrated that there was no association between these two variables for girls (Elliott & Huizinga, 1983; Gold, 1966).

Ethnicity. Ethnicity has been found to be related to delinquency (Cernkovich & Giordano, 1979; Elliott & Ageton, 1980; Giordano, 1978; Hindelang, 1978; Jensen, 1976; Wolfgang et al., 1972), but not when socioeconomic status is accounted for (Gold, 1970). African Americans commit more serious and more frequent delinquent acts than do whites (Elliott & Ageton, 1980). Furthermore, Polk (1967) reported that delinquency rates were highest in areas with a large ethnic population and more people in the lower class.

Age. Age is another social status variable that affects delinquency. Rates of crime and delinquency vary by age (Greenberg, 1977; Hirschi, 1969; LaGrange & White, 1985; Steffensmeier & Streifel, 1991; Thornberry et al., 1985; Warr, 1993a). Younger adolescents are less delinquent than older ones (Barnes et al., 1994; Johnson & Pandina, 1991) and less likely to engage in sexual activities regardless of gender and ethnicity (Lauritsen, 1994). For most offenses, there is a rapid onset of delinquency around ages 13 and 14, a peak in commission between ages 16 and 18, and a rapid decline thereafter (Steffensmeier & Streifel, 1991; Thornberry et al., 1995; Warr, 1993a).

Yet the effect of age on offending differs by the offense. Offenses that are less deviant for children (e.g., throwing things at cars, putting nails and other objects in streets) are committed less often by older adolescents than by younger ones (Clark & Haurek, 1966). Commission of status offenses and the use of drugs do not decrease as adolescents become older (Clark & Haurek, 1966; Warr, 1993a). Most, but not all, street crimes increase, then peak in midadolescence, and subsequently rapidly decline (Steffensmeier, Allan, Harew, &

Streifel, 1989). In addition, most street crimes are becoming more youth oriented during this century (Steffensmeier et al., 1989). However, the effect of age on delinquency varies by gender as well as the type of delinquency (Clark & Haurek, 1966). Females' delinquency does not peak in midadolescence (Clark & Haurek, 1966; Gold, 1970, p. 66; Seydlitz, 1990) as do males' delinquent deeds. Gold (1970) reported a small, steady increase in the delinquent behavior of females from age 13 to age 16, whereas Clark and Haurek (1966) and Seydlitz (1990) found nonsignificant decreases in females' delinquency between ages 11 and 19 for acts that peaked in midadolescence for males.

In addition, age affects the relationships between many theoretical concepts and delinquency (Agnew, 1992; Thornberry, 1987; White et al., 1987). Both Thornberry (1987) and Agnew (1992) suggest that the family is more important for younger adolescents, and peers are more influential during midadolescence. However, Thornberry claims that commitment to conventional activities and to the ideals of marriage and childbearing reduce delinquency for late adolescents and young adults, and school is more meaningful during midadolescence. Agnew, however, states that academic matters are more consequential for older adolescents. Similarly, research points out differences for adolescents who are early or late starters in delinquency (Simons, Wu, Conger, & Lorenz, 1994).

Moral Beliefs

Another way in which the community can influence adolescents' behavior is by teaching them to believe in the rules and the law. Belief in the law reduces delinquency (Agnew, 1985; Hindelang, 1973; Hirschi, 1969; Johnson, 1979; Lyerly & Skipper, 1981; Matsueda, 1982; Norland, Wessel, & Shover, 1981; Shover, Norland, James, & Thornton, 1979; Thomas & Hyman, 1978; Wiatrowski et al., 1981). Some studies involving various factors and their effects on delinquency have demonstrated that belief and definitions favorable to following the law are the strongest predictors of delinquency (Matsueda, 1982; Thomas & Hyman, 1978).

Some studies demonstrate an inverse relationship between religiousness or church attendance and delinquency (Elifson, Petersen, & Hadaway, 1983; Nye, 1958), whereas others show no evidence of this association (Dentler & Monroe, 1961; West, 1973). Elifson et al.

(1983) reported that religion had a greater inhibiting effect on victimless crimes than on crimes with victims. Of their three measures of religion—church attendance, religious salience, and orthodoxy—they found that religious salience had the greater negative effect on delinquency. They also demonstrated that religion is highly tied to the family and morality or belief in the law and has no independent effect on delinquency when family influences and morality are taken into account. Nye (1958) stated that youth were less delinquent if they attended church regularly. McCord et al. (1959) stated that if the mother was a strong Catholic, the son was less delinquent; otherwise, there was no relationship.

Research has shown that the effect of moral beliefs and religion vary by gender, ethnicity, and socioeconomic status. Moral beliefs are a significantly better inhibitor of females' delinquency than that of males (Johnson, 1979; Krohn & Massey, 1980; Smith & Paternoster, 1987). Moreover, religion is a better inhibitor of substance abuse and deviance for African Americans than for whites (Barnes et al., 1994). In contrast, belief in marriage and having children within marriage reduced engagement in sex for white males and females but not for African American males and females (Lauritsen, 1994). Socioeconomic status also appears to influence the effects of belief and religious attachment on delinquency. McGee (1992) found that belief in the law became less important as social class increased, whereas religious attachment increased in effectiveness as social class increased.

Summary

The relationship of the community to delinquency is the most controversial of all the areas discussed so far. Looking at the structure of the community rather than examining the behavior of families or individuals is much more difficult. The research shows that the type of neighborhood certainly mediates the possibility of delinquency. In neighborhoods where disorder is the norm, delinquency is more likely to occur. The debate continues whether poverty and racism, either as single causes or together, can define communities in such a way that many more young people are likely to become delinquent. Research states that poverty and racism are not sufficient conditions to produce delinquency; yet in examining current jail and prison populations, race/ethnicity and poverty appear to be directly linked to incarceration rates (Huizinga & Elliott, 1987). Furthermore, individual characteristics of young people are often used to identify those children at risk of becoming delinquent. Although gender is an important predictor of delinquency, it is not a universal predictor for young people. Many researchers have found that the relationship between socioeconomic status and delinquency is not direct; furthermore, it may vary by gender, ethnicity, and neighborhood. Tittle and Meier (1991) found that there were no contexts in which socioeconomic status consistently predicts delinquency. Age may prove to be an important factor in preventive efforts because delinquency often changes over time. Community frames the problems of delinquency but, as with all other explanations, does not provide a complete explanation.

CONCLUSION

This chapter synthesizes, although briefly, much of the existing literature concerning the influences of families, peers, schools, and communities on delinquency. We have not addressed the more political and conceptual aspects of delinquency nor some of the other agencies of social control, such as the juvenile and criminal justice systems.

Although the growing fear of crime has given impetus to the cry to do something, it must not be allowed to result in policies that focus attention only on some factors—such as dysfunctional families, delinquent gangs, and impoverished neighborhoods—while ignoring other equally important issues—such as schools, beliefs, and exposure to delinquent friends not related to gangs. The growing fear of juvenile crime is concentrated in responding to only some crimes and particular juveniles. Our collective and exaggerated fear of juvenile crime has led to policies and solutions that are simplistic and do not consider the multitude of relationships that produce situations and experiences that can result in juvenile delinquency. What we will do in this section is show how the research reviewed above can be used to create rational, informed, and feasible prevention and intervention strategies.

Males (1996), in his work *The Scapegoat Generation*, hypothesizes that it is not the juveniles who are the cause of the trouble in our culture; rather, it is adults, ranging from parents to institutional responses, who are responsible for both the behavior that causes juveniles to act out and the failed policies and programs that attempt to treat these children. He points out that the "unwillingness of American institutions to face the serious impacts of poverty, abuse, and adults' behaviors on teenagers has crippled realistic policies" (p. 30). We have, he says, more children in preventive programs such as therapy and drug and alcohol programs and more juveniles incarcerated than ever before. Yet efforts have failed; these children and youth are more at risk than ever before.

So much has not worked with juveniles in the past decade that we must reexamine earlier solutions to this complicated issue. Weis and Sederstrom (1981) recommend the following as elements of a program to reduce juvenile delinquency. First, they suggest that parental training is necessary. Parents need to learn how to show affection and support for their children, communicate openly with them, provide consistent discipline and positive reinforcement, and be models of law-abiding behavior. These skills can be enhanced through regular parenting training and family crisis intervention. Parent support groups are also advocated. In fact, research shows that parenting training is an effective strategy (Larzelere & Patterson, 1990; Rickel & Becker-Lausen, 1995).

As experts in the area of juvenile delinquency, Weis and Sederstrom (1981) are aware that peers must be included in any realistic delinquency reduction and prevention program. They advocate the creation of peer leadership groups that meet daily for an hour during school. Peer leadership groups should focus on school policy issues that are problems for students and should work with administrators to develop reasonable solutions. Peers can be effective in high delinquency neighborhoods as well. Weis and Sederstrom (1981) also suggest the creation of gang crisis programs and youth gang councils that would include current and former gang members.

The schools can also be altered to reduce delinquency (Polk, 1984; Weis & Sederstrom, 1981). Polk (1984) is concerned with the ways in which school experiences lead to alienation and tracking reduces self-esteem. To counter these forces, he recommends directly and realistically dealing with the issue of employment, finding new ways for students to achieve success, creating ways to keep students integrated into the school, and helping students to feel competent, regardless of the track they follow. Weis and Sederstrom's suggestions are similar but more specific. They advocate personalized instruction that tailors curricula to students' needs, establishes clear goals for students, and has individualized pacing and rewards. Such instruction should enhance cognitive skills and performance levels, increase the percentage of students experiencing academic success, strengthen attachment to teachers and school, and heighten commitment to education. All of these factors have been shown to reduce delinquency.

Weis and Sederstrom (1981) also recommend student involvement in decision making and school governance and suggest the implementation of interpersonal skills training and law-related education. In addition, they advocate prevocational education, career exploration, and cross-age tutoring. In fact, they would include students whose cognitive skills are sound but whose commitment to education is not, as tutors are a way to increase commitment. They also advise improving the school climate by enhancing teacher and administrator cooperation, and they propose having child development specialists in the schools to act as consultants for parents. They encourage the use of in-school suspension during which students must complete individualized lessons, and successful completion of these lessons must be necessary for release from suspension.

Weis and Sederstrom (1981) do not neglect those adolescents who are no longer in the traditional schools in their recommendations for changes that have the potential for reducing delinquency. They suggest the use of alternative schools that include personalized instruction; clear rewards for individual improvement; a goal-oriented emphasis in learning; low student-to-adult ratios in the classrooms; and caring, competent teachers, as opposed to the alternative schools that are used simply for punishment and that label students negatively. The alternative schools would attract youths in the neighborhood who have dropped out or have been expelled from school. They feel that enhanced school-community relations are necessary to lessen delinquency, and they recommend the creation of school-community councils made up of administrators, teachers, parents, and community members.

An aspect of the neighborhood included by Weis and Sederstrom (1981) is employment. They advocate both a vocational placement service operated through the school and a program for juniors and seniors interested in vocational training whereby they can earn credit for work experiences. They also urge the creation of school-work councils to strengthen the connection between schools and future employment. They suggest the establishment of vocational training and job placement programs for adolescents who have dropped out of school. These programs enable such youths to develop skills necessary for jobs and can provide roles to enhance commitment to conventional lines of action.

Protecting children is a far cry from the louder, simpler, and more vociferous voices that call for more punishment as a solution to a very complex problem. Goldstein (1990) states that "the world, in the youth's view, acts upon them in hostile, punitive, compelling, attractive, consciousness-clouding, or other ways, and delinquent behavior is the response" (p. 147). We agree. It is time to change how the world treats children in order to change their behavior.

NOTES

1. Additional references include Conger (1976); Dentler and Monroe (1961); Elliott and Voss (1974); Gold (1963, 1970); Gove and Crutchfield (1982); Hirschi (1969); Hindelang (1973); Johnson (1979); Krohn and Massey (1980); Meadow et al. (1981); McCord et al. (1959); Norland et al. (1981); Peterson (1974); Poole and Regoli (1979); and Shover et al. (1979).

2. Additional references include Elliott and Voss (1974); Frease (1973); Gold (1963, 1970); Hindelang (1973); Hirschi (1969); Hirschi and Hindelang (1977); Jensen (1976); Johnson (1979); Mann (1981); Pink (1982); Polk (1969); Polk and Burkett (1972); Polk and Pink (1972); Polk and Richmond (1972); Rankin (1980); Schafer and Polk (1972a); West (1973); and Wolfgang et al. (1972).

3. Additional references include Ageton (1983); Akers (1964); Dentler and Monroe (1961); Empey and Erickson (1966); Empey and Lubeck (1971); Frease (1973); Hagan et al. (1985); Hundleby and Mercer (1987); Johnson (1979); Polk and Halferty (1966); Thornberry and Farnworth (1982); and West (1973).

REFERENCES

Ageton, S. S. (1983). The dynamics of female delinquency. *Criminology, 21,* 555-584.

Agnew, R. (1985). Social control theory and delinquency: A longitudinal test. *Criminology, 23,* 47-61.

Agnew, R. (1991). The interactive effects of peer variables on delinquency. *Criminology, 29,* 47-72.

Agnew, R. (1992). Foundation for a general strain theory of crime and delinquency. *Criminology, 30,* 47-87.

Agnew, R., & Huguley, S. (1989). Adolescent violence toward parents. *Journal of Marriage and the Family, 51,* 699-711.

Akers, D. L. (1964). Socio-economic status and delinquent behavior: A retest. *Journal of Research in Crime and Delinquency, 1*, 38-46.

Albanese, J. S. (1993). *Dealing with delinquency: The future of juvenile justice* (2nd ed.). Chicago: Nelson-Hall.

Anderson, A. R., & Henry, C. S. (1994). Family system characteristics and parental behaviors as predictors of adolescent substance abuse. *Adolescence, 29*(114), 405-420.

Aseltine, R. H., Jr. (1995). A reconsideration of parental and peer influences on adolescent deviance. *Journal of Health and Social Behavior, 36*, 103-121.

Austin, R. L. (1978). Race, father-absence, and female delinquency. *Criminology, 15*, 487-505.

Barnes, G. M., Farrell, M. P., & Banerjee, S. (1994). Family influences on alcohol abuse and other problem behaviors among black and white adolescents in a general population sample. *Journal of Research on Adolescence, 4*, 183-201.

Beavers, W. R. (1982). Healthy, midrange, and severely dysfunctional families. In F. Walsh (Ed.), *Normal family processes* (pp. 45-66). New York: Guilford.

Biddle, B. J., Bank, B. J., & Marlin, M. M. (1980). Social determinants of adolescent drinking: What they think, what they do and what I think and do. *Journal of Studies on Alcohol, 41*, 215-241.

Blackwell, J. E. (1991). *The Black community: Diversity and unity.* New York: Harper-Collins.

Bowditch, C. (1993). Getting rid of trouble makers: High school discipline procedures and the production of dropouts. *Social Problems, 40*, 493-509.

Bowker, L. H. (1978). *Women, crime and the criminal justice system.* Lexington, MA: Lexington Books.

Brown, S. E. (1984). Social class, child maltreatment, and delinquent behavior. *Criminology, 22*, 259-278.

Burkett, S. R., & Jensen, E. L. (1975). Conventional ties, peer influence, and the fear of apprehension: A study of adolescent marijuana use. *Sociological Quarterly, 16*, 522-533.

Bursik, R. J., & Webb, J. (1982). Community change and patterns of delinquency. *American Journal of Sociology, 88*, 24-42.

Bursik, R. J., Jr., & Grasmick, H. G. (1993). Economic deprivation and neighborhood crime rates, 1960-1980. *Law & Society Review, 27*, 263-283.

Canter, R. J. (1982a). Family correlates of male and female delinquency. *Criminology, 20*, 149-167.

Canter, R. J. (1982b). Sex differences in self-report delinquency. *Criminology, 20*, 373-393.

Cernkovich, S. A., & Giordano, P. C. (1979). Delinquency, opportunity, and gender. *Journal of Criminal Law and Criminology, 70*, 145-151.

Cernkovich, S. A., & Giordano, P. C. (1987). Family relationships and delinquency. *Criminology, 25*, 295-321.

Cernkovich, S. A., & Giordano, P. C. (1992). School bonding, race, and delinquency. *Criminology, 30*, 261-291.

Chesney-Lind, M. (1989). Girls' crime and women's place: Toward a feminist model of female delinquency. *Crime & Delinquency, 35*, 5-29.

Clark, J. P., & Haurek, E. W. (1966). Age and sex roles of adolescents and their involvement in misconduct: A reappraisal. *Sociology and Social Research, 50,* 495-508.

Clark, J. P., & Wenninger, E. P. (1962). Socio-economic class and area as correlates of illegal behavior among juveniles. *American Sociological Review, 27,* 826-834.

Colvin, M., & Pauly, J. (1983). A critique of criminology: Toward an integrated structural-Marxist theory of delinquency production. *American Journal of Sociology, 89,* 513-551.

Conger, R. D. (1976). Social control and social learning models of delinquent behavior: A synthesis. *Criminology, 14,* 17-40.

Conger, R. D., Lorenz, F. O., Elder, G. H., Jr., Melby, J. N., Simons, R. L., & Conger, K. J. (1991). A process model of family economic pressure and early adolescent alcohol use. *Journal of Early Adolescence, 11,* 430-449.

Cook, P., & Laub, J. (1986). The (surprising) stability of youth crime. *Journal of Quantitative Criminology, 2,* 265-277.

Cullen, F. T., Golden, K. M., & Cullen, J. B. (1979). Sex and delinquency: A partial test of the masculinity hypothesis. *Criminology, 17,* 301-310.

Datesman, S. K., & Scarpitti, F. R. (1975). Female delinquency and broken homes: A re-assessment. *Criminology, 13,* 33-54.

Datesman, S. K., Scarpitti, F. R., & Stephenson, R. M. (1975). Female delinquency: An application of self and opportunity theories. *Journal of Research in Crime and Delinquency, 12,* 107-124.

Dembo, R., Grandon, G., La Voie, L., Schmeidler, J., & Burgos, W. (1986). Parents and drugs revisited: Some further evidence in support of social learning theory. *Criminology, 24,* 85-104.

Dentler, R. A., & Monroe, L. J. (1961). Social correlates of early adolescent theft. *American Sociological Review, 26,* 733-743.

Denton, R. E., & Kampfe, C. M. (1994). The relationship between family variables and adolescent substance abuse: A literature review. *Adolescence, 29*(114), 475-495.

Dinges, M. M., & Oetting, E. R. (1993). Similarity in drug use patterns between adolescents and their friends. *Adolescence, 28*(110), 253-266.

Elifson, K. W., Petersen, D. M., & Hadaway, C. K. (1983). Religiosity and delinquency: A contextual analysis. *Criminology, 21,* 505-527.

Elliott, D. S., & Ageton, S. S. (1980). Reconciling race and class differences in self-reported and official estimates of delinquency. *American Sociological Review, 45,* 95-110.

Elliott, D. S., & Huizinga, D. (1983). Social class and delinquent behavior in a national youth panel: 1976-1980. *Criminology, 21,* 149-177.

Elliott, D. S., Huizinga, D., & Ageton, S. S. (1985). *Explaining delinquency and drug use.* Beverly Hills, CA: Sage.

Elliott, D. S., & Voss, H. L. (1974). *Delinquency and dropout.* Lexington, MA: D. C. Heath.

Ellis, G. J. (1986). Societal and parental predictors of parent-adolescent conflict. In G. K. Leigh & G. W. Peterson (Eds.), *Adolescents in families* (pp. 155-178). Cincinnati, OH: South-Western.

Empey, L. T., & Erickson, M. L. (1966). Hidden delinquency and social status. *Social Forces, 44,* 546-554.

Empey, L. T., & Lubeck, S. G. (1971). *Explaining delinquency*. Lexington, MA: D. C. Heath.

Empey, L. T., & Stafford, M. C. (1991). *American delinquency: Its meaning and construction* (3rd ed.). Belmont, CA: Wadsworth.

Erickson, M. L., & Empey, L. T. (1965). Class position, peers, and delinquency. *Sociology and Social Research, 49,* 268-282.

Erickson, M. L., & Jensen, G. F. (1977). Delinquency is still group behavior: Toward revitalizing the group premise in the sociology of deviance. *Journal of Criminal Law and Criminology, 68,* 262-277.

Esbensen, F. A., & Elliott, D. S. (1994). Continuity and discontinuity in illicit drug use: Patterns and antecedents. *Journal of Drug Issues, 24,* 75-97.

Esbensen, F. A., & Huizinga, D. (1993). Gangs, drugs, and delinquency in a survey of urban youth. *Criminology, 31,* 565-587.

Eve, R. A. (1982, August). *Untangling the sex difference in delinquency: Social bonds, peers, gender roles and body images.* Paper presented at the annual meeting of the American Sociological Association, San Francisco.

Fagan, J. (1989). The social organization of drug use and drug dealing among urban gangs. *Criminology, 27,* 633-669.

Fagan, J., & Wexler, S. (1987). Family origin of violent delinquents. *Criminology, 25,* 643-669.

Foucault, M. (1979). *Discipline and punish: The birth of the prison.* New York: Vintage.

Frease, D. E. (1973). Delinquency, social class, and the schools. *Sociology and Social Research, 57,* 443-459.

Friday, P. C., & Hage, J. (1976). Youth crime in postindustrial societies. *Criminology, 14,* 347-367.

Giordano, P. C. (1978). Girls, guys, and gangs: The changing social context of female delinquency. *Journal of Criminal Law and Criminology, 69,* 126-132.

Giordano, P. C., & Cernkovich, S. A. (1979). On complicating the relationship between liberation and delinquency. *Social Problems, 26,* 467-481.

Giordano, P. C., Cernkovich, S. A., & De Maris, A. (1993). The family and peer relations of black adolescents. *Journal of Marriage and the Family, 55,* 277-287.

Giordano, P. C., Cernkovich, S. A., & Pugh, M. D. (1986). Friendships and delinquency. *American Journal of Sociology, 91,* 1170-1202.

Glaser, D. (1978). *Crime in our changing society.* New York: Holt, Rinehart & Winston.

Gold, M. (1963). *Status forces in delinquent boys.* Ann Arbor: University of Michigan, Institute for Social Research.

Gold, M. (1966). Undetected delinquent behavior. *Journal of Research in Crime and Delinquency, 3,* 27-46.

Gold, M. (1970). *Delinquent behavior in an American city.* Belmont, CA: Brooks/Cole.

Goldstein, A. P. (1990). *Delinquents on delinquency.* Champaign, IL: Research Press.

Gottlieb, D., & Chafetz, J. S. (1977). Dynamics of familial, generational conflict and reconciliation: A research note. *Youth & Society, 9,* 213-224.

Gottlieb, D., & Heinsohn, A. L. (1973). Sociology and youth. *Sociological Quarterly, 14,* 249-270.

Gove, W. R., & Crutchfield, R. D. (1982). The family and juvenile delinquency. *Sociological Quarterly, 23,* 301-319.

Greenberg, D. F. (1977). Delinquency and the age structure of society. *Contemporary Crises: Crime, Law, and Social Policy, 1,* 189-223.

Hagan, J. (1991). Destiny and drift: Subcultural preferences, status attainments, and the rushes and rewards of youth. *American Sociological Review, 56,* 567-582.

Hagan, J. (1993). Introduction: Crime in social and legal context. *Law & Society Review, 27,* 255-261.

Hagan, J., Gillis, A. R., & Simpson, J. (1985). The class structure of gender and delinquency: Toward a power control theory of common delinquent behavior. *American Journal of Sociology, 90,* 1151-1178.

Hagan, J., Gillis, A. R., & Simpson, J. (1990). Clarifying and extending power-control theory. *American Journal of Sociology, 95,* 1024-1037.

Hagedorn, J. M. (1994). Homeboys, dope fiends, legits, and new jacks. *Criminology, 32,* 197-219.

Harer, M. D., & Steffensmeier, D. (1992). The differing effects of economic inequality on black and white rates of violence. *Social Forces, 70,* 1035-1054.

Hays, R. D., & Revetto, J. R. (1990). Peer cluster theory and adolescent drug use: A reanalysis. *Journal of Drug Education, 20,* 191-198.

Hill, G. D., & Atkinson, M. P. (1988). Gender, familial control, and delinquency. *Criminology, 26,* 127-147.

Hindelang, M. J. (1971). Age, sex, and the versatility of delinquent involvements. *Social Problems, 18,* 522-535.

Hindelang, M. J. (1973). Causes of delinquency: A partial replication and extension. *Social Problems, 20,* 471-487.

Hindelang, M. J. (1978). Race and involvement in common law personal crimes. *American Sociological Review, 43,* 93-109.

Hirschi, T. (1969). *Causes of delinquency.* Berkeley: University of California Press.

Hirschi, T., & Hindelang, M. J. (1977). Intelligence and delinquency: A revisionist review. *American Sociological Review, 42,* 571-587.

Hirschi, T., Hindelang, M. J., & Weis, J. (1982). Reply to "On the use of self-report data to determine the class distribution of criminal and delinquent behavior." *American Sociological Review, 47,* 433-435.

Huff, C. R. (1989). Youth gangs and public policy. *Crime & Delinquency, 35,* 524-537.

Huizinga, D., & Elliott, D. S. (1987). Juvenile offenders: Prevalence, offender incidence, and arrest rates by race. *Crime & Delinquency, 33,* 206-224.

Hundleby, J. D., & Mercer, G. W. (1987). Family and friends as social environments and their relationship to young adolescents' use of alcohol, tobacco, and marijuana. *Journal of Marriage and the Family, 49,* 151-164.

Jaquith, S. N. (1981). Adolescent marijuana and alcohol use: An empirical test of differential association theory. *Criminology, 19,* 271-280.

Jarjoura, G. R. (1993). Does dropping out of school enhance delinquent involvement: Results from a large-scale national probability sample. *Criminology, 31,* 149-172.

Jenkins, P. H. (1995). School delinquency and school commitment. *Sociology of Education, 68,* 221-239.

Jensen, G. F. (1972). Parents, peers, and delinquent action: A test of the differential association perspective. *American Journal of Sociology, 78,* 562-575.

Jensen, G. F. (1976). Race, achievement and delinquency: A further look at delinquency in a birth cohort. *American Journal of Sociology, 82,* 379-387.

Jensen, G. F., & Brownfield, D. (1983). Parents and drugs: Specifying the consequences of attachment. *Criminology, 21,* 543-554.

Jensen, G. F., & Eve, R. (1976). Sex differences in delinquency: An experimentation of popular sociological explanations. *Criminology, 13,* 427-447.

Jensen, G. F., & Thompson, K. (1990). What's class got to do with it? A further examination of power-control theory. *American Journal of Sociology, 95,* 1009-1023.

Johnson, R. A., Su, S. S., Gerstein, D. R., Shin, H. Ch., & Hoffman, J. P. (1995). Parental influences on deviant behavior in early adolescence: A logistic response analysis of age and gender differentiated effects. *Journal of Quantitative Criminology, 11,* 167-193.

Johnson, R. E. (1979). *Juvenile delinquency and its origins.* New York: Cambridge University Press.

Johnson, R. E. (1986). Family structure and delinquency: General patterns and gender differences. *Criminology, 24,* 65-84.

Johnson, V., & Pandina, R. J. (1991). Effects of the family environment on adolescent substance use, delinquency, and coping styles. *American Journal of Drug and Alcohol Abuse, 17,* 71-88.

Johnstone, J.W.C. (1978). Juvenile delinquency and the family: A contextual interpretation. *Youth & Society, 9,* 299-313.

Joseph, J. (1995). Juvenile delinquency among African Americans. *Journal of Black Studies, 25,* 475-491.

Kafka, R. R., & London, P. (1991). Communication in relationships and adolescent substance use: The influence of parents and friends. *Adolescence, 26*(103), 567-598.

Kandel, D. B. (1980). Drug and drinking behavior among youth. *Annual Review of Sociology, 6,* 235-285.

Kandel, D. B., & Adler, I. (1982). Socialization into marijuana use among French adolescents: A cross-cultural comparison with the United States. *Journal of Health and Social Behavior, 23,* 295-309.

Kandel, D., & Davies, M. (1991). Friendship networks, intimacy, and illicit drug use in young adulthood: A comparison of two competing theories. *Criminology, 29,* 441-467.

Kaplan, H. B., Martin, S. S., & Robbins, C. (1982). Application of a general theory of deviant behavior: Self-derogation and adolescent drug use. *Journal of Health and Social Behavior, 23,* 274-294.

Kelly, D. H. (1974). Track position and delinquent involvement: A preliminary analysis. *Sociology and Social Research, 58,* 380-386.

Kelly, D. H., & Pink, W. T. (1982). School crime and individual responsibility: The perpetuation of a myth? *Urban Review, 14,* 47-63.

Kleck, G. (1982). On the use of self-report data to determine the class distribution of criminal and delinquent behavior. *American Sociological Review, 47,* 427-433.

Krohn, M. D., & Massey, J. L. (1980). Social control and delinquent behavior: An examination of the elements of the social bond. *Sociological Quarterly, 21,* 529-543.

Krohn, M., Thornberry, T., Collins-Hall, L., & Lizotte, A. (1995). School dropout, delinquent behavior, and drug use. In H. Kaplan (Ed.), *Drugs, crime and other deviant adaptations: Longitudinal studies* (pp. 163-183). New York: Plenum.

LaGrange, R. L., & White, H. R. (1985). Age differences in delinquency: A test of theory. *Criminology, 23,* 19-45.

Larzelere, R. E., & Patterson, G. R. (1990). Parental management: Mediator of the effect of socioeconomic status on early delinquency. *Criminology, 28,* 301-324.

Laub, J. H., & Sampson, R. J. (1988). Unraveling families and delinquency: A re-analysis of the Gluecks' data. *Criminology, 26,* 355-380.

Lauritsen, J. T. (1994). Explaining race and gender differences in adolescent sexual behavior. *Social Forces, 72,* 859-884.

Liska, A. E., & Reed, M. D. (1985). Ties to conventional institutions and delinquency: Estimating reciprocal effects. *American Sociological Review, 50,* 547-560.

Loeber, R., & Dishion, T. J. (1983). Early predictors of male adolescent delinquency: A review. *Psychological Bulletin, 94,* 68-99.

Loseke, B. R. (1991). Reply to Murray A. Straus: Readings on discipline and deviance. *Social Problems, 38,* 162-165.

Lyerly, R. R., & Skipper, J. K., Jr. (1981). Differential rates of rural-urban delinquency: A social control approach. *Criminology, 19,* 385-399.

Males, M. A. (1996). *The scapegoat generation: America's war on adolescents.* Monroe, ME: Common Courage Press.

Mann, D. W. (1981). Age and differential predictability of delinquent behavior. *Social Forces, 60,* 97-113.

Massey, D. S. (1990). American apartheid: Segregation and the making of the underclass. *American Journal of Sociology, 96,* 329-357.

Matsueda, R. L. (1982). Testing control theory and differential association: A causal modeling approach. *American Sociological Review, 47,* 489-504.

Matsueda, R. L., & Heimer, K. (1987). Race, family structure, and delinquency: A test of differential association and social control theories. *American Sociological Review, 52,* 826-840.

McCord, J. (1991). Family relationships, juvenile delinquency, and adult criminality. *Criminology, 29,* 397-417.

McCord, W., McCord, J., & Zola, I. (1959). *Origins of crime.* New York: Columbia University Press.

McGee, Z. T. (1992). Social class differences in parental and peer influence on adolescent drug use. *Deviant Behavior: An Interdisciplinary Journal, 13,* 349-372.

Meadow, A., Abramowitz, S. I., de la Cruz, A., & Bay, G. O. (1981). Self-concept, negative family affect, and delinquency: A comparison across Mexican social classes. *Criminology, 19,* 434-448.

Meier, R. F., Burkett, S. R., & Hickman, C. A. (1984). Sanctions, peers, and deviance: Preliminary models of a social control process. *Sociological Quarterly, 25,* 67-82.

Messner, S. F., & Krohn, M. D. (1990). Class, compliance structures, and delinquency: Assessing integrated structural-Marxist theory. *American Journal of Sociology, 96,* 300-328.

Miller, A. (1993). *Breaking down the wall of silence: The liberating experience of facing painful truth.* New York: Meridian.

Miller, A. (1994). *The drama of the gifted child: The search for the true self* (rev. ed.). New York: Basic Books.

Norland, S., & Shover, N. (1977). Gender roles and female criminality: Some critical comments. *Criminology, 15,* 87-104.

Norland, S., Wessel, R. C., & Shover, N. (1981). Masculinity and delinquency. *Criminology, 19,* 421-433.

Nye, I. (1958). *Family relationships and delinquent behavior.* New York: John Wiley.

O'Donnell, J., Hawkins, J. D., Catalano, R. F., Abbott, R. D., & Day, L. (1995). Preventing school failure, drug use, and delinquency among low-income children: Long-term intervention in elementary schools. *American Journal of Orthopsychiatry, 65*, 87-100.

Olson, D. H., Sprenkle, D. H., & Russell, C. S. (1979). Circumplex model of marital and family systems: I. Cohesion and adaptability dimensions, family types, and clinical applications. *Family Process, 18*, 3-28.

Osgood, D. W., O'Malley, P., Bachman, J., & Johnston, L. (1989). Time trends and age trends in arrests and self-reported illegal behavior. *Criminology, 27*, 389-417.

Patterson, G. R., & Dishion, T. J. (1985). Contribution of families and peers to delinquency. *Criminology, 23*, 63-79.

Peterson, E. T. (1974). *Parent-child relationships and juvenile delinquency.* (ERIC Document Reproduction Service No. ED 106 702)

Peterson, P. L., Hawkins, J. D., Abbott, R. D., & Catalano, R. F. (1994). Disentangling the effects of parental drinking, family management, and parental alcohol norms on current drinking by black and white adolescents. *Journal of Research on Adolescence, 4*, 203-227.

Pink, W. T. (1982). Academic failure, student social conflict, and delinquent behavior. *Urban Review, 14*, 141-180.

Polk, K. (1967). Urban social areas and delinquency. *Social Problems, 14*, 320-325.

Polk, K. (1969). Class, strain and rebellion among adolescents. *Social Problems, 17*, 214-224.

Polk, K. (1983). Curriculum tracking and delinquency: Some observations. *American Sociological Review, 48*, 282-284.

Polk, K. (1984). The new marginal youth. *Crime & Delinquency, 30*, 462-480.

Polk, K., & Burkett, S. R. (1972). Drinking and rebellion: A study of adolescent drinking. In K. Polk & W. Schafer (Eds.), *Schools and delinquency* (pp. 115-129). Englewood Cliffs, NJ: Prentice Hall.

Polk, K., & Halferty, D. (1966). Adolescents, commitment, and delinquency. *Journal of Research in Crime and Delinquency, 3*, 82-96.

Polk, K., & Pink, W. (1972). School pressures toward deviance: A cross-cultural comparison. In K. Polk & W. Schafer (Eds.), *Schools and delinquency* (pp. 129-145). Englewood Cliffs, NJ: Prentice Hall.

Polk, K., & Richmond, F. L. (1972). Those who fail. In K. Polk & W. Schafer (Eds.), *Schools and delinquency* (pp. 55-70). Englewood Cliffs, NJ: Prentice Hall.

Poole, E. D., & Regoli, R. M. (1979). Parental support, delinquent friends, and delinquency: A test of interaction effects. *Journal of Law and Criminology, 70*, 188-194.

Rankin, J. H. (1980). School factors and delinquency: Interactions by age and sex. *Sociology and Social Research, 64*, 420-435.

Rankin, J. H. (1983). The family context of delinquency. *Social Problems, 30*, 466-479.

Rankin, J. H., & Wells, L. E. (1987). The prevention effects of the family on delinquency. In E. H. Johnson (Ed.), *Handbook on crime and delinquency prevention* (pp. 257-275). Westport, CT: Greenwood.

Regan, T., & Vogt, V. (1983, April). *Critical analysis of male and female delinquency.* Paper presented at the annual meeting of the Midwest Sociological Association, Kansas City, MO.

Reiss, A. J., Jr., & Rhodes, A. L. (1961). The distribution of juvenile delinquency in social class structure. *American Sociological Review, 26*, 720-732.

Richards, P. (1979). Middle-class vandalism and age-status conflict. *Social Problems, 26*, 482-497.

Rickel, A. U., & Becker-Lausen, E. (1995). Intergenerational influences on child outcomes: Implications for prevention and intervention. In B. A. Ryan, G. R. Adams, T. P. Gullotta, R. P. Weissberg, & R. L. Hampton (Eds.), *The family-school connection: Theory, research, and practice* (pp. 315-340). Thousand Oaks, CA: Sage.

Rosen, L. (1985). Family and delinquency: Structure or function? *Criminology, 23*, 553-573.

Rosenbaum, J. L. (1989). Family dysfunction and female delinquency. *Crime & Delinquency, 35*, 31-44.

Sampson, R. J. (1987). Urban black violence: The effects of male joblessness and family disruption. *American Journal of Sociology, 93*, 348-382.

Sampson, R. J., & Laub, J. H. (1993). Structural variations in juvenile court processing: Inequality, the underclass, and social control. *Law & Society Review, 27*, 285-311.

Sampson, R. J., & Laub, J. H. (1994). Urban poverty and the family context of delinquency: A look at structure and process in a classic study. *Child Development, 65*, 523-540.

Sarri, R. (1983). Gender issues in juvenile justice. *Crime & Delinquency, 29*, 381-397.

Schafer, W. E. (1972a). Deviance in the public school: An interactional view. In K. Polk & W. Schafer (Eds.), *Schools and delinquency* (pp. 145-164). Englewood Cliffs, NJ: Prentice Hall.

Schafer, W. E. (1972b). Participation in interscholastic athletics and delinquency: A preliminary study. In K. Polk & W. Schafer (Eds.), *Schools and delinquency* (pp. 91-102). Englewood Cliffs, NJ: Prentice Hall.

Schafer, W. E., & Polk, K. (1972a). School career and delinquency. In K. Polk & W. Schafer (Eds.), *Schools and delinquency* (pp. 165-181). Englewood Cliffs, NJ: Prentice Hall.

Schafer, W. E., & Polk, K. (1972b). School conditions contributing to delinquency. In K. Polk & W. Schafer (Eds.), *Schools and delinquency* (pp. 182-239). Englewood Cliffs, NJ: Prentice Hall.

Schafer, W. E., Olexa, C., & Polk, K. (1972). Programmed for social class: Tracking in high school. In K. Polk & W. Schafer (Eds.), *Schools and delinquency* (pp. 33-54). Englewood Cliffs, NJ: Prentice Hall.

Seydlitz, R. (1990). The effects of gender, age, and parental attachment on delinquency: A test for interactions. *Sociological Spectrum, 10*, 209-225.

Seydlitz, R. (1991). The effects of age and gender on parental control and delinquency. *Youth & Society, 23*, 175-201.

Seydlitz, R. (1993a). Compared to what? Delinquent girls and the similarity or differences issue. In C. C. Culliver (Ed.), *Female criminality: The state of the art* (pp. 133-169). New York: Garland.

Seydlitz, R. (1993b). Complexity in the relationships among direct and indirect parental controls and delinquency. *Youth & Society, 24*, 243-275.

Shover, N., Norland, S., James, J., & Thornton, W. E. (1979). Gender roles and delinquency. *Social Forces, 58*, 162-175.

Siegel, L. J., & Senna, J. J. (1991). *Juvenile delinquency: Theory, practice and law* (4th ed.). St. Paul, MN: West.

Simons, R. L., Miller, M. G., & Aigner, S. M. (1980). Contemporary theories of deviance and female delinquency: An empirical test. *Journal of Research in Crime and Delinquency, 17,* 42-57.

Simons, R. L., Robertson, J. F., & Downs, W. R. (1989). The nature of the association between parental rejection and delinquent behavior. *Journal of Youth and Adolescence, 18,* 297-310.

Simons, R. L., Wu, C., Conger, R. D., & Lorenz, F. O. (1994). Two routes to delinquency: Differences between early and late starters in the impact of parenting and deviant peers. *Criminology, 32,* 247-275.

Simonson, C. E. (1991). *Juvenile justice in America.* New York: Macmillan.

Smith, C., & Thornberry, T. (1995). The relationship between childhood maltreatment and adolescent involvement in delinquency. *Criminology, 33,* 451-477.

Smith, D. A., & Paternoster, R. (1987). The gender gap in theories of deviance: Issues and evidence. *Journal of Research in Crime and Delinquency, 24,* 140-172.

Sommers, I., & Baskin, D. R. (1994). Factors related to female adolescent initiation into violent street crime. *Youth & Society, 25,* 468-489.

Steffensmeier, D. J., Allan, E. A., Harew, M. D., & Streifel, C. (1989). Age and the distribution of crime. *American Journal of Sociology, 94,* 803-831.

Steffensmeier, D. J., & Streifel, C. (1991). Age, gender, and crime across three historical periods: 1935, 1960, and 1985. *Social Forces, 69,* 869-894.

Stinchcombe, A. L. (1964). *Rebellion in high school.* Chicago: Quadrangle Books.

Straus, M. A. (1991). Discipline and deviance: Physical punishment of children and violence and other crime in adulthood. *Social Problems, 38,* 133-154.

Thomas, C. W., & Hyman, J. M. (1978). Compliance theory, control theory, and juvenile delinquency. In M. Krohn & R. L. Akers (Eds.), *Crime, law, and sanctions* (pp. 73-91). Beverly Hills, CA: Sage.

Thompson, W., Mitchell, J., & Dodder, R. A. (1984). An empirical test of Hirschi's control theory of delinquency. *Deviant Behavior, 5,* 11-22.

Thornberry, T. P. (1987). Toward an interactional theory of delinquency. *Criminology, 25,* 863-891.

Thornberry, T. P., & Farnworth, M. (1982). Social correlates of criminal involvement: Further evidence on the relationship between social status and criminal behavior. *American Sociological Review, 47,* 505-518.

Thornberry, T. P., Moore, M., & Christenson, R. L. (1985). The effect of dropping out of high school on subsequent criminal behavior. *Criminology, 23,* 3-18.

Tittle, C. R. (1983). Social class and criminal behavior: A critique of the theoretical foundation. *Social Forces, 62,* 334-358.

Tittle, C. R., & Meier, R. F. (1990). Specifying the SES/delinquency relationship. *Criminology, 28,* 271-299.

Tittle, C. R., & Meier, R. F. (1991). Specifying the SES/delinquency relationship by social characteristics of contexts. *Journal of Research in Crime and Delinquency, 28,* 430-455.

Tittle, C. R., Villemez, W., & Smith, D. A. (1982). One step forward, two steps back: More on the class/criminality controversy. *American Sociological Review, 47,* 435-438.

Tygart, C. E. (1991). Juvenile delinquency and number of children in a family. *Youth & Society, 22,* 525-536.

Warr, E. M., & Stafford, M. (1991). The influence of delinquent peers: What they think or what they do? *Criminology, 29,* 851-866.

Warr, M. (1993a). Age, peers, and delinquency. *Criminology, 31,* 17-40.

Warr, M. (1993b). Parents, peers, and delinquency. *Social Forces, 72,* 247-264.

Weis, J., & Sederstrom, J. (1981). *Reports of the National Juvenile Assessment Centers, the prevention of serious delinquency: What to do.* Washington, DC: U.S. Department of Justice.

Wellford, C. (1975). Labeling theory and criminology: An assessment. *Social Problems, 22,* 332-345.

Wells, E. L., & Rankin, J. H. (1988). Direct parental controls and delinquency. *Criminology, 26,* 263-285.

West, D. J. (1973). *Who becomes delinquent?* London: Heinemann.

White, H. R., Pandina, R. J., & LaGrange, R. L. (1987). Longitudinal predictors of serious substance use and delinquency. *Criminology, 25,* 715-740.

Wiatrowski, M. D., Griswold, D. B., & Roberts, M. K. (1981). Social control theory and delinquency. *American Sociological Review, 46,* 525-542.

Wiatrowski, M. D., Hernsell, S., Massey, C. R., & Wilson, D. L. (1982). Curriculum tracking and delinquency. *American Sociological Review, 47,* 151-160.

Wolfgang, M. E., Figlio, R., & Sellin, T. (1972). *Delinquency in a birth cohort.* Chicago: University of Chicago Press.

Wright, K. N., & Wright, K. E. (1994). *Family life, delinquency and crime: A policy maker's guide.* Washington, DC: U.S. Government Printing Office.

4. Adolescent Drug Use, Delinquency, and Other Behaviors

C. G. Leukefeld
T. K. Logan
R. R. Clayton
C. Martin
R. Zimmerman
A. Cattarello
R. Milich
D. Lynam

Empirical evidence supports a strong relationship between drug use and delinquency (Anglin & Hser, 1987; Hser, Anglin, & Booth, 1987; Inciardi & Pottinger, 1986; Sommers & Baskin, 1994). This association has been documented regardless of drug type, offense committed, and population sampled (Ball, Rosen, Flueck, & Nurco, 1981; Dembo et al., 1991; Elliott & Ageton, 1976; McGlothlin, Anglin, & Wilson, 1978; Otero-Lopez, Luengo-Martin, Miron-Redondo, Carrillo-DeLa-Penta, & Romero-Trinanes, 1994; Speckart & Anglin, 1985). There is also evidence that there are common underlying factors that contribute to drug abuse and delinquency (Clayton, 1995). Factors for both delinquency and drug use include family, peer, and personality variables that were common predictors (Otero-Lopez et al., 1994); low educational achievement as a common and early predictor (Stouthamer-Loeber & Loeber, 1988); family structure and conflict as common variables (Hawkins, Catalano, & Brewer, 1994); and childhood aggression as predictive of frequent adolescent drug use and delinquency (O'Donnell, Hawkins, & Abbott, 1995).

AUTHORS' NOTE: Support was provided by the National Institute on Drug Abuse as part of the Prevention Research Center at the University of Kentucky, NIDA Grant Number P50-DA05312. Requests for information should be sent to Carl Leukefeld, DSW, Center on Drug and Alcohol Research, University of Kentucky, 208 Medical Center, Annex 4, Lexington, KY 40536.

Drug use remains at an unacceptably high level among adolescents in the United States. Results from the national Monitoring the Future Study show that by eighth grade, 67% of students have tried alcohol, and more than one fourth (26%) say they have already been drunk at least once (U.S. Department of Health and Human Services, 1994). Almost one in five (19%) of the eighth graders surveyed said that they used inhalants, and 5% said that they had used inhalants in the past month. Marijuana was tried by one in every eight eighth graders (13%), and it had been used in the prior month by 5%. In addition, 12% of eighth graders said that they used prescription-type stimulants, and 3.6% had used them in the past month. Cigarettes had been tried by nearly half of eighth graders (45%); one in seven said they had smoked in the prior month, and only 52% believed that there was a great risk associated with being a pack-a-day smoker.

The data suggest that most students have used alcohol. Eighty-one percent of 10th graders and 87% of 12th graders reported trying alcohol. Trends in drug use among 8th- and 10th-grade Black, White, and Hispanic males and females showed an increase in drug use from 1991 to 1994. For high school seniors, drug use remained fairly stable across time. In 1993, 18% of Whites, 21.6% of Hispanics, and 14.5% of African Americans aged 12 to 17 years said that they had used illicit drugs. These numbers suggest that a large percentage of youth in the United States are at risk of proceeding to other drug use.

Drug use and abuse among preteens and young adults also places hardships on parents, schools, communities, and the country. Drug use and the associated consequences may be different for different age cohorts (Johnston, O'Malley, & Bachman, 1989). For example, a 13-year-old who uses and/or abuses alcohol potentially will have different problems associated with his or her alcohol use than will a 16-year-old who is also just learning to drive and is more likely to mix drinking with driving than the 13-year-old.

The consequences of use may vary for early users who discontinue use, early continuous users, and those who become users at a later age. Shedler and Block (1990) reported that adolescents who were early, frequent users of substances were relatively maladjusted. For example, at age 18, these adolescents reported less meaningful personal relationships, were not capable of investing in school and work, felt troubled and inadequate, and were impulsive. In addition, those adolescents who reported that they experimented with substances were psychologically healthier than either frequent users or abstainers at age 18.

The amount of drug and other substance use, as individuals move from childhood through adolescence to young adulthood, may affect adolescent development. Because the development and onset of substance use and/or abuse is different for each person, prevention and intervention strategies are more likely to be effective when prevention and prevention intervention programs are tailored to user characteristics (Gordon, 1983).

The purpose of this chapter is to examine selected etiological factors that are associated with adolescent drug use, abuse, and other problems, including delinquency. Selected etiological factors are reviewed in the following areas: individual, family, peer, school, neighborhood/social, and biological. In addition, developmental progression as well as risk/protective factors are presented as key concepts to more completely understand the relationship of drug use and delinquency. Finally, a model currently being tested by the authors is presented, and future implications are suggested.

ETIOLOGY

Individual Factors

Personality variables. Conduct disorder or antisocial personality has been correlated with drug abuse in general population samples (Lynam, 1996). Cadoret (1992) suggests that antisocial personality is an important factor in the transition from nonuse to use. Childhood conduct problems have been identified as a major risk factor for adult disorders characterized as antisocial behavior (Lynam, 1996). Thus, measures of aggressive behavior are more stable from childhood than are childhood measures of IQ. The connection between drug abuse and psychopathology has been identified repeatedly. For example, Weiss (1992) reports that a psychiatric disorder increases the vulnerability of patients to move from substance use to dependence.

Another personality variable that is often linked with substance use and/or abuse is self-esteem. The lack of self-esteem has been related to a wide variety of negative emotions and behaviors. For example, Overholser, Adams, Lehnert, and Brinkman (1995) found that low self-esteem was related to higher levels of depression, hopelessness, and suicidal ideation, and an increased likelihood of having previously attempted suicide. Abernathy, Massad, and Romano-Dwyer (1995) reported that self-esteem may be a factor in the smoking behavior of female adolescents in Grades 6 to 8 but not for males in any grade. Kaplan, Martin, and Robbins (1982) suggest that changes in self-derogation (e.g., low self-esteem) are related to drug use and other forms of delinquent behavior. However, the correlation of self-esteem and drug use has been shown to be low (Kaplan et al., 1982; White, Johnson, & Horwitz, 1986). Thus, the inconsistent findings for self-esteem and drug use may be due to self-esteem being measured inadequately, especially for adolescents, because self-esteem may be anchored to the situation and change with the shifting adolescent environment (Clayton, 1992).

Another example of an individual factor is sensation seeking. Sensation seeking has been a predictor of drug use initiation (Beck, Thombs, Mahoney, & Fingar, 1995). Sensation seeking (Zuckerman, 1979) has been defined as a need related to preferences for novel, complex, and ambiguous stimuli and has been measured as a personality trait and as a part of arousability (Pandina, 1992). Sensation seeking at the human level has a parallel construct at the animal level as novelty seeking (Bardo & Mueller, 1991). Research has explored possible relationships between personality dimensions—such as sensation seeking—and biological parameters (Gabel, Stadler, Bjorn, Shindledecker, & Bowden, 1994). One specific biological correlate that has been linked to sensation-seeking behavior is monoamine oxidase (MAO). However, although MAO platelets correlate with sensation seeking, platelet activity is not a direct measure of brain monoamine activity. Nevertheless, sensation seeking is usually described as a biologically based trait anchored in MAO so that the lower the MAO, the higher the sensation seeking (Zuckerman, 1983). MAO is discussed further as a biological factor later in this chapter.

Family Factors

The literature suggests that there is a relationship between teenage substance use and selected family characteristics. There are two broad categories of family characteristics: family drug use patterns and family atmosphere. Family drug use may influence adolescent substance abuse. Drug use by family members significantly increases the chances that other family members will also use drugs (Adler & Lotecka, 1973; Beardslee, Son, & Vaillant, 1986; Blum, 1972; Craig & Brown, 1975; Denton & Kampfe, 1994; Needle et al., 1986; Tec, 1974; Tolone & Dermott, 1975). In addition, parent habits and attitudes toward substance use have been found to be significantly related to those habits of their children (Adler & Lotecka, 1973; Cannon, 1976; Tec, 1974; Tolone & Dermott, 1975). Sibling drug use has also been found to be significantly related to adolescent drug use patterns (Craig & Brown, 1975; Needle et al., 1986). In addition, Denton and Kampfe (1994) suggest that availability and drug use modeling are major factors contributed by older siblings to younger sibling drug use.

Family atmosphere is a second broad category that may influence adolescent substance use and abuse. Family atmosphere includes family composition and family interaction. Family composition has a significant impact on adolescent substance abuse (Denton & Kampfe, 1994). For example, Kellam, Brown, Rubin, and Ensminger (1983) reported that there are 76 different family structures and suggest that one of the best predictors of drug use among adolescents was a single-parent family with the mother as the parent. Brook, Cohen, Whiteman, and Gordon (1992) reported that family-type variables were associated with movement from being a nonuser or light user to a moderate marijuana user. Several studies also indicate that children from broken homes (due to marital discord) are at higher risk for delinquency and drug use (Baumrind, 1983; Robins, 1980). Family conflict was found to be a stronger predictor of delinquency than was family structure (McCord, 1979; Rutter & Giller, 1983). In addition, the lack of parent-child closeness and the lack of maternal involvement was related to drug initiation (Brook, Lukoff, & Whiteman, 1980).

Family interaction is typically defined as involvement with family, family communication, and discipline. Reardon and Griffing (1983) suggest that positive child-parent association is vital to the development of a strong self-concept and to the prevention of drug abuse. Tec (1974) found that a high percentage of adolescents who abused drugs often reported low satisfaction with their families. Other studies have reported that although dissatisfaction varies according to the type of drug used by the adolescent, family environment is generally described by a drug-abusing adolescent as hostile, lacking understanding, lacking in love, lacking cohesiveness, lacking cooperation, and as a situation high in alienation (Adler & Lotecka, 1973; Gantman, 1978; Hamburg, Kraemer, & Jahnke, 1975; Pandina & Schuele, 1983; Rees & Wilborn, 1983; Streit, Halsted, & Pascale, 1974; Tolone & Dermott, 1975; Wechsler & Thum, 1973).

Common family characteristics among adolescent drug abusers include negative communication patterns; inconsistent, unclear behavior limits; and unrealistic parental expectations (Denton & Kampfe, 1994). Denton and Kampfe (1994) also suggest that there is a communication gap between family members of adolescents who are chemically dependent, which is supported by findings that adolescent drug abusers typically describe their parental communication as closed and unclear. Rigid communication patterns were also observed for these families.

The literature also suggests that discipline is important in family interactions. Research indicates that parents with drug-abusing adolescents view parenting as a job that requires suffering and sacrifice (Rees & Wilborn, 1983). These parents also reported a lack of confidence in child rearing. Although the literature indicates that there is a relationship between discipline and adolescent substance abuse, the nature of the relationship is not clear (Denton & Kampfe, 1994).

Peer and Peer Resistance Factors

Peer rejection in elementary grades has been related to drug use and abuse among adolescents. For example, Cole (1990) found that low peer acceptance elevated the risk for school problems and criminality. Peer drug use has been found to be highly associated with adolescent drug use (Akers, 1977; Elliott, Huizinga, & Ageton, 1985). Research also indicates that peer substance use is among the strongest predictors of substance use among youth (Brook et al., 1992; Newcomb, Maddahian, & Bentler, 1986). Brook et al. (1992) highlighted the impact of drug use by friends, time spent with friends, and the influence of deviance among friends on drug use. Brook et al. (1992) also reported that peer drug use and time spent with friends were predictive of movement from nonuse or light use of alcohol to moderate use and from nonuse or light use of marijuana to moderate use of marijuana.

Bauman and Ennett (1994) summarize peer influence by stating that friends make drugs available to each other, friends model drug use by their friends, and peer group support and norms favor drug use. Bauman and Ennett (1994) also suggest that peer influence is only a partial contributing factor. Two additional factors that may influence drug use are selection and friendship formation as well as attributing behavior to the behavior of friends (Holmes, 1968). Fischer and Bauman (1988) found support for this hypothesis with their findings that those adolescents who did not use drugs were much more likely to be reported as drug users by their friends who used drugs than by their friends who did not use drugs. This friendship selection hypothesis suggests that adolescents seek out specific types of people (Bauman & Ennett, 1994). For example, when drug behaviors conflict with peer groups, friendships may dissolve, leaving an adolescent to find others with similar drug-using habits. This model suggests that drug behaviors cause friendships, as opposed to the peer influence model, which suggests that peers influence drug behavior. This is similar to the feathering and flocking phenomenon described by Elliot et al. (1985).

Oetting and Beauvais (1987) suggest that adolescent drug use is related to peer influence as the dominant variable in their peer cluster theory. A key link among peers may be sensation seeking, and that a larger number of sensation seekers in peer clusters increases the likelihood of drug use (Donohew, Rice, & Clayton, 1994). A conceptual underpinning for research on peer pressure resistance for drug initiation and use is Sutherland's (1947) theory of differential association, which emphasizes that criminal drug use behavior is learned in intimate networks (Pentz et al., 1989). Thus, an individual commits criminal acts because he or she has learned rationalizations and attitudes that are favorable to law violations, as opposed to rationalizations and attitudes unfavorable to the violation of the law (Akers, 1994). These adolescent rationalizations and attitudes are most likely to be learned through associations at school and in neighborhoods.

School Factors

School failure is predictive of adolescent drug abuse and is related to the frequency and levels of illicit drug use (Jessor, 1976; Robins, 1980; Smith & Fogg, 1978). Good school performance reduced the likelihood of frequent drug use (Hundleby & Mercer, 1987). Cernkovich and Giordano (1992) examined the relationship of school bonding to delinquency and reported that although school bonding explains a reasonable amount of the variance, school factors were as important as peer and family factors for delinquency involvement. Students who liked school and spent time on homework had decreased levels of drug use (Kelly & Balch, 1971). Pentz et al. (1989) reported that school smoking policy has a marginal effect on adolescent smoking, and that the use of punitive measures to regulate smoking has no effect, but a policy to stop smoking—and particularly to prevent smoking—was related to lower recent smoking.

Neighborhood and Social Factors

Rates of delinquent and criminal behavior tend to vary by geographic location (Reiss, 1986; Stark, 1987). For example, urban areas tend to have higher rates of crime and other forms of unconventional behavior (Fischer, 1975). Within specific urban areas, there are different rates of delinquency, crime, and substance abuse. Thus, alcohol and other drug use must be viewed in the context of the socioeconomic conditions in which adolescents live. Wilson (1987) emphasized the need to study unemployment and crime in low-income communities or neighborhoods using a macrolevel causal link that flows from joblessness and residential isolation of the minority poor to escalating problems of urban crime. The same can be said for drug use, which is connected to neighborhood disorganization and extreme economic deprivation. In addition, neighborhood social disorganization levels have been found to be predictive of individual drug use, delinquency, and their mediating factors (Cattarello, 1993; Gottfredson & McNeil, 1991; Simcha-Fagan & Schwartz, 1986). However, a detailed understanding of the relationship of economic resources and the context in which an adolescent lives to drug abuse is still incomplete. An important consideration is the relationship of the flow of drug-trafficking money into impoverished neighborhoods and the increased reliance of the residents on that money (Clayton, 1992).

Biological Factors

In general, studies have shown that genetic factors can influence behavior, including alcohol use (Cloninger, Bohman, & Sigvardsson, 1981; Goodwin, 1976, 1979). Although the literature on the genetic and biological factors related to alcoholism is extensive, the literature on their influence on drug use is more limited (Pickens et al., 1991). Biochemical measures that correlate with externalizing behaviors, such as substance abuse and conduct disorder, include MAO platelets, plasma dopamine beta hydroxylase (DBH), and plasma testosterone and estradiol. (Testosterone is the principal sex hormone for males, and estrogen is the principal sex hormone for females.) These markers have been studied in various populations with findings relevant to substance use.

MAO is an essential enzyme in the cells of most tissues that catalyzes the oxidation of monoamines such as norepinephrine and serotonin. MAO is also a biochemical marker that has been correlated with heavy alcohol consumption. In addition, low platelet activity is associated with the same personality traits found to be correlated with heavy alcohol consumption (LaGrange, Jones, Erb, & Reyes, 1995). Research suggests that there is a correlation between sensation seeking and drug use initiation (Clayton, Cattarello, & Walden, 1991; Donohew, Lorch, & Palmgreen, 1991). For 18-year-old boys, low MAO correlated with increased impulsivity and monotony avoidance on the Zuckerman Sensation Seeking Scale. In addition, tobacco, alcohol, and drug abuse have been negatively correlated with MAO (Von Knorring, 1984). Buchsbaum, Coursey, and Murphy (1976) found low MAO correlated with criminality and sensation seeking in male college students. In addition, chronic alcoholism is associated with lower platelet MAO activity (Sullivan, Stanfield, Schanberg, & Cavenar, 1978). Interestingly, Cederblad, Oreland, and Zachrisson (1992) found that girls with externalizing disorders were more likely to have low platelet MAO than were males with externalizing disorders. These externalizing disorders included alcohol and marijuana abuse, conduct disorder, and/or attention deficit disorder. Cederblad et al. (1992) also found that boys whose fathers were alcohol abusers had lower levels of MAO. It is interesting to note that given the higher rate of externalizing disorders in men, they have lower MAO than females (Cederblad et al., 1992), and MAO is relatively stable across age.

DBH is the synthesizing enzyme that converts to dopamine and norepinephrine. DBH has been negatively correlated with alcohol abuse and has a negative correlation with the personality traits associated with alcoholism, including sensation seeking, extroversion, and impulsivity (LaGrange et al., 1995). DBH also has been associated with externalizing disorders in children. Rogeness, Javors,

Maas, and Macedo (1990) reported that lower DBH is associated with undersocialized conduct disorder. In contrast to MAO, there are no gender distinctions, but DBH increases with age (Ciaranello & Boehme, 1981). This is intriguing, given the developmental increase in substance use vulnerability. Quay (1987), based on the work of Gray, Owen, Davis, and Tsaltas (1983), postulated that externalizing disorders are associated with decreased noradrenergic function, making DBH a possible marker with the effect of age on drug use.

One biological system that is particularly relevant when investigating the evolution of substance use through adolescence and into adulthood is the hypothalamic-pituitary-gonadotropin axis (HPGA). Two hormones of this axis show particular promise in identifying individuals at risk for initiating and maintaining substance use. The first is testosterone. Testosterone has been associated with cigarette smoking in adolescent males and females (Bauman, Foshee, Koch, Haley, & Downeon, 1989). Testosterone has also been correlated with alcohol consumption in adolescent and college-age males but not females (LaGrange et al., 1995; Udry, 1991). Testosterone concentrations are positively correlated with sensation seeking in college-age men (Daitzman, Zuckerman, Sammelwitz, & Ganjam, 1978). Testosterone also correlates with a number of problem behaviors, such as early sexual intercourse, aggression, violence, impulsivity, and extroverted personality (Daitzman et al., 1978; Daitzman & Zuckerman, 1980; Mattson, Schalling, Olweus, Low, & Svensson, 1980; Olweus, Mattson, Schalling, & Low, 1980; Udry, Talbert, & Morris, 1985). Testosterone may also be correlated with drug experimentation.

The second HPGA hormone of importance is estradiol. Estrogen is higher in male smokers and adult male alcoholics as compared to controls (King, Errico, & Parson, 1995; Klaiber & Broverman, 1988). Martin, Mainous, Oler, and Mainous (1995) found that both testosterone and estradiol were correlated with substance use in adolescent high school students and that estradiol levels were found to be higher in females who were currently using cigarettes and alcohol. Furthermore, females with both estradiol and testosterone levels at or above the medium were significantly more likely to use alcohol. There was also a trend toward increased likelihood of cigarette smoking for females high in both estradiol and testosterone. Relatively little attention has been given to the possible impact of testosterone and estradiol on initiation or maintenance of drug use in young adulthood. Given the developmental links in high-risk behaviors and testosterone, this hormone seems particularly important to better understand drug use.

Researchers are also investigating a newly discovered gene that was uncovered from twin and adoption studies over the past 20 years, the D4 dopamine receptor gene (Bower, 1996). This gene is thought to contribute to sensation seeking, which is also called novelty seeking. D4 has been identified in some cases of attention deficit hyperactivity disorder (ADHD) (Bower, 1996). It is hypothesized that the D4 gene may provide an individual with receptors that respond to dopamine by promoting novelty-seeking behavior (Bower, 1996, p. 4).

Developmental Patterning

Longitudinal studies are becoming more rigorous and sophisticated from both the design and analytic perspective (Leukefeld & Bukoski, 1991; Leukefeld & Clayton, 1995). However, many longitudinal studies do not differentiate outcome and preceding etiologic pathway(s) with respect to drug use and drug abuse, nor do they systematically examine drug use progression (Clayton & Leukefeld, 1994; Glantz & Pickens, 1992; Leukefeld & Clayton, 1995). There are relatively invariant patterns of change and developmental stages of drug use initiation (Kandel, 1975). However, there also has been discussion about stage comprehensiveness and gender differences (Donovan & Jessor, 1984; Kandel & Logan, 1984). What the developmental stages model of drug use suggests is that most of those individuals who use any drug, use multiple drugs. Furthermore, progression involves more than simply adding a new drug class; it also involves progression to greater quantities/frequencies with former classes. Questions remain about whether early onset represents dynamic developmental forces and about the interaction of individual variables on early onset (Clayton & Leukefeld, 1994; Nagin & Farrington, 1992a, 1992b). Rutter (1989) suggests that developmental patterning should incorporate several issues. One important factor to consider is development in the social context. For example, social development theory suggests that bonding to family, school, and prosocial peers predicts deviance, including drug use (Hawkins & Weis, 1985). To the extent that an individual is bonded, the likelihood of deviance or drug use diminishes. Research on delinquency and drug use is based in large part on Hirschi's (1969) social control theory and Hawkins and Weis's (1985) social development model. In this conceptual orientation, involvement, attachment, belief, and commitment are the elements of the social bond that, if the bonding is positive, protect the young person.

Other factors that Rutter (1989) considers to be important include (a) timing of experiences; (b) intrinsic and experiential factors such as school experience and self-esteem; (c) continuities and disconti-nuities in behavior (continuities in behavior may occur as a result of earlier learning, whereas discontinuities in behavior may produce changes in people that are the result of physiological events, such as puberty, and new experiences); (d) parallels and differences between normal and abnormal development (e.g., five alcoholic beverages over a weekend may be considered abnormal for a sixth grader, but may not be considered abnormal for a 12th grader); (e) heterotypic and homotypic continuities (because behaviors may change in form but still reflect the same basic process), key life transitions, risk and protective factors, indirect chain effects including transitions that occur during the course of development, such as high school, college, marriage, and having children; (f) mediating mechanisms, including genetic and biological influences, the environment in which the adolescent lives, cognitive and social skills, habits, coping styles, and links between experiences; and (g) age as an index of maturational and experiential factors.

Risk and Protective Factors

A dominant taxonomy in the drug prevention field used to sum-marize the etiology of drug use and abuse is risk and protective factors (Hawkins, Catalano, & Miller, 1992). Risk factors can be defined as an individual attribute, individual characteristic, situ-ational condition, or environmental context that increases the prob-ability of drug use or abuse or a transition in level of involvement with drugs (Clayton, 1992, p. 15). A protective factor is defined as something that inhibits, reduces, or buffers the probability of drug use, abuse, or a transition in the level of involvement with drugs. Conduct disorder and antisocial personality at a young age, low self-esteem, family drug use, family atmosphere problems, poor family communication, peer drug use, poor school factors, and living in impoverished neighborhoods have been shown in a number of studies to be risk factors (Clayton, 1992; Hawkins et al., 1992; Stouthamer-Loeber et al., 1993).

There are several assumptions that can be made about risk and protective factors: (a) A single risk or protective factor can have multiple outcomes, (b) several risk or protective factors can affect a single outcome, (c) drug abuse may alter risk and protective factors, and (d) the relationship of risk and protective factors to each other and to transitions in drug abuse may be influenced by age-graded norms (Clayton, 1995). Although counting the number of risk factors present is associated with drug use (Newcomb & Bentler, 1986), the existing literature does not provide guidance about the relative predictive power of the various risk factors. Furthermore, little systematic research has been conducted concerning the relationship of protective factors to risk factors in predicting drug use (Clayton, 1995).

DELINQUENCY

Stouthamer-Loeber et al. (1993) examined risk and protective factors in three separate samples and found that some protective and risk effects co-occurred. In other words, the presence or absence of a protective factor could promote or inhibit delinquent behavior. For example, a high level of school motivation could work as a protective factor to inhibit delinquent behavior, whereas a low level of school motivation could be a risk factor and serve to increase the likelihood of delinquent behavior. Variables such as school motivation, peer delinquency, supervision, and relationship to partners were more likely to show both protective and risk effects than simply protective effects or simply risk effects. In fact, there were no variables that had only protective effects, and only a few variables had predominantly risk effects. One specific variable that did have a predominant risk effect was attention deficit disorder and oppositional defiant behavior. Stouthamer-Loeber et al. (1993) suggest that attention deficit disorder and oppositional defiant behavior was related to the likelihood of delinquency, whereas the absence of these symptoms may not predispose a person to nondelinquency. This fits with their overall findings and hypothesis that risk and protective factors are not independent and unrelated variables.

In 1991, juveniles were responsible for about one in five violent crimes (Snyder & Sickmund, 1995). Youth violence in the United States has also increased in recent decades. This increase has been especially dramatic in the past few years (Allen-Hagen & Sickmund, 1993). In fact, between 1965 and 1991, the violent crime arrest rate for juveniles tripled; and between 1987 and 1991, the rate increased 50%, which was twice the level of increase for adults.

Some researchers believe that delinquency and substance abuse are caused by the same underlying factors, rather than one causing the other (Snyder & Sickmund, 1995). Others consider alcoholism and drug use as risk factors that contribute to juvenile delinquency and violence (Greenwood, 1995). Anecdotal evidence, from interviews with youth participants in a variety of correctional programs, suggests that drug selling has replaced theft as the primary source of illegal income for many youth (Greenwood, 1995). Furthermore, deviant attitudes and behaviors have been shown to be strong predictors of drug use and problem alcohol use among adolescents (Ellickson & Hays, 1991; Huba & Bentler, 1983; Smith & Fogg, 1978). Generally, the more serious a youth's involvement in delinquency, the more serious his or her involvement with drugs. Changes in drug use have been shown to produce large changes in delinquent behavior, whereas changes in delinquency have been shown to have a smaller impact on changes in drug use (Snyder & Sickmund, 1995). For example, the Drug Use Forecasting (1993) annual report on juvenile arrestees/detainees reports that cocaine and marijuana are the two most commonly used drugs among juvenile arrestees/detainees. The report also indicates that those arrestees/detainees who attend school were less likely than those not attending school to test positive for cocaine.

Studies have reported that school failure is highly related to both official and self-reported delinquent behavior (Empey & Lubeck, 1971; Gold, 1978; Siegel & Senna, 1988). The relationship between academic performance and delinquency has also been consistent across time for chronic delinquents (Joseph, 1996; Shannon, 1982; West & Farrington, 1977).

The correlation between self-reported delinquency and number of delinquent friends is one of the strongest and most consistent findings (Akers, Krohn, Lanza-Kaduce, & Radosevich, 1979; Elliott et al., 1985; Matsueda & Heimer, 1987; Reiss & Rhodes, 1964; Warr & Stafford, 1991). Warr and Stafford (1991) called this the "sticky friends" phenomenon. Elliott et al. (1985) note that adolescents can be introduced to drug use and delinquency by friends and called this "feathering" and "flocking." Jessor and Jessor (1977) and others have shown that problem behaviors tend to cluster in the same individuals and that being prone to deviance can be measured at fairly early stages of life, particularly through factors such as conduct disorder and ADHD (Huizinga, Loeber, & Thornberry, 1994; Loeber & Dishion, 1983; Patterson, 1993; Tremblay, 1993). In other words, childhood aggression has been shown to be highly predictive of later delinquent behavior and substance abuse (Farrington, 1991; Loeber, 1988; Loeber & Dishion, 1983). Early onset of aggression (5 to 10 years old) has been associated with higher rates and severity of adolescent and adult antisocial behavior and adolescent substance abuse (Kellam et al., 1983; O'Donnell, Hawkins, Catalano, Abbott, & Day, 1995). Moffitt (1993) suggests that the etiologic pathways differ for adolescents who are life course persistent versus adolescents limited in their deviance. Thus, factors related to substance abuse are different for those who use substances during adolescence than for those youth who use substances throughout their lives or at least for longer than their adolescence. One goal of research should be to better understand the interlocking aspects of multiple problem behaviors and to examine whether variables predict longitudinal outcomes (Bry, McKeon, & Pandina, 1982; Clayton, 1992; Newcomb et al., 1986).

RESEARCH IMPLICATIONS

Existing studies have examined a host of important variables to consider when thinking about prevention intervention programs for adolescent drug use, drug abuse, and delinquency. Several longitudinal studies (i.e., Brook et al., 1992; Brunswick, Messeri, & Titus, 1992; Elliot et al., 1985; Jessor & Jessor, 1977; Kandel, 1975; Kaplan et al., 1982; Kellam, 1994; Kellam et al., 1983; Newcomb et al., 1986; Tarter & Mezzich, 1992) have contributed to the prevention intervention literature. These studies have investigated (a) the sequencing of drug use (e.g., Newcomb & Bentler, 1986; Newcomb et al., 1986); (b) the risk of progressing from one drug type/stage to another (e.g., Kandel & Davies, 1992); (c) onset as multifactorial with predisposing variables/risk factors that together, rather than alone, are predictive (e.g., Bry et al., 1982; Newcomb et al., 1986); and (d) the importance of interaction between individual variables or characteristics and social variables or factors (Newcomb & Bentler, 1986). Several of these studies involve a number of data collection waves (e.g., Brook et al., 1992; Brunswick et al., 1991; Kandel, 1975; Newcomb et al., 1986). Several studies include an entire cohort in one community (Brook et al., 1992; Kaplan et al., 1982). Most of the studies include multiple levels and waves of data collection and use individual subject psychosocial questionnaire data (Brook et al., 1992; Brunswick et al., 1991; Elliot et al., 1985; Jessor & Jessor, 1975; Kandel, 1975; Kaplan et al., 1982; Kellam et al., 1983). However, a comparison of these studies on explicit criteria (age of subjects at first contact, size of the sample, number of waves of data collection, theoretical basis of study, analytical techniques used, size of community from which subjects were selected, and attrition) reveals gaps in the literature. The following section presents a study in which the authors are currently engaged. The study is designed to examine adolescent drug use, drug abuse, and delinquency longitudinally.

TRANSITION INTO ADULTHOOD STUDY

The Transition into Adulthood Study is a longitudinal and natural history follow-up study. The study began in 1987 at the University of Kentucky as a prospective, longitudinal, cohort-sequential evaluation of the effectiveness of the Drug Abuse Resistance Education (DARE) program in Lexington, Kentucky. The 5-year study of DARE began with the entire 1987-1988 sixth-grade cohort attending 31 elementary schools in Lexington, 23 of which were randomly selected to participate in the DARE program and 8 of which were randomly selected as comparison schools.

DARE's effectiveness was tested using analysis of variance (Clayton, Cattarello, & Walden, 1991; Clayton, Cattarello, Day, & Walden, 1991) as well as hierarchical linear modeling (HLM; Bryk & Raudenbush, 1992). HLM is a multilevel modeling technique that revealed a few short-term DARE effects, but they decayed after the third data collection period. Specifically, Clayton, Cattarello, and Johnstone (1996) reported that exposure to DARE resulted in a temporary "stabilization" of negative attitudes toward drugs. However, over time, the decline in negative attitudes in the intervention group approached that of the comparison group. In addition, short-term

DARE effects were noted in estimates of the peer drug use levels. However, no program effects were observed on actual drug use. These findings are consistent with findings from other school-based program evaluations (Ellickson, Bell, & McGuigan, 1993; Ellickson & Bell, 1991; Ennett et al., 1994; Harmon, 1993; Ringwalt, Ennett, & Holt, 1991; Ringwalt et al., 1994).

In 1992, data collection was extended in Lexington to investigate social bonding in relation to drug use, and to expand the focus to also include delinquency (both in and out of school, truancy, aggressivity, and violence; Robbins, 1993). In addition, Donohew and Clayton obtained peer network data to test the hypothesis that a key linkage among peers may be homogamy on sensation seeking, and that the larger the number of sensation seekers in peer clusters, the greater the likelihood of drug use and abuse (Donohew et al., 1994).

Although testing DARE's effectiveness was the major thrust of the original study, both the original and the follow-up study were also designed to explore etiologic pathway(s) to drug use. There are many known or presumed risk and protective factors for adolescent drug use (Clayton, 1992; Clayton & Leukefeld, 1994; Hawkins et al., 1992). For example, Cattarello (1993) used HLM to test the influence of neighborhood social disorganization on social bonds, peer associations, and drug use with data from the study (Bryk & Raudenbush, 1992). The results indicated that neighborhood characteristics significantly influenced individual levels of attachment to the family; attitudes toward marijuana; number of friends using cigarettes, alcohol, and marijuana; and past-year marijuana and alcohol use. In addition, all three measures of social bonding/attachment—commitment and belief—significantly predicted the likelihood of associating with drug-using peers, whereas drug-specific beliefs were the only indicator of the social bond to affect drug use directly. Therefore, it is possible that some of the influence of social bonds on drug use is indirect through peer associations (Oetting & Beauvais, 1987).

The study continued data collection for the first cohort of students as they transitioned into adulthood. The study's primary purpose was to examine the predictive efficacy of sensation seeking compared to other theoretically relevant predictor variables. However, sensation seeking was one individual risk factor of interest. Figure 4.1 presents a model that includes major factors discussed in the first section of this chapter. The variables incorporated into the model are social bonding and social development theory, including attachment to family, commitment to school, and peer relationships; social disorganization, including economic level, overcrowding, mobility, family disruption, and heterogeneity; intrapersonal variables, including self-esteem and sensation seeking; and outcome variables, including drug use in the past year or use in the past month. The key mediating variables in the model are peer pressure resistance and peer association using peer cluster theory (Oetting & Beauvais, 1987) as a predominant factor to understand drug use. As noted in the model, it is suggested that almost all of the other variable influences will be indirect through peers as the mediating variable.

In addition to aiding in the testing of complex hypotheses about the relationships among critical variables over time, covariance structure analysis will be used to provide a basis for testing exploratory relationships among variables. Because of the multitude of variables measured and the large number of related correlations among variables, Huba and Bentler's (1982) statistical approach is planned which uses the results of canonical correlation analyses as antecedent to the covariance structure analysis as a starting point.

To measure the variables in the model, two data collection procedures are being used—a survey and in-depth laboratory measures. First, a comprehensive survey will be administered to all participants who have completed at least three previous surveys from the 6th through the 10th grade. The survey was adapted from the previous surveys and has maintained the same format that subjects were accustomed to using. The survey includes the following measures: demographic measures including gender, age, race, living arrangements, children, education, job history, income, and a measure of major life events that have occurred in the past year; self-esteem; family attachment; general drug attitudes; peer relations; peer pressure resistance; cigarette use; alcohol use; drug use; impulsivity; sensation seeking; negative and positive drug use utilities; friends' drug use; diet; a measure of disorders including somatization, obsessive-compulsive, interpersonal sensitivity, depression, anxiety, hostility, phobic anxiety, paranoid ideation, and psychoticism; a measure of ADHD; criminal behavior; HIV risk behaviors; neighborhood variables; onset of puberty; and honesty.

A second part of the study consists of in-depth laboratory measures. Subjects for the laboratory part of the study have been selected using a stratified random sampling procedure and oversampling (a) those who had used multiple drugs or had heavy or frequent use of

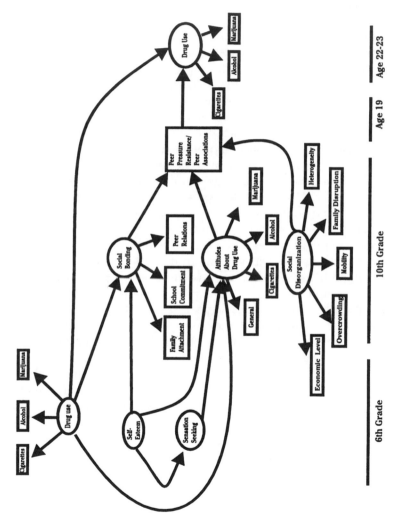

Figure 4.1. Major factors in drug use

any substance, and (b) those who had not tried any drug through the 10th grade. Three hundred of the 1,215 subjects who completed the first survey are being recruited to participate in the laboratory study. Face-to-face interview data, medical information, performance measures, and biochemical correlates are being collected including (a) a retrospective life history of use of a number of classes of drugs (onset, frequency, quantity by year); (b) a retrospective life history on various forms of delinquency and criminal behavior; (c) psychological variables that would allow classification into *DSM-IV* diagnostic categories; (d) a medical history and current medical/physical status; (e) performance measures indicative of disinhibition, cognitive abilities, and executive function; and (f) biochemical correlates— blood to measure various neuroendocrine functions (e.g., plasma dopamine estradiol, plasma testosterone, MAO platelets, and D4 allele). A urine sample is also collected to determine current drug use.

IMPLICATIONS

The selected etiological factors reviewed in this chapter are associated with several problem behaviors, suggesting that problem behaviors can share common pathways and underlying causes. In fact, everyday experiences for many suggest that there are certain adolescents who are more prone to problem behaviors, whereas others seem to be invulnerable.

For the practitioner, the literature reviewed in this chapter suggests that comprehensive prevention programming that focuses on underlying problem behavior clusters, although targeting specific problem behaviors, could be effective in changing those selected problem behaviors. It is also important to note that individually directed prevention may be a key factor for engaging the adolescent prevention interventions. An additional point is that there is limited research that has systematically focused on these changes over time in real-world settings. However, there are data to suggest that prevention interventions should be targeted on substance use early and at the beginning of the developmental progression. These early prevention interventions could be effective in preventing the use of gateway drugs as well as reducing the risk of using other substances further along the drug use trajectory (Cazares, 1994). Thus, examining drug use and drug use progression can be enhanced by testing multivariate models that incorporate biological, social, and psychological factors like the model presented in this chapter, although the model is not without limitations.

   Although major etiological factors related to substance use, abuse, and delinquency have been identified in the research literature, there is no single comprehensive theoretical model that incorporates etiological factors taken together. In fact, this may not be possible. However, there are examples. Lettieri, Sayers, and Pearson (1980) identified 43 different theories of substance use, and Petraitis, Flay, and Miller (1995) identified 14 multivariate theories of substance use. Yet each of these approaches toward comprehensiveness is limited. Thus, additional research is needed to better understand the complex nature of substance use to include developmental, biological, psychological, and sociological factors together in order to better comprehend interactions between variables as well as mediating variables.

   Understanding both the causes and effects of multiple pathways in and out of substance use and abuse has implications for both prevention and intervention programming. Additional research is also needed to assess the roles and interactions between school, family, neighborhoods, and personality factors to increase the effectiveness and efficiency of universal and targeted prevention programming (Gordon, 1983). For example, Donohew et al. (1991) found that substance use public service announcements are more effective with high sensation seekers if they are targeted to the high sensation seeker.

   Additional research is needed to examine biobehavioral prevention interventions, especially for children with antecedent behaviors that appear to be related to the onset of drug use and abuse, such as early signs of aggression, poor impulse control, oppositional behaviors, sensation-seeking behavior, poor concentration and inattention, and conduct disorder (Lynam, 1996). For example, if children can be diagnosed at ages 5 to 10 as being at risk for substance abuse or delinquency, prevention interventions can be targeted specifically to those children. As another example, and eliminating issues related to personal freedom, biochemical markers could be used to identify people at risk for substance abuse or juvenile delinquency. Thus, interventions could be tailored and individually targeted. Further examination of the predictive validity of risk and protective factors is also needed to improve the efficacy of drug abuse prevention interventions. An especially important focus is to increase our knowledge and practice experience related to interactions between risk and protective factors within the context of gender and culture.

Timing interventions and sequencing is important. Research has shown that younger, less addicted individuals will do better in treatment, and earlier detection may help the abuser before more severe problems develop (McLellan, Luborsky, O'Brien, Woody, & Druley, 1982). This suggests the need to design early intervention and treatment programs specifically for adolescents and to develop assessment procedures that are sensitive to specific risk factors related to later substance abuse. Just as multiple pathways into and out of substance use and abuse should be investigated, multiple interventions should be examined for developing research-based interventions.

Finally, the approach used in the past has been to treat all substance abusers with a universal approach. This review of etiological factors within a developmental perspective underscores the idea that interventions should be targeted and should focus on individual needs, incorporating the idea that "one size does not fit all."

REFERENCES

Abernathy, T., Massad, L., & Romano-Dwyer, L. (1995). The relationship between smoking and self-esteem. *Adolescence, 30*(120), 899-907.

Adler, P., & Lotecka, L. (1973). Drug use among high school students: Patterns and correlates. *International Journal of Addictions, 8,* 537-548.

Akers, R. (1977). *Deviant behavior: A social learning approach* (2nd ed.). Belmont, CA: Wadsworth.

Akers, R. (1994). *Criminological theories: Introduction and evaluation.* Los Angeles: Roxbury.

Akers, R., Krohn, L., Lanza-Kaduce, L., & Radosevich, M. (1979). Social learning and deviant behavior: A specific test of general theory. *American Sociological Review, 44,* 636-655.

Allen-Hagen, B., & Sickmund, M. (1993, July 1-4). Juveniles and violence: Juvenile offending and victimization. *OJJDP Fact Sheet.*

Anglin, D., & Hser, Y. (1987). Addicted women and crime. *Criminology, 25,* 359-397.

Ball, J., Rosen, L., Flueck, J., & Nurco, D. (1981). Lifetime criminality of heroin addicts in the United States. *Journal of Drug Issues, 12,* 225-239.

Bardo, M., & Mueller, C. (1991). Sensation seeking and drug abuse prevention from a biological perspective. In L. Donohew, H. Sypher, & W. Bukoski (Eds.), *Persuasive communication and drug abuse prevention* (pp. 195-207). Hillsdale, NJ: Lawrence Erlbaum.

Bauman, K., & Ennett, S. (1994). Peer influence on adolescent drug use. *American Psychologist, 49,* 820-822.

Bauman, K., Foshee, V., Koch, G., Haley, N., & Downeon, M. (1989). Testosterone and cigarette smoking in early adolescence. *Journal of Behavioral Medicine, 2,* 425-433.

Baumrind, D. (1983). Specious causal attributions in the social sciences: The reformulated steppingstone theory of heroin use: An exemplar. *Journal of Personality and Social Psychology, 45,* 1289-1298.

Beardslee, W., Son, L., & Vaillant, G. (1986). Exposure to parental alcoholism during childhood and outcome in adulthood: A prospective longitudinal study. *British Journal of Psychiatry, 149,* 584-591.

Beck, K., Thombs, D., Mahoney, C., & Fingar, K. (1995). Social context and sensation seeking: Gender differences in college student drinking motivations. *International Journal of Addictions, 30,* 1101-1115.

Blum, R. (1972). White middle-class families. In W. E. Henry & N. Sanford (Eds.), *Horatio Alger's children* (pp. 65-94). London: Jossey-Bass.

Bower, B. (1996). Gene tied to excitable personality. *Science News, 149,* 4.

Brook, J., Lukoff, I., & Whiteman, M. (1980). Initiation into adolescent marijuana use. *Journal of Genetic Psychology, 137,* 133-142.

Brook, J. S., Cohen, P., Whiteman, M., & Gordon, A. S. (1992). Psychosocial risk factors in the transition from moderate to heavy use or abuse of drugs. In M. D. Glantz & R. W. Pickens (Eds.), *Vulnerability to drug abuse* (pp. 359-388). Washington, DC: American Psychological Association Press.

Brunswick, A. F., Messeri, P. A., & Titus, S. P. (1992). Predictive factors in adult substance abuse: A prospective study of African American adolescents. In M. D. Glantz & R. W. Pickens (Eds.), *Vulnerability to drug abuse* (pp. 419-472). Washington, DC: American Psychological Association Press.

Bry, B., McKeon, P., & Pandina, R. (1982). Extent of drug use as a function of the number of risk factors. *Journal of Abnormal Psychology, 91,* 273-279.

Bryk, A. S., & Raudenbush, W. W. (1992). *Hierarchical linear models.* Newbury Park, CA: Sage.

Buchsbaum, M. S., Coursey, R. D., & Murphy, D. L. (1976). The biochemical high-risk paradigm: Behavioral and familial correlates of low platelet monoamine oxidase activity. *Science, 194,* 339-341.

Cadoret, R. J. (1992). Genetic and environmental factors in initiation of drug use and the transition to abuse. In M. D. Glantz & R. W. Pickens (Eds.), *Vulnerability to drug abuse* (pp. 91-144). Washington, DC: American Psychological Association Press.

Cannon, S. (1976). *Social functioning patterns of families of offspring receiving treatment for drug abuse.* New York: Libra.

Cattarello, A. (1993). *Neighborhood influences on adolescents' social bond: Peer association and drug use: A multilevel analysis.* Unpublished doctoral dissertation, University of Kentucky, Lexington.

Cazares, A. (1994). Prevention intervention research, focus and perspective. In A. Cazares & L. Beatty (Eds.), *Scientific methods for prevention intervention research* (NIDA Research Monograph No. 139).

Cederblad, M., Oreland L., & Zachrisson, E. (1992). Thrombocyte monoamine oxidase activity and behavior deviances in adolescence. *Developmental Pharmacal Therapy, 18,* 184-190.

Cernkovich, S. A., & Giordano, P. C. (1992). School bonding, race, and delinquency. *Criminology, 30,* 261-291.

Ciaranello, R., & Boehme, R. (1981). Biochemical genetics of neurotransmitter enzymes and recepters: Relationships to schizophrenia and other major psychiatric disorders. *Clinical Genetics, 19,* 358-372.

Clayton, R. (1992). Transitions in drug use: Risk and protective factors. In M. D. Glantz & R. W. Pickens (Eds.), *Vulnerability to drug abuse* (pp. 15-52). Washington, DC: American Psychological Association Press.

Clayton, R. (1995). *Community treatment and prevention approaches to drugs and violence: What works?* Paper submitted to the Drugs-Violence Task Force of the U.S. Sentencing Committee, Tallahassee, FL.

Clayton, R. R., Cattarello, A., Day, E., & Walden, K. P. (1991). Persuasive communication and drug prevention: An evaluation of the D.A.R.E. program. In L. Donohew, H. Sypher, & W. Bukoski (Eds.), *Persuasive communication and drug abuse prevention* (pp. 295-313). Hillsdale, NJ: Lawrence Erlbaum.

Clayton, R. R., Cattarello, A., & Johnstone, B. (1996). *The effectiveness of Project DARE: Five-year follow-up results.* Manuscript submitted for publication.

Clayton, R. R., Cattarello, A., & Walden, K. P. (1991). Sensation seeking as a potential mediating variable for school-based prevention intervention: A two-year follow up of D.A.R.E. *Health Communication, 3,* 229-239.

Clayton, R. R., & Leukefeld, C. G. (1994). *Drug use and its progression to drug abuse and dependence: Implications for needle exchange and bleach distribution programs.* Paper prepared for the National Academy of Sciences, Panel on Needle Exchange and Bleach Distribution Programs. Washington, DC: U.S. Government Printing Office.

Cloninger, C. R., Bohman, M., & Sigvardsson, S. (1981). Inheritance of alcohol abuse: Cross fostering analysis of adopted men. *Archives of General Psychiatry, 39,* 861-868.

Cole, J. (1990). Toward a theory of peer rejection. In S. Asher & J. Cole (Eds.), *Peer rejection in childhood* (pp. 365-401). Cambridge, UK: Cambridge University Press.

Craig, S., & Brown, B. (1975). Comparison of youthful heroin users and nonusers from one urban community. *International Journal of Addictions, 10,* 53-64.

Daitzman, R. J., & Zuckerman, M. (1980). Disinhibitory sensation seeking, personality, and gonadal hormones. *Personality and Individual Differences, 1,* 103-110.

Daitzman, R. J., Zuckerman, M., Sammelwitz, P., & Ganjam, V. (1978). Sensation seeking and gonadal hormones. *Journal of Biological Science, 10,* 401-408.

Dembo, R., Williams, L., Getreu, A., Schmeidler, J., Berry, E., Wish, E., & La Voie, L. (1991). A longitudinal study of the relationships among marijuana/hashish use, cocaine use and delinquency in a cohort of high risk youths. *Journal of Drug Issues, 21,* 271-312.

Denton, R., & Kampfe, C. (1994). The relationship between family variables and adolescent substance abuse: A literature review. *Adolescence, 29*(114), 475-495.

Donohew, L., Lorch, E., & Palmgreen, P. (1991). Sensation seeking and targeting of televised anti-drug PSA's. In L. Donohew, H. E. Sypher, & W. J. Bukoski (Eds.), *Persuasive communication and drug abuse prevention* (pp. 209-226). Hillsdale, NJ: Lawrence Erlbaum.

Donohew, L., Rice, R., & Clayton, R. (1994). *Sensation seeking, peer networks, and drug use among junior and senior high students.* Manuscript submitted for publication.

Donovan, J., & Jessor, R. (1984). *The structure of problem behavior in adolescence and young adulthood* (Research report no. 10, young adult follow-up study). Boulder: Institute of Behavioral Science, University of Colorado.

Drug Use Forecasting. (1993). *Annual report on juvenile arrestees/detainees: Drugs and crime in America's cities.* Washington, DC: National Institute of Justice.

Ellickson, P., Bell, R., & McGuigan, K. (1993). Preventing adolescent drug use: Long-term results of a junior high program (Project Alert). *American Journal of Public Health, 83,* 856-861.

Ellickson, P., & Hays, R. (1991). Antecedents of drinking among young adolescents with different alcohol use histories. *Journal of Studies on Alcohol, 52,* 398-408.

Ellickson, P. L., & Bell, R. M. (1991). Drug prevention in junior high: A multi-site longitudinal test. *Science, 247,* 1299-1305.

Elliott, D., & Ageton, S. (1976). *The relationship between drug use and crime among adolescents: Drug use and crime: Report of Panel on Drug Use and Criminal Behavior.* Research Triangle, NC: Research Triangle Institute.

Elliott, D., Huizinga, D., & Ageton, S. (1985). *Explaining delinquency and drug use.* Beverly Hills, CA: Sage.

Empey, L., & Lubeck, S. (1971). *The Silverlake experiment: Testing delinquency theory and community interaction.* Chicago: Aldine.

Ennett, S. T., Rosenbaum, D. P., Flewilling, R. L., Bieler, G. S., Ringwalt, C. L., & Bailey, S. L. (1994). Long-term evaluation of Drug Abuse Resistance Education. *Addictive Behaviors, 19,* 113-125.

Farrington, D. (1991). Childhood aggression and adult violence. In D. Pepler & K. Rubin (Eds.), *The development and treatment of childhood aggression* (pp. 5-29). Hillsdale, NJ: Lawrence Erlbaum.

Fischer, C. (1975). Toward a subcultural theory of urbanism. *American Journal of Sociology, 80,* 311-326.

Fischer, L., & Bauman, K. (1988). Influence and selection in the friend-adolescent relationship: Findings from studies of adolescent smoking and drinking. *Journal of Applied Social Psychology, 18,* 289-314.

Gabel, S., Stadler, J., Bjorn, J., Shindledecker, R., & Bowden, C. L. (1994). Sensation seeking in psychiatrically disturbed youth: Relationship to biochemical parameters and behavior problems. *Journal of the American Academy of Child and Adolescent Psychiatry, 33,* 123-129.

Gantman, C. (1978). Family interaction patterns among families with normal, disturbed, and drug-abusing adolescents. *Journal of Youth and Adolescence, 7,* 429-440.

Glantz, M. D., & Pickens, R. W. (1992). Vulnerability to drug abuse: Introduction and overview. In M. D. Glantz & R. W. Pickens (Eds.), *Vulnerability to drug abuse* (pp. 1-14). Washington, DC: American Psychological Association Press.

Gold, M. (1978). School experiences, self-esteem, and delinquent behavior: A theory for alternative schools. *Crime & Delinquency, 24,* 294-295.

Goodwin, D. W. (1976). *Is alcoholism hereditary?* New York: Oxford University Press.

Goodwin, D. W. (1979). Alcoholism and heredity. *Archives of General Psychiatry, 36,* 57-61.

Gordon, R. (1983). An operational classification of disease prevention. *Public Health Reports, 98,* 107-109.

Gottfredson, D. C., & McNeil, R. T., III. (1991). Social area influences on delinquency: A multilevel analysis. *Crime & Delinquency, 28,* 197-226.

Gray, J. A., Owen, S., Davis, N., & Tsaltas, E. (1983). Psychological and physiological relations between anxiety and impulsivity. In M. Zuckerman (Ed.), *Biological bases of sensation seeking, impulsivity, and anxiety* (pp. 181-217). Hillsdale, NJ: Lawrence Erlbaum.

Greenwood, P. (1995). Juvenile crime and juvenile justice. In J. Wilson & J. Petersilia (Eds.), *Crime* (pp. 15-38). San Francisco: ICS.

Hamburg, B., Kraemer, H., & Jahnke, W. (1975). A hierarchy of drug use in adolescence: Behavioral and attitudinal correlates of substantial drug use. *American Journal of Psychiatry, 132,* 1155-1163.

Harmon, M. A. (1993). Reducing the risk of drug involvement among early adolescents: An evaluation of Drug Abuse Resistance Education (D.A.R.E.). *Evaluation Review, 17,* 221-239.

Hawkins, D., Catalano, R., & Brewer, D. (1994, July). *Preventing serious, violent and chronic delinquency and crime: Effective strategies from conception to age six.* Paper presented for the National Council on Crime and Delinquency for the Office of Juvenile Justice and Delinquency Prevention, U.S. Department of Justice.

Hawkins, J. D., Catalano, R. F., & Miller, J. Y. (1992). Risk and protective factors for alcohol and other drug problems in adolescence and early adulthood: Implications for substance abuse prevention. *Psychological Bulletin, 112,* 64-105.

Hawkins, J., & Weis, J. (1985). The social development model: An integrated approach to delinquency prevention. *Journal of Primary Prevention, 6,* 73-97.

Hirschi, T. (1969). *Causes of delinquency.* Berkeley: University of California Press.

Holmes, D. (1968). Dimensions of projection. *Psychological Bulletin, 69,* 248-268.

Hser, Y., Anglin, D., & Booth, M. (1987). Sex differences in addict careers: Initiation of use. *American Journal of Drug and Alcohol Abuse, 13,* 231-251.

Huba, G., & Bentler, P. (1983). Causal models of the development of law abidance and its relationship to psychosocial factors and drug use. In W. S. Laufer & J. M. Dau (Eds.), *Personality theory, moral development, and criminal behavior* (pp. 165-215). Lexington, MA: Lexington Books.

Huba, G. J., & Bentler, P. M. (1982). On the usefulness of latent variable causal modeling testing theories of naturally occurring events. *Journal of Personality and Social Psychology, 43,* 604-611.

Huizinga, D., Loeber, R., & Thornberry, T. P. (1994). *Urban delinquency and substance abuse: Initial findings.* Washington, DC: Office of Juvenile Justice and Delinquency Prevention.

Hundleby, J., & Mercer, G. (1987). Family and friends as social environments and their relationship to young adolescents' use of alcohol, tobacco, and marijuana. *Journal of Clinical Psychology, 44,* 125-134.

Inciardi, J., & Pottinger, A. (1986). Drug use and crime among two cohorts of women narcotics users: An empirical assessment. *Journal of Drug Issues, 14,* 91-106.

Jessor, R. (1976). Predicting time of onset of marijuana use: A developmental study of high school youth. *Journal of Consulting and Clinical Psychology, 44,* 125-134.

Jessor, R. R., & Jessor, S. (1977). *Problem behavior and psychosocial development: A longitudinal study of youth.* San Diego, CA: Academic Press.

Johnston, L. D., O'Malley, P. M., & Bachman, J. G. (1989). *Drug use, drinking and smoking: National survey results from high school, college, and young adult populations, 1975-1988* (DHEW Pub. No. ADM89-1638). Washington, DC: U.S. Government Printing Office.

Joseph, J. (1996). School factors and delinquency: A study of African American youths. *Journal of Black Studies, 26,* 340-355.

Kandel, D. B. (1975). Stages in adolescent involvement in drug use. *Science, 190,* 912-914.

Kandel, D. B., & Davies, M. (1992). Progression to regular marijuana involvement: Phemonology and risk factors for near-daily use. In M. D. Glantz & R. W. Pickens (Eds.), *Vulnerability to drug abuse* (pp. 211-254). Washington, DC: American Psychological Association Press.

Kandel, D. B., & Logan, S. A. (1984). Problems of drug use from adolescence to young adulthood: Periods of risk initiation, continued use, and discontinuation. *American Journal of Public Health, 74,* 660-666.

Kaplan, H. B., Martin, S. S., & Robbins, C. (1982). Application of a general theory of deviant behavior: Self-derogation and adolescent drug use. *Journal of Health and Social Behavior, 23,* 274-294.

Kellam, S. G. (1994). Testing theory through developmental epidemiologically based prevention research. In A. Cazares & L. Beatty (Eds.), *Scientific methods for prevention intervention research* (NIDA Research Monograph No. 139).

Kellam, S. G., Brown, C., Rubin, B., & Ensminger, M. (1983). Paths leading to teenage psychiatric symptoms and substance abuse: Developmental epidemiological studies in Woodlawn. In S. Guze, F. Earls, & J. Barrett (Eds.), *Childhood psychopathology and development* (pp. 17-51). New York: Raven.

Kelly, D., & Balch, R. (1971). Social origins and school failure: A reexamination of Cohne's theory of working-class delinquency. *Pacific Social Review, 14,* 413-430.

King, A. C., Errico, A. L., & Parson, O. A. (1995). Eysenck's personality dimensions and sex steroids in male abstinent alcoholics and nonalcoholics: An exploratory study. *Biological Psychiatry, 38,* 103-113.

Klaiber, E. L., & Broverman, D. M. (1988). Dynamics of estradiol and testosterone and seminal fluid indexes in smokers and nonsmokers. *Fertility and Sterility, 50,* 630-634.

LaGrange, L., Jones, T. D., Erb, L., & Reyes, E. (1995). Alcohol consumption: Biochemical and personality correlates in college student population. *Addictive Behavior, 20,* 93-103.

Lettieri, D., Sayers, M., & Pearson, H. (Eds.). (1980). *Theories on drug abuse: Selected contemporary perspectives* (Research Monograph No. 30). Rockville, MD: National Institute on Drug Abuse.

Leukefeld, C. G., & Bukoski, W. J. (1991). Drug abuse prevention evaluation methodology: A bright future. *Journal of Drug Education, 51,* 191-201.

Leukefeld, C. G., & Clayton, R. R. (Eds.). (1995). *Drug prevention practice in substance abuse.* Binghamton, NY: Haworth.

Loeber, R. (1988). Behavioral precursors and accelerators of delinquency. In W. Buikhuisen & S. Mednick (Eds.), *Explaining criminal behavior* (pp. 51-67). Leiden, The Netherlands: Brill.

Loeber, R., & Dishion, T. (1983). Early predictors of male delinquency: A review. *Psychological Bulletin, 94,* 68-99.

Lynam, D. (1996). The early identification of chronic offenders: Who is the fledgling psychopath? *Psychological Bulletin, 120*, 209-234.

Martin, C. A., Mainous, A., Oler, M., & Mainous, R. (1995, October). *Hormonal changes in puberty: Correlates with substance use.* Paper presented at the annual meeting of the American Academy of Child and Adolescent Psychiatry, San Antonio, TX.

Matseuda, R., & Heimer, K. (1987). Race, family structure, and delinquency: A test of differential association and social control theories. *American Sociological Review, 52*, 826-840.

Mattson, A., Schalling, D., Olweus, D., Low, H., & Svensson, J. (1980). Plasma testosterone aggressive behavior and personality: Dimensions in young adult delinquents. *Journal of the American Academy of Child Psychiatry, 19*, 476-490.

McCord, J. (1979). Some child-rearing antecedents of criminal behavior in adult men. *Journal of Personality and Social Psychology, 37*, 1477-1486.

McGlothlin, W., Anglin, D., & Wilson, B. (1978). Narcotic addiction and crime. *Criminology, 16*, 293-315.

McLellan, A., Luborsky, L., O'Brien, C., Woody, G., & Druley, K. (1982). Is treatment for substance abuse effective? *Journal of the American Medical Association, 247*, 1423-1428.

Moffitt, T. E. (1993). Adolescence-limited and life-course persistent antisocial behavior: A developmental taxonomy. *Psychological Review, 100*, 674-701.

Nagin, D. S., & Farrington, D. P. (1992a). The onset and persistence of offending. *Criminology, 30*, 501-524.

Nagin, D. S., & Farrington, D. P. (1992b). The stability of criminal potential from childhood to adulthood. *Criminology, 30*, 235-260.

Needle, R., McCubbin, H., Wilson, M., Reineck, R., Lazar, A., & Mederer, H. (1986). Interpersonal influences in adolescent drug use—The role of older siblings, parents, and peers. *International Journal of Addictions, 21*, 739-766.

Newcomb, M. D., Maddahian, E., & Bentler, P. (1986). Risk factors for drug use among adolescents: Concurrent and longitudinal analyses. *American Journal of Public Health, 76*, 525-531.

O'Donnell, J., Hawkins, J., & Abbott, R. (1995). Predicting serious delinquency and substance use among aggressive boys. *Journal of Consulting and Clinical Psychology, 63*, 529-537.

O'Donnell, J., Hawkins, J., Catalano, R., Abbott, R., & Day, L. (1995). Preventing school failure, drug use and delinquency among low-income children: Long-term intervention in elementary schools. *American Journal of Orthopsychiatry, 65*, 101-113.

Oetting, G., & Beauvais, F. (1987). Peer cluster theory, socialization characteristics, and adolescent drug use: A path analysis. *Journal of Counseling Psychology, 34*, 205-213.

Olweus, D., Mattson, A., Schalling, D., & Low, H. (1980). Testosterone, aggression, physical, and personality dimensions in normal adolescent males. *Psychosomatic Medicine, 42*, 253-269.

Otero-Lopez, J., Luengo-Martin, A., Miron-Redondo, L., Carrillo-DeLaPenta, M., & Romero-Trinanes, E. (1994). An empirical study of the relations between drug abuse and delinquency among adolescents. *British Journal of Criminology, 34*, 459-478.

Overholser, J., Adams, D., Lehnert, K., & Brinkman, D. (1995). Self-esteem deficits and suicidal tendencies among adolescents. *Journal of the American Academy of Child and Adolescent Psychiatry, 34,* 919-928.

Pandina, R. (1992). Arousability as a risk factor in drug abuse. In M. D. Glantz & R. W. Pickens (Eds.), *Vulnerability in drug abuse* (pp. 179-209). Washington, DC: American Psychological Association Press.

Pandina, R., & Schuele, J. (1983). Psychosocial correlates of alcohol and drug use of adolescent students and adolescents in treatment. *Journal of Studies on Alcohol, 44,* 950-973.

Patterson, G. R. (1993). Orderly change in a stable world: The antisocial trait as a chimera. *Journal of Consulting and Clinical Psychology, 61,* 911-919.

Pentz, M. A., Dwyer, J. H., MacKinnon, D. P., Flay, B. R., Hansen, W. B., Wang, E. Y., & Johnson, C. A. (1989). A multi-community trial for primary prevention of adolescent drug abuse: Effects on drug use prevalence. *Journal of the American Medical Association, 161,* 3259-3266.

Petraitis, J., Flay, B., & Miller, T. (1995). Reviewing theories of adolescent substance use: Organizing pieces in the puzzle. *Psychological Bulletin, 117,* 67-86.

Pickens, R., Svikis, D., McGue, M., Lykken, D., Heston, L., & Clayton, P. (1991). Heterogeneity in the inheritance of alcoholism. *Archives of General Psychiatry, 48,* 19-28.

Quay, H. C. (1987). The behavior reward and inhibition system in childhood behavior disorders: In L. M. Bloomingdale (Ed.), *Attention deficit disorder* (3rd ed.). New York: Spectrum.

Reardon, B., & Griffing, P. (1983). Factors related to the self-concept of institutionalized, white, male, adolescent drug abusers. *Adolescence, 18,* 29-41.

Rees, C., & Wilborn, B. (1983). Correlates of drug abuse in adolescents: A comparison of families of drug abusers with families of nondrug users. *Journal of Youth and Adolescents, 12,* 55-63.

Reiss, A. (1986). Why are communities important in understanding crime? In A. Reiss & M. Tonry (Eds.), *Communities and crime* (pp. 115-159). Chicago: University of Chicago Press.

Reiss, A. J., Jr., & Rhodes, A. (1964). An empirical test of differential association theory. *Journal of Research in Crime and Delinquency, 1,* 5-18.

Ringwalt, C., Ennett, S. T., & Holt, K. D. (1991). An outcome evaluation of Project DARE (Dare Abuse Resistance Education). *Health Education Research, 6,* 327-337.

Ringwalt, C., Green, J., Ennett, S., Lachan, R., Clayton, R., and Leukefeld, C. (1994). *Past and future directions of the D.A.R.E. program: An evaluation review.* Washington, DC: U.S. Department of Justice, Office of Justice Programs, National Institute of Justice.

Robbins, C. (1993). *Progress report: School experiences and adolescent substance abuse.* Lexington: University of Kentucky Press.

Robins, L. (1980). The natural history of drug abuse. *Acta Psychiatric Scandinavia, 62,* 7-20.

Rogeness, G. A., Javors, M. A., Maas, J. W., Macedo, C. A. (1990). Cathecolamines and diagnosis in children. *Journal of the American Academy of Child Adolescent Psychiatry, 29,* 234-241.

Rutter, M. (1989). Pathways from childhood to adult life. *Journal of Child Psychology and Psychiatry, 30,* 23-51.

Rutter, M., & Giller, H. (1983). *Juvenile delinquency: Trends and perspectives.* New York: Guilford.

Shannon, L. (1982). *Assessing the relationship of adult criminal careers to juvenile careers: A summary.* Washington, DC: U.S. Government Printing Office.

Shedler, J., & Block, J. (1990). Adolescent drug use and psychological health: A longitudinal inquiry. *American Psychologist, 45,* 612-630.

Siegel, L., & Senna, J. (1988). *Juvenile delinquency: Theory, practice, and laws.* St. Paul, MN: West.

Simcha-Fagan, O., & Schwartz, J. E. (1986). Neighborhood and delinquency: An assessment of contextual effects. *Criminology, 24,* 667-703.

Smith, G., & Fogg, C. (1978). Psychological predictors of early use, late use, and non-use of marijuana among teenage students. In D. B. Kandel (Ed.), *Longitudinal research on drug use: Empirical findings and methodological issues* (pp. 101-113). Washington, DC: Hemisphere-Wiley.

Snyder, H., & Sickmund, M. (1995). *Juvenile offenders and victims: 1995 update on violence.* Pittsburgh: U.S. Department of Justice, Office of Juvenile Justice and Delinquency Prevention, National Center for Juvenile Justice.

Sommers, I., & Baskin, D. (1994). Factors related to female adolescent initiation into violent street crime. *Youth & Society, 25,* 468-489.

Speckart, G., & Anglin, D. (1985). Narcotics use and crime: An analysis of existing evidence for a causal relationship. *Behavioral Science and the Law, 3,* 259-283.

Stark, R. (1987). Deviant places: A theory of the ecology of crime. *Criminology, 25,* 893-909.

Stouthamer-Loeber, M., & Loeber, R. (1988). The use of predictive data in understanding delinquency. *Behavioral Sciences and the Law, 6,* 334-354.

Stouthamer-Loeber, M., Loeber, R., Farrington, D., Zhang, Q., Van Kammen, W., & Maguin, E. (1993). The double edge of protective and risk factors for delinquency: Interrelations and developmental patterns. *Development and Psychopathology, 5,* 683-701.

Streit, F., Halsted, D., & Pascale, P. (1974). Differences among youthful users and nonusers of drugs based on their perceptions of parental behavior. *International Journal of Addictions, 9,* 749-755.

Sullivan, J. L., Stanfield, C. N., Schanberg, S., Cavenar, J. (1978). Platelet monoamine oxidase and serum dopamine-B-hydroxylase activity in chronic alcoholics. *Archives of General Psychiatry, 35,* 1209-1212.

Sutherland, E. (1947). *Criminology* (4th ed.). Philadelphia: Lippincott.

Tarter, R. E., & Mezzich, A. C. (1992). Ontogeny of substance abuse: Perspectives and findings. In M. D. Glantz & R. W. Pickens (Eds.), *Vulnerability to drug abuse* (pp. 149-178). Washington, DC: American Psychological Association Press.

Tec, N. (1974). Parent-child drug abuse: Generational continuity or adolescent deviancy? *Adolescence, 4,* 351-364.

Tolone, W., & Dermott, D. (1975). Some correlates of drug use among high school youth in a midwestern rural community. *International Journal of Addictions, 10,* 761-777.

Tremblay, J. (1993). Early disruptive behavior, poor school achievement, delinquent behavior and delinquent personality: Longitudinal analyses. *Journal of Consulting and Clinical Psychology, 60,* 64-72.

U.S. Department of Health and Human Services. (1994). *National survey results on drug use from the Monitoring the Future study, 1975-1993: Vol. 1: Secondary students.* Washington, DC: National Institute on Drug Abuse.

Udry, J. R. (1991). Predicting alcohol use by adolescent males. *Journal of Biosocial Science, 23,* 381-386.

Udry, J. R., Talbert, L. M., & Morris, N. M. (1985). Biosocial foundation for adolescent female sexuality. *Demography, 23,* 217-230.

Von Knorring, O. (1984). Personality traits related to monoamine oxidase activity in platelets. *Psychology Research, 12,* 11-26.

Warr, M., & Stafford, M. (1991). The influence of delinquent peers: What they think or what they do? *Criminology, 29,* 851-866.

Wechsler, H., & Thum, D. (1973). Teen-age drinking, drug use, and social correlates. *Quarterly Journal of Studies on Alcohol, 34,* 1220-1227.

Weiss, R. D. (1992). The role of psychopathology in the transition from drug use to abuse and dependence. In M. D. Glantz & R. W. Pickens (Eds.), *Vulnerability to drug abuse* (pp. 137-148). Washington, DC: American Psychological Association Press.

West, D., & Farrington, D. (1977). *The delinquent way of life.* London: Heinemann.

White, H., Johnson, V., & Horwitz, A. (1986). An application of three deviance theories to adolescent substance use. *International Journal of Addictions, 21,* 347-366.

Wilson, W. J. (1987). *The truly disadvantaged.* Chicago: University of Chicago Press.

Zuckerman, M. (1979). *Sensation seeking: Beyond the optimal level of arousal.* Hillsdale, NJ: Lawrence Erlbaum.

Zuckerman, M. (Ed.). (1983). *Biological bases of sensation seeking, impulsivity, and anxiety.* Hillsdale, NJ: Lawrence Erlbaum.

5. Life Imitating Art: Adolescents and Television Violence

Robert D. Sege

Decades of social science research have examined the relationship between exposure to media violence and childhood and adolescent violence. There is no doubt that American society is quite violent by modern standards: Our homicide rate is four times higher than that of the next leading developed country (Fingerhut & Kleinman, 1990). Although this phenomenon is complex and multifactorial, with deep historical roots, one of the best documented causes of the modern upsurge in violence appears to be childhood exposure to television violence. Comstock and Strasburger (1990) published a definitive review of the topic, concluding that "the literature gives little comfort to those who assert that . . . violence on TV does not influence behavior" (p. 32).

Although the overall size of the effect is disputed, the relationship between media exposure and aggressive behavior is no longer controversial. A supported model of these relationships is shown here as Figure 5.1, reproduced from the influential book *The Early Window* (Liebert, 1988), first published in 1983. Overall, those studies that analyzed the relationship between aggressive behavior and television violence have determined that a preference for violent programs at a young age results in increased viewing of these programs, which leads to the learning of TV behavior, which in turn is related to subsequent aggressive behavior. Apparent in the diagram is that the inverse relationship between aggressive behavior and preference for violent television in childhood has not been demonstrated.

After a brief historical overview, this chapter will review some of the salient arguments and point the interested reader to important original studies and complex reviews of certain aspects of the topic.

AUTHOR'S NOTE: I would like to thank David Stone, William Dietz, and Karen Victor for their critical reading of this manuscript. Preparation of this manuscript was funded by a Generalist Physician Faculty Scholarship from the Robert Wood Johnson Foundation.

129

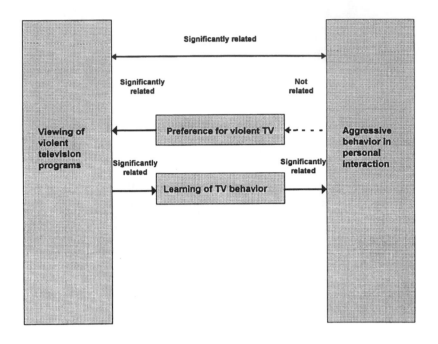

Figure 5.1. Relationship Between Viewing of Violent Programs and Aggressive Behavior

SOURCE: Reprinted from Liebert, 1988.

HISTORICAL PERSPECTIVE

In a sense, the mass exposure of television is a giant social experiment, and there has been concern about the effects of television viewing on children almost since television first made its appearance. Violence on television has long been suggested to be a source of antisocial influence on children. In *The Magic Years,* Selma Fraiberg, referring to the influence of television, wrote:

> We need to consider what it means to be a child who receives moral education from his parents and is entertained in his own living room, with the consent of his parents, by a constant flow of visitors . . . whose views on society and human values would have been barely tolerated in a Neanderthal cave. . . . When murder and violence are

offered as an entertainment diet, how is the child helped to give up pleasure in the destructive act? (Fraiberg, 1959, pp. 270-271)

The issue of violence on television and its effects on children and adolescents has been the subject of periodic scientific review and government policy recommendations. Donnerstein, Slaby, and Eron (1996) reviewed a series of government reports, including the 1972 Surgeon General's report, a review conducted in 1982 by the National Institute of Mental Health, and recent congressional testimony on the subject. Each of these reports concluded that a substantial body of evidence supported the notion that television violence had a deleterious effect on the children who watched it. It was not until the mid-1990s, however, that formal rating and enforcement was required.

The 1972 Surgeon General's Scientific Advisory Committee on Television and Social Behavior reported that "the present entertainment offerings of the television medium may be contributing, in some measure, to the aggressive behavior of many normal children. Such an effect has been shown in a wide variety of situations" (Surgeon General, 1972, p. 5). Ten years later, the National Institute of Mental Health (1982) updated this report and concluded:

> The consensus among most of the research community is that violence on television does lead to aggressive behavior by children and teenagers who watch the programs. . . . In magnitude, television violence is as strongly correlated with aggressive behavior as any other behavioral variable that has been measured. (p. 6)

In 1992, the House and Senate committees began hearing testimony on violence in children's television (Eron, 1992; Slaby, 1992). This testimony has led to a new federal requirement that all new television sets sold in the United States in 1998 and beyond have a specialized computer chip—the V-chip—that will allow parents to block excessively violent programming from their television. This chip will interpret ratings broadcast along with the show itself and allow parents to block the viewing of excessively violent programming. The industry was given 1 year to develop a voluntary rating system, after which time the FCC would develop a system of its own devising. Unlike motion pictures developed for cinematic release, television programming will be rated by the producers of each show. At this writing, the industry has proposed an age-based rating system, similar in concept and nomenclature to the motion picture rating system. The American Academy of Pediatrics and other advocacy organizations have indicated that they will oppose this system and push instead for a system that simply describes the levels of violence and sexuality depicted in the programming.

The American Academy of Pediatrics Committee on Communication advocates that children and adolescents be restricted to no more than 2 hours of television per day (Shelov et al., 1995). Other recent articles have advised pediatricians to counsel parents to monitor the programs children watch, to remove television sets from children's bedrooms, and to discuss the content of television programming with their children (Sege & Dietz, 1994; Shelov & Hannemann, 1991).

To better understand the impetus for the growing consensus that exposure to violence on television has deleterious consequences, it is important to review the research literature pertaining to three questions: (a) How much violence do children see on television? (b) How is violence portrayed on television? and (c) What evidence supports a link between childhood exposure to television violence and subsequent aggressive behavior?

HOW MUCH VIOLENCE DO CHILDREN SEE ON TELEVISION?

The business of television is delivering audiences to advertisers: This is how profits are made and careers determined. No matter how socially conscious an individual creative artist may be, there is no escaping that television is paid for by advertisers who need to reach as large an audience as possible. Television producers have learned that people, including children, will tune in to dramatic shows that depict personal danger—including interpersonal violence. The result is that violence on television is ubiquitous. On any Sunday evening, particularly during sweeps week (when agencies such as the A. C. Nielsen rating service measure audience size), a channel surfer settling down in front of the TV set will have the opportunity to see multiple people, often women, killed in the opening scenes of television programs. Previews of feature films—as well as the films themselves—often feature stylized grotesque and horrible interpersonal violence.

Television news producers have also discovered that portrayals of violence and violent criminals attract large audiences. Overall, in the United States, the mid-1990s have seen a slow but clear decline in the rate of actual violence. These rates are reflected both in criminal victimization studies produced by the National Institute of Justice (Bureau of Justice Statistics, 1993), and in police and FBI reports. In the same period, however, competitive pressures have increased, and television and cable outlets have increased the portrayal of violence and violent crime. In Boston, acquisition of one network-affiliated television station by an aggressive media company led to a 200% increase in the portrayal of violent crime in nightly television news despite a reported 10% reduction in actual violent crime.

Violent acts (defined as acts intended to injure or harm others) appear 8 to 12 times per hour on prime-time television (Dietz & Strasburger, 1991). Dietz and Strasburger further noted that much of the violent fare on television is actually aimed at children. Children's cartoons, for example, often have 25 to 50 acts of violence per hour, about twice the rate of adult television. Children and adolescents view an average of 4 hours of television per day (Nielsen, 1990). When averaged over the year, they spend more time watching television than they do in any other activity except sleep. Thus, American children and teens spend more time watching television than they do going to school. Combining the amount of time spent viewing television and the violent content of children's programming results in an estimate that American children view, on average, 10,000 to 12,000 violent acts per year on television (Sege & Dietz, 1994). A recent review by Donnerstein et al. (1996) estimates that American children see 8,000 murders and 100,000 total acts of violence by the time they finish grade school, and double that total by the time they enter their 20s.

HOW IS VIOLENCE PORTRAYED
ON TELEVISION?

Although other media have been widely discussed in the popular press, the ubiquity of television exposure has made it the most important, and best studied, mass medium influencing American children. The effects of viewing violence depend on the context in which it is seen and on the social messages that accompany the presentation. Several factors peculiar to media violence determine its impact on individual and community opinion:

- Both heroes and villains use violence as an acceptable means of achieving their ends, making violence normative behavior.
- Mass media violence, unlike real violence, is seldom painful.
- Aspects of both viewer and program content interact to influence the effect on aggressive behavior.

Violence Portrayed as Socially Acceptable

On television, violence is used effectively by both hero and villain. In fact, violence is often used as the first and most effective way of resolving situations of conflict. American heroes, from Rambo to the police on *NYPD Blue*, use violence either directly or indirectly to solve problems. Heroes receive social affirmation for the use of violence, and in addition, heroes—with whom children are likely to identify—are seldom, if ever, hurt through the use of violence.

Does this matter? The classic study by Bandura and his colleagues (Bandura, Ross, & Ross, 1963) demonstrated the effect of the social affirmation of violence on television. They performed a laboratory experiment in which preschoolers were shown a short film segment (on a simulated TV screen) in which an actor hit and kicked a clown doll in certain characteristic ways. Three different versions of the film were used: in the first version, the episode ended directly after the actor hit and kicked the clown doll; the second set of children saw a version in which the actor was rewarded following his attack on the doll; the third group saw a version of the film in which the actor was punished.

After viewing one of the three films, each preschooler was led into a room where there was a clown doll identical to the one he or she had just seen on film. Two groups of children tended to attack the doll: those children who had been exposed to the version that ended immediately after the actor attacked the doll and those who had seen the version in which the actor was rewarded. Furthermore, their stylized attacks used the same sequence of moves the actor had employed—apparently in imitation of what they had just viewed on television. However, those children who had been exposed to the scene in which the actor was punished for hitting and kicking the clown doll did not attack the doll nearly as often. Bandura argued that children learn social mores from observing adults. This social learning may take as its foundation either direct observation or observations of television and other media. Since that time, many studies have further amplified these original results. For example, Singer and Singer (1981) demonstrated that an aggressive effect of television violence exposure in preschoolers lasted at least 2 years, and that this effect was not explained by differences in parental disciplinary styles.

Violence Without Pain

Television violence does not hurt—at least not for long. Violence on television and violence in the mass media, including television, serves a variety of dramatic functions. In children's cartoons, for example, violence is funny. Wile E. Coyote has faced innumerable episodes of apparent death and dismemberment, only to reappear after the commercial break. In other dramatic shows, the heroes are often spared the effects of violence. Villains, even when they are killed, rarely suffer, and they are not often mourned. Children and teens internalize this concept of violence without pain. In her book *Deadly Consequences* (Prothrow-Stith & Weissman, 1991), Deborah Prothrow-Stith recalls an account of an adolescent who is treated for a gunshot wound at Boston City Hospital. He was shocked, dismayed, and angry that it hurt. On TV, he explained to his doctor, it never seemed to hurt so much.

Aspects of Program and Viewer That Enhance the Effect of Television Violence

In their authoritative review, Comstock and Strasburger (1990, p. 39) found 14 circumstances in which violence on television is more likely to have behavioral consequences:

1. Reward or lack of punishment for the perpetrator of violence
2. Portrayal of the violence as being justified
3. Cues in the portrayal that mimic real life (e.g., a victim with the same name as someone in real life whom the viewer dislikes)
4. Portrayal of the perpetrator as being similar to the viewer
5. Depiction of behavior that has vengeful motives

6. Depiction of violence without consequences—violence without pain, suffering, sorrow, or remorse

7. Real-life violence

8. Uncriticized violence

9. Violence that pleases the viewer

10. Violence without associated humor in the story

11. Abuse that includes physical violence as well as verbal abuse

12. Aggression against females by males engaged in sexual conquest

13. Portrayals—whether violent or not—that leave the viewer in an aroused state

14. Viewers who are angry or provoked before viewing a violent portrayal or who are frustrated afterward

Comstock and Strasburger then reduced these circumstances to four dimensions: efficacy (Does the violence work for the protagonist?), normativeness (Is the violence justified?), pertinence to the viewer's life circumstance, and susceptibility of the viewer. Thus, each viewers' past experience and values interact with the programming. Certain program elements affect certain individuals strongly, whereas others have little or no effect. This view clearly places the viewing of television violence as a risk factor that, when combined with individual factors, may lead to an increase in aggressive behavior. This situation is analogous to other, more traditional health problems: asbestos exposure combined with smoking to produce lung cancer, and cholesterol intake interacting with certain genetic factors to accelerate atherosclerosis in certain individuals.

THE LINK BETWEEN ADOLESCENT BEHAVIOR AND VIEWING VIOLENCE IN THE MASS MEDIA

Theoretical Models

Early researchers proposed relatively simple models for the effects of television violence on children. Children observed television violence, saw that it was socially rewarded, and began to imitate those behaviors. This simple model failed to account for the wide variation in observed effects in individual children. Donnerstein et al. (1996) cite two current theoretical models that help explain some of the more complicated interactions involved. They summarize these results as follows:

> Children who are heavy viewers of television violence will see characters solving interpersonal problems by behaving aggressively. To the extent that these children identify with the aggressive character ... they will fantasize about and encode in memory the aggressive characters they observe. . . . [The] aggressive behavior becomes habitual [and] it will interfere with social and academic success. These academic and social fillers may lead to . . . more regular television viewing. . . . The self-perpetuating cycle of aggression, academic and social failure, violence viewing, and fantasizing then continues. (p. 234)

Note that this summary reports that certain qualities of the child and program must interact to produce a behavioral outcome: The children must first identify with the aggressive television character.

The same authors offer a second explanation for the influence of televised violence on children. A single exposure to violent images in television or media can cause anxiety and discomfort for most adolescents, whereas repeated exposure to violence simply desensitizes adolescents to its emotional effects. In one experiment, young adult viewers exposed to violent films over a 5-day period reported less anxiety after the fifth day then they did after the first. They also responded less sympathetically with real-world victims of violence. Thus, heavy TV viewers became accustomed to violence and displayed a blunted affective response to it. This altered emotional response to violent images may generalize to real situations, explaining the observed increase in violence-prone behaviors among heavy viewers.

In general, this normalization of violence has three effects (American Psychological Association Commission on Violence and Youth, 1993): increased likelihood of aggression, the increased likelihood of being a victim, and the bystander effect. Which type of effect each individual will experience is influenced largely by other temperamental and environmental variables. The aggressor effect is perhaps the most easily understood. Children who identify with violent characters in the mass media are likely to use aggression in their own lives. The other effects are more subtle, yet equally important. By repeated exposures to media violence, children accept violence as simply a normal part of life, and they learn that those who object to it may find themselves victims of even more serious attacks. Some children resign themselves to violence, fail to seek help, and are more likely to become victims themselves. This effect is associated with a learned helplessness, an unwillingness to reach for assistance.

Among teenagers in particular, the bystander effect may be the most important. Bystanders encourage the protagonists to fight, or refrain from intervening to prevent the fight, because they feel that physical violence is an important and normal part of everyday life. This bystander effect is associated with a particular philosophical view of the world—that it is a mean place populated with people who are essentially out only for themselves. Recent work with adolescent and young adult victims of violence indicates that many teens fight simply to avoid being perceived as "suckers" (Rich & Stone, 1996).

Several descriptive studies have documented that exposure to repeated violence on television programming produces subtle shifts in how adult Americans view the world and in fact contributes to this rather pessimistic perspective. Researchers at the Annenberg School for Communication, led by George Gerbner (Gerbner, Gross, & Signorielli, 1980), have studied adults who watch large amounts of television. Using an instrument they call "The Mean World Test," they find that adults who view large amounts of television are more likely to view the world with feelings of danger, mistrust, intolerance, gloom, and hopelessness then are other adults with less television exposure. Interestingly, my own experience administering this survey to medical students in the preclinical years confirms this effect even among highly educated Americans. Thus, images from television alter the view of adults toward the real world. This has far-reaching consequences, both in terms of policy making and in terms of individual actions. For example, fueled by the belief in a "mean world," many more Americans own handguns now than did a decade ago (Denno et al., 1996), despite decreases in the overall rates of violent crime. This increase has occurred despite the well-documented increased personal risk of injury or death associated with handgun ownership (Kellerman et al., 1993).

Preschool children appear to be extremely vulnerable to this effect because they have not yet acquired the ability to sort fantasy from reality (Flavell, 1986). Researchers at Yale University led by Singer (Singer & Rapaczynski, 1984) used an adaptation of Gerbner's mean world instrument—"The Scary World" test—to demonstrate similar effects on the worldview of children. The test included questions relevant to the experiences of young children: "Do you think that most people are mean or most people are friendly? Is it all right to hit someone? What scares you the most?" High scores on this scale correlated with increased television viewing.

The ubiquitous nature of violence on television leads American children and adults to believe that violence is prevalent at higher rates than it actually is, and that it is inevitable and unavoidable. Given adults' influence in shaping children's and adolescents' behaviors and attitudes, the effect of TV violence on adults is likely to have an indirect effect on children and adolescents. From these viewing experiences, children, for their part, learn to accept violence as an important component of everyday life.

Experimental Evidence

Over the past 30 years, evidence has accrued linking childhood and adolescent viewing of television violence with subsequent violence. Each of these studies infers an association based on a limited set of observations, and, like all scientific studies of human behaviors, is subject to a variety of potential errors in interpretation. However, the results of hundreds of studies, using a variety of experimental approaches and involving thousands of subjects, suggest a causal link (Donnerstein et al., 1996). This review includes samples of some of these studies to provide the reader with an idea of the quality and breadth of the research that has been accomplished to date. From the research, summarized in recent review articles (Eron, 1995; Sege & Dietz, 1994), it appears that the most important developmental period for the childhood viewing of television occurs in the preadolescent years, and perhaps in the preschool years.

In field studies, investigators look at the short-term impact of viewing specific films on children. Although experimental techniques differ, the basic experimental protocol is quite simple: children in a controlled environment (e.g., a boarding school) are exposed to a mainstream film that is classified by the researchers as either violent or nonviolent. In the ensuing time period, usually 2 to 3 weeks, the number of violent incidents and fights among the students who watch the film is recorded. Meta-analysis of these experiments has shown the clear and consistent association between the viewing of violent films and violence at the school in the short term (Wood, Wong, & Chachere, 1991). By design, these studies are unable to show which children are particularly vulnerable to this effect, the duration of the effect, or whether television viewed in private is as potent a stimulus as group viewing of a film. However, these studies suggest that the viewing of media violence precedes the increase in aggressive behavior, and that no increase is seen after viewing nonviolent "control" films. This time sequence, unavailable from cross-sectional studies or purely observational studies, forms one basis for establishing a causal link.

In a classic observational study begun in the 1960s, Heusmann and Eron (1984; Huesmann, 1986) examined the long-term influences on a cohort of 8-year-old children living in a county in New York State. Data were collected concerning these 8-year-olds, including socioeconomic status, parenting styles, size of family, and the quantity and quality of television viewing. These children were subsequently followed for 22 years. By the end of the time in the study period, those boys who were reported viewing and preferring violent TV were much more likely to have been arrested for violent crime than were their cohorts. In fact, television variables were one of the strongest predictors of subsequent violence. In their view, preference for viewing violent television appears to precede actual aggressive behavior (Huesmann, Lagerspetz, & Eron, 1984). Interestingly, however, they found a much weaker association between television violence viewing among 18-year-olds and their subsequent violence history up to age 30. This suggests that the most vulnerable period for television viewing may occur closer to the 8-year-old time point than the 18-year-old time point.

This extraordinary study, which covered all of the youth in a particular county for 22 years, is unlikely to be repeated. Because it was an observational study—no randomization or experimental manipulation occurred—it is impossible to rule out the possibility that another variable, unobserved and uncategorized, accounted for the simultaneous occurrence of increased viewing frequency and choice of violent programming at age eight and subsequent criminal convictions at age 30. However, it is interesting to note that the same study failed to show a relationship between aggressive behavior at age eight and subsequent viewing of TV violence at age 19. Thus, in this study, viewing TV violence portended subsequent aggressive behavior, but the reciprocal relationship—aggressive behavior predicting subsequent television viewing preferences—was not observed. These observations extend the experimental evidence offered in the smaller scale, short-term studies described above.

Among the more controversial studies implicating television viewing with subsequent violent behavior are those performed by Brandon Centerwall (Centerwall, 1989, 1992), who examined homicide trends in the United States, white South Africa, and Canada before, during, and after the introduction of television in each country. These countries were selected because they are predominantly English speaking and use American programming material. The three countries each had television introduced at different times, allowing for international comparisons as controls. Centerwall found that the introduction of television presaged a doubling of the homicide rate in each of these countries by 10 to 12 years. In fact, in the United States, the homicide rate doubled first among those populations who were exposed to television first—urban, northeastern populations, and among whites prior to minorities, because television was originally a luxury for minority individuals.

Standing alone, this approach is subject to a variety of criticisms. Other contemporary trends and events may account for the observations. In South Africa, for example, there was a struggle over the apartheid regime; in the United States, the Vietnam War intervened. These epidemiological data should most properly be viewed as confirmation of the predictions of the smaller scale studies described above. If the laboratory experiments, field studies, and longitudinal observations were accurate, then we would expect the observed increases in national homicide rates to occur. The fact that they do follow, and that they follow in the same sequence in which television was introduced, lends credence to the other, more rigorous studies.

CONCLUSION

Collectively, these studies provide strong epidemiological evidence that childhood viewing of television results in the increased risk of subsequent violence. In establishing that cigarette smoking caused cancer, the 1964 Surgeon General's Report on Smoking and Health (Public Health Service, 1964) established criteria by which epidemiological causality can be established. In a recent review (Sege & Dietz, 1994), we argued that the research connecting childhood exposure to televised violence and subsequent aggression met these criteria. Specifically, studies such as the ones described above establish (a) time sequence of variables—exposure to violence in each case predated the aggressive behavior studied; (b) consistency, strength, and specificity of association—the preponderance of evidence, including studies conducted with vastly different designs, each established the same specific association between exposure and subsequent behavior; and (c) coherence—there are theories of childhood learning that provide an explanatory model for the observed results.

REFERENCES

American Psychological Association Commission on Violence and Youth. (1993). *Violence & youth: Psychology's response.* Washington, DC: Author.

Bandura, A., Ross, D., & Ross, S. A. (1963). Imitation of film-mediated aggressive models. *Journal of Abnormal Social Psychology, 66,* 3-11.

Bureau of Justice Statistics. (1993). *Highlights from 20 years of surveying crime victims: The national crime victimization survey, 1973-92* (NCJ-144525). Washington, DC: U.S. Department of Justice.

Centerwall, B. S. (1989). Exposure to television as a risk factor for violence. *American Journal of Epidemiology, 129,* 643-652.

Centerwall, B. S. (1992). Television and violence: The scale of the problem and where to go from here. *Journal of the American Medical Association, 267,* 3059-3063.

Comstock, G., & Strasburger, V. (1990). Deceptive appearances: Television violence and aggressive behavior. *Journal of Adolescent Health, 11,* 31-44.

Denno, D., Grossman, D., Britt, J., & Bergman, A. B. (1996). Safe storage of handguns. *Archives of Pediatrics, 150,* 927-931.

Dietz, W. H., & Strasburger, V. C. (1991). Children, adolescents and television. *Current Problems in Pediatrics, 21,* 8-31.

Donnerstein, E., Slaby, R. G., & Eron, L. D. (1996). The mass media and youth aggression. In L. D. Eron, J. H. Gentry, & P. Schlegel (Eds.), *Reason to hope: A psychosocial perspective on violence and youth* (pp. 219-250). Washington, DC: American Psychological Association Press.

Eron, L. D. (1992, June 18). Testimony before the Senate Committee on Governmental Affairs. *Congressional Record, 88,* S8538-S8539.

Eron, L. D. (1995). Media violence. *Pediatric Annals, 24,* 84-87.

Fingerhut, L. A., & Kleinman, J. C. (1990). International and interstate comparisons of homicide among young males. *Journal of the American Medical Association, 263,* 3292-3294.

Flavell, J. H. (1986). The development of children's knowledge about the appearance-reality distinction. *American Psychologist, 41,* 418-425.

Fraiberg, S. H. (1959). *The magic years.* New York: Macmillan.

Gerbner, G. L., Gross, M. M., & Signorielli, N. (1980). The "mainstreaming" of America: Violence profile number 11. *Journal of Communication, 33,* 10-29.

Huesmann, L. R. (1986). Psychological processes promoting the relation between exposure to media violence and aggressive behavior by the viewer. *Journal of Social Issues, 42,* 125-139.

Huesmann, L. R., & Eron, L. D. (1984). Cognitive processes and the persistence of aggressive behavior. *Aggressive Behavior, 10,* 243-251.

Huesmann, L. R., Lagerspetz, K., & Eron, L. D. (1984). Intervening variables in the TV violence-aggression relation: Evidence from two countries. *Developmental Psychology, 20,* 746-775.

Kellerman, A. L., Rivara, F. P., Rushforth, N. B., Banton, J. G., Reay, D. T., Francisco, J. T., Locci, A. B., Prodzinski, J., Hackman, B. B., & Somes, G. (1993). Gun ownership as a risk factor for homicide in the home. *New England Journal of Medicine, 329,* 1084-1091.'

Liebert, R. M. (1988). *The early window: Effects of television on children and youth* (6th ed.). Needham, MA: Allyn and Bacon.

National Institute of Mental Health. (1982). *Television and behavior, Volume 1: Summary report.* Washington, DC: U.S. Government Printing Office.

Nielsen, A. C. C. (1990). *1990 Nielsen report on television.* New York: Nielsen Media Research.

Prothrow-Stith, D., & Weissman, M. (1991). *Deadly consequences: How violence is destroying our teenage population and a plan to begin solving the problem.* New York: HarperCollins.

Public Health Service. (1964). *Smoking and health: Report of the advisory committee to the Surgeon General.* Washington, DC: U.S. Government Printing Office.

Rich, J. A., & Stone, D. A. (1996). The experience of violent injury for young African-American men: The meaning of being a "sucker." *Journal of General Internal Medicine, 11,* 77-82.

Sege, R., & Dietz, W. (1994). Television viewing and violence in children: The pediatrician as agent for change. *Pediatrics, 94,* 600-607.

Shelov, S. P., Bar-On, M., Beard, L., Hogan, M., Holyrod, H. J., Prentice, P., Sherry, S. N., & Strasburger, V. (1995). Children, adolescents, and television (Report of the American Academy of Pediatrics Committee on Communications). *Pediatrics, 96,* 786-787.

Shelov, S. P., & Hannemann, R. E. (Eds.). (1991). *Caring for your baby and young child: Birth to age 5.* New York: Bantam.

Singer, J.S.D., & Rapaczynski, W. (1984). Family patterns and television viewing as predictors of children's beliefs and aggression. *Journal of Communication, 37,* 74-89.

Singer, J. L., & Singer, D. G. (1981). *Television, imagination, and aggression: A study of pre-schoolers.* Hillsdale, NJ: Lawrence Erlbaum.

Slaby, R. (1992). *Television violence: Effects and remedies.* Testimony before the Subcommittee on Crime and Criminal Justice of the U.S. House of Representatives' Committee on Judiciary Affairs. Washington, DC: U.S. Government Printing Office.

Surgeon General's Scientific Advisory Committee on Television and Social Behavior. (1972). *Television and growing up: The impact of televised violence.* Washington, DC: U.S. Government Printing Office.

Wood, W., Wong, F., & Chachere, J. (1991). Effects of media violence on viewer's aggression in unconstrained social interaction. *Psychological Bulletin, 109,* 371-383.

6. Violent Offending in Adolescence: Epidemiology, Correlates, Outcomes, and Treatment

Charles M. Borduin
Cindy M. Schaeffer

Violent crimes committed by adolescents are a significant social and clinical problem. As a social problem, adolescent violent crime has extremely detrimental emotional, physical, and economic effects on victims, victims' families, and the larger community (Gottfredson, 1989). Violent adolescents also consume much of the resources of the child welfare, juvenile justice, and special education systems and are overrepresented in the "deep end" of these systems (Melton & Hargrove, in press; Melton & Spaulding, in press), with considerable cost to the public treasury and intrusion on family integrity and youth autonomy. As a clinical problem, adolescent violent and antisocial behavior accounts for one third to one half of all adolescent referrals for mental health services (Gilbert, 1957; Herbert, 1978; Robins, 1981). The immediate costs for these services and for continued contact with the mental health system well into adulthood are difficult to estimate but are undoubtedly exorbitant (Kazdin, 1995).

The purpose of the present chapter is to discuss important conceptual issues and research findings pertaining to the nature and treatment of violent criminal behavior in adolescents. More specifically, the chapter begins with an examination of the definitional and methodological difficulties surrounding the study of adolescent violent behavior, followed by a discussion of the epidemiology of violent crimes among adolescents. Next, we review research findings pertaining to the precursors and course of aggressive and violent behavior among children and adolescents. Recent empirical work on the correlates and causes of violent criminal behavior in adolescents is then reviewed. The final section examines contemporary research on the evaluation of treatment and service program outcomes with adolescent violent offenders.

DEFINING ADOLESCENT VIOLENT BEHAVIOR

Adolescent violent behavior has been studied by many different disciplines, including psychology, psychiatry, criminology, and sociology. Although the terms "aggressive," "assaultive," and "antisocial" have all been used in the research literature to refer to adolescent behaviors that are physically harmful to others, the term "violent" is usually reserved for those adolescents who have been adjudicated for crimes against people (e.g., physical assault, armed robbery, homicide). To date, however, there have been relatively few empirical studies focusing exclusively on adolescents who have committed violent crimes. Moreover, within this small extant literature, there has been considerable variability between studies in the severity and chronicity of violent offending, with samples drawn from the community (e.g., Walsh & Beyer, 1987), psychiatric hospitals (e.g., Truscott, 1992), and juvenile detention facilities (e.g., Lewis, Shankok, Pincus, & Glaser, 1979).

Although the empirical base regarding adolescent violent offenders is limited, there have been numerous studies that have more broadly examined serious behavior problems (e.g., conduct disorders) or criminal activity (e.g., index offenses) in adolescents and that can help to shed light on adolescent violent behavior. Indeed, factor-analytic work (e.g., Donovan & Jessor, 1985; Donovan, Jessor, & Costa, 1988; Jessor & Jessor, 1977; McGee & Newcomb, 1992) and longitudinal studies (e.g., Farrington, 1989, 1991) have indicated that diverse adolescent problem behaviors (e.g., property offending, violence, substance use, school problems, early sexual intercourse) reflect a single underlying dimension of deviance. Nevertheless, other factor-analytic studies (e.g., Loeber & Schmaling, 1985a; Quay, 1986) suggest that there are at least two dimensions or groupings of child and adolescent antisocial behavior (i.e., an aggressive dimension composed of oppositional symptoms and "overt" behaviors such as physical fighting and bullying, and a nonaggressive dimension consisting of "covert" delinquent behaviors such as truancy, theft, and association with deviant peers). Of course, it is possible that aggressive and nonaggressive adolescent offenders share some common psychosocial problems and also have some psychosocial difficulties that are unique.

Keeping these conceptual issues in mind, this chapter will draw from diverse empirical studies to review what is known about the development, course, and treatment of violent adolescent offending. Although we consider adolescent sexual offending to be a form of interpersonal violence, little is known about the causes and correlates of adolescent sexual offending or the relation of sexual assaults to other violent criminal acts (Henggeler, 1989). Accordingly, studies that examine adolescent sexual offenders exclusively are not included. For a thorough examination of the topic of adolescent sexual offending, the reader is referred to reviews by Barbaree, Marshall, and Hudson (1993); Becker, Harris, and Sales (1993); and Davis and Leitenberg (1987).

EPIDEMIOLOGY

The prevalence of antisocial behavior in adolescents has been estimated using a number of different methods, including annual crime statistics and survey studies of delinquency and psychiatric disorders. Prevalence rates often vary according to factors such as geographical location, age, and gender.

Prevalence

In 1994, male and female adolescents under 18 years of age were arrested for 107,000 and 17,000 violent crimes, respectively, and together accounted for 19% of all violent crimes (Federal Bureau of Investigation, 1995). These numbers reflect a marked increase in the prevalence and severity of youth violence in the past decade. Indeed, since 1985, the overall violent crime rate among adolescents has increased by 75%, including a 97% increase in aggravated assaults and a 150% increase in murders (Federal Bureau of Investigation, 1995). Although there is some evidence that the violent crime rate for adolescents may have finally leveled off (Federal Bureau of Investigation, 1996), these statistics remain especially disturbing when one considers that arrest data significantly underestimate rates of criminal behavior in juveniles (Dunford & Elliott, 1984).

Epidemiological surveys have examined self-reported rates of violent behavior within nationally representative samples of adolescents. Using a sample of 1,719 11- to 17-year-olds from the United States, Elliott and his colleagues (Elliot, Huizinga, & Morse, 1985; Huizinga & Elliot, 1987) found the following prevalence rates for several types of violent behaviors reported by youths: strong armed robbery, 3%; aggravated assault, 6%; gang fights, 12%; and minor assault on another youth, 48%. In a more recent survey using a Canadian sample of 1,232 12- to 16-year-olds, Offord, Boyle, and Racine (1991) reported prevalence rates for boys and girls, respectively, of 12.3% and 7.1% for physical assault, and 29.5% and 21.0% for fighting.

Information about the prevalence of youth violence also can be gleaned from epidemiological surveys of psychiatric disorders in preadolescents and adolescents. More specifically, the psychiatric diagnosis of conduct disorder (i.e., a persistent pattern of antisocial behavior, including bullying or threatening others, cruelty to people or animals, using weapons, or fighting) is based largely on behaviors that involve harm to others and is applied frequently to youths with histories of criminal violence. The following prevalence estimates of conduct disorder among youths have been reported: 3.4% among 11-year-olds in New Zealand (Anderson, Williams, McGee, & Silva, 1987); 4% and 10% among 11-year-olds from rural and urban settings, respectively, in England (Graham, 1979; Rutter, Cox, Tupling, Berger, & Yule, 1975; Rutter, Tizard, Yule, Graham, & Whitmore, 1976); 10.4% and 4.1% among 12- to 16-year-old boys and girls, respectively, in Canada (Offord et al., 1991); and 6% among 14- to 16-year-olds in the United States (Kashani et al., 1987).

Other statistics also point to the high prevalence of violence among adolescents. For example, national surveys indicate that as many as 11.4% of high school males own a gun (Callahan & Rivera, 1992) and that 15% of males or females in high school carried a handgun to school in the previous year (O'Donnell, 1995). Adolescents are also frequent targets of violent crime: 11.5% and 12.3% are victims of simple assault and aggravated assault, respectively, from nonfamily perpetrators, the vast majority (85%) of whom are adolescent peers (Boney-McCoy & Finkelhor, 1995).

In summary, from 5% to 10% of adolescents report involvement in violent crime. Moreover, a large proportion of youth have access to violent weapons or are themselves victims of violence.

Gender Differences

Several studies have demonstrated large gender differences in the prevalence of conduct disorders and antisocial behavior in adolescents. Male adolescents evidence considerably higher rates of conduct disorder and serious antisocial behaviors than do female adolescents, with male-female prevalence ratios ranging from 3:1 to 12:1 (American Psychiatric Association, 1994; Graham, 1979; McDermott, 1996; Quay, 1986). Likewise, prevalence rates of specific types of antisocial behavior are much higher for males than females. For example, based on National Youth Survey data for White adolescents, Huizinga and Elliott (1987) reported a male-female prevalence ratio of 3:1 for index (i.e., serious and violent) offenses.

PRECURSORS AND OUTCOMES

Aggression tends to be highly stable in individuals (Loeber, 1982) and across generations (Huesmann, Lefkowitz, Eron, & Walder, 1984). In fact, the stability of aggressive behavior in males is only slightly lower than the stability of intelligence (Olweus, 1979). It follows from the stability of such behavior that the prognosis is likely to be poor (Kazdin, 1995). However, it is important to recognize that many individuals who show aggressive and antisocial behaviors during childhood do not display a pattern of serious antisocial behavior during adolescence. Indeed, aggressive behaviors can be seen in most children over the course of normal development (Kazdin, 1995), and the proportion of youths who engage in aggressive behaviors gradually decreases from the preschool years to adolescence (Loeber, 1982). Nevertheless, childhood risk factors can be identified that predict violent behavior in adolescence.

Over the past 15 years, a number of longitudinal studies have evaluated the developmental links between adolescent violent behavior and its childhood precursors. In addition, several longitudinal studies have examined the course (i.e., stability) of aggression and violent behavior during adolescence and into early adulthood. In the subsections that follow, we summarize the results of some of the recent work in these areas.

Childhood Precursors

There is evidence that precursors of aggression and other externalizing behaviors are already evident in infancy and toddlerhood, and that these behaviors are highly stable. Indeed, for boys, noncompliance with parental directives at 18 months predicts child aggression at 24 months, which in turn predicts a wide array of externalizing behavior problems, including aggression, at 36 months (Shaw, Keenan, & Vondra, 1994). Furthermore, aggressive behaviors among toddlers show strong stability over a 6-month period (from 18 to 24 months of age), especially for those toddlers exhibiting aggression in multiple settings (Keenan & Shaw, 1994). One-year stability of aggressive behavior has been found for first-, second-, and third-grade boys and girls (Dumas, Neese, Prinz, & Blechman, 1996), and 3-year stability has been reported for conduct disorder symptoms, including aggression, in boys 7 through 12 years of age (Lahey et al., 1995).

The emergence of aggressive behaviors in young children may reflect insecure attachment to caregivers and difficulty in emotional regulation. Lyons-Ruth (1996) has suggested that hostility from caregivers, coupled with a lack of caregiver responsiveness to infant cues, leads to a disorganized attachment style during infancy (characterized by apprehensive, avoidant, and oppositional behavior) and to subsequent aggression during childhood. Similarly, Landy and Peters (1992) have proposed that aggression in early childhood is related to a disruption in mother-child bonding, which interferes with the infant's developing capacity to regulate affective responses. Longitudinal research is needed to examine the contribution of these early developmental processes to aggressive and violent behavior during childhood and adolescence.

Although aggression during childhood is among the strongest predictors of delinquency and antisocial behaviors during adolescence (Huesmann et al., 1984; Magnusson, Stattin, & Duner, 1983), the continuity of aggression and other antisocial behaviors is not the same for all individuals. To understand the persistence and progression of deviant behaviors from childhood to adolescence, it is important to appreciate that particular *patterns* of such behaviors during childhood are also relevant. Indeed, researchers (e.g., Loeber, 1982) have concluded that the risk of a later deviant outcome is higher for those children whose problem behavior (a) is more frequent, (b) is more varied, (c) occurs in multiple settings (e.g., both at home and at school), or (d) occurs at an earlier age. Of course, these risk factors can be intercorrelated; for example, a youth who exhibits a variety of problem behaviors at an early age probably also exhibits these behaviors at a relatively high rate and in multiple settings.

In an excellent review of risk factors that influence the course of antisocial and violent behavior, Loeber (1990) described an "aggressive-versatile path" that is distinct from other forms of conduct problems. The aggressive-versatile path begins in the preschool years and involves a great variety of aggressive and nonaggressive conduct problems, as well as hyperactivity. Children on this path tend to have poor relationships with peers and adults and engage in numerous and serious offenses as adolescents. Although evidence for the existence of this developmental path is far from complete, it seems clear that aggressive youths progress more rapidly in the development of antisocial behaviors and are less likely to show remission of their behaviors than are those youth whose behaviors do not involve aggression (see Moffitt, 1993, for an extended discussion of this issue).

Short- and Long-Term Outcomes

A number of prospective studies have shown that aggression and other conduct problems in early adolescence portend criminal behavior in adulthood. For example, in a community sample of 1,027 subjects, Stattin and Magnusson (1989) found a strong association between teacher ratings of boys' and girls' aggressiveness at age 13 and their involvement in criminal activities at age 26. High ratings of aggressiveness were characteristic of both boys and girls who later committed frequent and serious crimes, especially crimes involving violence against people or property damage. For both sexes, the relationship between aggressiveness and crime was largely independent of intelligence and family education. Similarly, in a community sample of 632 subjects who were followed from ages 8 to 30, Huesmann et al. (1984) found that for both boys and girls, the relationship between early aggressiveness (as rated by peers) and serious antisocial behavior (including criminal convictions, spouse abuse, and self-reported physical aggression) in adulthood was still significant after partialing out IQ. Finally, in a community sample of 411 boys, Farrington, Loeber, and Van Kammen (1990) found that a composite measure of conduct problems (based on teacher, mother, and peer ratings) at age 10 significantly predicted criminal convictions at age 25.

It is also evident from longitudinal research that violent and chronic juvenile offenders are at increased risk of committing serious and repeated crimes during adulthood. Indeed, Farrington (1995) found that nearly 75% of juveniles who were convicted of at least one criminal offense (either a violent or a property crime) were reconvicted between ages 17 and 24, and nearly 50% were reconvicted between ages 25 and 32; other researchers (e.g., Lattimore, Visher, & Linster, 1995; Stattin & Magnusson, 1991) have reported a similar continuity in offending for juveniles who commit serious offenses. Moreover, although serious juvenile offenders generally commit fewer crimes at age 30 than at age 20 (Nagin & Land, 1993), their criminal "careers" show a relatively stable pattern of offending into their 30s and do not decline until around 40 years of age (Blumstein & Cohen, 1987) or beyond (Moffitt, 1993). In general, there is agreement that individuals who display high rates of serious antisocial behavior, especially violence, during adolescence are more likely to continue their criminal behavior during adulthood than are youths who mainly commit status offenses or nonviolent crimes (for reviews, see Loeber, 1990, and Moffitt, 1993).

Violent and other serious juvenile offenders are also at increased risk for substance use and abuse in adulthood, although it appears that this risk is moderated by gender. In a prospective study using a national probability sample of 2,411 adolescents, Windle (1990) found that various types of self-reported antisocial behaviors (including both violent and property offenses) at ages 14 and 15 were uniformly related to substance use (including alcohol, cigarettes, marijuana, and other illicit substances) at ages 18 and 19 in men but not in women; for women, property offenses (e.g., vandalism) but not other types of offenses at ages 14 and 15 were linked to substance use at ages 18 and 19. Similarly, in other prospective studies by Farrington (1991) and Pulkkinen and Pitkanen (1993), teacher and peer ratings of adolescent aggression predicted illicit drug use, problem drinking, and arrests for alcohol abuse at ages 25 to 32 years, especially among males. In another recent study using data from the St. Louis sample ($N = 2,572$) of the NIMH Epidemiological Catchment Area Project, Lewis and Bucholz (1991) found that serious antisocial behavior before age 15 (as retrospectively reported by subjects) was significantly associated with alcoholism in early adulthood among both men and women, but the odds of developing alcoholism following a childhood history of antisocial behavior were more than twice as high for women as for men.

Serious and violent offending in adolescence has also been associated with difficulties in physical health, educational/vocational attainment, and interpersonal relations in adulthood. Regarding physical health, some evidence suggests that antisocial youths have higher rates of hospitalization for physical problems in adulthood than do clinical or normal controls (Robins, 1966), and the long-term use of drugs and alcohol noted previously for serious juvenile offenders likely contributes to future health-related difficulties in this population (see Newcomb & Bentler, 1987). Regarding educational and vocational performance, chronic delinquency predicts school dropout and decreased educational ambitions during early adulthood (Laub & Sampson, 1994); and chronic delinquency (Laub & Sampson, 1994; Sampson & Laub, 1990, 1993) and adolescent aggression (Farrington, 1991) have been linked with unemployment, job instability, and lower-status jobs during early to middle adulthood. Persistent juvenile offending (Laub & Sampson, 1994) and aggression in youths (Farrington, 1991; Huesmann et al., 1984) also predict difficulties in close interpersonal relations, including increased divorce/separation, increased spouse/partner abuse, and decreased relationship satisfaction in young adults and adults. Taken together, these findings suggest that aggression and other serious antisocial behavior during adolescence can disrupt developmental tasks and role performance during early adulthood.

Economic Costs of Criminal Behavior
During Adulthood

Although the economic costs of adult criminal behavior to society have not been fully delineated, available data suggest that such costs are substantial. For example, in 1992, the average annual cost of housing an adult prison inmate was approximately $18,000, and it was estimated that almost 13,000 new cells (at a cost of $108,000 per cell) would be needed by 1996 to house a projected increase in federal detainees (U.S. General Accounting Office, 1992). Moreover, in 1994, almost $5 billion was spent to construct new prisons in the United States (Mendel, 1995). Recent federal legislation, such as the $30.2 billion Violent Crime Control and Law Enforcement Act of 1994, provided additional funding for prison construction as well as for increased law enforcement and incarceration time. The economic costs related to victimization from serious crime are also considerable. Indeed, using several national data sets, Miller, Cohen, and Rossman (1993) estimated that, in 1987, physical injury to victims of violent crime resulted in about $10 billion in health-related costs (medical, psychological, emergency response, insurance administration); more than $23 billion in lost productivity (wages, fringe benefits, housekeeping); and almost $145 billion in reduced quality-of-life costs (pain and suffering). Although these costs pertain to victims of both adolescent and adult violent offenders, adult offenders in their twenties (age 20 to 29 years) and thirties (age 30 to 39 years) accounted for 49% and 25%, respectively, of all people arrested for violent offenses in 1987 (Bureau of Justice Statistics, 1990).

CORRELATES AND CAUSES

A large number of studies have evaluated correlates of serious antisocial behavior and conduct disorder in adolescents (for reviews, see Henggeler, 1989; Kazdin, 1995; Quay, 1987a). In general, these correlates pertain to the individual adolescent and to the key systems (family, peer, school) in which the adolescent is embedded. A number of other studies have evaluated multidimensional causal models of antisocial and violent behavior in adolescents (for a review, see Henggeler, 1991). This section reviews the major findings that have emerged in these areas of research.

Individual Adolescent Characteristics

There is a substantial body of empirical research showing that conduct disorder and aggressive behavior in adolescents are associated with lower IQ scores, even after controlling for race, social class, and test motivation (Lynam, Moffitt, & Stouthamer-Loeber, 1993; Rutter & Giller, 1983). Evidence also suggests that there is a sizable discrepancy between the performance IQs and verbal IQs of conduct-disordered adolescents, and that the association between conduct disorder and overall IQ is due to the relatively low verbal IQs of these adolescents (Quay, 1987b). Although some researchers have observed an association between the size of the performance IQ/verbal IQ discrepancy and the seriousness (i.e., aggressiveness) of antisocial behavior in adolescents (e.g., Walsh, Petee, & Beyer, 1987), other researchers have not found such an association (e.g., Cornell & Wilson, 1992; Tarter, Hegedus, Alterman, & Katz-Garris, 1983).

The association of low verbal IQ with conduct-disordered or aggressive behavior might be a result of the linkage between low verbal IQ and the delayed development of higher-order cognitive abilities.

For example, researchers have concluded that delinquents in general, and aggressive delinquents in particular, have lower moral reasoning maturity than do nondelinquents (e.g., Arbuthnot, Gordon, & Jurkovic, 1987), and that aggressive youths have poorer abstract reasoning and problem-solving abilities than do nonaggressive youths (e.g., Seguin, Pihl, Harden, Tremblay, & Boulerice, 1995).

Several researchers have also suggested that social skills deficits are linked with aggressive behavior in adolescents. However, in a review of this literature, Henggeler (1989) concluded that findings have been inconsistent, especially when the influences of mediating factors such as IQ are considered. In contrast, recent studies of sociocognitive deficits in aggressive adolescents and adolescent violent offenders (for reviews, see Akhtar & Bradley, 1991; Crick & Dodge, 1994) have consistently found evidence of hostile attributional biases (i.e., a propensity to infer hostile intentions in ambiguous interpersonal situations). The association between hostile attributional biases and aggressive behavior seems to be independent of verbal IQ, social class, or race (see Dodge, Price, Bachorowski, & Newman, 1990; Graham, Hudley, & Williams, 1992). Moreover, such attributional biases are linked to forms of aggression that involve interpersonal deficits (undersocialized aggression) but not to deviant behaviors classified as socialized aggression or socialized delinquency (Dodge et al., 1990). Interestingly, there is growing evidence that mothers of aggressive boys share the propensity to infer hostility in ambiguous situations and may, in effect, model a hostile attributional bias for their sons (e.g., Bickett, Milich, & Brown, 1996; Dix & Lochman, 1990; MacKinnon-Lewis et al., 1994).

Family Characteristics

Research suggests that the family relations of violent delinquents are more disturbed than the family relations of nonviolent delinquents or nondelinquent adolescents. Indeed, a number of studies have demonstrated that violent juvenile offending is associated with low levels of family warmth and supportiveness (e.g., Borduin & Henggeler, 1987; Borduin, Henggeler, Hanson, & Pruitt, 1985) and high rates of marital and family conflict (e.g., Borduin, Pruitt, & Henggeler, 1986; Mann, Borduin, Henggeler, & Blaske, 1990). Likewise, studies using community samples have found that adolescent self-reported delinquent behavior, including violence, is linked with low parental affection and family cohesion (Gorman-Smith, Tolan, Zelli, & Huesmann, 1996; Haapasalo & Tremblay, 1994; Loeber & Schmaling, 1985b; Olweus, 1980; Patterson & Stouthamer-Loeber, 1984) and high marital and family conflict (Jouriles, Bourg, & Farris, 1991; Tolan & Lorion, 1988). Evidence also suggests that affective relations in families of female serious juvenile offenders may be even more dysfunctional than those in families of male offenders (e.g., Henggeler, Edwards, & Borduin, 1987).

Lax and ineffective parental discipline (see Henggeler, 1989; Snyder & Patterson, 1987; Weiss, Dodge, Bates, & Pettit, 1992) and poor parental monitoring (Gorman-Smith et al., 1996) also have been linked consistently with aggression and delinquency in adolescents. However, whether these parenting practices lead to aggressive and antisocial behavior or are the result of such behavior is unclear. Indeed, longitudinal research (Vuchinich, Bank, & Patterson, 1992) with preadolescent boys and their parents has indicated bidirectional effects between parental discipline practices and child antisocial behavior (also see Lytton, 1990; Rutter, 1994).

The effects of witnessing or experiencing family violence on the development of aggressive behavior in children and adolescents have received a great deal of attention from researchers. Studies suggest that violent delinquent adolescents are more likely to have been physically abused by a parent or to have witnessed violence between their parents than are nonviolent or nondelinquent adolescents (for a review, see Widom, 1989). Studies also suggest that the chronicity of family violence is linked more strongly to later aggression in youths than is the severity of the violence (Widom, 1989). Further research is needed to identify whether the relation of family violence to children's aggressive behavior is direct or, instead, is moderated by a third variable known to be associated with violence (e.g., parental rejection).

Peer Relations

The peer group is important to psychosocial development because it provides adolescents with a sense of belonging, emotional support, and behavioral norms. Within peer groups of many violent adolescents, the sense of belonging and emotional support are evident; however, the group behavioral norms often conflict with societal norms. Moreover, violent behavior often serves an adaptive function for these adolescents because it can be collaborative and can elicit continued peer support and acceptance. In fact, a high percentage of assaultive behavior is carried out with peers (Emler, Reicher, & Ross, 1987; Strasburg, 1978), and the youth's involvement with deviant peers is a powerful predictor of both the frequency and the seriousness of his or her antisocial behavior (e.g., Hanson, Henggeler, Haefele, & Rodick, 1984; Lyon, Henggeler, & Hall, 1992; Smith, Visher, & Jarjoura, 1991; White, Pandina, & LaGrange, 1987). Although there is some evidence that adolescent violent offenders (i.e., those convicted of aggravated assault or assault/battery) are more aggressive toward their peers than are nonviolent offenders or nonoffenders (Blaske, Borduin, Henggeler, & Mann, 1989), it is unclear whether this aggression is more likely to be directed toward prosocial peers or toward deviant peers.

Although involvement with deviant peers can contribute to violent behavior, positive family relations and prosocial peer support tend to mitigate the negative effects of deviant peers. For example, Poole and Rigoli (1979) found that high involvement with delinquent peers was strongly predictive of antisocial behavior under conditions of low family support but only slightly predictive of antisocial behavior under conditions of high family support; boys who had highly delinquent friends and nonsupportive family relations reported 500% more criminal activity than did boys with highly delinquent friends and supportive family relations. Similarly, in a study using a community sample of 10-year-old boys, Dishion, Patterson, Stoolmiller, and Skinner (1991) found that high levels of parental discipline skill and monitoring buffered the negative effects of child involvement with deviant peers.

School and Academic Performance

Poor school performance (e.g., low grades, special class placement, general reading problems, retention, suspension) and subsequent dropping out of high school have been linked consistently with aggressive behavior (see Hinshaw, 1992) and serious delinquency (see Elliott & Voss, 1974). Furthermore, this linkage seems to be independent of pertinent mediating variables such as conduct problems during childhood (Maughan, Gray, & Rutter, 1985) and IQ (Berrueta-Clement, Schweinhart, Barnett, & Weikart, 1987). Academic underachievement and dropping out of school also have been associated with higher rates of criminal activity during early adulthood (e.g., Thornberry, Moore, & Christenson, 1985).

School characteristics also can contribute to aggressive and violent behavior. Hellman and Beaton (1986) reported that violent behavior in junior high schools was related to low student attendance and to high student-teacher ratios. Aggressive behavior in senior high schools was associated with instability in the student population (i.e., high rates of transfers and new admissions) and with poor academic quality of the school. These relations between school characteristics and in-school aggressive behaviors emerged even after controlling for crime rates in the local communities.

Multidimensional Causal Models

Although the above studies have contributed significantly to our understanding of the different factors associated with violence in adolescents, it should be noted that these studies generally possess three important methodological limitations. First, in light of the correlational nature of the studies, it is impossible to determine whether the observed correlates led to the violent behavior, whether the violent behavior led to the correlates, or whether the association is reciprocal. For example, does parental rejection lead to aggressive behavior, does aggressive behavior lead to parental rejection, or are parental rejection and aggressive behavior part of a reciprocal causal structure, mutually influencing one another over time? Second, the association between a particular psychosocial variable and violence may be spurious (i.e., the result of their joint association with a third variable). For example, low levels of sociomoral reasoning may be linked with aggression because both sociomoral reasoning and aggression are associated with authoritarian discipline strategies. Third, most of the extant studies have tapped only a small subset of the correlates of violent behavior. Thus, it is not possible to examine the interrelations among the correlates of violent behavior to determine which variables have direct versus indirect effects on such behavior, or which variables are no longer linked with violent behavior when the effects of other correlates are controlled.

To address the inherent limitations of correlational research, several research groups have developed empirically based multidimensional causal models of serious antisocial behavior in adolescents. For example, Elliott, Huizinga, and Ageton (1985) used a longitudinal design with a representative national sample of adolescents (N = 1,725) to assess the psychosocial determinants of delinquent behavior, including violent and other serious crimes. Path analyses showed that serious delinquency (i.e., index offenses) at Time 1 and involvement with delinquent peers at Time 2 (1 year later) had direct effects on serious delinquent behavior at Time 2, especially for males; in addition, serious delinquent behavior at Time 2 was predicted indirectly by family difficulties and school difficulties, which predicted involvement with delinquent peers. Similarly, in a cross-sectional study using 553 male adolescents and their mothers drawn from 12 New York City neighborhoods, Simcha-Fagan and Schwartz (1986) found that association with delinquent peers, school attachment, neighborhood criminal subculture, and age had direct effects on severe self-reported delinquent behavior (including violent crime); furthermore, family residential stability, neighborhood organizational participation, and neighborhood residential stability had indirect effects on severe delinquency through their direct association with school attachment. These and other causal modeling studies reviewed by Henggeler (1991) provide consistent support for the view that variance in violent and other serious delinquent behavior is contributed to directly or indirectly by variables at the individual, family, peer, school, and community levels.

It is possible that the variables that lead to violent behavior in adolescents may not be the same as the variables that maintain such behavior. For example, individual (e.g., hostile attributional biases) and family (e.g., parental rejection, low family warmth) variables may represent key determinants of the onset of violent criminal activity among younger adolescents, whereas peer (e.g., association with deviant peers) and school (e.g., low achievement, dropping out) variables may be linked more strongly with continued participation and even escalation in violent criminal activity in middle and later adolescence. Indeed, in a cross-sectional study that included community samples of 12-year-old (n = 122), 15-year-old (n = 138), and 18-year-old (n = 81) boys, LaGrange and White (1985) found considerable differences between age groups in the strengths of the predictors of delinquent behavior. Although this study had some significant methodological limitations (e.g., samples were quite small and included few serious offenders), the findings suggest that age is an important mediating variable that should be considered in the development of future causal models of violent criminal offending in adolescence. Moreover, longitudinal research is needed to elucidate characteristics of the developmental pathway to violent criminal offending in adolescence and adulthood (see Loeber, 1990; Moffitt, 1993).

TREATMENT

The preceding review has several important implications regarding the design of effective treatments of violent criminal behavior in adolescents. First, because most violent offenders commit both violent and nonviolent crimes (Osgood, Johnston, O'Malley, & Bachman, 1988), treatments should possess the flexibility to address a broad range of antisocial behaviors. Second, the multicausal nature of adolescent violent behavior suggests that treatments must consider variables that reflect major determinants of such behavior (e.g., adolescent cognitions, family relations, peer relations, and school performance). Third, the intransigence and stability of violent and aggressive behaviors suggest that treatments must be intensive and must be delivered with ecological validity.

Unfortunately, few treatments incorporate each of the aforementioned implications. Hence, it is not surprising that most treatments with violent and serious juvenile offenders have had little success. Indeed, reviewers have argued that the major limitation of such treatments is their relatively narrow focus and failure to address the multiple determinants of violent behavior in youths' naturally occurring systems (e.g., Andrews et al., 1990; Borduin, 1994; Henggeler, 1989; Mulvey, Arthur, & Reppucci, 1993; Zigler, Taussig, & Black, 1992).

The following review examines the contemporary outcome literature regarding serious and violent juvenile offending. In general, we conclude that most treatments have beneficial effects on instrumental outcomes (Rosen & Proctor, 1981) that are the focus of the particular treatment (e.g., role playing to learn social skills). Because of their narrow focus and lack of ecological validity, however, most of these treatments have had minimal effects on ultimate outcomes such as recidivism and self-reported delinquency. On the other hand, broadbased, multifaceted treatments that occur in youths' natural environments have demonstrated considerable success recently regarding both instrumental and ultimate outcomes.

Cognitive and Behavioral Skills Training

Skills training approaches assume that aggressive juvenile offenders lack cognitive and interpersonal skills for managing challenges in family, peer, and school situations. Thus, through techniques such as modeling and behavioral rehearsal, offenders are taught strategies for improving problem solving, moral reasoning, anger control, and interpersonal relations.

Guerra and Slaby (1990) conducted what may be the best designed evaluation of a cognitive and behavioral skills training approach with aggressive juvenile offenders. In contrast with most of the research in this area, the investigators focused on a seriously aggressive sample of incarcerated adolescents, included an attention-placebo condition, and examined the generalization of their results. Findings, however, paralleled the vast majority of outcomes in this area (Henggeler, 1989). Relative to youths in the control conditions, those who received cognitive and behavioral skills training showed (a) greater improvements on instrumental outcomes (e.g., social problem-solving measures), (b) modest changes in behavior problems inside the institutional setting, and (c) no differences in aggressive behavior outside the institution at a 24-month follow-up.

Based on these and other findings, reviewers have noted that the effectiveness of problem-solving skills training and moral reasoning training have not been demonstrated with samples of serious adolescent offenders, such as violent offenders (Gordon & Arbuthnot, 1987; Henggeler, 1989; Kazdin, 1987; Mulvey et al., 1993; Tate, Reppucci, & Mulvey, 1995). On the other hand, a multifaceted and intense cognitive and skills training approach used with incarcerated violent offenders (i.e., Aggression Replacement Training; Goldstein & Glick, 1987) has shown some generalization to the natural environment at a 4-month follow-up, and the authors recommended that treatment also encompass factors in the offenders' interpersonal systems that contribute to aggressive behavior.

Family Therapy

Family therapy approaches attempt to change aspects of family relations that correlate with aggression and violence (e.g., lax parental discipline, conflict, low affection). A growing consensus among reviewers is that to be potentially effective, treatments of serious antisocial behavior should be family based (Henggeler, Borduin, & Mann, 1992; Miller & Prinz, 1990; Mulvey et al., 1993).

Behavioral parent training (Patterson, 1982) is the best researched family-based treatment for aggression, and this approach has shown considerable success with young children (Miller & Prinz, 1990). Behavioral parent training, however, has had limited success when used with serious adolescent offenders. For example, Bank, Marlowe, Reid, Patterson, and Weinrott (1991) evaluated the effectiveness of such training with families of violent and chronic juvenile offenders and found that treatment had minimal influence on family functioning and no long-term effect on recidivism.

Functional family therapy (FFT; Alexander & Parsons, 1982) integrates treatment strategies from systems theory and behavior therapy and has been regarded as one of the most promising treatments of antisocial behavior in adolescents (Kazdin, 1988). The initial evaluation of FFT was a well-designed study conducted with adolescent status offenders; FFT was effective at decreasing subsequent status offenses but not criminal offenses (Alexander & Parsons, 1973; Parsons & Alexander, 1973). More recently, quasi-experimental studies with significant methodological shortcomings have supported its effectiveness in ameliorating more serious antisocial behavior, including violence (Barton, Alexander, Waldron, Turner, & Warburton, 1985; Gordon, Arbuthnot, Gustafson, & McGreen, 1988).

Peer-Based Interventions

Guided-Group Interaction (GGI) and its derivatives (e.g., Positive Peer Culture) are the most widely used peer-based treatments for delinquency. In general, GGI provides daily group discussions aimed at confronting negative behavior and reinforcing positive behavior. Gottfredson (1987) concluded that GGI-like approaches have proliferated in spite of little support for their effectiveness. In fact, based on aforementioned findings that association with deviant peers is a powerful predictor of antisocial behavior, treating delinquents in groups may exacerbate their problems. Feldman, Caplinger, and Wodarski (1983) support this contention; in a well-designed study, aggressive adolescents showed the greatest behavioral gains when placed in groups with prosocial peers. In contrast, behavior frequently deteriorated in antisocial adolescents placed in groups with similar youths.

Individualized/Wraparound Care

Human service agencies that provide treatment to juvenile offenders often lack the flexibility and coordination that are needed to meet the multiple and changing needs of these youths. Although numerous examples of interagency collaboration in the treatment of serious juvenile offenders have been reported over the past 15 years (see Barnum & Keilitz, 1992), these examples usually involve efforts to "fit" youths into some combination of available programs (or "components") and tend to ignore youth needs not addressed by existing services (see Melton & Pagliocca, 1992). However, a newer and more promising approach to interagency collaboration, known as "individualized care," or "wraparound" services, involves a commitment to complete flexibility in arranging services for individual youth and families (Burchard & Clarke, 1990). In this approach, an interdisciplinary team (comprised of the youth, parents, and representatives of relevant agencies) develops a service plan that addresses both the short- and long-term needs of the youth and family, and treatment or service providers are selected on the basis of their ability to meet these needs. Moreover, the team modifies and redesigns the service plan (and funding for the purchase of treatment or services) to address developing and changing needs of the individual youth/family. Thus, unlike "component" service approaches, which tend to be time limited and to lack flexibility in service planning and delivery, individualized/wraparound care is intended to provide integrated treatment and services to the youth and family as long as the treatment/services are needed (Burchard & Clarke, 1990).

One promising example of the individualized care or wraparound services model is the Alaska Youth Initiative (AYI; see Burchard, Burchard, Sewell, & VanDenBerg, in press; Sewell & Whitbeck, 1992; VanDenBerg & Minton, 1987). The AYI, which began in 1986, was designed initially to support the return of adjudicated delinquents from out-of-state placements; the project later evolved into an integrative model of care in an effort to better serve these youth in their own communities and prevent further placements. The AYI provides truly individualized treatment and services, in some cases developing and funding needed treatments or services when they do not exist. The treatments and services are intensive, are provided by skilled therapists/service personnel, and are implemented in youths' own homes. Another important feature of the AYI is its emphasis on provider accountability, which is accomplished through routine monitoring of the performance of service vendors. The AYI has helped to reduce the number of youths placed in residential settings (e.g., psychiatric hospitals, correctional facilities) and to increase the number of youths served in their own homes or specialized foster care (Child Welfare League of America, 1992). Nevertheless, controlled evaluations of short- and long-term outcomes must be conducted before more definite conclusions can be drawn about the effectiveness of the AYI project or other examples of the individualized care model (e.g., Project Wraparound in Vermont; Burchard & Clarke, 1990).

Multisystemic Therapy

To date, Multisystemic Therapy (MST; Henggeler & Borduin, 1990) has received the most empirical support as an effective treatment of serious and violent criminal behavior in adolescents (for reviews, see Levesque, 1996; Tate et al., 1995). MST is an intensive, time-limited, home- and family-based treatment approach that is predicated on a social-ecological (Bronfenbrenner, 1979) view of behavior, in which criminal behavior is maintained by characteristics of the individual youth and the key social systems in which youths are embedded (i.e., family, peer, school, neighborhood). Importantly, MST interventions are consistent with findings from causal models of violent juvenile offending and, as such, are designed to address a broad range of factors that may contribute to identified problems. Using treatment strategies derived from strategic family therapy (Haley, 1987), structural family therapy (Minuchin, 1974), behavioral parent training (Schaefer & Briesmeister, 1989), and cognitive-behavioral therapy (Braswell & Bloomquist, 1991), MST directly addresses intrapersonal, familial, and extrafamilial factors that are known to be associated with adolescent violent and serious crime. Because different combinations of these factors are relevant for different adolescents, MST interventions are individualized and highly flexible. Moreover, to optimize the ecological validity of interventions, MST is conducted directly in the natural ecologies (home, school, community) of the youth and family.

Rigorous evaluation of outcome has been a cornerstone in the development of MST. In an initial outcome study conducted with inner-city juvenile offenders (Henggeler et al., 1986), many of whom were violent, MST had strong effects on numerous measures of instrumental outcome (i.e., decreased reported behavior problems, decreased association with deviant peers, and improved family relations). In a subsequent study of serious juvenile offenders (Henggeler et al., 1991), MST was relatively effective in reducing recidivism for drug-related crimes. Likewise, Henggeler, Melton, and Smith (1992) established the efficacy of MST in the treatment of serious and violent adolescent offenders with regard to key measures of ultimate outcome (e.g., re-arrests, self-reported delinquency, time incarcerated), as well as with regard to cost savings, at a 59-week follow-up; results from a 2-year follow-up (Henggeler, Melton, Smith, Schoenwald, & Hanley, 1993) further support the long-term efficacy of MST. Similarly, Borduin et al. (1995; also see Borduin, Henggeler, Blaske, & Stein, 1990; Mann et al., 1990) demonstrated the relative effectiveness of MST regarding numerous instrumental and ultimate outcomes in the treatment of violent and chronic juvenile offenders. Most importantly, substantial between-group differences in criminal behavior and violent offending were demonstrated at a 4-year follow-up.

The results from these outcome studies clearly support the efficacy of MST in the treatment of violent criminal behavior in adolescents. The success of MST, especially in comparison with results from other treatment approaches, is attributed primarily to (a) the match between MST intervention foci and empirically identified correlates/causes of violent behavior (e.g., parental discipline, family affective relations, peer associations, school performance, or hostile attributions) and (b) the individualized and flexible use of well-validated interventions in the natural environment (Henggeler, Borduin, & Mann, 1992). That is, MST is effective because it addresses the multiple determinants of violent behavior in youths' naturally occurring systems. Treatments that address only a small subset of the possible determinants of violent behavior or that minimize the ecological validity of interventions (e.g., office-based or institution-based treatment) are almost certain to be ineffective in a substantial number of cases.

SUMMARY

This chapter has highlighted important conceptual issues and research findings in several areas related to violent antisocial behavior in adolescents. The extant literature indicates that violent behavior is highly stable over time and is linked with deleterious psychosocial outcomes during adolescence and adulthood. Although there are still gaps in our knowledge regarding the extent to which various forms of juvenile offending are associated with unique correlates and causes, there is at least some evidence to suggest that adolescent violent offenders and nonviolent offenders may follow different developmental paths. Furthermore, although our understanding of violent antisocial behavior in adolescents is far from complete, multidimensional causal models of such behavior have pointed to the complex and reciprocal interplay between important characteristics of violent adolescents and the social systems in which they are embedded. Moreover, in contrast to the conclusions of many reviewers, it is proposed that adolescent violence can be treated effectively. To be effective, however, such treatments should possess the flexibility to address a broad range of antisocial behaviors, be capable of addressing the multiple factors that can maintain such behaviors, and be intensive and ecologically valid.

REFERENCES

Akhtar, N., & Bradley, E. J. (1991). Social information processing deficits of aggressive children: Present findings and implications for social skills training. *Clinical Psychology Review, 11*, 621-644.

Alexander, J. F., & Parsons, B. V. (1973). Short-term behavioral intervention with delinquent families: Impact on family process and recidivism. *Journal of Abnormal Psychology, 81*, 219-225.

Alexander, J. F., & Parsons, B. V. (1982). *Functional family therapy*. Monterey, CA: Brooks/Cole.

American Psychiatric Association. (1994). *Diagnostic and statistical manual of mental disorders* (4th ed.). Washington, DC: Author.

Anderson, J. C., Williams, S., McGee, R., & Silva, P. A. (1987). DSM-III disorders in preadolescent children: Prevalence in a large sample from the general population. *Archives of General Psychiatry, 44*, 69-76.

Andrews, D. A., Zinger, I., Hoge, R. D., Bonta, J., Gendreau, P., & Cullen, F. T. (1990). Does correctional treatment work? A clinically relevant and psychologically informed meta-analysis. *Criminology, 28*, 369-404.

Arbuthnot, J., Gordon, D. A., & Jurkovic, G. J. (1987). Personality. In H. C. Quay (Ed.), *Handbook of juvenile delinquency* (pp. 139-183). New York: John Wiley.

Bank, L., Marlowe, J. H., Reid, J. B., Patterson, G. R., & Weinrott, M. R. (1991). A comparative evaluation of parent-training interventions for families of chronic delinquents. *Journal of Abnormal Child Psychology, 19*, 15-33.

Barbaree, H. E., Marshall, W. L., & Hudson, S. M. (1993). *The juvenile sex offender.* New York: Guilford.

Barnum, R., & Keilitz, I. (1992). Issues in systems interactions affecting mentally disordered juvenile offenders. In J. P. Cocozza (Ed.), *Responding to the mental health needs of youth in the juvenile justice system* (pp. 49-87). Seattle, WA: National Coalition for the Mentally Ill in the Criminal Justice System.

Barton, C., Alexander, J. F., Waldron, H., Turner, C. W., & Warburton, J. (1985). Generalizing treatment effects of functional family therapy: Three replications. *American Journal of Family Therapy, 13,* 16-26.

Becker, J. V., Harris, C. D., & Sales, B. D. (1993). Juveniles who commit sexual offenses: A critical review of research. In G. C. Nagayama-Hall, R. Hirschman, J. R. Graham, & M. S. Zaragoza (Eds.), *Sexual aggression: Issues in etiology, assessment, and treatment* (pp. 215-228). Washington, DC: Taylor & Francis.

Berrueta-Clement, J. R., Schweinhart, L. J., Barnett, W. S., & Weikart, D. P. (1987). The effects of early educational intervention on crime and delinquency in adolescence and early adulthood. In J. D. Burchard & S. N. Burchard (Eds.), *Prevention of delinquent behavior* (pp. 220-240). Newbury Park, CA: Sage.

Bickett, L. R., Milich, R., & Brown, R. T. (1996). Attributional styles of aggressive boys and their mothers. *Journal of Abnormal Child Psychology, 24,* 457-472.

Blaske, D. M., Borduin, C. M., Henggeler, S. W., & Mann, B. J. (1989). Individual, family, and peer characteristics of adolescent sex offenders and assaultive offenders. *Developmental Psychology, 25,* 846-855.

Blumstein, A., & Cohen, J. (1987). Characterizing criminal careers. *Science, 237,* 985-991.

Boney-McCoy, S., & Finkelhor, D. (1995). Psychosocial sequelae of violent victimization in a national youth sample. *American Psychologist, 63,* 726-736.

Borduin, C. M. (1994). Innovative models of treatment and service delivery in the juvenile justice system. *Journal of Clinical Child Psychology, 23*(Suppl.), 19-25.

Borduin, C. M., & Henggeler, S. W. (1987). Post-divorce mother-son relations of delinquent and well-adjusted adolescents. *Journal of Applied Developmental Psychology, 8,* 273-288.

Borduin, C. M., Henggeler, S. W., Blaske, D. M., & Stein, R. (1990). Multisystemic treatment of adolescent sexual offenders. *International Journal of Offender Therapy and Comparative Criminology, 34,* 105-113.

Borduin, C. M., Henggeler, S. W., Hanson, C. L., & Pruitt, J. A. (1985). Verbal problem solving in families of father-absent and father-present delinquent boys. *Child and Family Behavior Therapy, 7,* 51-63.

Borduin, C. M., Mann, B. J., Cone, L., Henggeler, S. W., Fucci, B. R., Blaske, D. M., & Williams, R. A. (1995). Multisystemic treatment of serious juvenile offenders: Long-term prevention of criminality and violence. *Journal of Consulting and Clinical Psychology, 63,* 569-578.

Borduin, C. M., Pruitt, J. A., & Henggeler, S. W. (1986). Family interactions in Black, lower-class families with delinquent and nondelinquent adolescent boys. *Journal of Genetic Psychology, 147,* 333-342.

Braswell, L., & Bloomquist, M. L. (1991). *Cognitive-behavioral therapy with ADHD children: Child, family, and school interventions.* New York: Guilford.

Bronfenbrenner, U. (1979). *The ecology of human development: Experiments by nature and design.* Cambridge, MA: Harvard University Press.

Burchard, J., Burchard, S., Sewell, R., & VanDenBerg, J. (in press). *One kid at a time—The Alaska Youth Initiative: A demonstration of individualized services.* Washington, DC: Georgetown University Press.

Burchard, J., & Clarke, R. (1990). The role of individualized care in a service delivery system for children and adolescents with severely maladjusted behavior. *Journal of Mental Health Administration, 17,* 48-60.

Bureau of Justice Statistics. (1990). *Tracking offenders, 1987.* Washington, DC: U.S. Department of Justice.

Callahan, C. M., & Rivera, F. P. (1992). Urban high school youth and handguns: A school-based survey. *Journal of the American Medical Association, 267,* 3038-3042.

Child Welfare League of America. (1992). *Sharing innovations: The program exchange compendium.* Washington, DC: Author.

Cornell, D. G., & Wilson, L. A. (1992). The PIQ>VIQ discrepancy in violent and nonviolent delinquents. *Journal of Clinical Psychology, 48,* 256-261.

Crick, N. R., & Dodge, K. A. (1994). A review and reformulation of social information processing mechanisms in children's social adjustment. *Psychological Bulletin, 115,* 74-101.

Davis, G. E., & Leitenberg, H. (1987). Adolescent sex offenders. *Psychological Bulletin, 101,* 417-427.

Dishion, T. J., Patterson, G. R., Stoolmiller, M., & Skinner, M. L. (1991). Family, school, and behavioral antecedents to early adolescent involvement with antisocial peers. *Developmental Psychology, 27,* 172-180.

Dix, T., & Lochman, J. E. (1990). Social cognition and negative reactions to children: A comparison of mothers of aggressive and nonaggressive boys. *Journal of Social and Clinical Psychology, 9,* 418-438.

Dodge, K. A., Price, J. M., Bachorowski, J., & Newman, J. M. (1990). Hostile attributional biases in severely aggressive adolescents. *Journal of Abnormal Psychology, 99,* 385-392.

Donovan, J. E., & Jessor, R. (1985). Structure of problem behavior in adolescence and young adulthood. *Journal of Consulting and Clinical Psychology, 53,* 890-904.

Donovan, J. E., Jessor, R., & Costa, F. M. (1988). Syndrome of problem behavior in adolescence: A replication. *Journal of Consulting and Clinical Psychology, 56,* 762-765.

Dumas, J. E., Neese, D. E., Prinz, R. J., & Blechman, E. A. (1996). Short-term stability of aggression, peer rejection, and depressive symptoms in middle childhood. *Journal of Abnormal Child Psychology, 24,* 105-119.

Dunford, F. W., & Elliott, D. S. (1984). Identifying career offenders using self-reported data. *Journal of Research in Crime and Delinquency, 21,* 57-86.

Elliott, D. S., Huizinga, D., & Ageton, S. S. (1985). *Explaining delinquency and drug use.* Beverly Hills, CA: Sage.

Elliott, D. S., Huizinga, D., & Morse, B. J. (1985). *The dynamics of deviant behavior: A national survey progress report.* Boulder, CO: Behavioral Research Institute.

Elliott, D. S., & Voss, H. (1974). *Delinquency and dropout.* Lexington, MA: D. C. Heath.

Emler, N., Reicher, S., & Ross, A. (1987). The social context of delinquent conduct. *Journal of Child Psychology and Psychiatry, 28,* 99-109.

Farrington, D. P. (1989). Early predictors of adolescent aggression and adult violence. *Violence and Victims, 4,* 79-100.

Farrington, D. P. (1991). Childhood aggression and adult violence: Early precursors and later-life outcomes. In D. J. Pepler & K. H. Rubin (Eds.), *The development and treatment of childhood aggression* (pp. 5-29). Hillsdale, NJ: Lawrence Erlbaum.

Farrington, D. P. (1995). The development of offending and antisocial behavior from childhood: Key findings from the Cambridge Study in Delinquent Development. *Journal of Child Psychology and Psychiatry and Allied Disciplines, 36,* 929-964.

Farrington, D. P., Loeber, R., & Van Kammen, W. B. (1990). Long-term criminal outcomes of hyperactivity-impulsivity-attention deficit and conduct problems in childhood. In L. Robins & M. Rutter (Eds.), *Straight and devious pathways from childhood to adulthood* (pp. 62-81). New York: Cambridge University Press.

Federal Bureau of Investigation. (1995). *Uniform crime reports.* Washington, DC: U.S. Government Printing Office.

Federal Bureau of Investigation. (1996). *Uniform crime reports.* Washington, DC: U.S. Government Printing Office.

Feldman, R. A., Caplinger, T. E., & Wodarski, J. S. (1983). *The St. Louis conundrum: The effective treatment of antisocial youths.* Englewood Cliffs, NJ: Prentice Hall.

Gilbert, G. M. (1957). A survey of "referral problems" in metropolitan child guidance centers. *Journal of Clinical Psychology, 13,* 37-42.

Goldstein, A. P., & Glick, B. (1987). *Aggression replacement training: A comprehensive intervention for aggressive youth.* Champaign, IL: Research Press.

Gordon, D. A., & Arbuthnot, J. (1987). Individual, group, and family interventions. In H. C. Quay (Ed.), *Handbook of juvenile delinquency* (pp. 290-324). New York: John Wiley.

Gordon, D. A., Arbuthnot, J., Gustafson, K. E., & McGreen, P. (1988). Home-based behavioral systems family therapy with disadvantaged juvenile delinquents. *American Journal of Family Therapy, 16,* 243-255.

Gorman-Smith, D., Tolan, P. H., Zelli, A., & Huesmann, L. R. (1996). The relation of family functioning to violence among inner-city minority youth. *Journal of Family Psychology, 10,* 115-129.

Gottfredson, G. D. (1987). Peer group interventions to reduce the risk of delinquent behavior: A selective review and a new evaluation. *Criminology, 25,* 671-714.

Gottfredson, G. D. (1989). The experiences of violent and serious victimization. In N. A. Weiner & M. E. Wolfgang (Eds.), *Pathways to criminal violence* (pp. 202-234). Newbury Park, CA: Sage.

Graham, P. (1979). Epidemiological studies. In H. C. Quay & J. S. Werry (Eds.), *Psychopathological disorders of childhood* (2nd ed., pp. 185-209). New York: John Wiley.

Graham, S., Hudley, C., & Williams, E. (1992). Attributional and emotional determinants of aggression among African-American and Latino young adolescents. *Developmental Psychology, 28,* 731-740.

Guerra, N. G., & Slaby, R. G. (1990). Cognitive mediators of aggression in adolescent offenders: 2. Intervention. *Developmental Psychology, 26,* 269-277.

Haapasalo, J., & Tremblay, R. E. (1994). Physically aggressive boys from ages 6 to 12: Family background, parenting behavior, and prediction of delinquency. *Journal of Consulting and Clinical Psychology, 62,* 1044-1052.

Haley, J. (1987). *Problem-solving therapy* (2nd ed.). San Francisco: Jossey-Bass.

Hanson, C. L., Henggeler, S. W., Haefele, W. F., & Rodick, J. D. (1984). Demographic, individual, and family relationship correlates of serious and repeated crime among adolescents and their siblings. *Journal of Consulting and Clinical Psychology, 52,* 528-538.

Hellman, D. A., & Beaton, S. (1986). The pattern of violence in urban public schools: The influence of school and community. *Journal of Research in Crime and Delinquency, 23,* 102-127.

Henggeler, S. W. (1989). *Delinquency in adolescence.* Newbury Park, CA: Sage.

Henggeler, S. W. (1991). Multidimensional causal models of delinquent behavior and their implications for treatment. In R. Cohen & A. W. Siegel (Eds.), *Context and development* (pp. 211-231). Hillsdale, NJ: Lawrence Erlbaum.

Henggeler, S. W., & Borduin, C. M. (1990). *Family therapy and beyond: A multisystemic approach to treating the behavior problems of children and adolescents.* Pacific Grove, CA: Brooks/Cole.

Henggeler, S. W., Borduin, C. M., & Mann, B. J. (1992). Advances in family therapy: Empirical foundations. In T. H. Ollendick & R. J. Prinz (Eds.), *Advances in clinical child psychology* (Vol. 15, pp. 207-241). New York: Plenum.

Henggeler, S. W., Borduin, C. M., Melton, G. B., Mann, B. J., Smith, L. A., Hall, J. A., Cone, L., & Fucci, B. R. (1991). Effects of multisystemic therapy on drug use and abuse in serious juvenile offenders: A progress report from two outcome studies. *Family Dynamics of Addiction Quarterly, 1,* 40-51.

Henggeler, S. W., Edwards, J., & Borduin, C. M. (1987). Family relations of female juvenile delinquents. *Journal of Abnormal Child Psychology, 15,* 199-209.

Henggeler, S. W., Melton, G. B., & Smith, L. A. (1992). Family preservation using multisystemic therapy: An effective alternative to incarcerating serious juvenile offenders. *Journal of Consulting and Clinical Psychology, 60,* 953-961.

Henggeler, S. W., Melton, G. B., Smith, L. A., Schoenwald, S., & Hanley, J. H. (1993). Family preservation using multisystemic treatment: Long-term follow-up to a clinical trial with serious juvenile offenders. *Journal of Child and Family Studies, 2,* 83-93.

Henggeler, S. W., Rodick, J. D., Borduin, C. M., Hanson, C. L., Watson, S. M., & Urey, J. R. (1986). Multisystemic treatment of juvenile offenders: Effects on adolescent behavior and family interaction. *Developmental Psychology, 22,* 132-141.

Herbert, M. (1978). *Conduct disorders of childhood and adolescence: A behavioural approach to assessment and treatment.* Chichester, UK: John Wiley.

Hinshaw, S. P. (1992). Externalizing behavior problems and academic underachievement in childhood and adolescence: Causal relationships and underlying mechanisms. *Psychological Bulletin, 111,* 127-155.

Huesmann, L. R., Lefkowitz, M. M., Eron, L. D., & Walder, L. O. (1984). Stability of aggression over time and generations. *Developmental Psychology, 20,* 1120-1134.

Huizinga, D., & Elliott, D. S. (1987). Juvenile offenders: Prevalence, offender incidence, and arrest rates by race. *Crime & Delinquency, 33,* 206-223.

Jessor, R., & Jessor, S. L. (1977). *Problem behavior and psychosocial development: A longitudinal study of youth.* New York: Cambridge University Press.

Jouriles, E. N., Bourg, W. J., & Farris, A. M. (1991). Marital adjustment and child conduct problems: A comparison of the correlation across samples. *Journal of Consulting and Clinical Psychology, 59,* 354-357.

Kashani, J., McGee, R., Clarkson, S., Anderson, J., Walton, L., Williams, S., Silva, P., Robins, A., Cytryn, M., & McKnew, D. (1987). Depression in a sample of

9-year-old children: Prevalence and associated characteristics. *Archives of General Psychiatry, 40,* 1217-1223.

Kazdin, A. E. (1987). Treatment of antisocial behavior in children: Current status and future directions. *Psychological Bulletin, 102,* 187-203.

Kazdin, A. E. (1988). *Child psychotherapy: Developing and identifying effective treatments.* New York: Pergamon.

Kazdin, A. E. (1995). *Conduct disorders in childhood and adolescence* (2nd ed.). Thousand Oaks, CA: Sage.

Keenan, K., & Shaw, D. S. (1994). The development of aggression in toddlers: A study of low-income families. *Journal of Abnormal Child Psychology, 22,* 53-77.

LaGrange, R. L., & White, H. R. (1985). Age differences in delinquency: A test of theory. *Criminology, 23,* 19-45.

Lahey, B. B., Loeber, R., Hart, E. L., Frick, P. J., Applegate, B., Zhang, Q., Green, S. M., & Russo, M. F. (1995). Four-year longitudinal study of conduct disorder in boys: Patterns and predictors of persistence. *Journal of Abnormal Psychology, 104,* 83-93.

Landy, S., & Peters, R. D. (1992). Toward an understanding of a developmental paradigm for aggressive conduct problems during the preschool years. In R. D. Peters, R. J. McMahon, & V. L. Quinsey (Eds.), *Aggression and violence throughout the lifespan* (pp. 1-30). Newbury Park, CA: Sage.

Lattimore, P. K., Visher, C. A., & Linster, R. A. (1995). Predicting rearrest for violence among serious youthful offenders. *Journal of Research in Crime and Delinquency, 32,* 54-83.

Laub, J. H., & Sampson, R. J. (1994). Unemployment, marital discord, and deviant behavior: The long-term correlates of child misbehavior. In T. Hirschi & M. R. Gottfredson (Eds.), *The generality of deviance* (pp. 235-252). New Brunswick, NJ: Transaction Books.

Levesque, R. J. R. (1996). Is there still a place for violent youth in juvenile justice? *Aggression and Violent Behavior, 1,* 69-79.

Lewis, C. E., & Bucholz, K. K. (1991). Alcoholism, antisocial behavior, and family history. *British Journal of Addiction, 86,* 177-194.

Lewis, D. O., Shankok, S. S., Pincus, H., & Glaser, G. H. (1979). Violent juvenile delinquents: Psychiatric, neurological, psychological, and abuse factors. *Journal of the American Academy of Child Psychiatry, 18,* 307-319.

Loeber, R. (1982). The stability of antisocial and delinquent child behavior: A review. *Child Development, 53,* 1431-1446.

Loeber, R. (1990). Development and risk factors of juvenile antisocial behavior and delinquency. *Clinical Psychology Review, 10,* 1-41.

Loeber, R., & Schmaling, K. B. (1985a). Empirical evidence for overt and covert patterns of antisocial conduct problems: A meta-analysis. *Journal of Abnormal Child Psychology, 13,* 337-352.

Loeber, R., & Schmaling, K. B. (1985b). The utility of differentiating between mixed and pure forms of antisocial child behavior. *Journal of Abnormal Child Psychology, 13,* 315-336.

Lynam, D., Moffitt, T., & Stouthamer-Loeber, M. (1993). Explaining the relation between IQ and delinquency: Class, race, test motivation, or self-control? *Journal of Abnormal Psychology, 102,* 187-196.

Lyon, J. M., Henggeler, S. W., & Hall, J. A. (1992). The family relations, peer relations, and criminal activities of Caucasian and Hispanic-American gang members. *Journal of Abnormal Child Psychology, 20,* 439-449.

Lyons-Ruth, K. (1996). Attachment relationships among children with aggressive behavior problems: The role of disorganized early attachment patterns. *Journal of Consulting and Clinical Psychology, 64,* 64-73.

Lytton, H. (1990). Child and parent effects in boys' conduct disorder: A reinterpretation. *Developmental Psychology, 26,* 683-697.

MacKinnon-Lewis, C., Volling, B. L., Lamb, M. E., Dechman, K., Rabiner, D., & Curtner, M. E. (1994). A cross-contextual analysis of boys' social competence: From family to school. *Developmental Psychology, 30,* 325-333.

Magnusson, D., Stattin, H., & Duner, A. (1983). Aggression and criminality in a longitudinal perspective. In K. T. Van Dusen & S. A. Mednick (Eds.), *Antecedents of aggression and antisocial behavior* (pp. 277-302). Boston: Kluwer-Nijhoff.

Mann, B. J., Borduin, C. M., Henggeler, S. W., & Blaske, D. M. (1990). An investigation of systemic conceptualizations of parent-child coalitions and symptom change. *Journal of Consulting and Clinical Psychology, 58,* 336-344.

Maughan, B., Gray, G., & Rutter, M. (1985). Reading retardation and antisocial behaviour: A follow-up into employment. *Journal of Child Psychology and Psychiatry, 26,* 741-758.

McDermott, P. A. (1996). A nationwide study of developmental and gender prevalence for psychopathology in childhood and adolescence. *Journal of Abnormal Child Psychology, 24,* 53-66.

McGee, L., & Newcomb, M. D. (1992). General deviance syndrome: Evaluations at four ages from early adolescence to adulthood. *Journal of Consulting and Clinical Psychology, 60,* 766-776.

Melton, G. B., & Hargrove, D. S. (in press). *Planning mental health services for children and youth.* New York: Guilford.

Melton, G. B., & Pagliocca, P. M. (1992). Treatment in the juvenile justice system: Directions for policy and practice. In J. J. Cocozza (Ed.), *Responding to the mental health needs of youth in the juvenile justice system* (pp. 107-139). Seattle, WA: National Coalition for the Mentally Ill in the Criminal Justice System.

Melton, G. B., & Spaulding, W. J. (in press). *No place to go: Civil commitment of minors.* Lincoln: University of Nebraska Press.

Mendel, R. A. (1995). *Prevention or pork? A hard-headed look at youth-oriented anti-crime programs.* Washington, DC: American Youth Policy Forum.

Miller, G. E., & Prinz, R. J. (1990). Enhancement of social learning family interventions for childhood conduct disorder. *Psychological Bulletin, 108,* 291-307.

Miller, T. R., Cohen, M. A., & Rossman, S. B. (1993). Victim costs of violent crime and resulting injuries. *Health Affairs, 12,* 186-197.

Minuchin, S. (1974). *Families and family therapy.* Cambridge, MA: Harvard University Press.

Moffitt, T. E. (1993). Adolescence-limited and life-course-persistent antisocial behavior: A developmental taxonomy. *Psychological Review, 100,* 674-701.

Mulvey, E. P., Arthur, M. A., & Reppucci, N. D. (1993). The prevention and treatment of juvenile delinquency: A review of the research. *Clinical Psychology Review, 13,* 133-167.

Nagin, D. S., & Land, K. C. (1993). Age, criminal careers, and population heterogeneity: Specification and estimation of a nonparametric, mixed Poisson model. *Criminology, 31*, 327-362.

Newcomb, M. D., & Bentler, P. M. (1987). The impact of late adolescent substance use on young adult health status and utilization of health services: A structural-equation model over four years. *Social Science and Medicine, 24*, 71-82.

O'Donnell, C. R. (1995). Firearm deaths among children and youth. *American Psychologist, 50*, 771-776.

Offord, D. R., Boyle, M. H., & Racine, Y. A. (1991). The epidemiology of antisocial behavior in childhood and adolescence. In D. J. Pepler & K. H. Rubin (Eds.), *The development and treatment of childhood aggression* (pp. 31-53). Hillsdale, NJ: Lawrence Erlbaum.

Olweus, D. (1979). Stability of aggressive reaction patterns in males: A review. *Psychological Bulletin, 86*, 852-875.

Olweus, D. (1980). Familial and temperamental determinants of aggressive behavior in adolescent boys: A causal analysis. *Developmental Psychology, 16*, 644-660.

Osgood, D. W., Johnston, L. D., O'Malley, P. M., & Bachman, J. G. (1988). The generality of deviance in late adolescence and early adulthood. *American Sociological Review, 53*, 81-93.

Parsons, B. V., & Alexander, J. F. (1973). Short-term family intervention: A therapy outcome study. *Journal of Consulting and Clinical Psychology, 41*, 195-201.

Patterson, G. R. (1982). *A social learning approach to family intervention: III. Coercive family process*. Eugene, OR: Castalia.

Patterson, G. R., & Stouthamer-Loeber, M. (1984). The correlation of family management practices and delinquency. *Child Development, 55*, 1299-1307.

Poole, E. D., & Rigoli, R. M. (1979). Parental support, delinquent friends, and delinquency: A test of interaction effects. *Journal of Criminal Law and Criminology, 70*, 188-193.

Pulkkinen, L., & Pitkanen, T. (1993). Continuities in aggressive behavior from childhood to adulthood. *Aggressive Behavior, 19*, 249-263.

Quay, H. C. (1986). Conduct disorders. In H. C. Quay & J. S. Werry (Eds.), *Psychopathological disorders of childhood* (3rd ed., pp. 35-72). New York: John Wiley.

Quay, H. C. (Ed.). (1987a). *Handbook of juvenile delinquency*. New York: John Wiley.

Quay, H. C. (1987b). Intelligence. In H. C. Quay (Ed.), *Handbook of juvenile delinquency* (pp. 106-117). New York: John Wiley.

Robins, L. N. (1966). *Deviant children grown up*. Baltimore: Williams & Wilkins.

Robins, L. N. (1981). Epidemiological approaches to natural history research: Antisocial disorders in children. *Journal of the American Academy of Child and Adolescent Psychiatry, 20*, 566-580.

Rosen, A., & Proctor, E. K. (1981). Distinctions between treatment outcomes and their implications for treatment evaluation. *Journal of Consulting and Clinical Psychology, 49*, 418-425.

Rutter, M. (1994). Family discord and conduct disorder: Cause, consequence, or correlate? *Journal of Family Psychology, 8*, 170-186.

Rutter, M., Cox, A., Tupling, C., Berger, M., & Yule, W. (1975). Attainment and adjustment in two geographical areas: 1. The prevalence of psychiatric disorder. *British Journal of Psychiatry, 126*, 493-509.

Rutter, M., & Giller, H. (1983). *Juvenile delinquency: Trends and perspectives*. New York: Guilford.

Rutter, M., Tizard, J., Yule, W., Graham, P., & Whitmore, K. (1976). Research report: Isle of Wight studies, 1964-1974. *Psychological Medicine, 6*, 313-332.

Sampson, R. J., & Laub, J. H. (1990). Crime and deviance over the life course: The salience of adult social bonds. *American Sociological Review, 55*, 609-627.

Sampson, R. J., & Laub, J. H. (1993). *Crime in the making: Pathways and turning points through life*. Cambridge, MA: Harvard University Press.

Schaefer, C. E., & Briesmeister, J. M. (Eds.). (1989). *Handbook of parent training: Parents as co-therapists for children's behavior problems*. New York: John Wiley.

Seguin, J. R., Pihl, R. O., Harden, P. W., Tremblay, R. E., & Boulerice, B. (1995). Cognitive and neuropsychological characteristics of physically aggressive boys. *Journal of Abnormal Psychology, 104*, 614-624.

Sewell, R., & Whitbeck, J. (1992, May). *Individualized "wrap-around" care: A promising service approach for youth who experience severe emotional disturbance and who have been adjudicated delinquent*. Paper presented at the meeting of Community Action for the Mentally Ill Offender, Seattle, WA.

Shaw, D. S., Keenan, K., & Vondra, J. I. (1994). Developmental precursors of externalizing behavior: Ages 1 to 3. *Developmental Psychology, 30*, 355-364.

Simcha-Fagan, O., & Schwartz, J. E. (1986). Neighborhood and delinquency: An assessment of contextual effects. *Criminology, 24*, 667-703.

Smith, D. A., Visher, C. A., & Jarjoura, C. R. (1991). *Journal of Research in Crime and Delinquency, 28*, 6-32.

Snyder, J., & Patterson, G. R. (1987). Family interaction and delinquent behavior. In H. C. Quay (Ed.), *Handbook of juvenile delinquency* (pp. 216-243). New York: John Wiley.

Stattin, H., & Magnusson, D. (1989). The role of early aggressive behavior in the frequency, seriousness, and types of later crime. *Journal of Consulting and Clinical Psychology, 57*, 710-718.

Stattin, H., & Magnusson, D. (1991). Stability and change in criminal behaviour up to age 30. *British Journal of Criminology, 31*, 327-346.

Strasburg, P. A. (1978). *Violent delinquents*. New York: Monarch.

Tarter, R. E., Hegedus, A. M., Alterman, A. I., & Katz-Garris, L. (1983). Cognitive capacities of juvenile violent, nonviolent, and sexual offenders. *Journal of Nervous and Mental Disease, 171*, 564-567.

Tate, D. C., Reppucci, N. D., & Mulvey, E. P. (1995). Violent juvenile delinquents: Treatment effectiveness and implications for future action. *American Psychologist, 50*, 777-781.

Thornberry, T. P., Moore, M., & Christenson, R. L. (1985). The effect of dropping out of high school on subsequent criminal behavior. *Criminology, 23*, 3-18.

Tolan, P. H., & Lorion, R. P. (1988). Multivariate approaches to the identification of delinquency-proneness in adolescent males. *American Journal of Community Psychology, 16*, 547-561.

Truscott, D. (1992). Intergenerational transmission of violent behavior in adolescent males. *Aggressive Behavior, 18*, 327-335.

U.S. General Accounting Office. (1992). *Federal jail bedspace: Cost savings and greater accuracy possible in the capacity extension plan* (Publication No. GAO/GGD-92-141).

VanDenBerg, J., & Minton, B. (1987). Alaska native youth: A new approach to serving emotionally disturbed children and youth. *Children Today, 16*(5), 15-18.

Vuchinich, S., Bank, L., & Patterson, G. R. (1992). Parenting, peers, and the stability of antisocial behavior in preadolescent boys. *Developmental Psychology, 28,* 510-521.

Walsh, A., & Beyer, J. A. (1987). Violent crime, sociopathy, and love deprivation among adolescent delinquents. *Adolescence, 22,* 705-717.

Walsh, A., Petee, J. A., & Beyer, T. A. (1987). Intellectual imbalance and delinquency: Comparing high verbal and high performance IQ delinquents. *Criminal Justice and Behavior, 14,* 370-379.

Weiss, B., Dodge, K. A., Bates, J. E., & Pettit, G. S. (1992). Some consequences of early harsh discipline: Child aggression and a maladaptive social information processing style. *Child Development, 63,* 1321-1335.

White, H. R., Pandina, R. J., & LaGrange, R. L. (1987). Longitudinal predictors of serious substance use and delinquency. *Criminology, 25,* 715-740.

Widom, C. S. (1989). Does violence beget violence? A critical examination of the literature. *Psychological Bulletin, 106,* 2-28.

Windle, M. (1990). A longitudinal study of antisocial behaviors in early adolescence as predictors of late adolescent substance use: Gender and ethnic group differences. *Journal of Abnormal Psychology, 99,* 86-91.

Zigler, E., Taussig, C., & Black, K. (1992). Early childhood intervention: A promising preventative for juvenile delinquency. *American Psychologist, 47,* 997-1006.

7. Youth Gangs: A Developmental Perspective

Daniel J. Flannery
C. Ronald Huff
Michael Manos

Adolescence as a developmental period is characterized by significant changes and transformations in family and peer relationships (Montemayor & Flannery, 1990; Paikoff & Brooks-Gunn, 1991; Steinberg, 1989). Peers often gain influence during adolescence, usually at the expense of parents. Youth seek out more time with their peers and report a high degree of satisfaction from their peer relations (Larson & Richards, 1989). For some youth, spending time with peers has a positive influence on socialization, providing opportunities to become more involved in community organizations and activities like Boy Scouts, school band, athletics, or church activities. For others, spending time with peers becomes a mechanism for opportunity to engage in deviant behavior such as truancy, substance use, theft, or assault (Gottfredson & Hirschi, 1990).

For better or worse, peers are an important influence in adolescence, affecting development in multiple domains. The purpose of this chapter is to provide an overview of one specific form of peer group relationship, the youth gang, and to provide a developmental framework for understanding what gangs are, why adolescents in particular may become gang members, and how developmental issues can inform prevention and intervention efforts. We begin by providing a general definition of gangs. This is followed by a discussion of different kinds of gang activity, including recent data on the role of drugs in gangs. We then examine gangs from a developmental perspective, focusing on reasons why some kids may join gangs (including risk factors), the developmental needs that gangs may meet for some youth, and the role of parents and families in gang activity. Where pertinent, we discuss the role of gender and ethnicity in gangs and gang-member activity. We also provide a brief overview, within a developmental framework, of factors associated with suc-

175

cessful prevention and intervention programs, and we discuss programs that have shown iatrogenic effects. Finally, we review some of the macrosocial or individual factors that appear to preclude youth involvement in prosocial settings or prohibit attachment to school and other institutions, and why socially appropriate groups have lost their appeal to many youth.

DEFINING GANGS

As Howell (1994) and Klein (1995) state, no accepted standard definition of a gang currently exists. State and local jurisdictions tend to develop their own definition and form policies based on those local criteria. However, several common criteria are typically used to define gangs: (a) There exists a formal organizational structure; (b) the group has an identified leader or leadership hierarchy; (c) the group is usually, but not always, identified with a specific territory or turf; (d) there exists recurrent interaction among the members of the group; and (e) the members of the group engage in delinquent or criminal behavior. The last criterion, participating in delinquent or criminal behavior, is the characteristic that distinguishes gangs from other, more prosocially focused adolescent groups. Curry, Ball, and Fox's (1994) law enforcement survey for 1991 estimated that there were 4,881 gangs in the United States with 249,324 members.

Who belongs to a gang? Gang members typically range in age from 14 to 24, with the peak age of gang membership around age 17, although in some cities the gang members are somewhat older. Evidence exists that children as young as 8 are gang involved or gang "wannabes" (Embry, Flannery, Vazsonyi, Powell, & Atha, 1996; Huff, 1996). To some degree, gang membership depends on where one lives. In established gang cities such as Los Angeles or Chicago, the majority of gang members tend to be adults, whereas in cities reporting recent or emerging gang problems, up to 90% of gang members are estimated to be juveniles. Certainly not every youth is involved in gang activity. Most reports estimate that between 5% and 8% of youth are at high risk for engaging in violent, gang-related activities (Tolan & Guerra, 1994). Although no reliable national data exist, a recent Denver study estimated that 7% of inner-city, high-risk juveniles were gang involved (Esbensen & Huizinga, 1993).

Based on research in Colorado, Florida, and Ohio, Huff (1996) identified a developmental progression from "hanging out" with the gang (being a gang "wannabe") to joining the gang and getting arrested. Gang members responded that they first began associating with the gang at about age 13 and joined, on average, about 6 months later. They were then arrested for the first time at about age 14, 1 year after beginning to associate with a gang and about 6 months after joining. Arrests for property crimes peaked 1 to 2 years before arrests for either drug offenses or violent offenses. Rather than gang membership providing protection, Huff found that a high percentage of gang leaders' declining arrest rates was due to incarceration and homicide. The gang lifestyle places individuals at much higher risk than would normally be expected.

Gangs are also appearing in more and more cities, particularly smaller communities (Maxson & Klein, 1996). Curry et al. (1994) reported that more than 90% of the nation's largest cities report youth gang problems, up from about 50% in 1983. This increase is mostly due to family migration and local gang genesis rather than to relocation, suggesting that gang formation is not due solely to the recruitment of youth to "other city" gangs. Even very young children report exposure to gang activity at school (Embry et al., 1996). In Tucson, 42% of youth in Grades K through 5 reported seeing gang activity at school in a given week (Embry et al., 1996). This trend among young people is of concern because the Tucson data were collected from self-contained elementary schools, limiting the possibility that youth were reporting gang activity of older peers, or, conversely, suggesting that older peers were coming to elementary schools to recruit younger members.

The racial and ethnic composition of gangs is rapidly changing. Until the mid-1900s, the majority of gangs in the United States were white and composed of various European backgrounds. By the 1970s, an estimated 80% of gang members were either African American or Hispanic, and in the past few years, Asian groups have been emerging rapidly. The ethnic composition and social class position of gang members has remained fairly constant, with gangs comprised of recently migrated youth and those of lower socioeconomic status (Howell, 1994; Miller, 1982; Spergel, 1991).

Female gang membership is also increasing (Chesney-Lind, Sheldon, & Joe, 1996), although girls still account for a relatively small percentage of gang-involved youth (3.5% to 6%; Curry et al., 1994).

In 1992, 40 cities reported female gangs with an estimated 7,205 members (Curry, Fox, Ball, & Stone, 1992). Historically, the stereotype of girls in gangs and delinquent girls in general was that these girls were either tomboys or sex objects (Campbell, 1990) or a form of male property (Jankowski, 1991). Girls' delinquency was viewed as interpersonal and sexual, whereas boys' offending was viewed as aggressive and more criminal in nature (Chesney-Lind & Sheldon, 1992). Recent data on girls' participation in gangs, their activities, and their motivations for joining are discussed below.

ACTIVITY: WHAT DO GANGS
AND GANG MEMBERS DO?

In this section, we provide an overview of gang member activity, including the social role of the gang and the role of firearms and drugs in gangs. Huff (1996) recently completed several studies of current and former gang-involved youth compared to at-risk youth in Cleveland, metropolitan Denver, and south Florida. He used detailed, semistructured, individual interviews conducted by graduate students and youth workers. For the Cleveland sample, Huff found that gang-involved youth were, on average, younger when first arrested (age 14 for gang members vs. never arrested for most nongang members) and had been arrested more often than their at-risk peers (median of three arrests for gang members vs. zero for nongang youth). Gang-involved youth were significantly more likely to have guns or knives in school, carry a concealed weapon, use or sell drugs, and engage in theft and property crimes. These trends also held for comparisons of the collective criminal behavior of gangs and nongang peer groups (Huff, 1996). These results reflect the criminogenic nature of gangs and the powerful socializing influence of the peer group in a gang member's life.

The Social Role of Gangs

Joe and Chesney-Lind's (1995) interviews with gang members in Hawaii show the social role of the gang for young people. They identified two primary mechanisms for group solidarity through gangs, particularly in disorganized and chaotic neighborhoods. First, boredom with lack of resources and high visibility of crime in neglected communities create the conditions for turning to others who are similarly situated, that is, peer groups that offer a social outlet. Second, the stress on families from living in marginalized areas combined with financial struggles create tension and, in many cases, violence at home. Patterson and his colleagues have demonstrated the role of economic stress and violence on disrupted family management practices that lead to school failure and delinquency (Patterson, DeBaryshe, & Ramsey, 1989). In these families, high levels of physical and sexual abuse and assault, particularly among siblings (Finkelhor & Dziuba-Leatherman, 1994), exist. The group or gang, then, is perceived by both girls and boys as providing safe refuge and a surrogate family.

With respect to "normative" adolescent activities, Huff's recent data shed some light on what gang members and nongang members have in common and how they differ (Tables 7.1 and 7.2). The only activity that is more common for nongang members is involvement in sporting activities. Although varying proportions of nongang youth engage in these activities, gang members are significantly more likely to "party"; attend musical concerts; "hang out"; "cruise" for the opposite sex; engage in fighting, drinking, drug use, and drug sales; and put up and cross out graffiti. These data illustrate how the activities of youth gang members are in some respects very similar to activities of non-gang-member youth.

Activities of Boys Versus Girls

Recent analyses of arrest patterns have shown consistently that for boys suspected of gang activity, the most common arrest was "other assaults," mostly fighting with other males (Federal Bureau of Investigation, 1994). Boys also report engaging in frequent drinking, cruising, and looking for trouble (Huff, 1996). Female suspected gang members tend to be chronic, but not serious, offenders who are arrested most commonly for larceny theft, followed by status offenses such as running away. Serious violent offenses (murder, sexual assault, robbery, and aggravated assault) accounted for 23% of the most serious offenses of boys suspected of gang membership, but none of the girls' most serious offenses. Girls are three times more likely than boys to be involved in "property offenses," an important consideration given Huff's (1996) recent findings that property offenses are often a major precursor of more serious gang activity. In

Table 7.1   Comparison of Gang and Nongang Member Activities

Activity	Gang (%)	Nongang (%)	p
Dances, parties	89.4	66.0	**
Sports, events	46.7	77.8	**
Concerts	61.7	40.0	*
"Hang out"	100.0	87.5	*
"Cruise"	86.4	54.5	**
Fighting	93.6	20.5	***
Drinking	87.0	31.8	***
Drug use	34.0	7.0	**
Drug sales	72.3	9.1	***
Put up graffiti	95.7	46.9	***
Cross out graffiti	89.1	46.9	***

$*p < .05; **p < .01; ***p < .001.$

jurisdictions that track female gang activity, girls accounted for 13.6% of gang-related property offenses, 12.7% of the drug crimes, but only 3.3% of the crimes of violence (Curry et al., 1994). Joe and Chesney-Lind (1995) report that, if anything, the presence of girls in a gang tends to depress the occurrence of violence. They quote one 14-year-old Filipino boy: "If we not with the girls, we fighting. If we not fighting, we with the girls" (Joe & Chesney-Lind, 1995, p. 424).

In 1994, girls accounted for about 25% of all arrests of youth in the United States (Federal Bureau of Investigation, 1995). As with boys, arrests of girls for violent crimes have increased steadily and significantly in the past decade. From 1985 to 1994, arrests of girls for murder were up 64%, robbery arrests were up 114%, and aggravated assault arrests were up 136%. Similar to males, however, serious crimes of violence represent a small proportion of all girls' delinquency: 2.3% in 1984 and 3.4% in 1993. Girls are more likely to fight with a parent or sibling, for example, whereas boys are more likely to fight with friends or strangers.

For girls, fighting and violence are part of their life in the gang but not necessarily something they seek out. In qualitative interviews, girls consistently mention protection from neighborhood and family violence as major reasons why they join gangs (Chesney-Lind et al., 1996). Chesney-Lind and her colleagues assert that, in general, female gang activity is not an expression of "liberation," nor are female

Table 7.2 Comparison of Gang and Nongang Member Criminal Behavior

Crime	Gang (%)	Nongang (%)	p
Shoplifting	30.4	14.3	n.s.(.058)
Check forgery	2.1	0.0	n.s.
Credit card theft	6.4	0.0	n.s.
Auto theft	44.7	4.1	***
Theft (other)	51.1	14.3	***
Sell stolen goods	29.8	10.2	*
Assault rivals	72.3	16.3	***
Assault own members	30.4	10.2	*
Assault police	10.6	14.3	n.s.
Assault teachers	14.9	18.4	n.s.
Assault students	51.1	34.7	n.s.
Mug people	10.6	4.1	n.s.
Assault in streets	29.8	10.2	*
Bribe police	10.6	2.0	n.s.
Burglary (unoccupied)	8.5	0.0	*
Burglary (occupied)	2.1	2.0	n.s.
Guns in school	40.4	10.2	***
Knives in school	38.3	4.2	***
Concealed weapons	78.7	22.4	***
Drug use	27.7	4.1	**
Drug sales (school)	19.1	8.2	n.s.
Drug sales (other)	61.7	16.7	***
Drug theft	21.3	0.0	***
Arson	8.5	0.0	*
Kidnap	4.3	0.0	n.s.
Sexual assault	2.1	0.0	n.s.
Rape	2.1	0.0	n.s.
Robbery	17.0	2.0	*
Intimidate/assault victims or witnesses	34.0	0.0	***
Intimidate/assault shoppers	23.4	6.1	*
Drive-by shooting	40.4	2.0	***
Homicide	15.2	0.0	**

*$p < .05$; **$p < .01$; ***$p = .001$; n.s. = not significant.

gang members the hyperviolent, amoral individuals portrayed in popular media accounts. Rather, gang membership reflects the attempts of young women to cope with a bleak and harsh present as well as a dismal future. This sense of hopelessness about the future and need to cope with the here and now permeate both male and female gang activity and youths' motivations for membership.

Use of Firearms

Gangs and gang members are engaging in more violent offenses, experiencing more serious injuries, and using more lethal weapons in the commission of delinquent and criminal acts. Sheley and Wright (1993) recently surveyed male incarcerated offenders and males in 10 inner-city high schools about their use of and access to firearms. Although their findings cannot be generalized to other populations, they were somewhat sobering. Approximately 83% of inmates (average age 17) and 22% of students said that they possessed guns, and more than half of the inmates said that they had carried guns all or most of the time in the year or two before being incarcerated. This compared to 12% of high school students who reported regularly carrying guns to school; nearly one in four reported that they did so "now and then." Perhaps even more disconcerting was the ease with which both incarcerated and high school males reported they could acquire a gun. Only 13% of inmates and 35% of high school males said they would have a lot of trouble getting a gun; nearly half of all respondents indicated that they would "borrow" one from family or friends, more than those who said they would get one "off the street" (54% of inmates and 37% of students). The most frequently endorsed reason for owning or carrying a gun was self-protection. These inner-city youth were convinced they were not safe in their neighborhoods and their schools.

Although not a primary focus of their study, Sheley and Wright (1993) identified members of the incarcerated and student cohorts who reported being in quasi-gangs, unstructured gangs, and structured gangs. Especially for the inmates but to some extent for students, moving from nongang member to gang member was associated with increased frequency of possessing and carrying guns. For members of both structured and unstructured gangs, the most commonly owned weapon was a revolver. Ownership of military-style weapons among gang-affiliated inmates was high, averaging 53% across gang types. In the street environment inhabited by these juvenile offenders, owning and carrying guns were virtually universal behaviors (Sheley & Wright, 1993). Furthermore, the inmate respondents reported that they regularly experienced both threats of violence and violence itself. A total of 84% reported that they had been threatened with a gun or shot at during their lives; 45% of the student sample reported being threatened or shot at on the way to or from school. The researchers also found that firearms were a common element in the drug business; 89% of inmates and 75% of students who dealt drugs carried guns regularly.

Drug Use and Gang Activity

Recent research has demonstrated that although some gang members are involved in the distribution and sale of drugs, and although some gangs have evolved specifically for the purpose of drug distribution, drug trafficking is not a primary gang activity (Klein, Maxson, & Cunningham, 1991; Huff, 1996). Furthermore, most of the homicides involving gang members are over turf battles, not drug violence. In a study conducted in two smaller cities outside Los Angeles, Klein et al. (1991) found that gang members were involved in about 17% of arrests for cocaine sales and about 12% of arrests connected to other drug sales. Firearms were involved in only about 10% of the cases, and violence was present in only about 5% of the incidents. Block and Block's (1994) Chicago study of the city's four largest and most criminally active street gangs found only 8 out of 285 gang-motivated homicides between 1987 and 1990 to be related to drugs. Approximately 90% of violent crimes, including homicides, involving youth gangs in the Boston area between 1984 and 1994 were unrelated to drug dealing or drug use.

Drugs and Firearms

The combination of drugs and firearms appears to contribute a great deal to both the contextual and situational determinants of violence and gang activity. Youth involved in gangs who carry weapons for self-protection and status seeking and who also may be involved with drugs are at high risk for violence. These youth are often impulsive and frequently lack the cognitive problem-solving skills to settle disputes calmly. Fistfights turn into more lethal confrontations because guns are present. This "sequence" can be exacerbated by the socialization problems (e.g., poor parental monitoring) associated with extreme poverty, the high proportion of single-parent households, educational failures, and the pervasive sense of hopelessness about one's life and economic situation (Blumstein, 1995). The number of murders by adolescents, gun-related homicides by 10- to 17-year-old offenders, the homicide arrest rates for 14- to 17-year-old males, and the number of drug arrests have all increased significantly in the past decade.

Huff (1995, 1996) found a significant disparity in profit from drug selling between gang and nongang youth. The typical gang member was much more likely than his at-risk peers to be selling drugs, usually on a daily basis. At-risk youth who sold drugs also did so on a daily basis. However, gang members reported, on average, nearly 50% more in earnings per week ($1,000 vs. $675) with far fewer customers (30 vs. 80 per week). Thus, the average earnings per transaction for gang members was $33.33 compared to $8.44 for nongang/at-risk youth. Gang membership has high potential for profit making and presents an additional motivation for remaining in a gang.

Wilkinson and Fagan (1996; Fagan, 1996), using detailed individual interviews with incarcerated and at-risk youth, have found alcohol to be present in nearly 40% of violent incidents, with subjects reporting that the use of alcohol prior to conflict increased the chances of the conflict being handled violently. Respondents also characterized violent events as "shocking" life experiences, where alcohol "juiced up" a seemingly harmless situation into a physical assault. Furthermore, problematic alcohol use predicted involvement in violent behaviors for both males and females, regardless of gang involvement (Fagan, 1990).

In addition to alcohol use, other situational factors significantly affect the onset, escalation, desistance, and injury outcomes of assaults (Sampson & Lauritsen, 1993). Third parties, for example, are important to how a situation is handled. In Fagan's (1996) recent work, individuals explained how disputes that could have been "squashed" or "deaded" were continued by third parties who would provoke combatants with comments like "don't let him play you like that," appealing to courage, respect, and power as reasons to fight back. Even if events were squashed one day, disputes were often continued at school or in the neighborhood at a later time.

DEVELOPMENTAL PERSPECTIVE

A developmental perspective of youth gangs needs to ground itself in understanding what is normal for children and adolescents as a framework for understanding how normal development may have gone "awry." Recent advances in research on adolescent violence show promise in this regard. Specifically, the study of individual risk factors has focused recently on understanding the cognitive underpinnings of antisocial behavior (e.g., attitudes, beliefs, and information-processing skills; Kendall & Hollon, 1979) and has moved from a dependence on static, simplistic definitions of outcome to an articulation of the sequence of behaviors that mark increasing risk for chronic and serious antisocial behavior (Loeber & Hay, 1994). An emphasis on how developmental sequences are altered rather than a focus on changing static behavioral outcomes has helped advance our thinking about prevention and intervention (Kellam & Rebok, 1992). Furthermore, there has been a growing recognition of the impact of context on individual risk (Tolan & Loeber, 1993), particularly with emphases on family factors in the etiology of antisocial behavior and how family factors interact with and unfold in specific cultural and community contexts (Henggeler & Borduin, 1990).

There are many developmental tasks and transformations for adolescents that may influence whether a young person joins a gang. For most youth, delinquent and violent behavior does not suddenly emerge in adolescence. Although risk for gang membership is multifactored, multifaceted, and complex in its etiology, there are several factors that exert a great deal of influence on determining who is at highest risk for gang involvement. We briefly review some of the risk factors at the individual, family, and neighborhood levels. Individual risk includes exposure to and victimization from violence. Under family risk, we include a discussion of peer group influence. Macrosocial risk factors are also examined. Gang membership and gang-related violence are strongly associated with local economic, school, and peer group factors that need to be taken into account (Klein, 1995; Spergel, 1991, 1995). Several excellent reviews of risk for youth violence and delinquency are available (Earls, 1994; Fraser, 1996; Reiss & Roth, 1993; Yoshikawa, 1994).

Individual-Level Risk Factors

At the individual level, those youth who exhibit an antisocial personality at an early age are most at risk for becoming delinquent adolescents and antisocial adults (Elliott, 1994; Farrington et al., 1993). Aggressive behavior in kindergarten and first grade is an important predictor of delinquency in adolescence (Huesmann, Eron, Leftkowitz, & Walder, 1984; Tremblay, Masse, Leblanc, Schwartzman, & Ledingham, 1992), and, in one longitudinal study, this relationship persisted until the age of 30 (Eron & Huesmann, 1990). A child's early aggressive behavior interacts with family factors to place young children at high risk for delinquency and gang membership. Children who have histories of coercive, intimidating social relations from a very early age experience limited social opportunities with other children and adults (Kupersmidt & Coie, 1990). Of course, not all aggressive children end up becoming delinquent or gang-involved adolescents (Tolan, Guerra, & Kendall, 1995).

Young children who suffer from a combination of a mood disorder (e.g., major depression, bipolar disorder), conduct disorder, and associated attention deficit hyperactivity disorder are at particularly high risk for criminal offending, school failure, and incarceration as adolescents and young adults (Farrington, 1991; Loeber, 1982). In the longitudinal studies that have followed young children through adolescence and into adulthood, low verbal intelligence has been shown to be the best predictor of aggressive behavior at age 8 (as rated by both teachers and parents), delinquent behavior in adolescence, and violent criminal offending in late adolescence (Huesmann et al., 1984). The effects of IQ on later delinquency remain even after controlling for the effects of socioeconomic status on delinquent behavior. There is also growing evidence of prenatal factors being associated with adolescent delinquency. Low birth weight, being small for gestational age, and anoxia at birth have all been associated with adolescent delinquency and violence (Kandel & Mednick, 1991).

One cannot discuss gangs from an individual developmental perspective without mentioning the significant link between exposure to violence, victimization from violence, and risk for violence perpetration (Martinez & Richters, 1993; Richters & Martinez, 1993), particularly among African American youth (DuRant, Cadenhead, Pendergrast, Slaven, & Linder, 1994; Fitzpatrick & Boldizar, 1993). The developmental impact of chronic exposure to violence and victimization by violence can be significant for children and adolescents (Flannery et al., 1996). In general, males are more likely than females to be victims of assault and violence and to witness violent acts. Furthermore, symptoms of posttraumatic stress are commonly reported among children and adolescents exposed to violence (Bell & Jenkins, 1991; Garbarino, Durbrow, Kostelny, & Pardo, 1992; Singer, Anglin, Song, & Lunghofer, 1995).

Family conflict and assault also have been linked to increases in interpersonal assaultive behavior among youth. Sibling assault is one of the most commonly reported forms of youth victimization (Finkelhor & Dziuba-Leatherman, 1994). Coupled with high family conflict and poor parental management, violence between siblings creates a home environment with high potential for child victimization and exposure to violence, and for learning interaction styles that lead to further violent behavior (Cicchetti & Lynch, 1993). Other family factors related to victimization and violent youth behavior include poor parental monitoring (Patterson et al., 1989; Steinberg, 1987) and accessibility of firearms in the home (Ropp, Visintainer, Uman, & Treloar, 1992).

Research over the past few years has shown consistently that intentional injury victimization increases one's risk of subsequently perpetrating violence. Prothrow-Stith (1995), in her book *Deadly Consequences*, discusses her experience as a young emergency department physician in Boston. She was often faced with young patients who told her that the person who injured them would soon be at the hospital for treatment of his own injuries, usually involving the use of firearms. The consensus is that advances in emergency medical care keep the homicide rates among young people from skyrocketing beyond their already epidemic proportions.

Several theories have been advanced about why individuals sometimes alternate between the role of offender and victim. Singer (1981) argues that victims of crime may become offenders because of norms that justify retaliation. Conversely, offenders may become victims because they hold values that support the initiation of violence to resolve disputes (i.e., "victim precipitation"). Sparks (1982) suggested that offenders make ideal victims because they are likely to be viewed by other offenders as vulnerable targets who are unlikely to call police, as compared to nonoffender victims. Gottfredson (1984) supported the victimogenic potential of offending by showing the relationship between victimization and self-reported criminal behavior.

In their most recent work, Rivara, Shepherd, Farrington, Richmond, and Cannon (1995) examined criminal records of males ages 10 to 24 treated for injuries in emergency departments compared to males treated for unintentional injury. They found that assault patients were significantly more likely in the past to have been formally warned or convicted of a violent crime. In addition, they found that differences between injury groups was most pronounced for males 10 to 16 years old, who had significantly different and less extensive criminal histories than did their older counterparts. Rivara et al. (1995) did find, however, that all of their 10- to 16-year-old offenders had convictions in the year following treatment of an injury. This showed that the incident in which they were injured did not deter them from further criminal activity and supports the risk for an intentional injury victim subsequently perpetrating violence and assault against others.

The relationship between victimization and assault perpetration is particularly salient for gang-involved youth. Huff (1996) found that gang-involved youth in Cleveland were significantly more likely to assault rivals (72% vs. 16%) and to be victims of assault (34% vs. 0%) than were their nongang peers. Furthermore, gang members were more likely to be assaulted by other members of their own gangs than their at-risk peers were of being assaulted by their peers. The notion that gang membership somehow protects a member from being victimized by violence or from perpetrating assault against others is a dangerous falsehood for young people to endorse. Sanchez-Jankowski (1991) showed that the longer a gang remains viable, the greater the potential for criminal victimization to occur for its members. Savitz, Rosen, and Lalli (1982) also found that membership in a fighting gang was related to increased chances of victimization. Finally, it should be noted that Huff's interviews in Cleveland, south Florida, and Denver consistently revealed that youth are far more likely to be assaulted if they join a gang (as part of the initiation and thereafter) than if they politely refuse to join (Huff, 1995, 1996).

Family-Level and Peer-Related Risk

Patterson and his colleagues have a model of early versus late starters in delinquent activity that incorporates child antisocial behavior as a precursor to early childhood behavior problems and poor parent management. These lead to school failure and rejection by peers, precursors of adolescent delinquency and violence. According to Patterson and Yoerger (1993), there exist two primary routes to delinquency, each with a different set of determinants and long-term outcomes. The critical determinant is age at first arrest. If a child is arrested prior to age 14, he or she is considered an early starter. If arrested after the age of 14, the child is considered to be a late starter. The primary assumptions of both models is that disrupted parenting practices directly determine a child's antisocial behavior, and that these, in turn, place a child at risk for early arrest (Patterson et al., 1989). Second, it is assumed that the majority of adult criminal offenders are early starters. This latter assumption is consistent with the evidence for the chronicity and stability of aggressive, violent behavior shown across longitudinal studies (Eron & Huesmann, 1990; Farrington, 1991; Patterson, Reid, & Dishion, 1992).

Several other findings and assumptions that underlie their coercion model are important to mention. First is the assumption that, as the frequency of antisocial behavior increases, the severity shifts from the trivial to more severe acts (Patterson & Bank, 1989). Second, Patterson and colleagues have found that parents of antisocial children are noncontingent in many of their interactions with their children. They are essentially ineffective disciplinarians who punish frequently, inconsistently, and ineffectively, and they tend to ignore or fail to reinforce prosocial behaviors. Patterson et al.'s model focuses on five parenting constructs shown to be important predictors of antisocial and delinquent child behavior: discipline, monitoring, family problem solving, involvement, and positive reinforcement (Patterson et al., 1992).

Their program of research has demonstrated how child antisocial behaviors directly determine school failure, rejection by peers, and involvement with deviant peers and indirectly determine depressed mood and substance use. All of these factors place youth at greater risk for gang involvement. In the coercion model, child antisocial behavior is viewed as merely the first step in a long-term dynamic process resulting in adolescent delinquency and adult antisocial behavior. What is crucial, from a developmental perspective, is understanding that early childhood behavior is the marker for who is at risk for early adolescent gang involvement and for participation in the aggressive, criminal, and violent behavior characteristic of many gang-involved youth.

The influence of peers on gang involvement and activity is significant. Goldstein (1991) asserts that establishing a stable sense of identity and striving for peer acceptance are two central features of adolescent development fostered by gang involvement. Contacts with deviant peers are readily available to most adolescents. Cairns and Cairns (1991) showed that most adolescents develop support networks of some kind. For most adolescents, the peer group provides at least one of those social networks. For some adolescents, the gang becomes the primary support network, made up mostly of other deviant peers and rejected youth who are not attached to school or home, and who live in families where parents are not interested in or are unable to monitor effectively who they are with and what they are doing. In their struggle to establish an identity, the gang can provide a context for establishing a system of values, beliefs, and goals.

Physical, emotional, cognitive, and social developmental tasks merge during early and middle adolescence, forcing young people to cope with many issues, expectations, and responsibilities that they may not yet be capable of handling on their own. For gang-involved youth, it is the peer group that provides both girls and boys with a safe refuge and a surrogate family. Patterson and others have shown that the most antisocial youth are those most committed to a deviant peer group. Being relatively free from adult supervision and free from any attachment to school, religion, or family, hanging out with other rejected youth provides a great deal of opportunity to engage in delinquent activity (Gottfredson & Hirschi, 1990; O'Donnell, Hawkins, & Abbott, 1995). The sooner the antisocial child is out on the streets, the more exposed he or she is to higher levels of antisocial behavior and violence and the more opportunities he or she has to perpetrate criminal acts.

Macrosocial/Community-Level Risk

Several macrosocial or community-level factors contribute to gang membership, gang activity, crime rates, and violence. Examples of macrolevel risk factors include neighborhood resident mobility, levels of disorganization, population density, heterogeneity, unemployment, and income inequality (e.g., the spatial proximity of middle class and poor). Each of these has been related to higher levels of gang activity, crime, and violence (Coulton, Korbin, & Su, in press; Sampson & Lauritsen, 1993). A major dimension of social disorganization relevant to violence is the ability of a community to supervise and control teenage peer groups, particularly gangs (Sampson & Groves, 1989). There is much evidence that adolescent delinquency is most often a group activity, and thus the capacity of the community to control group-level dynamics is a key theoretical mechanism linking community characteristics with crime and gang activity (Sampson & Lauritsen, 1993).

Skogan (1986) reviews some of the "feedback" processes that may further increase levels of crime and gang activity in a community. These include (a) physical and psychological withdrawal from community life, (b) weakening of the informal social control processes that inhibit crime, (c) a decline in the organizational life and mobilization capacity of the neighborhood, (d) deteriorating business conditions, (e) the importation and domestic production of delinquency and deviance, and (f) further dramatic changes in the composition of the population. So, if people shun their neighbors and withdraw from their community, there will be fewer opportunities to form friendship networks that may help provide appropriate adult supervision of youth group activity (Sampson & Lauritsen, 1993).

IMPLICATIONS FOR ADOLESCENT DEVELOPMENT

During adolescence, multiple developmental tasks converge to make this an important time for gang activity and involvement. Gangs can be an attractive alternative to an at-risk youth struggling to fulfill unmet needs and resolve emerging developmental issues. Gang membership jeopardizes adolescent psychosocial development in general and particularly threatens the adequate resolution of primary adolescent developmental tasks, including achieving effective relations with peers of both genders, achieving a masculine or feminine social role, achieving an appropriate body image and becoming competent in using the body, achieving emotional autonomy, preparation for marriage and family life, preparing for an economic career, developing a value-based ideology, and aspiring to participate responsibly in the community (Straus, 1994). Gang membership, which may substitute for an adolescent's desire to be a member of an accepting and supportive social network, cannot replace the support and adequate supervision that a parent can provide. Furthermore, membership in a social network that tolerates and approves of violence is a strong predictor of violent behavior (Callahan & Rivara, 1992; Webster, Gainer, & Champion, 1994). This is a particular irony for those youth who initially join a gang for protection. Females who join a gang for protection from abusive parents have, in most cases, simply placed themselves at greater risk (although perhaps different) for sexual and physical victimization (Portillas & Zatz, 1995). Because victimization leads to an increased risk for perpetrating violence, the attainment of any "normative" developmental tasks in adolescence is problematic at best.

Gang membership places young people at risk for a variety of negative outcomes. Gang membership is highly associated with earlier onset of delinquency and victimization from violence (Widom, 1989). For both genders, gang involvement has been associated with earlier onset of sexual intercourse, unsafe sex, and early pregnancy or the fathering of a child (Morris et al., 1996). Gang members also more frequently report suicidal ideation and suicide attempts, often involving heavy substance abuse.

Recently, researchers have begun to specifically examine outcomes for gang-involved females. Moore and Hagedorn (1996) assert that no matter what the cultural context, and no matter what the economic opportunity structure, there appears to be one constant in the later life of women in gangs. Most of them have children, and children have more effect on women's lives than on men's. For women, but rarely for men, the new responsibilities associated with child rearing may speed up the process of maturing out of the gang. As Chesney-Lind and Brown (in press) point out, in an environment of extreme poverty and deprivation, developmental tasks are subordinate to the imperatives of short-term survival on the streets. There is little hope for the future, especially for females in this environment: Recent data suggest that the future awaiting gang girls is bleak indeed; 94% will go on to have children, and 84% will raise them without spouses. One third of them will be arrested, and the vast majority will be dependent on welfare (Campbell, 1990).

PREVENTION AND INTERVENTION

As the developmental and criminological literature illustrates, child aggressive, antisocial behavior is highly predictive of adolescent delinquency, violence, and gang involvement. To systematically prevent adolescent gang activity, we endorse a primary prevention approach with the goal of reducing child aggressive and antisocial behavior (Tolan et al., 1995). By the early elementary school years, aggression is predictive of later aggressive and antisocial behavior. This suggests that interventions should begin by the first grade, especially given the significant increase in aggression between the first and second grades (Tremblay, Kurtz, Masse, Vitaro, & Phil, 1995). It is important to note, however, that postintervention aggression scores are typically lower than developmentally expected increases and not lower than preintervention scores. Similar results were found for high-risk K through 5 children in Tucson (Flannery et al., 1996). These findings for aggression highlight the need to use normative developmental information as a measuring stick for intervention effectiveness (Kendall & Grove, 1988).

Tolan et al. (1995) point out that even among aggressive children, less than half continue to engage in high rates of aggressive behavior, and relatively few go on to escalate their involvement in serious antisocial behavior. We need to identify multiple-risk pathways that may contain different combinations of risk factors or may be differentiated by the relative influence of risk factors common to pathways. Especially needed are studies of how intervention components affect the risk of children who differ by gender, ethnicity, socioeconomic status, and other major demographic markers. Evidence also exists for the significant influence of social-cognitive factors on delinquency and violence and their legitimacy as a focus of intervention efforts. The work of Dodge (Crick & Dodge, 1994) and of Guerra and her colleagues (Guerra, Huesmann, & Hanish, 1994; Guerra, Huesmann, Tolan, Acker, & Eron, 1995) demonstrates the link between attributional bias, social information-processing skills, and individual beliefs with aggressive and antisocial behavior. Each of these is a potentially modifiable skill through preventive interventions. For example, Guerra et al. (1995) reported that normative beliefs supporting the legitimacy of aggression predict aggression during elementary school, and O'Donnell et al. (1995) showed that attitudes toward substance use and aggression predicted involvement in both behaviors for adolescents. Family variables, particularly communication skills and management practices, are also increasingly the focus of both prevention efforts with young children and interventions with adolescents (Dishion & Andrews, 1995).

The influence of peers has been a major focus of this chapter. Given the impact of association with antisocial peers, peer rejection, and the support network provided by peers in a gang, peer relations has become a major focus of prevention and intervention efforts. Successful interventions are not merely exercises in teaching youth to cope with peer pressure to engage in antisocial acts. Lack of effective social skills and social problem solving are critical elements in the escalation of minor conflicts into serious altercations (Dodge, 1993). The tendency of delinquent youth to interpret ambiguous or neutral events as reflective of hostile intent is problematic in the classroom, at home, and on the streets. Many gang-involved youth speak about the necessity of retaliation for being "disrespected" or "dissed" because of how someone else looked at them or their girlfriend, for example.

One of the dangers of peer-focused interventions is attempting to conduct group therapy with all antisocial youth. A social network effect was described by O'Donnell, Manos, and Chesney-Lind (1987) in programs such as the Juvenile Awareness Project at Rahway State Prison in New Jersey and the Group Guidance Project (Klein, 1971). These programs were associated with an increase in delinquency, gang membership, and cohesiveness of gangs because they brought fringe members into contact with active gang members who recruited them. Activities of programs that promote prosocial affiliation or disrupt existing affiliations do so by creating opportunities for youth to participate meaningfully within different networks. The Ladino Hills Project (Klein, 1971), for example, offered employment as an alternative to gang membership. Although the number of offenses per gang member did not change, follow-up data indicated decreases in gang membership, gang cohesiveness, and in the total number of gang offenses. In a sense, interventions with a focus on social networks emphasize forming more gangs. But these gangs are of a different nature. Developing prosocial networks that bring youth into contact with others who can provide what the gang provides holds promise for prevention efforts and takes advantage of a developmental task that is a powerful influence in the lives of children and youth. It is imperative that prosocial peers be included in group settings for long-term gain (Tremblay et al., 1995). Moreover, Goldstein and Glick (1994) report some success in implementing aggression replacement training with New York City gangs.

But even programs that alter social networks are likely to be ineffective if they do no more than attempt to control behavior or

translate competitive entrepreneurial initiative (e.g., drug trafficking) into low-level job opportunities (Jankowski, 1991). A pervasive
sense of hopelessness about the future in a prosocial world drives
many youth to seek the power and opportunity that gang membership affords. A young person with low bonding to school and family,
with unlikely access to higher education, with fewer opportunities
to enter the legal labor market, and with little likelihood of being
socioeconomically mobile will tend to continue gang involvement
into adulthood (Wilson, 1987). For some youth, economic, political,
and social forces compel gang membership. Although it is beyond
the scope of this chapter to pursue such issues, until these forces are
successfully redirected, the developmental tasks confronted by some
youth will require that gangs persist.

Clearly, many demographic variables, including gender, ethnicity,
family composition, and neighborhood disorganization, affect en-
trance into a gang, how long a youth stays in a gang, and how and
why he or she leaves a gang. Most research to date on aggressive and
delinquent behavior has focused on white, middle-class youth,
whereas research on gang-involved youth has focused on ethnic
minority youth. There is little work that spans the developmental
literature on aggression and delinquent behavior and the sociologi-
cal/criminological work on gangs. Huff's (1995, 1996) recent studies
directly comparing gang-involved and at-risk youth highlight the
need to begin examining the continuum of aggressive behavior,
delinquency, gang involvement, and antisocial behavior for both
groups of adolescents. Factors that predict which youth will go from
being at risk to being involved in a gang are not yet well understood
beyond a descriptive level. The relative influence of normative beliefs, stress, poverty, exposure to violence and victimization, and
ethnicity may all contribute differentially to this process. The relative
effectiveness of any preventive intervention also may vary tremen-
dously depending on which factors are pertinent for a particular
adolescent or group.

Finally, all of the research to date on youth at risk for engaging in
aggressive, delinquent behavior and gang activity points to the need
for multicomponent, multicontext interventions. To date, those that
have shown the most promise include a focus on the individual (e.g.,
attitudes about aggression), the influence of close interpersonal relations (e.g., problem solving, peer pressure, family conflict), and the
contexts within which development takes place (e.g., home, school,
peer group). Promising programs include aggression replacement

training with delinquent youth (Goldstein & Glick, 1994), multisystemic family therapy (Henggeler, Melton, & Smith, 1992), the Seattle Social Development Project (Hawkins et al., 1992), and the Peace-Builders youth violence prevention project (Embry et al., 1996; Flannery et al., 1996). Each of these approaches takes into account a combination of intrapersonal, interpersonal, and contextual factors in attempting to reduce delinquency, violent behavior, or gang involvement. Certainly, the relative importance of environmental risk factors, compared with individual risk factors, may vary with age and by context. This has been demonstrated quite well by Finkelhor in his model of "developmental victimology" for children exposed to and victimized by violence (Finkelhor, 1995). Young children may be more affected by context (e.g., persistent family violence) than adolescents, who may have more resources to avoid becoming victims of violence.

MACROSOCIAL ISSUES THAT
DELIMIT INTERVENTION

Gang activity and violence are likely to be fostered by the same macrostructural factors at the community level that have been linked to other forms of deviance and negative child and adolescent outcomes (Huff, 1993). For example, highly mobile communities have been shown to have lower density of acquaintanceships, which limits their ability to control crime, socialize their youth, and care for members with special needs (Freudenburg, 1986). There exists considerable evidence that the density of friendship networks, parental control over teen peer groups, and participation in voluntary organizations—all aspects of community organization—are good predictors of rates of crime and delinquency within a community (Figueira-McDonough, 1991). Rates of delinquency are related to the community instability that develops in neighborhoods that experience significant population turnover (Bursik & Webb, 1982). Durkin, Davidson, Kuhn, O'Connnor, and Barlow (1994) found that high census tract proportions of low-income households, single-parent families, non-high school graduates, and unemployment were significant predictors of violence and delinquency among children younger than 17 years of age. These findings are consistent with those of Coulton, Korbin, Su, and Chow (1995), who showed that impoverishment, population instability, child care burden (e.g., ratio of children to adults), and geographic/economic isolation (i.e., whether a neighborhood had a contiguous census tract with at least 40% poor residents) were all related to increased risk of child victimization and delinquency.

In a recently completed study, the RAND Corporation examined the cost-effectiveness of several crime-prevention strategies that involve early intervention in the lives of people at risk of pursuing a criminal career (Greenwood, Model, Rydell, & Chiesa, 1996). Focusing on California, RAND contrasted California's "three-strikes" policy, which guarantees extended sentences for repeat offenders, with four different approaches: (a) home visits by child care professionals, beginning before birth and extending through the first 2 years of childhood, followed by 4 years of day care; (b) parent training for families with aggressive or acting-out children; (c) 4 years of cash and other graduation incentives for disadvantaged high school students; and (d) monitoring and supervision of high school-age youth who have already exhibited delinquent behavior. All of the examined programs, with the exception of home visits and day care, were appreciably more effective at reducing serious crimes than was the three-strikes policy. Graduation incentives for disadvantaged youth proved the most cost-effective approach, averting nearly $260 million from serious crimes compared to about $60 million for the three-strikes option. These findings have serious implications for policymakers who believe that increased incarceration time for juvenile offenders will systematically and over time reduce the youth crime rate.

SUMMARY

In this chapter, we have provided an overview of youth gangs from a developmental perspective and presented social and criminological literature integrated with research on development and risk to underscore the importance of including multiple disciplines in our prevention and intervention strategies. Gang membership increases in adolescence because adolescence is a developmental transition period in which peers take on a significant support and influence role, and this is done often at the expense of parents and families. The gang can provide a vehicle for identity formation and a setting where an at-risk youth can find acceptance and reinforcement for rejecting social norms and engaging in deviant, delinquent, and sometimes violent behavior. Adolescence is a transitional period when the need to meet multiple developmental tasks makes the gang an attractive alternative to at-risk youth.

Although the challenges are complex and long-term systematic change difficult to achieve, the cost of doing nothing is too high. We know that if we start early and identify at-risk youth in the early elementary years, we can promote prosocial competence and reduce the incidence of aggressive, antisocial behavior. Gang violence is not an insurmountable social malady. Youth seek out gang involvement typically to meet normal developmental tasks and to fulfill needs that all adolescents and all individuals have. Prothrow-Stith is fond of saying that children will eventually get our time, our money, our attention, and our resources. It is up to us, as parents, researchers, educators and advocates, to decide when that will be. Will it be when children are young, eager to learn, and perhaps not yet exposed to high levels of violence and victimization? Or will it be later, after our children reach adolescence, have failed at school, and have chosen to meet their needs through gangs? Before systems can change, individuals must take action and make their choices.

REFERENCES

Bell, C., & Jenkins, E. (1991). Traumatic stress and children. *Journal of Health Care for the Poor and Underserved, 2,* 175-185.

Block, C. R., & Block, R. (1994). *Street gang crime in Chicago* [Research in brief]. Washington, DC: U.S. Department of Justice, Office of Justice Programs, National Institute of Justice.

Blumstein, A. (1995). Violence by young people: Why the deadly nexus? *National Institute of Justice Journal,* pp. 2-9.

Bursik, R. J., & Webb, J. (1982). Community change and patterns of delinquency. *American Journal of Sociology, 88,* 24-41.

Cairns, R. B., & Cairns, B. D. (1991). Social cognition and social networks: A developmental perspective. In D. J. Pepler & K. H. Rubin (Eds.), *The development and treatment of childhood aggression* (pp. 249-274). Hillsdale, NJ: Lawrence Erlbaum.

Callahan, C. M., & Rivara, F. P. (1992). Urban high school youth and hand-guns. *Journal of the American Medical Association, 267,* 3038-3042.

Campbell, A. (1990). Female participation in gangs. In C. R. Huff (Ed.), *Gangs in America* (pp. 163-183). Newbury Park, CA: Sage.

Chesney-Lind, M., & Brown, M. (in press). Girls and violence: An overview. In D. Flannery & R. Huff (Eds.), *Youth violence: Prevention, intervention, and social policy.* Washington, DC: American Psychiatric Press.

Chesney-Lind, M., Brown, M., Leisen, M. B., Perrone, P., Kwasck, D., Marker, N., & Kato, D. (1996). *Perspectives on juvenile delinquency and gangs: An interim report to Hawaii's state legislature.* Honolulu: University of Hawaii at Manoa, Center for Youth Research, Social Science Research Institute.

Chesney-Lind, M., & Sheldon, R. G. (1992). *Girls, delinquency and juvenile justice.* Pacific Grove, CA: Brooks/Cole.

Chesney-Lind, M., Sheldon, R., & Joe, L. K. (1996). Girls, delinquency and gang membership. In C. R. Huff (Ed.), *Gangs in America* (pp. 185-204). Thousand Oaks, CA: Sage.

Chicchetti, D., & Lynch, M. (1993). Toward an ecological/transactional model of community violence and child maltreatment: Consequences for children's development. *Psychiatry, 56,* 96-118.

Coulton, C., Korbin, J., & Su, M. (in press). Measuring neighborhood context for young children in an urban area. *American Journal of Community Psychology.*

Coulton, C., Korbin, J., Su, M., & Chow, J. (1995). Community level factors and child maltreatment rates. *Child Development, 66,* 1262-1276.

Crick, N. R., & Dodge, K. A. (1994). A review and reformulation of social information-processing mechanisms in children's social adjustment. *Psychological Bulletin, 115,* 74-101.

Curry, G. D., Ball, R. A., & Fox, R. J. (1994). *Gang crimes and law enforcement recordkeeping* [Research in brief]. Washington, DC: U.S. Department of Justice, National Institute of Justice, Office of Justice Programs.

Curry, G. D., Fox, R. J., Ball, R. A., & Stone, D. (1992). *National assessment of law enforcement anti-gang information resources* [Draft 1992 Final Report]. Morgantown: West Virginia University, National Assessment Survey.

Dishion, T. J., & Andrews, D. W. (1995). Preventing escalation in problem behaviors with high-risk young adolescents: Immediate and 1-year outcomes. *Journal of Consulting and Clinical Psychology, 63,* 538-548.

Dodge, K. A. (1993). Social-cognitive mechanisms in the development of conduct disorder and depression. *Annual Review of Psychology, 44,* 559-584.

DuRant, R., Cadenhead, C., Pendergrast, R., Slaven, G., & Linder, C. W. (1994). Factors associated with the use of violence among urban black adolescents. *American Journal of Public Health, 84,* 612-617.

Durkin, M., Davidson, L., Kuhn, L., O'Connor, P., & Barlow, B. (1994). Low-income neighborhoods and the risk of severe pediatric injury: A small area analysis in Northern Manhattan. *American Journal of Public Health, 84,* 587-592.

Earls, F. J. (1994). Violence and today's youth. *Critical Issues for Children and Youth, 4,* 4-23.

Elliot, D. E. (1994). Serious violent offenders: Onset, developmental course, and termination. *Criminology, 32,* 1-21.

Embry, D., Flannery, D., Vazsonyi, A., Powell, K., & Atha, H. (1996). PeaceBuilders: A theoretically driven, school-based model for early violence prevention. *American Journal of Preventive Medicine, 12,* 91-100.

Eron, L. D., & Huesmann, R. (1990). The stability of aggressive behavior—Even unto the third generation. In M. Lewis & S. M. Miller (Eds.), *Handbook of developmental psychopathology* (pp. 147-156). New York: Plenum.

Esbensen, F. A., & Huizinga, D. (1993). Gangs, drugs, and delinquency in a survey of urban youth. *Criminology, 31,* 565-589.

Fagan, J. (1990). Social processes of delinquency and drug use among urban gangs. In C. R. Huff (Eds.), *Gangs in America* (1st ed., pp. 183-223). Newbury Park, CA: Sage.

Fagan, J. (1996). Gangs, drugs and neighborhood change. In C. R. Huff (Ed.), *Gangs in America* (2nd ed., pp. 39-74). Thousand Oaks, CA: Sage.

Farrington, D. P. (1991). Antisocial personality from childhood to adulthood. *The Psychologist, 4,* 389-394.

Farrington, D. P., Loeber, R., Elliot, D. S., Hawkins, J. D., Kandel, D. B., Lein, M. W., McCord, J., Rowe, D. C., & Tremblay, R. E. (1993). Advancing knowledge about the onset of delinquency and crime. In B. B. Lahey & A. E. Kazdin (Eds.), *Advances in clinical child psychology* (Vol. 12, pp. 283-342). New York: Plenum.

Federal Bureau of Investigation. (1994). *Crime in the United States—1993.* Washington, DC: U.S. Department of Justice.

Federal Bureau of Investigation. (1995). *Crime in the United States.* Washington, DC: U.S. Department of Justice.

Figueira-McDonough, J. (1991). Community structure and delinquency: A typology. *Social Service Review, 65,* 69-91.

Finkelhor, D. (1995). The victimization of children: A developmental perspective. *American Journal of Orthopsychiatry, 65,* 177-193.

Finkelhor, D., & Dziuba-Leatherman, J. (1994). Victimization of children. *American Psychologist, 49,* 173-183.

Fitzpatrick, K., & Boldizar, J. (1993). The prevalence and consequence of exposure to violence among African American youth. *Journal of the American Academy of Child and Adolescent Psychiatry, 32,* 424-430.

Flannery, D. J., Vazsonyi, A., Embry, D., & Atha, H. (1996). *Longitudinal follow-up of PeaceBuilders violence prevention program* (Centers for Disease Control and Prevention, Cooperative Agreement #U81/CCU513508-01).

Fraser, M. W. (1996). Aggressive behavior in childhood and early adolescence: An ecological-developmental perspective on youth violence. *Social Work, 41,* 347-361.

Freudenburg, W. R. (1986). The density of acquaintanceship: An overlooked variable in community research. *American Journal of Sociology, 92,* 27-63.

Garbarino, J., Durbrow, N., Kostelny, K., & Pardo, C. (1992). *Children in danger: Coping with the consequences of community violence.* San Francisco: Jossey-Bass.

Goldstein, A. P. (1991). *Delinquent gangs: A psychological perspective.* Champaign, IL: Research Press.

Goldstein, A. P., & Glick, B. (1994). *The prosocial gang: Implementing aggression replacement training.* Thousand Oaks, CA: Sage.

Gottfredson, M. (1984). *Victims of crime: The dimensions of risk* (Home Office Research Study #81). London: Her Majesty's Stationery Office.

Gottfredson, M., & Hirschi, T. (1990). *A general theory of crime.* Stanford, CA: Stanford University Press.

Greeenwood, P. W., Model, K. E., Rydell, P., & Chiesa, J. (1996). *Diverting children from a life of crime: Measuring costs and benefits.* Santa Monica, CA: RAND.

Guerra, N. G., Huesmann, L. R., & Hanish, L. (1994). The role of normative beliefs in children's social behavior. In N. Eisenberg (Ed.), *Social development* (pp. 140-158). Thousand Oaks, CA: Sage.

Guerra, N. G., Huesmann, L. R., Tolan, P. H., Acker, R., & Eron, L. F. (1995). Stressful events and individual beliefs as correlates of economic disadvantage and aggression among urban children. *Journal of Consulting and Clinical Psychology, 63,* 518-528.

Hawkins, J. D., Catalano, R. F., Morrison, D. M., O'Donnell, J., Abbott, R. D., & Day, L. E. (1992). The Seattle Social Development Project: Effects of the first four years on protective factors and problem behaviors. In J. McCord & R. Tremblay (Eds.), *The prevention of antisocial behavior in children* (pp. 139-161). New York: Guilford.

Henggeler, S. W., & Borduin, C. M. (1990). *Family therapy and beyond: A multi-systemic approach to treating the behavior problems of children and adolescents.* Pacific Grove, CA: Brooks/Cole.

Henggeler, S. W., Melton, G. B., & Smith, L. A. (1992). Family preservation using multisystemic therapy—An effective alternative to incarcerating serious juvenile offenders. *Journal of Consulting and Clinical Psychology, 60,* 953-961.

Howell, J. C. (1994). Recent gang research: Program and policy implications. *Crime & Delinquency, 40,* 495-515.

Huesmann, L. R., Eron, L. D., Leftkowitz, M. M., & Walder, L. O. (1984). Stability of aggression over time and generations. *Developmental Psychology, 20,* 1120-1134.

Huff, C. R. (1993). Gangs and public policy: Macrolevel interventions. In A. P. Goldstein & C. R. Huff (Eds.), *The gang intervention handbook* (pp. 463-475). Champaign, IL: Research Press.

Huff, C. R. (1995). *Final report to the National Institute of Justice regarding the criminal behavior of gang members.* Columbus: Ohio State University Press.

Huff, C. R. (1996). The criminal behavior of gang members and nongang at-risk youth. In C. R. Huff (Ed.), *Gangs in America* (2nd ed., pp. 75-102). Thousand Oaks, CA: Sage.

Jankowski, M. S. (1991). *Islands in the street: Gangs and American urban society.* Berkeley: University of California Press.

Joe, K. A., & Chesney-Lind, M. (1995). Just every mother's angel: An analysis of gender and ethnic variations in youth gang membership. *Gender & Society, 9,* 408-430.

Kandel, E., & Mednick, S. A. (1991). Perinatal complications predict violent offending. *Criminology, 29,* 519-529.

Kellam, S. G., & Rebok, G. W. (1992). Building developmental and etiological theory through epidemiologically based preventive intervention trials. In J. McCord & R. E. Tremblay (Eds.), *Preventing antisocial behavior: Interventions from birth through adolescence* (pp. 62-195). New York: Guilford.

Kendall, P. C., & Grove, W. (1988). Normative comparisons in therapy outcome. *Behavioral Assessment, 10,* 147-158.

Kendall, P. C., & Hollon, S. D. (1979). *Cognitive-behavioral interventions: Theory, research, and procedures.* New York: Academic Press.

Klein, M. (1971). *Street gangs and street workers.* Englewood Cliffs, NJ: Prentice Hall.

Klein, M. (1995). *The American street gang: Its nature, prevalence, and control.* New York: Oxford University Press.

Klein, M. W., Maxson, C. L., & Cunningham, L. C. (1991). "Crack," street gangs, and violence. *Criminology, 29,* 623-650.

Kupersmidt, J. B., & Coie, J. D. (1990). Preadolescent peer status, aggression, and school adjustment as predictors of externalizing problems in adolescence. *Child Development, 61,* 1350-1362.

Larson, R., & Richards, M. H. (Eds.). (1989). The changing life space of early adolescence [Special issue]. *Journal of Youth and Adolescence, 18*(6).

Loeber, R. (1982). The stability of antisocial and delinquent child behavior: A review. *Child Development, 53,* 1431-1446.

Loeber, R., & Hay, D. F. (1994). Developmental approaches to aggression and conduct problems. In M. Rutter & D. F. Hay (Eds.), *Development through life: A handbook for clinicians* (pp. 288-316). Boston: Blackwell Scientific.

Martinez, P., & Richters, J. E. (1993). The NIMH community violence project: II. Children's distress symptoms associated with vilence exposure. *Psychiatry, 56,* 22-35.

Maxson, C. L., & Klein, M. W. (1996). Defining gang homicide: An updated look at member and motive approaches. In C. R. Huff (Ed.), *Gangs in America* (2nd ed., pp. 3-20). Thousand Oaks, CA: Sage.

Miller, W. B. (1982). *Crime by youth gangs and groups in the United States.* Washington, DC: U.S. Department of Justice, Office of Juvenile Justice and Delinquency Prevention.

Montemayor, R., & Flannery, D. (1990). Making the transition from childhood to early adolescence. In R. Montemayor, G. Adams, & T. Gullotta (Eds.), *Advances in adolescent development, Vol. 2: From childhood to adolescence: A transitional period?* (pp. 291-301). Newbury Park, CA: Sage.

Moore, J. W., & Hagedorn, J. M. (1996). What happens to girls in the gang? In C. R. Huff (Ed.), *Gangs in America* (2nd ed., pp. 205-220). Thousand Oaks, CA: Sage.

Morris, R. E., Harrison, E. A., Knox, G. W., Romanjhauser, E., Marques, D. K., & Watts, L. L. (1996). Health risk behavioral survey from 39 juvenile correctional facilities in the United States. *Journal of Adolescent Health, 117,* 334-375.

O'Donnell, C., Manos, M., & Chesney-Lind, M. (1987). Diversion and neighborhood delinquency programs in open settings: A social network interpretation. In E. Morris & C. Braukman (Eds.), *Behavioral approaches to crime and delinquency: Application, research and theory* (pp. 251-271). New York: Plenum.

O'Donnell, J., Hawkins, J. D., & Abbott, R. D. (1995). Predicting serious delinquency and substance use among aggressive boys. *Journal of Consulting and Clinical Psychology, 63,* 529-537.

Paikoff, R. L., & Brooks-Gunn, J. (1991). Do parent-child interactions change during puberty? *Psychological Bulletin, 110,* 47-66.

Patterson, G., DeBaryshe, B., & Ramsey, B. (1989). A developmental perspective on antisocial behavior. *American Psychologist, 44,* 329-335.

Patterson, G. R., & Bank, L. (1989). Some amplifying mechanisms for pathologic process in families. In M. R. Gunner & E. Thelem (Eds.), *Systems and development: The Minnesota symposia on child psychology* (Vol. 22, pp. 167-210). Hillsdale, NJ: Lawrence Erlbaum.

Patterson, G. R., Reid, J. B., & Dishion, T. J. (1992). *A social learning approach: IV. Antisocial boys.* Eugene, OR: Castalia.

Patterson, G. R., & Yoerger, K. (1993). Developmental models for delinquent behavior. In S. Hodgins (Ed.), *Mental disorders and crime* (pp. 140-172). Newbury Park, CA: Sage.

Portillas, E., & Zatz, M. S. (1995, November). *Not to die for: Positive and negative aspects of Chicano youth gangs.* Paper presented at the annual meeting of the American Society of Criminology, Boston.

Prothrow-Stith, D. (1995). *Deadly consequences.* New York: HarperCollins.

Reiss, A. J., Jr., & Roth, J. (1993). *Understanding and preventing violence.* Washington, DC: National Academy Press.

Richters, J., & Martinez, P. (1993). The NIMH community violence project: I. Children as victims of, and witnesses to violence. *Psychiatry, 56,* 7-21.

Rivara, F., Shepherd, J., Farrington, D., Richmond, P. W., & Cannon, P. (1995). Victim as offender in youth violence. *Annals of Emergency Medicine, 26,* 609-615.

Ropp, L., Visintainer, P., Uman, J., & Treloar, D. (1992). Death in the city: An American childhood tragedy. *Journal of the American Medical Association, 267,* 2905-2910.

Sampson, R. J., & Groves, W. B. (1989). Testing social-disorganization theory. *American Journal of Sociology, 94,* 774-802.

Sampson, R. J., & Lauritsen, J. (1993). Violent victimization and offending: In-dividual, situational, and community-level risk factors. In A. J. Reiss, Jr., & J. A. Roth (Eds.), *Understanding and preventing violence. Vol. 3: Social influences* (pp. 1-114). Washington, DC: National Academy Press.

Sanchez-Jankowski, M. (1991). *Islands in the street: Gangs and American urban society.* Berkeley: University of California Press.

Savitz, L., Rosen, L., & Lalli, M. (1982). Delinquency and gang membership as related to victimization. *Victimology, 5,* 152-160.

Sheley, J. F., & Wright, J. D. (1993). *Gun acquisition and possession in selected juvenile samples.* Washington, DC: U.S. Department of Justice, National Institute of Justice, Office of Juvenile Justice and Delinquency Prevention.

Singer, S. (1981). Homogenous victim-offender populations: A review and some research implications. *Journal of Criminal Law and Criminology, 72,* 779-788.

Singer, M., Anglin, T., Song, L., & Lunghofer, L. (1995). Adolescents' exposure to violence and associated symptoms of psychological trauma. *Journal of the American Medical Association, 273,* 477-482.

Skogan, W. (1986). Fear of crime and neighborhood change. In A. J. Reiss & M. Tonry (Eds.), *Communities and crime* (pp. 203-229). Chicago: University of Chicago Press.

Sparks, R. (1982). *Research on victims of crime.* Washington, DC: U.S. Government Printing Office.

Spergel, I. A. (1991). *Youth gangs: Problem and response.* Washington, DC: U.S. Department of Justice, Office of Juvenile Justice and Delinquency Prevention.

Spergel, I. A. (1995). *The youth gang problem: A community approach.* New York: Oxford University Press.

Steinberg, L. (1987). Familial factors in delinquency: A developmental perspective. *Journal of Adolescent Research, 2,* 255-268.

Steinberg, L. (1989). Pubertal maturation and family relations: Evidence for the distancing hypothesis. In G. Adams, R. Montemayor, & T. Gullotta (Eds.), *Advances in adolescent development* (Vol. 1, pp. 71-97). Newbury Park, CA: Sage.

Straus, M. (1994). *Violence in the lives of adolescents.* New York: Norton.

Tolan, P., & Guerra, N. (1994). *What works in reducing adolescent violence: An empirical review of the field.* Boulder, CO: Center for the Study and Prevention of Violence.

Tolan, P. H., Guerra, N. G., & Kendall, P. C. (1995). A developmental perspective on antisocial behavior in children and adolescents: Toward a unified risk and intervention framework. *Journal of Consulting and Clinical Psychology, 63,* 579-584.

Tolan, P. J., & Loeber, R. (1993). Antisocial behavior. In P. H. Tolan & B. J. Cohler (Eds.), *Handbook of clinical research and practice with adolescents* (pp. 307-331). New York: John Wiley.

Tremblay, R. E., Kurtz, L., Masse, L. C., Vitaro, F., & Phil, R. O. (1995). A bimodal preventive intervention for disruptive kindergarten boys: Its impact through adolescence. *Journal of Consulting and Clinical Psychology, 63,* 560-568.

Tremblay, R., Masse, B., Leblanc, M., Schwartzman, A. E., & Ledingham, J. E. (1992). Early disruptive behavior, poor school achievement, delinquent behavior, and delinquent personality: Longitudinal analyses. *Journal of Consulting and Clinical Psychology, 60,* 64-72.

Webster, D. W., Gainer, P. S., & Champion, H. R. (1994). Weapon carrying among inner-city junior high school students: Defensive behavior vs. aggressive delinquency. *American Journal of Public Health, 83,* 1604-1608.

Widom, C. S. (1989). The cycle of violence. *Science, 244,* 160-166.

Wilkinson, D. L., & Fagan, J. (1996). Understanding the role of firearm violence: They dynamics of gun events among adolescent males. *Law and Contemporary Problems, 59,* 55-90.

Wilson, W. J. (1987). *The truly disadvantaged: The inner city, the underclass and public policy.* Chicago: University of Chicago Press.

Yoshikawa, H. (1994). Prevention as cumulative protection: Effects of early family support and education on chronic delinquency and its risks. *Psychological Bulletin, 115,* 28-54.

8. A Comprehensive Review of Community-Based Approaches for the Treatment of Juvenile Offenders

Cassandra A. Stanton
Aleta L. Meyer

The treatment of juvenile offenders and the prevention of crimes committed by youths are pressing issues that have serious social and political ramifications. Reviews of the juvenile offender literature demonstrate equivocal findings that suggest a pessimistic view of the efficacy of traditional treatments, such as residential care or low-security incarceration (e.g., Mulvey, Arthur, & Reppucci, 1993). In contrast, it seems that community-based approaches to the treatment of juvenile offenders may have more potential for effecting long-term change in these difficult-to-treat youth (e.g., Tate, Reppucci, & Mulvey, 1995). Community-based programs offer several advantages above and beyond the traditional adult treatments that are often applied to juvenile offenders. First, juvenile offenders are adolescents—they are still children—and they should be treated differently from adults. Second, these children are products of the communities in which they live and deserve to have the community care for and be responsible for them. Third, incarcerated inmates, whether child or adult, learn strategies for being a more skilled criminal. A fourth advantage of community-based approaches is that they can be more cost-effective than institutional approaches. The question remains, however, as to whether or not community-based approaches that appear to make good sense actually result in the desired outcome of rehabilitating the youthful offender into a contributing member of the community.

This chapter will begin with a straightforward presentation of the desired outcomes of adolescence and a brief discussion of ecological perspectives on adolescent development. The second section will briefly review the history of treatment for juvenile offenders in the United States. A thorough examination of the effectiveness of community-based treatment approaches for juvenile offenders will then

be presented. Finally, those elements common to effective community-based programs will be summarized to provide suggestions for
the future development, implementation, and evaluation of these
interventions.

ECOLOGICAL PERSPECTIVES
ON ADOLESCENT DEVELOPMENT

In 1977, Bronfenbrenner challenged those who sought to understand child development to move outside of the laboratory into
real-world settings. He offered the following description of the field:
"The science of the strange behavior of children in strange situations
with strange adults for the briefest periods of time" (Bronfenbrenner,
1977, p. 513). Bronfenbrenner's contribution to the field did not end
with that challenge; instead, he offered a model of human development in context that has set the tone for the profession. This ecological
model delineates four interrelated types of settings or systems:

MICROSYSTEM: the complex of relationships between the developing person and the environment in an immediate setting containing
the person (e.g., family, peer group, school)

MESOSYSTEM: the interrelations among major settings containing
the developing person at a particular point in his or her life (e.g.,
family-school, peer group-family)

EXOSYSTEM: an extension of the mesosystem embracing specific
social structures, both formal and informal, that do not themselves
contain the developing person but impinge upon or encompass the
immediate setting in which the person is found, and thereby delimit,
influence, or even determine what goes on there (e.g., impact of work
on children in families, local and state governments)

MACROSYSTEM: the system of cultural values and beliefs as well as
historical events (e.g., wars, hurricanes, changes in national leadership), both of which may affect the other ecological systems. (Bronfenbrenner, 1977, p. 515)

In other words, individuals are viewed as being nested within a
complex of interconnected systems that encompasses individual,

family, and extrafamilial (peer, school, neighborhood) factors. Behavior is viewed as the result of a reciprocal interplay between the child and these systems and the relations of the systems to each other.

A specific application of this model to adolescent development was outlined by Hill (1983). In this model, adolescents are influenced by three forces of change (biological, cognitive, and social transitions) within four specific contexts (family, school, peer group, and work). Ideally, the contexts in which adolescents develop support a successful transition into adulthood, whereby the young adult is competent to carry out the following three roles simultaneously and responsibly—that of citizen, worker, and procreator (Garbarino, 1982). Given that these desired outcomes (that adolescents become responsible citizens, workers, and family members) do not happen at the rate we would like (e.g., Lerner, 1995; Task Force, 1989), efforts designed to address juvenile delinquency must go above and beyond getting the youth "back on track" with other youth.

One specific illustration is that of the school-to-work transition, in which the youth's attainment of the role of responsible worker is considered one of the primary goals of adulthood. According to Glover and Marshall (1993), "America has the worst approach to school-to-work transition of any industrialized nation" (p. 588). Schools prepare youth inadequately for the modern day world of work, where the ability to work in groups and apply higher-order thinking to new problems and information is required (Task Force, 1989; William T. Grant Foundation, 1988). Ideally, a society provides clarity and continuity for the transition to adulthood via explicit markers of the attainment of adult status and experiences throughout childhood and adolescence that prepare the youth for future rights and responsibilities (Benedict, 1943). Such a transition can promote strong bonds between youth and society's institutions that, according to social control theory (Gottfredson & Hirschi, 1990), provide the necessary groundwork for prosocial behavior. Perhaps a critical contributing factor to why some youth learn to behave in socially irresponsible ways is our society's failure to adequately facilitate transition to adulthood roles or provide strong bonds between youth and larger social institutions.

An extremely useful enhancement of Bronfenbrenner's social ecology model for considering the transition to adulthood is the developmental contextualism framework (e.g., Ford & Lerner, 1992; Lerner, 1995). According to this framework, when the adolescent transition results in poor developmental outcomes (i.e., adolescents are not successfully transitioning to the roles of worker, citizen, and family member/procreator), there is a lack of fit between individuals and their context (Lerner & Lerner, 1987). In terms of the focus of this chapter, when a youth becomes involved in the justice system and is described as a juvenile offender in need of treatment, something has not gone well with the developmental process. The unique contribution of this framework is its focus on the individual differences that result from interactions between individuals and unique environments (i.e., diversity) as well as its focus on the ways in which youth cocreate their own environments (e.g., their family, their peer group, their school, their treatment program; Lerner, 1982, 1991). This attention to the ways in which diversity and context interact to create a level of "goodness of fit" provides a standard for determining which interventions work best with which individuals (Lerner, 1995). These issues, of goodness of fit and of how to promote a positive transition to adulthood for juvenile offenders, will be revisited toward the end of the chapter.

REVIEW OF TREATMENT APPROACHES

Traditional approaches to therapy have tended to target the individual and focus on unidimensional attempts to implement behavior change. Although these individual therapeutic approaches have been the strategies used most frequently for treating delinquents in general both within institutions and in the community, they have not been demonstrated to be effective in strong controlled studies with juvenile offenders (Mulvey et al., 1993; Tate et al., 1995). Approaches that take a social-ecological perspective and focus on multiple systems and techniques to address behavior, cognition, and attitude may be more effective in eliciting significant change that will last (e.g., Henggeler & Borduin, 1995; Henggeler, Melton, & Smith, 1992; Henggeler, Schoenwald, & Pickrel, 1995; Scherer, Brondino, Henggeler, Melton, & Hanley, 1994).

The history of treating juvenile offenders can be traced back to the 19th century, when such youths were placed in refuge homes and often treated inhumanely (Basta & Davidson, 1988). The idea was that punishment and segregation served to rehabilitate the youth and protect society. Flowers (1990) summarized arguments for and against this traditional approach that suggest even today that there are many who argue that placing adolescents, particularly habitual and violent delinquent offenders, in correctional facilities may both deter and punish teenage crime. However, others argue that institutionalizing youth may do more harm than good, resulting in the treatment of teenagers as criminals rather than as minors, depriving them of normal familial and environmental settings, stigmatizing them with a lasting label, and socializing them toward delinquent and criminal habits. Although theoretical and political arguments continue to address these issues, neither of these positions has received adequate empirical support (e.g., Mulvey et al., 1993). The following sections present an empirically based review of various strategies for treating the juvenile offender, from residential to cognitive-behavioral to innovative treatment programs.

Residential Treatment Programs

The passage of the Juvenile Justice and Prevention Act of 1974 marked the beginning of a major federal effort to prohibit the incarceration of juvenile offenders in jails, detention centers, correctional facilities, and other institutional settings (Kobrin & Klein, 1983). As an alternative to placing juveniles in training schools and adult institutions, community-based and diversionary correctional programs gained popularity as more humane, cost-effective alternatives for rehabilitating youth (Flowers, 1990). In addition, residential treatment programs and community-based corrections for juvenile offenders provide an alternative living arrangement for youths whose home environments are unsafe or inappropriate. These programs include foster care placements or group homes that provide a supportive living arrangement with adult supervision and often mandated treatment.

In the 1960s and 1970s, the trend toward deinstitutionalization led to group home treatment programs gaining popularity as a form of residential treatment for adolescents who had experienced behavioral problems and needed more intensive treatment and supervision than could be provided in a foster care home (Haghighi & Lopez, 1993). Group homes generally consist of approximately 10 to 20 youths who live together under the guidance of house parents (residential staff workers and counselors). Unlike many alternatives for juveniles, group homes provide a family-type atmosphere where the youth and house parents often establish familial ties. Stewart, Vockell, and Ray (1986) traced 906 juvenile offenders during a 3-year period and found that there was a significant reduction in the recidivism rates of juvenile offenders who had been in a family-type atmosphere group home. In other words, it seems that the creation of a more functional microsystem (a group home to replace the family) might be a promising component of efforts to treat juvenile offenders.

The Teaching Family Model, developed at Achievement Place in Kansas, has been one of the most tested and modeled residential treatment programs for youthful offenders. Achievement Place itself is a collection of family-style homes, each managed by a specially trained married couple (teaching parents) who teach specific programs and skills. A behavior change program is employed as a merit system. Several evaluations of the Teaching Family homes have found that they significantly reduce residents' delinquent behavior and substance use compared to youths in other group homes (Braukmann et al., 1987; Kirigan, Braukmann, Atwater, & Wolf, 1982). Cross-cultural replication of success with the Teaching Family Model in The Netherlands showed similar improvements in social competence and decreases in delinquent behavior (Slot, Jagers, & Dangel, 1992). However, nearly all evaluations indicate that behavioral improvements disappear once the youths have left the home (Braukmann et al., 1987; Kirigan et al., 1982). Thus, it appears that the Achievement Place model is successful in reducing offending while the youth is present in the newly formed microsystem, but that this success does not always transfer to the community when the youth has returned to the previously established environment.

More recently, Haghighi and Lopez (1993) examined the efficacy of a group home treatment program in reforming juvenile offenders. The treatment program included a therapeutic living community, involvement in community services projects, employment assistance, athletic activities, and educational and vocational activities. Of the 152 reviewed cases that had gone through the program, 95 adolescents successfully completed the group home treatment program and did not appear in the juvenile justice system within a 2-year period. The remaining 57 juveniles had been referred to another agency or had committed a subsequent crime. Apparently, addressing more than one microsystem and the relationships between those systems had a positive impact. In addition, the efficacy of the group home program in decreasing recidivism was found to be enhanced in cases where the first occasion of intervention was in the early stages of delinquent behavior and in those without a history of time served in state detention facilities.

As an innovative alternative to residential placement or detention, Raider (1994) examined whether electronic monitoring of juveniles in their communities would provide a more humane and cost-effective means of detention. The program used electronic monitoring for 21 juveniles in their homes and was positively regarded by the youth and family members. Its efficacy as a treatment approach has yet to be demonstrated. However, electronic monitoring offers a mechanism for maintaining juveniles in their communities with their families while simultaneously providing treatment and services to both the offender and his or her family. While this option does not have the potential benefit of temporarily replacing a dysfunctional environment with one that is more functional, it does have the benefit of continuity over time.

Diversionary Programs

Diversionary programs are another commonly used, noninstitutional alternative for dealing with juvenile delinquents (Flowers, 1990). Juveniles are diverted from the juvenile justice system by police, the courts, and agencies outside the system. Police diversion programs, informal probation, runaway shelters, and alternative schools seek to educate and work with troubled youths outside the formal process of the juvenile court. One type of diversion program involves inmates in a penitentiary setting sharing real-life accounts of prison life as a form of deterrence. Despite their popularity and simplicity, prisoner-run delinquency prevention programs have not been found to be efficacious in reducing recidivism rates (Locke, Johnson, Kirigin-Kamp, Atwar, & Gerrard, 1986). For example, Cook and Spirrison (1992) evaluated the effects of a nonconfrontational, prisoner-run, juvenile delinquency program and found that participation in the prison-based program did not reduce the recidivism risk of the 97 adjudicated juvenile delinquent males. However, adolescents attending the program were significantly less likely to drop out of school than were the 79 adjudicated juvenile delinquent controls. Although recidivism may not have been affected by this deterrence program, this approach may effectively address one part of the total system and act to deter certain aspects of delinquent behavior. Future research is needed to examine the efficacy of an educational approach in conjunction with other methods.

Probation and Aftercare

Probation refers to a juvenile court disposition imposed on an adjudicated delinquent by a judge and is the most common sentence ordered by the juvenile court (Flowers, 1990). Contingent upon following some restriction and conditions imposed by the court, probation enables juvenile offenders to remain within their community under the official supervision of a probation officer. Although it may be beneficial to maintain the youth in their natural environments, it may not provide the necessary additional intervention and support. Similar to electronic monitoring, probation may not have the desired long-term effects for deterring and inhibiting future offenses (e.g., Jackson, 1982).

Aftercare is the juvenile justice system's synonym for parole and refers to the release of juveniles from the institutional setting and the support services provided for the youths' transition back into the community (Flowers, 1990). Aftercare programs serve a dual role of supervising high-risk parolees and providing services to facilitate their readjustment to community living. Intensive probation supervision is a popular form of aftercare that is used with both adults and juveniles to provide frequent and intense contact between the probation officer and the youth. Although there are few systematic evaluations of intensive probation programs for juveniles, Barton and Butts (1990) found that adolescent offenders assigned to a community aftercare group showed no higher rates of rearrest or self-reported delinquency than other forms of probation programs. Furthermore, a cost analysis indicated that institutional placements were approximately three times more expensive than community supervision.

Cognitive-Behavioral Interventions

Cognitive-behavioral approaches assume that an angry, aggressive state is mediated through a person's expectations and appraisals, and that the likelihood of violence is increased or decreased as a result of this cognitive process along with a learning history that reinforces antisocial behaviors (Tate et al., 1995). These intervention programs tend to focus on skill building, social skills training, anger management, and problem solving. Although cognitive-behavioral treatment programs have been found to be effective, treatment gains appear to be more promising in those programs that combine a strong ecological approach with cognitive-behavioral training, individualized contracts, and family therapy (Bank, Marlowe, Reid, & Patterson, 1991; Guerra & Slaby, 1990; Hagan & Robert, 1992; Howell & Enns, 1995). Furthermore, a meta-analysis of more than 400 juvenile program evaluations found that behavioral, skill-oriented, and multimodal methods produced the largest effects and that positive effects were in the community rather than institutional settings (Lipsey, 1992).

Anger management/social skills training. The most well-studied example of social skills training is aggression replacement therapy, a multimodal, psychoeducational intervention that can be used with aggressive juveniles in institutions, schools, mental health clinics, or other community-based organizations (Glick & Goldstein, 1987). The intervention program includes a psychoeducational curriculum of prosocial behaviors, anger control training, and moral reasoning training. The multimodal approach of aggression replacement training has been found to increase constructive prosocial behaviors, but its effectiveness for reducing violent or criminal behavior has yet to be determined (Tate et al., 1995). Other programs that use cognitive-behavioral and anger management techniques within a community, school-based setting to effect change in the antisocial behavior of at-risk youth have been found to directly decrease problematic behavior (Larson, 1992).

Cognitive problem-solving interventions. One of the more promising approaches to the treatment of antisocial aggression is based on a social cognitive development model that suggests that aggressive behavior patterns result from both external social events experienced by the juvenile and his or her constitutional propensities (e.g., cognitive resources; Guerra & Slaby, 1990). Guerra and Slaby (1990) designed a 12-session intervention program based on this model to remediate cognitive factors identified as correlates of aggression. One hundred and twenty male and female adolescents incarcerated for aggression offenses participated in either the cognitive mediation training program, an attention control group, or a no-treatment control group. Results indicated that juveniles who received the cognitive mediation training showed increased skills in solving social problems; decreased endorsement of beliefs supporting aggression; and decreased aggressive, impulsive, and inflexible behaviors. However, there were no significant differences in recidivism rates between the groups that got the cognitive treatment and those that did not receive treatment. These results suggest initial support for the use of cognitive mediation training in altering the social behavior of adolescent offenders. However, the small magnitude of the cognitive and behavior change produced suggests that this specific intervention may be more effective when used in conjunction with other interventions that address the external social events that play a role in the etiology of antisocial behavior.

Social System Treatment Interventions

Peer group interventions. Guided-group interaction (GGI) and its derivatives (e.g., positive peer culture, peer group counseling, and peer culture development) have been widely used in school and residential settings to prevent or decrease delinquent behavior (Gottfredson, 1987). The GGI treatment model consists of daily group discussions aimed at confronting and censuring negative behavior and supporting and reinforcing positive behavior. Unfortunately, evaluations of school-based programs using GGI derivatives have been described as methodologically flawed and have not provided evidence that this approach to treatment is effective (Gottfredson, 1987). Henggeler (1989) hypothesized that these programs have been ineffective because they work primarily with artificially created peer groups rather than the offenders' actual friendship network. Broad-based interventions that emphasize change in the adolescents' natural environment, including peer relations in the community, have been shown to be more efficacious (Borduin et al., 1995; Henggeler & Borduin, 1995).

Restitution and mediation. Restitution is a community-based treatment approach that requires the juvenile offender to pay the victim directly to compensate for his or her loss, perform a useful service to the victim, and/or perform a comparable amount of public service. In addition, mediation between the offender and victim can be a component of the restitution program. Schneider (1986) examined the recidivism rates at four random-assignment experiments conducted simultaneously in four communities. The results showed that restitution may have a small but important effect on recidivism. In two of the four studies, the juveniles in restitution had fewer recontracts with the court during the 2- to 3-year follow-up. Schneider concluded that the mechanism of the positive effect might be attributed to processes such as reduced stigmatization, greater understanding of the effects of the crime on the victim, deterrence, and more intense supervision.

More recently, Roy (1993) compared the effectiveness of a Victim Offender Reconciliation Program for juvenile offenders operated in Indiana with a juvenile probate court-administered restitution program in Michigan. Effectiveness was measured according to the impact of the two programs on offender repayments to their victims and on offender recidivism. Both programs were equally effective in rates of successful completion of restitution contracts, and there were no differences between the samples in rates of offender recidivism during the 2-year follow-up period. Offenders with prior offense records were more likely to commit further offenses despite participation in either type of restitution program. These results suggest that although restitution may be effective with some populations, additional forms of treatment may be needed to address the complex histories of repeat offenders.

The New Mexico Center for Dispute Resolution has developed a service continuum of mediation and conflict resolution programs for children, youth, and families and has demonstrated that these programs can be effective in responding to some of the needs of at-risk juveniles and their families (Smith, 1995). At this center, a continuum of services is provided for youth and families at risk for involvement in the juvenile justice system. The underlying goal of the program is to equip youth and their families with basic communication and conflict resolution skills; model alternatives to violence; and improve youth functioning in the environments of home, school, and community. Smith (1995) suggests that youth exposed to mediation and conflict resolution at each stage of their development have the potential to build a foundation for lifelong social and interpersonal skills. Thus, the use of mediation may contribute to the establishment of new norms of social interaction. Although the efficacy of the Victim-Juvenile Offender Mediation Program has not yet been demonstrated, this comprehensive package of prevention, education, skills building, mediation, and restitution directed at offenders and their families may prove to be an effective means of preventing recidivism and treating troubled youth, given its attention to individual differences and context.

Multimodal Treatment Approaches

Comprehensive prevention, intervention, and rehabilitation programs in community settings have been designed for groups of high-risk, sentenced, delinquent youths. For example, Stein et al. (1992) evaluated the effectiveness of the Colorado OSAP Project, a community-based, unsecured, residential project that works in conjunction with multiagencies to provide effective education, drug-free alternatives, prosocial bonding, self-competency development, and transitions skills to juvenile offenders. Thirty juveniles were interviewed at intake and release. Although there were individual successes, the group did not change significantly over time. Similarly, Wooldredge, Hartman, Latessa, and Holmes (1994) investigated whether a community program created specifically for male, African American, juvenile felons was more effective than community supervision alone for preventing recidivism. Participating youths were 160 community program clients and 160 regular probationers. Results indicated that the community program did no better than regular probation for preventing recidivism among these juveniles. Still, despite these discouraging results, broadly based and individually tailored interventions have been suggested as the most promising direction for the treatment of juvenile offenders (Mulvey et al., 1993). In support of this position, empirical evidence from a multisystemic approach strongly suggests that certain comprehensive interventions show the promise of success (Tate et al., 1995).

Multisystemic therapy. Multisystemic therapy (MST; Henggeler & Borduin, 1990) is a family-based, therapeutic approach that is viewed by many as the most promising treatment for reducing the number of incarcerated youth and remediating their antisocial behavior with a cost-effective strategy (Tate et al., 1995). In fact, MST is the only treatment program to date that has demonstrated short- and long-term efficacy with chronic, serious, and violent juvenile offenders with well-controlled studies (e.g., Borduin et al., 1995; Henggeler et al., 1995; Henggeler, Schoenwald, Pickrel, Rowland, & Santos, 1994).

MST interventions are child-focused, family-centered, and directed toward solving multiple problems across the numerous contexts in which youths are embedded (family, peers, schools, and neighborhood). Based on a combined theoretical foundation of so-cial-ecological and family systems models, services are provided in home and community settings to enhance cooperation and promote generalization. Consistent with Bronfenbrenner's (1979) theory of social ecology, Henggeler and Borduin (1990) describe individuals as being nested within a complex of interconnected systems that encom-pass individual, family, and extrafamilial (peer, school, neighbor-hood) factors. The multisystemic therapy approach posits that be-havior problems can be maintained by problematic transactions within any given system or between some combination of pertinent systems. Therefore, the treatment approach is not limited to interven-tions within the family but encourages treatment of problems in other systems as needed. The MST approach emphasizes the impor-tance of working within the context of the child's environment and developmental level with intervention techniques that are not neces-sarily systemic (e.g., cognitive-behavioral therapy, parent training; Henggeler & Borduin, 1990). Interventions are tailored to the specific needs of the adolescent, the family, and surrounding systems.

Henggeler et al. (1992) studied the efficacy of MST delivered through a community mental health center as compared with usual services offered by the Department of Youth Services in the treatment of 84 serious juvenile offenders and their multiproblem families. Offenders were randomly assigned to treatment conditions. In com-parison with youths who had received usual services, youths who had received MST had fewer arrests and self-reported offenses, and they spent an average of 10 fewer weeks incarcerated, according to archival data at posttreatment assessment. In addition, families in the MST condition reported increased family cohesion and decreased youth aggression in peer relations. Whereas MST was found to be significantly more effective than usual services in this study, it was also found to be far more cost-effective. The cost per client for treatment in the MST group was approximately $2,800, as compared to the estimated cost of $16,300 for the average course of institutional treatment. Furthermore, long-term follow-up at 2.4 years demon-strated the capacity of MST to interrupt criminal careers and main-tain reduced arrest rates (Henggeler, Melton, Smith, Schoenwald, & Hanley, 1993). In an even more impressive investigation, Borduin et al. (1995) examined the long-term effects of MST versus individual therapy on the prevention of criminal behavior of 176 juvenile of-fenders. Results from a multiagent and multimethod assessment indicated MST to be more effective than individual therapy in reducing antisocial behavior. In addition, results of a 4-year follow-up indicated MST to be more effective at reducing re-arrest rates than was individual treatment.

Moreover, MST has been found to be effective across cultural, regional, and treatment setting variables. Scherer et al. (1994) conducted MST with rural African American and Caucasian families who had chronic or violent adolescents at imminent risk for incarceration. Preliminary findings from The Diffusion of Multisystemic Family Preservation Services Project (MFP) indicated improvements in the amount of problem behavior and mother psychological distress. Results were consistent with the previous success MST has shown in the treatment of serious juvenile offenders in urban areas (Henggeler et al., 1993). Furthermore, despite its origin in early clinical trials to deliver home-based services through a university-based setting, MST has demonstrated success in community settings because it explicitly bridges the gap between university-based psychotherapy studies and dissemination into community-based programs (Henggeler et al., 1995). MST's emphasis on the delivery of empirically based interventions through theoretically based and highly individualized, flexible, and comprehensive strategies makes it the most promising treatment available for the complex problems of youthful offenders.

Innovative Community-Based Treatments

Additional alternative treatment approaches are emerging that use innovative techniques for skill building and rehabilitation. Adventure-based counseling models are a new trend that is based in social-ecological models of working within a positive environment to build self-esteem, learn interpersonal skills, and model prosocial behavior. Gillia and Simpson (1991) studied 29 adolescents involved in Project Choices, an adventure-based, 8-week residential treatment program for drug-abusing adjudicated adolescents. Although methodologically fairly weak, there was some evidence that the program had a positive effect.

Fashimpar (1991) compared the effectiveness over 2 years of two traditional approaches to rehabilitating delinquents (probation vs. probation and recreation) with an innovative minibike club. The minibike club was based on ecological and behavioral systems models of treatment and included bike maintenance, minibike trail riding, and group meetings. The effectiveness of all three treatment programs were compared to a control group of delinquents with regard to criminal offenses, status offenses, grade point average (GPA), school absences, and self-esteem. Results show that the minibike club offered the greatest potential for rehabilitating delinquents. Social group approaches to rehabilitation appear to have promise as effective alternatives to treatment as compared to probation casework or the deterrent effect of arrest. This is a novel approach to using a positive social environment as a means for behavior and attitude change.

Summary of Community-Based Treatment Approaches

The empirical literature on interventions with juvenile offenders traditionally has been hampered by methodological flaws. These flaws include a lack of understanding of how programs were implemented differently in various sites, small sample sizes, a lack of comparison and control groups, an overemphasis on the outcome of the treatment program, and a lack of understanding of how previously examined interventions function once disseminated. In contrast, recent research on multisystemic therapy offers a promising treatment for these complex and difficult-to-treat problems in children and adolescents. Not only is this approach embedded in the juvenile offender's multiple contexts, it is also intrinsic to the priorities of the cultural contexts of academia and applied settings. As has been demonstrated through efforts to improve school-based prevention programs as well as *many* program evaluations (Guba & Lincoln, 1989), a respect for the priorities of the members of multiple settings results in the best outcomes for youth (Meyer, Miller, & Herman, 1993).

COMMUNITY-BASED TREATMENT APPROACHES AND THE ADOLESCENT TRANSITION

The preceding review of community-based approaches to the treatment of the juvenile offender reinforces the value of using an ecological perspective. As was demonstrated by the available research on the effectiveness of residential, diversionary, and probation programs for juvenile delinquents, not only do these efforts cost more and produce fewer desirable outcomes, it is hard to understand how they might contribute to the positive socialization of youth toward adulthood. In contrast, another way of summarizing the goals of a multisystemic approach is to determine what is necessary to promote the goodness of fit between an individual adolescent and the contexts of his or her development. In addition, the review demonstrated how treatments that do not include the long-term systems and settings with which the juvenile interacts produce only short-term effects, if any at all.

Interestingly, an important component of the solution to the problem of juvenile offenders appears to be the construction of valued connections between the adolescent and social institutions such as family, school, and community—a virtual mirror of the social control theory of deviance, whereby individuals who do not have strong bonds to society's institutions act in unconventional and deviant ways (Gottfredson & Hirschi, 1990). Moreover, the particular strategies used in the various treatment modalities (e.g., problem solving, anger management, mediation, and restitution) are made up of knowledge, attitudes, and skills necessary for being responsible workers, citizens, and family members. For example, model citizens choose nonviolent means of communication (mediation) and take responsibility for their own actions (restitution); responsible procreators communicate respectfully with their family members (anger management) and think ahead to the consequences of various options in a potentially sexual situation (problem solving). Community approaches to treatment may be most effective in rehabilitating youthful offenders to the extent to which treatment approaches are adapted specifically for the strengths and weaknesses of individual adolescents and their developmental contexts (Lipsey, 1992). Furthermore, the success of an intervention ultimately may lie in the extent to which the adolescent's existing systems can be altered to support the youth's choice to cocreate his or her future life in a responsible manner.

Understanding the effectiveness of juvenile offender treatment modalities and finding cost-effective ways of measuring treatment success is difficult. However, until evaluation efforts move beyond measuring program outcomes such as "reduced recidivism" and "weeks incarcerated," advances in the field will be limited. By focusing on these outcomes, it is not possible to discern whether youth in various programs who have lower recidivism rates are actually contributing to society in positive ways or instead have simply become more skilled at not getting caught when engaged in criminal activity. Evaluation efforts that include outcome measures such as education level, employment status, and parent status would greatly enhance the knowledge base in this area. If the expectation of treatment outcome goes beyond reducing offenses and advances to maximizing each adolescent's adaptive development, then we may have the potential to not only reduce the number of criminals but also to increase the number of functional and productive members in our communities.

FUTURE TRENDS

Although methodological flaws in much of the existing treatment literature for juvenile offenders limits the extent to which conclusive remarks can be made, comprehensive social programs that include treatment strategies targeting the systems that affect the juvenile's development appear to be the most promising. Solid research on the efficacy of these treatment packets is well underway and suggests that a multisystemic approach is the trend for the future (Borduin et al., 1995; Henggeler et al., 1992; Scherer et al., 1994). Furthermore, innovative programs that are finding creative ways to intervene in the development of criminality and to encourage, educate, and promote healthy reconciliation with the community are gaining popularity (Fashimpar, 1991; Gillia & Simpson, 1991). However, in order to begin examining the efficacy of these new treatment trends, advances in program evaluation are essential. Despite growing empirical knowledge, solid and controlled evaluations of social programs for juveniles are needed to determine the direction of the field and provide concrete evidence to promote these treatment trends. An investment of funds at the level of evaluation ultimately will provide the government and justice systems with evidence as to which social programs are the most cost-effective.

Some in the field of social program evaluation have been proponents of comparing the effectiveness of various social programs and selecting the best from that pool to be disseminated widely in a fashion similar to the *Consumer Reports* approach to product evaluation (Scriven, 1981). In contrast, after spending time working within the system of change in social programs, others (e.g., Weiss, 1988) have come to argue that "once initiated, they [social programs] seem to have lives of their own [sic]" (Shadish, Cook, & Leviton, 1991, p. 105). With these two positions in mind, that of disseminating only the most effective interventions and that of recognizing how change within social programs is a complex and time-consuming process, suggestions for future directions in community-based treatment will be made. These suggestions focus on where to prioritize resources for present and future programming.

Grounded in the empirical findings of the excessively high cost of residential treatment settings compared to the cost of community-based efforts, our primary suggestion for present programming is to move away from the punishment model of institutional treatment and move toward strategies that are comprehensive and take into account issues specifically related to adolescence. For example, according to Camp and Camp (1993), it cost $105.27 per day in 1992 to house a youth in a correctional facility. In contrast, the per diem cost of MST in 1994 was only $31.43 (Henggeler et al., 1992). Making similar comparisons between the cost of institutionalization and intensive supervision programs, Barton and Butts (1990) found that over the course of 4 years (from 1983 to 1986), the State of Michigan was able to avoid $11.5 million in additional costs that would have been spent on institutionalization (had all eligible juvenile offenders been placed in such settings). Given the fact that MST has been found to be more effective than institutionalization (Tate et al., 1995) and that intensive supervision is no better or worse than institutionalization (Barton & Butts, 1990), there is strong support for the idea that community-based efforts can reduce costs related to recidivism (i.e., court costs, additional time in incarceration, victim costs).

Many questions remain unanswered with regard to what constitutes the best community-based strategies for the future. These questions include, but are not limited to, the following:

- What is the comparative impact of each strategy in terms of reducing negative behavior (e.g., recidivism) and increasing positive behavior (e.g., level of education, employment status)?
- What are the important differences and similarities in program impact across gender, ethnicity, and socioeconomic status?
- Which strategies are most effective for which individuals in which contexts?

- How does the juvenile offender cocreate the therapeutic environment?
- How can our understanding of the treatment of the juvenile offender inform prevention strategies?

The preceding review of the literature indicated that the most fruitful endeavors for understanding how to effectively treat the juvenile offender with community-based approaches combined individually tailored, comprehensive strategies with rigorous evaluation (e.g., the evaluations of MST). Thus, it might seem that the only way to conduct program evaluation in the future is to try to replicate these intensive research strategies. Although the outcomes of such evaluation can help set the standard for the field (in terms of community-based approaches to the treatment of juvenile offenders), it is unrealistic and undesirable for each and every local community to attempt such extensive inquiry. Expectations for local programs to muster the expertise and resources necessary for such evaluations can be immobilizing and can lead to an abandonment of any type of evaluation. Because the very process of evaluation improves program implementation (Gottfredson, 1984), it is unwise to intimidate local communities by requesting overly comprehensive evaluation. Instead, the future trends for improving the state-of-the-art, community-based treatment approaches for the juvenile offender include two evaluation tracks: (a) evaluation for the purpose of guiding theory and setting the standard of best practices for the field, and (b) evaluation for the purpose of enhancing program replication, adaptation, and implementation in local settings.

Evaluations to Guide Theory and Set the Standard for Best Practices

Since Lewin's (1946) introduction of the action research paradigm, many models have been developed to help manifest his vision of a cyclical process of problem definition, fact finding, theory building and goal setting, action, and evaluation that leads to problem redefinition, and so forth. Two of those models, one focused on university-community collaborations and another that evolved from a combination of action research with organizational development methods to promote community collaboration, will be presented here. Both of these models have the capacity to not only help design and refine efforts but to inform our understanding of the development of delinquency as well as the development of adolescents in general.

In Lerner's (1995) guidebook addressing the program and policy needs of *America's Youth in Crisis,* which was sponsored by the National 4-H Council, he outlines the mission of the American Land Grant University as teaching, research, and service. Given this mission, universities are in an optimal position to collaborate with local communities. Lerner (1995) continues with a step-by-step guide as to how developmental contextualism can guide this collaboration and inform our understanding of human development in context. This type of collaboration can facilitate understanding about which interventions work best with which individuals (e.g., gender and cultural differences) as well as understanding about how juvenile offenders affect the program environment itself.

Another model for applied research evolved from the need to form a common language and mode of operation for research and applied settings. This model, called Program Development Evaluation (PDE), was developed by Gottfredson (1984) and designed to stimulate researcher-implementer collaboration. Through a combination of organizational development strategies and action research, PDE facilitates a process that allows researchers to state their theoretical rationale in a way that is (a) sensible to those implementing programs and (b) consistent with research and evaluation.

Evaluations to Enhance Replication,
Modification, and Implementation

Implied, but not explicitly stated, is the fact that progress in treating the juvenile offender demands as much change from the individuals and systems who implement the programs as it does from those served by the programs. Even though change will likely result in positive outcomes, many of the stakeholders in this field, as in any field, will want to maintain the status quo. Therefore, small-scale evaluations that help promote buy-in and accountability from local efforts are the most promising. Moreover, given that MST is being found to be very cost effective, local programs may begin to receive support from their local governments to change. If this saved money can be transformed into benefits such as (a) being able to provide appropriate services for all those who need them, (b) being able to improve the retention of direct-service providers through competitive salaries, (c) being able to provide more staff training, and (d) being able to address issues that can reduce staff burnout, then the process of changing services may be easier. In other words, for programs to be replicated with integrity as well as adapted to the needs of the local community, evaluation must be user-friendly.

This goal, to make evaluation user-friendly and useful, has guided the Empowerment Evaluation special interest group within the American Evaluation Association. Through processes that increase the self-awareness and accountability of agencies, empowerment evaluation can facilitate quality program implementation at minimal cost (Fetterman, Kaftarian, & Wandersman, 1996). One particularly empowering evaluation technique is that of Concept-Mapping and Pattern-Matching, computer software that evolved from rigorous multidimensional scaling methods (Trochim, 1989). This system flows from brainstorming to action plans, using the input of as many stakeholders as desired. Although the action plan may look similar to those developed by other working groups, because it evolves from the individual working group, it can have greater meaning to those involved. In addition to providing an action plan, the software provides simple means for determining the degree to which action plan strategies are met over time. These resources are just a few of many available to agencies that treat juvenile offenders who are attempting internal change.

CONCLUDING REMARKS

As the introductory comments argued, and as supported by the empirical information presented, community-based strategies to treat juvenile offenders make the most sense. It is vital that in addition to treating the adolescent offender, we provide education, counseling, and support to the various systems (e.g., family, school, peers) that affect the adolescent. Removing troubled youth from their communities to punish them, protect others, or rehabilitate in an artificial or controlled environment does not take into account the developmental needs of the adolescent or the larger social issues. Treatment effects gained in a residential or institutional setting are often lost when the adolescent is returned to a dysfunctional environment that has not received intervention. By implementing change in the systems within the juvenile's community, a supportive environment can be formed to rehabilitate the targeted offender and potentially maximize the healthy development of other children affected by those systems. The treatment of juvenile offenders should move away from the punishment model of controlling criminality and concentrate on developing, implementing, and evaluating comprehensive social programs that seek to build communities that support the adaptive and prosocial development of all children. Although such progress will require great effort, the futures of our children and our communities are worth the investment of our best research efforts and commitment to social change.

REFERENCES

Bank, L., Marlowe, J. H., Reid, J. B., & Patterson, G. R. (1991). A comparative evaluation of parent-training interventions for families of chronic delinquents. *Journal of Abnormal Child Psychology, 19*, 15-33.

Barton, W. H., & Butts, J. A. (1990). Viable options: Intensive supervision programs for juvenile delinquents. *Crime & Delinquency, 36*, 238-256.

Basta, J. M., & Davidson, W. S. (1988). Treatment of juvenile offenders: Study outcomes since 1980. *Behavioral Science & the Law, 6*, 355-384.

Benedict, R. (1943). *Patterns of culture.* Boston: Houghton Mifflin.

Borduin, C. M., Mann, B. J., Cone, L. T., Henggeler, S. W., Fucci, B. R., Blaske, D. M., & Williams, R. A. (1995). Multisystemic treatment of serious juvenile offenders: Long-term prevention of criminality and violence. *Journal of Consulting and Clinical Psychology, 63*, 569-578.

Braukmann, C. J., & Wolfe, M. M. (1987). Behaviorally based group homes for juvenile offenders. In E. K. Morris & C. J. Braukmann (Eds.), *Behavioral approaches to crime and delinquency: A handbook of application, research, and concepts* (pp. 135-159). New York: Plenum.

Bronfenbrenner, U. (1977). Toward an experimental ecology of human development. *American Psychologist, 32*, 513-531.

Bronfenbrenner, U. (1979). *The ecology of human development.* Cambridge, MA: Harvard University Press.

Camp, G. M., & Camp, C. G. (1993). *The corrections yearbook.* South Salem, NY: Criminal Justice Institute.

Cook, D. D., & Spirrison, C. L. (1992). Effects of a prisoner-operated delinquency deterrence program: Mississippi's Project Aware. *Journal of Offender Rehabilitation, 17*, 89-99.

Fashimpar, G. A. (1991). From probation to mini-bikes: A comparison of traditional and innovative programs for community treatment of delinquent adolescents. *Social Work With Groups, 14*, 105-118.

Flowers, R. B. (1990). *The adolescent criminal: An examination of today's juvenile offender.* Jefferson, NC: McFarland.

Ford, D., & Lerner, R. (1992). *Developmental systems theory: An integrative approach.* Newbury Park, CA: Sage.

Garbarino, J. (1982). *Children and families in the social environment.* Hawthorne, NY: Aldine.

Gillia, H. L., & Simpson, C. (1991). Project Choices: Adventure-based residential drug treatment for court-referred youth. *Journal of Addictions and Offender Counseling, 12,* 12-27.

Glick, B., & Goldstein, A. P. (1987). Aggression replacement training. *Journal of Counseling and Development, 65,* 356-362.

Glover, R., & Marshall, R. (1993). Improving the school-to-work transition of American adolescents. *Teachers College Record, 94,* 588-610.

Gottfredson, G. (1984). A theory-ridden approach to program evaluation: A method for stimulating researcher-implementer collaboration. *American Psychologist, 39,* 1101-1112.

Gottfredson, G. D. (1987). Peer group interventions to reduce the risk of delinquent behavior: A selective review and new evaluation. *Criminology, 25,* 671-714.

Gottfredson, M., & Hirschi, T. (1990). *A general theory of crime.* Stanford, CA: Stanford University Press.

Guba, E., & Lincoln, Y. (1989). *Fourth generation evaluation.* Newbury Park, CA: Sage.

Guerra, N. G., & Slaby, R. G. (1990). Cognitive mediators of aggression in adolescent offenders: II. Intervention. *Developmental Psychology, 26,* 269-277.

Hagan, M. K., & Robert, P. (1992). Recidivism rates of youth completing an intensive treatment program in a juvenile correctional facility. *International Journal of Offender Therapy and Comparative Criminology, 36,* 349-358.

Haghighi, B., & Lopez, A. (1993). Success/failure of group home treatment programs for juveniles. *Federal Probation, 57,* 53-58.

Henggeler, S. W. (1989). *Delinquency in adolescence.* Newbury Park, CA: Sage.

Henggeler, S. W., & Borduin, C. M. (1990). *Family therapy and beyond: A multisystemic approach to treating the behavior problems of children and adolescents.* Pacific Grove, CA: Brooks/Cole.

Henggeler, S. W., & Borduin, C. M. (1995). Multisystemic treatment of serious juvenile offenders and their families. In I. M. Schwartz & P. AuClaire (Eds.), *Home-based services for troubled children* (pp. 113-130). Lincoln: University of Nebraska Press.

Henggeler, S. W., Melton, G. B., & Smith, L. A. (1992). Family preservation using multisystemic therapy: An effective alternative to incarcerating serious juvenile offenders. *Journal of Consulting and Clinical Psychology, 60,* 953-961.

Henggeler, S. W., Melton, G. B., Smith, L. A., Schoenwald, S. K., & Hanley, J. H. (1993). Family preservation using multisystemic treatment: Long term follow-up to a clinical trial with serious juvenile offenders. *Journal of Child and Family Studies, 2,* 283-293.

Henggeler, S. W., Schoenwald, S. K., & Pickrel, S. G. (1995). Multisystemic therapy: Bridging the gap between university- and community-based treatment. *Journal of Consulting and Clinical Psychology, 63,* 709-717.

Henggeler, S. W., Schoenwald, S. K., Pickrel, S. G., Rowland, M. D., & Santos, A. B. (1994). The contribution of treatment outcome research to the reform of children's mental health services: Multisystemic therapy as an example. *Journal of Mental Health Administration, 21,* 229-239.

Hill, J. (1983). Early adolescence: A framework. *Journal of Early Adolescence, 3,* 1-21.

Howell, A. J., & Enns, R. A. (1995). A high risk recognition program for adolescents in conflict with the law. *Canadian Psychology, 36,* 149-161.

Jackson, P. C. (1982). Some effects of parole supervision on recidivism. *British Journal of Criminology, 23,* 17-30.

Kirigin, K. A., Braukmann, C. J., Atwater, J., & Wolf, M. M. (1982). An evaluation of Teaching Family (Achievement Place) group homes for juvenile offenders. *Journal of Applied Behavioral Analysis, 15*(1), 1-16.

Kobrin, S., & Klein, M. W. (1983). *Community treatment of juvenile offenders. The DSO experiments.* Beverly Hills, CA: Sage.

Larson, J. (1992). Anger and aggression management techniques through the Think First curriculum. *Journal of Offender Rehabilitation, 18,* 101-117.

Lerner, R. (1982). Children and adolescents as producers of their own environment. *Developmental Review, 2,* 342-370.

Lerner, R. (1991). Changing organism-context relations as the basic process of development: A developmental-contextual perspective. *Developmental Psychology, 27,* 27-32.

Lerner, R. (1995). *America's youth in crisis: Challenges and options for programs and policies.* Thousand Oaks, CA: Sage.

Lerner, R., & Lerner, J. (1987). Children in their contexts: A goodness of fit model. In J. Lancaster, J. Altmann, A. Rossi, & L. Sherrod (Eds.), *Parenting across the lifespan: Biosocial dimensions* (pp. 377-404). Chicago: Aldine.

Lewin, K. (1946). Action research and minority problems. *Journal of Social Issues, 2,* 34-46.

Lipsey, M. W. (1992). Juvenile delinquency treatment: A meta-analytic inquiry into the variability of effects. In T. D. Cook, H. Cooper, D. S. Corray, H. Hartmann, L. V. Hedges, R. J. Light, T. A. Louis, & F. Mostereller (Eds.), *Meta-analysis for explanation: A casebook* (pp. 83-127). New York: Russell Sage.

Locke, T. P., Johnson, G. M., Kirigin-Kamp, K., Atwater, J. D., & Gerrard, M. (1986). An evaluation of a juvenile education program in a state penitentiary. *Evaluation Review, 10,* 281-298.

Meyer, A., Miller, S., & Herman, M. (1993). Balancing the priorities of evaluation with the priorities of the setting: A focus on positive youth development programs in school settings. *Journal of Primary Prevention, 12,* 95-113.

Mulvey, E. P., Arthur, M. W., & Reppucci, N. D. (1993). The prevention and treatment of juvenile delinquency: A review of the research. *Clinical Psychology Review, 13,* 133-167.

Raider, M. C. (1994). Juvenile electronic monitoring: A community based program to augment residential treatment. *Residential Treatment for Children and Youth, 12,* 37-48.

Roy, S. (1993). Two types of juvenile restitution programs in two Midwestern counties: A comparative study. *Federal Probation, 57,* 48-53.

Scherer, D. G., Brondino, M. J., Henggeler, S. W., Melton, G. B., & Hanley, J. H. (1994). Multisystemic Family Preservation Therapy: Preliminary findings from a study of rural and minority serious adolescent offenders. *Journal of Emotional and Behavioral Disorders, 2,* 198-206.

Schneider, A. L. (1986). Restitution and recidivism rates of juvenile offenders: Results from four experimental studies. *Criminology, 24,* 533-552.

Scriven, M. (1981). Product evaluation. In N. L. Smith (Ed.), *New techniques for evaluation* (pp. 121-166). Beverly Hills, CA: Sage.

Shadish, W., Cook, T., & Leviton, L. (1991). *Foundations of program evaluation.* Newbury Park, CA: Sage.

Slot, N. W., Jagers, H. D., & Dangel, R. F. (1992). Cross-cultural replication and evaluation of the Teaching Family Model of community-based residential treatment. *Behavioral Residential Treatment, 7,* 341-354.

Smith, M. (1995). Mediation for children, youth, and families: A service continuum. *Mediation Quarterly, 12,* 277-283.

Stein, S. A., Garcia, F., Mailer, B., Embree, B. J., Garrett, C. J., Unrein, D., Burdick, M. A., & Fishburn, S. Y. (1992). A study of multiagency collaborative strategies: Did juvenile delinquents change? *Journal of Community Psychology, 20,* 88-105.

Stewart, M. J., Vockell, E. L., & Ray, R. E. (1986). Decreasing court appearances of juvenile status offenders. *Social Caseworker: The Journal of Contemporary Social Work, 67,* 74-79.

Task Force on Education of Young Adolescents. (1989). *Turning points: Preparing American youth for the 21st century.* New York: Carnegie Corporation.

Tate, D. C., Reppucci, N. D., & Mulvey, E. P. (1995). Violent juvenile delinquents: Treatment effectiveness and implications for future action. *American Psychologist, 50,* 777-781.

Weiss, C. (1988). Evaluation for decisions: Is anybody there? Does anybody care? *Evaluation Practice, 9,* 15-28.

William T. Grant Foundation Commission on Work, Family, and Citizenship. (1988). *The forgotten-half: Non-college bound youth in America.* Washington, DC: Author.

Wooldredge, J., Hartman, J., Latessa, E., & Holmes, S. (1994). Effectiveness of culturally specific community treatment for African American juvenile felons. *Crime & Delinquency, 40,* 589-598.

9. Incarcerated Juvenile Offenders: Integrating Trauma-Oriented Treatment With State-of-the-Art Delinquency Interventions

Evvie Becker
Annette U. Rickel

"There is very little reverence for children in Chicago," wrote British journalist William T. Stead in 1894 in *If Christ Came to Chicago* (quoted in Hawes, 1991, p. 32). Stead's work documented what he considered to be appalling conditions for children at the turn of the century, chronicling examples of young boys who carried messages in and out of jails and sold newspapers in the bordellos.

What would Stead say today about children in Chicago? One hundred years later, James Garbarino and others have documented conditions in Chicago (and elsewhere) that rival and, indeed, surpass those that shocked Stead. For example, in interviews in Chicago housing projects, Garbarino (1995) found "virtually all the children have firsthand experience with shooting by the time they are five years old" (p. 75). Also in Chicago, a wider survey of 1,035 African American children aged 10 to 19 found 75% of boys and 10% of girls had witnessed the shooting, stabbing, robbing, or killing of another person (Shakoor & Chalmers, 1991). Others have documented high levels of family violence in the lives of children and adolescents, particularly in areas of poverty, where violence in the home co-occurs with violence in the streets (American Psychological Association, 1996; Osofsky, Wewers, Hann, & Fick, 1993).

Beginning with a historical perspective, the chapter that follows outlines the ways in which violent conditions inflicted upon youth interact with other societal and individual factors to perpetuate adolescent involvement in crime, and the implications of those interactions for treatment of youthful offenders. New findings regarding treatment for the most recalcitrant offenders are described, with suggestions for integration with other emerging treatment modalities. The message herein is one of hope despite the pessimistic times in which we find ourselves. As the American Psychological Association Commission on Violence and Youth (1993) concluded:

> Many factors, both individual and social, contribute to an individual's propensity to use violence, and many of these factors are within our power to change. Although we acknowledge that the problem of violence involving youth is staggering and that there are complex macrosocial, biomedical, and other considerations that must be addressed in a comprehensive response to the problem, there is overwhelming evidence that we can intervene effectively in the lives of young people to reduce or prevent their involvement in violence. (p. 14)

THE "CORRECTIONAL" SYSTEM:
WHERE HAS ALL THE "CORRECTION" GONE?

Shortly after the publication of Stead's tract, described above, on the plight of Chicago's children, social workers and club women in Chicago advocated successfully for a separate trial court for juveniles in that city (Hawes, 1991). The legislature passed the Illinois Juvenile Court Act of 1899, the first in the United States, creating a separate court for youth under age 16 who had violated a law or ordinance and guaranteeing a right to request and receive a jury trial. Furthermore, this legislation allowed individuals to complain to the court regarding any child who was delinquent, but also any who were believed to be neglected, and the court was granted broad power to remove children from their homes and place them in a variety of settings, from institutions to foster care. In 1901, in an attempt to broaden the reach of the court to help children further, the law was expanded to include children who associated with questionable companions, frequented dangerous or immoral establishments, or who exhibited other behavior that today might be termed "high risk." The legality of a separate juvenile court was upheld by the Pennsylvania Supreme Court in 1906.

Early in the 20th century, the idea that delinquency was a psychiatric problem to be treated, rather than punished, gathered strength and momentum. William A. Healy's first youth guidance clinic, the Juvenile Psychopathic Institute, was established in Chicago in 1909 to treat youthful offenders. The system developed at the beginning of the century included training, reform schools, and other institutional settings, and also community rehabilitation efforts through probation and suspended sentences (National Research Council, 1993).

Throughout the first half of the century, the trend continued, and in the flurry of change that characterized the decades of the 1960s and 1970s, the move toward deinstitutionalization of psychiatric patients and the developmentally delayed affected the juvenile population as well (Zigler, Taussig, & Black, 1992). The Juvenile Justice and Delinquency Prevention Act of 1974 required that juvenile status offenders be provided alternatives to institutionalization (status offenses for juveniles are crimes resulting from the age of the perpetrator; e.g., truancy, violations of liquor or driving laws, running away). Consequently, the number of juveniles held in public facilities dropped by 60% by the end of the 1970s, and juveniles detained in adult facilities dropped by more than 80,000 youth.

Simultaneously, however, other forces worked to move juveniles away from their own facilities and back toward processes similar to those of adults in the justice system. The U.S. Supreme Court's 1967 Gault decision extended the Fifth and Sixth Amendment protections to juveniles, increasing the similarity of juvenile court proceedings to the adult process. Meanwhile, many states were engaged in a movement toward punishment and deterrence in juvenile cases and away from rehabilitation and treatment. States became increasingly willing to allow adolescents to be tried in adult courts. The concentration of racial minorities in poverty areas has confounded the problem, with inequality and discrimination prevalent in the criminal justice system for youth and for adults (American Bar Association, 1993; National Research Council, 1993).

Gradually, this movement has grown, so that, after the initial decrease at the end of the 1970s, noted above, the population of juveniles in public facilities began to increase again. By 1989, the population of juveniles in public facilities was 19% greater than it was in 1975 (National Research Council, 1993). Increasing violence among youth and escalating severity of violence have contributed to the public's fear of juvenile offenders. Treatment and rehabilitation have given way to punishment and retribution as the focus has shifted to community protection (Tate, Reppucci, & Mulvey, 1995).

Lack of solid evidence of the effectiveness of interventions with juvenile offenders has been cited as one reason for this trend (Tate et al., 1995; Zigler et al., 1992). Yet the rejection of treatment and rehabilitation by the public is also due in part to politicians who play upon the public's fears, calling for more jails and tougher sentencing as a means of political gain.

"The United States has been engaged in an unprecedented imprisonment binge," wrote Irwin and Austin (1994, p. 1), who suggested that politicians choose to focus on crime because it is a safe political issue when compared to root problems of greater complexity (e.g., economic issues such as unemployment and spiraling costs of living).

Calls for adjudicating youthful offenders as adults have come from legislators but also from the courts, where judges have shown a willingness to try juveniles as adults and to consider homicide by juveniles as a capital offense. All of these trends, together with stiffer punishments for adult offenders, have led to large increases in the number of inmates in state and federal prisons. This population tripled from 1980 to 1994, from 329,821 to more than a million (Kupers, 1996). In the federal penal system, rehabilitation is no longer even a goal.

Deteriorating conditions resulting from this overcrowding not only fail to rehabilitate, they may actually increase the rage, psychiatric symptomatology, and resultant violence of the incarcerated offender. Frequent fighting, racial strife, fear of violence (including assault and rape), staff brutality, anonymity, and boredom are among the factors that may lead a criminal to a greater propensity for violence after imprisonment than before incarceration, particularly if he or she has significant psychiatric problems and/or a traumatic history (Kupers, 1996).

Juveniles who are placed within the adult criminal justice system are exposed to all of these conditions, as well as to experienced offenders as role models, and they are particularly vulnerable to victimization in prison. Yet at no other time in our history have the effects of violence and victimization on children and youth been better articulated. The effects of violence at home, in the media, or in the streets, as well as the effects of poverty on children have been documented extensively (American Psychological Association, 1993, 1996). Among the problems associated with exposure to violence for children include difficulties with emotional regulation, an increase in aggressive behaviors, a negative self-image, symptoms of post-traumatic stress disorder, and difficulties in interpersonal relationships (Osofsky, 1995).

White House conferences on children and youth have been held periodically since the beginning of this century, with the debate shifting from a focus on families as the source of answers to the belief that experts had the solutions (Rickel & Allen, 1987). The 1960 fifth White House conference focused on increasing violence in the United States, specifically for adolescent individuals and youth gangs, and in 1970 and 1971, a conference for youth was held separately from that for children's issues.

Yet ever since the 1930 White House Conference on Children asserted that a child had a right to a "secure and loving home," children and youth have been subjected to family violence, street violence, multiple foster placements, abusive foster homes, drawn-out termination-of-parental-rights proceedings, latchkey situations, and lack of adequate food and housing, all contributing to the failure to fulfill on this historic promise to our children.

Nevertheless, most American youth are better off today than they were in 1641, when Massachusetts adopted a law that provided that any offspring 16 or older who cursed or struck a parent would be put to death, and 5 years later added that the death penalty could be applied to those 16 or older who failed to obey their parents (Hawes, 1991). Just 200 years ago, infanticide was not only permitted but accepted as the right of a father to manage his property (Zigler & Gordon, 1982), and only in 1938 was the first permanent child labor law finally enacted as part of the Fair Labor Standards Act.

The historical perspective suggests that solutions may lie in the convergence of multiple approaches to serving children and families. Multilevel solutions are suggested by history, and, as will be shown, are supported by research evaluations of effective treatment approaches.

VIOLENT HISTORIES, VIOLENT YOUTH

A six-year-old girl once told me that her job was to find her two-year-old sister whenever the shooting started and get her to safety in the bathtub of their apartment. "The bathroom is the safest place," she told me. Being responsible for the safety of another, younger child is a big responsibility for a six-year-old girl. Too big, I think. (Garbarino, 1995, p. 64)

As this anecdote illustrates, many children in the United States today have good reason to feel unsafe when their lives are threatened daily by the violence around them. But as Garbarino (1995) further observes, children living in more benign settings also report feeling unsafe: A Harris poll found that 35% of youth worried about being shot; another survey found that 12% of children felt unsafe, and the majority reported feeling only "somewhat" safe. Kidnapping and family dissolution are also worries for a large number of children.

These fears reflect the increasingly violent society in which we live. The United States continues to be a world leader—but not for our educational system, nor for our thriving economy. Rather, America leads the world for our rates of violence. The United States has the highest homicide rate of any industrialized country, a rate far above the country with the next highest rate (American Psychological Association, 1993). Only countries that are "profoundly distressed," such as Colombia, have similar homicide rates, according to Garbarino (1995), who computed the odds for children living in Northern Ireland before the 1994 IRA cease-fire and found that children in the United States are 15 times more likely to be killed than are children in Northern Ireland.

The psychological costs of this threat are tremendous. A recent study of 96 low-income, multiethnic youth in alternative high schools in Miami found that more than 93% had witnessed at least one violent event in their community, 44% had been victims of at least one of these violent events, and 41.6% had witnessed a murder (Berman, Kurtines, Silverman, & Serafini, 1996). Posttraumatic stress disorder (PTSD) symptoms were common among these students. For the large majority who had witnessed violence, an average number of 10 PTSD symptoms were reported. Examining the PTSD symptom reports for their clinical significance, 34.5% met the full criteria for a PTSD diagnosis, and 48.8% were symptomatic without meeting the full criteria; 16.7% were without symptoms. Similar findings have been reported for low-income, African American youth aged 7 to 18: Both victimization and witnessing violence were significantly related to reported PTSD symptoms, which were moderately high in this sample (Fitzpatrick & Boldizar, 1993).

As testimony in a 1993 hearing on youth and violence before the U.S. Senate Labor Subcommittee on Children indicated (*Keeping Every Child Safe*, 1993), victims may be inner-city youth in Bridgeport, as reported by a 16-year-old honor student in a magnet school who had lost several friends to shootings, or they may be adolescents in suburbia, such as the son of a suburban Virginia woman who was taken into the woods and shot by a friend, an Eagle Scout, just before he went off to college.

Victims may be visitors from other countries, such as German tourists murdered in Florida or the Japanese exchange student killed in Louisiana. Or they may be federal workers and children in day care, such as those killed in the Oklahoma City bombing. Yet race and ethnicity, primarily because of the concentration of ethnic minorities in poverty areas, are factors in the risk of death: A young African American female is four times more likely to be a victim of homicide than a young, non-African American female; a young African American male has a likelihood of being a homicide victim that is 11 times greater than that for young non-African American males. For young African Americans of both genders, homicide is the leading cause of death (American Psychological Association, 1993).

Guns are readily available to children in many communities. The rate of penetrating trauma in the emergency room at Children's National Medical Center in Washington, DC, increased by 1,740% from 1986 to 1989 (American Psychological Association, 1993). In Los Angeles County, military surgeons had to be brought in to teach medical residents at Martin Luther King Hospital how to deal with the overwhelming numbers of gunshot wounds and other traumatic injuries resulting from violence.

Consequent to this culture heavily laden with violent images, children are themselves becoming ever more violent, and at younger ages. We hear the horrifying stories, such as the teenager who opened fire on a public swimming pool filled with children, or those cited by Coudroglou (1996): a 13-year-old who shoots a friend in an argument over a girlfriend, dumping the body in a garbage can; a 6-year-old and twin 8-year-olds who beat and kick a 4-week-old infant within inches of its life because it cried while they were burglarizing the home; three preteens who throw a 5-year-old down 14 stories, killing him because he refused to steal for them; a 10-year-old who shoots and kills his 5-year-old sister when she refuses to go to her room; a group of 10- to 15-year-olds who gang rape a 13-year-old girl.

Statistics support the conclusion that youth violence is increasing: Between 1984 and 1991, homicides committed by youth during the commission of another crime increased by 200%, and homicides resulting from interpersonal conflict increased by 83% (Cornell, 1993).

Adolescent homicide perpetrators are far more likely to use a handgun than are adults who kill, and juveniles are more likely to have an accomplice.

As Coudroglou (1996) concludes, however, these incidents "ought to spark an agonizing inquiry into why otherwise ordinary people do bad things; why children and adolescents replace the joy of play with the horror of violence" (p. 324).

VIOLENCE AND VICTIMIZATION IN THE LIVES OF YOUTHFUL OFFENDERS

"Does violence beget violence?" Widom (1989a, 1989b) asked in her landmark work examining the relationship between a documented history of child maltreatment and records of criminal activity as juveniles and as adults. She found a strong relationship between a history of either physical abuse or neglect and later violent behavior. Other studies have reported a relationship between a history of sexual abuse and sexual offending by youth, although neglect, physical abuse, and witnessing family violence were more prevalent among adolescent sexual offenders than was sexual victimization (Kaplan, Becker, & Cunningham-Rathner, 1988; Pierce & Pierce, 1987).

Subsequent findings have indicated that while the link is not inevitable between maltreatment as a child and later violent or abusive behavior, the greater the violence and victimization in the home, the more likely a child will engage in violent or abusive behavior (American Psychological Association, 1996). Osofsky (1995) notes the importance of including measures of family violence when studies are conducted of children and youth exposed to community violence. She cites her own and other researchers' findings that indicate considerable co-occurrence of family and neighborhood violence.

Family patterns in the homes of delinquent juveniles have been studied for a number of years. Duncan, Kennedy, and Patrick (1995) summarize long-standing findings in this area that suggest that families of delinquents, compared to those of nondelinquents, are "cold and conflictual," and "rigid and less cohesive" (p. 250).

Studies have continued to document relationships among violence exposure, victimization, and delinquency (Rickel & Becker-Lausen, 1995). For example, one study of 50 abused women and 80 of their children, aged 11 to 12 years, revealed that among youth exposed to family violence, the earlier the abuse began in the lives of the children, the more frequent and severe was the youth's own participation in offending behavior (Kruttschnitt & Dornfeld, 1993).

Likewise, studies of 225 African American adolescents aged 11 to 19 (44% male), living in or near public housing projects, have documented the relationship between exposure to violence and youth violence (DuRant, Cadenhead, Pendergrast, Slavens, & Linder, 1994; DuRant, Pendergrast, & Cadenhead, 1994). Results indicated that 16.2% of the variance in frequency of fighting by the teen in the past year was explained by exposure to violence and victimization, school grades, and number of sexual partners. Exposure to violence and victimization, hopelessness, and the anticipation of future socioeconomic status accounted for 15% of variability in the frequency of gang fighting. Results overall were strongest for relationships among the youth's self-reported use of violence and exposure to violence (particularly victimization), family conflict, and severity of punishment or discipline. Researchers also found a relationship between depression and use of violence that was independent of violence exposure.

Similar findings were reported by Bell and Jenkins (1991, 1993) in studies of inner-city children and African American youth in Chicago. Among 536 inner-city children (in Grades 2 through 8), those who witnessed a shooting or a stabbing, as well as those exposed to family fighting, were more likely to report their own involvement in fighting. Among another sample of 1,035 youth aged 10 to 19, those who had perpetrated violence had also been witnesses and victims of violence.

Bell and Jenkins (1994) further note the resulting posttraumatic stress symptoms, lowered self-esteem, and decline in cognitive performance that are likely to occur in these children, and the anger, despair, and psychic numbing related to exposure to chronic and repeated trauma. They suggest that victims of family and community violence will have difficulty benefiting from interventions unless the symptoms of trauma are addressed.

Research with a sample of 1,140 incarcerated adult male felons (most of whom had not experienced combat-related trauma) found a relationship between PTSD and arrest and incarceration for expressive violence, when demographic variables, antisocial personality, and problem drinking were controlled (Collins & Bailey, 1990).

Among subjects with at least one PTSD symptom and expressive violence arrest, PTSD symptoms occurred in the same year as the arrest or earlier, supporting the directionality necessary for ultimately establishing a causal link.

However, studies of child maltreatment history and delinquency have failed to consistently document a clear-cut relationship between the two (Leiter, Myers, & Zingraff, 1994; Schwartz, Rendon, & Hsieh, 1994). For example, Zingraff, Leiter, Myers, and Johnsen (1993) found that although maltreated children had higher rates of delinquency than nonmaltreated children, the effects decreased substantially when demographic variables and family structure were controlled. Specific types of maltreatment failed to predict any type of offending behavior.

The latter finding is consistent with maltreatment researchers' recent recommendations that investigators move away from studies of specific forms of abuse (e.g., sexual abuse) in favor of investigating broader maltreatment as an aggregate variable (Elliott, Briere, McNeil, Cox, & Bauman, 1995; Finkelhor & Dziuba-Leatherman, 1994; Sanders & Becker-Lausen, 1995).

THE TRAUMA PERSPECTIVE

The still broader formulation of psychological trauma, which has emerged from a combination of studies on child maltreatment, combat veterans, natural disasters and other phenomena, provides a more comprehensive framework in which to consider the concept of juvenile offending behavior. From this perspective, it is possible to examine the accumulation of risk factors for children and youth from the various elements, including poverty, racism, and community violence, in addition to family violence and victimization (Garbarino, 1993).

Pynoos, Steinberg, and Goenjian (1996) note that the trend in trauma research and treatment has been a movement from broad categories of trauma to more narrow formulations, as specific features of traumatic experiences become more clearly delineated. Although this would seem to contradict the recommendations of maltreatment researchers noted above, in fact it does not. The narrowing of the field described by Pynoos et al. differs from the simple naming of types of abuse (i.e., physical abuse, sexual abuse, or neglect) criticized by others in the field. Examples listed by the authors make clear the distinction between the differentiation of traumatic experiences and simplistic categories of abuse: "Exposure to direct life threat . . . Being trapped or without assistance . . . Proximity to violent threat . . . Number and nature of threats during a violent episode . . . Witnessing of atrocities . . . Degree of brutality and malevolence" (pp. 336-337). These examples and others of this nature have been found to be associated with symptoms of PTSD. Trauma research and treatment are discussed in greater detail in the next section.

TRAUMATIC LIFE EXPERIENCES:
RESEARCH AND TREATMENT

"Experiencing trauma is an essential part of being human; history is written in blood," van der Kolk and McFarlane (1996, p. 3) state at the beginning of their edited volume, *Traumatic Stress,* one of several recent comprehensive works on trauma research and treatment. Trauma may be defined simply as any life event or experience that overwhelms one's ability to cope. Traumatic experiences in childhood may cause changes in cognitive, affective, behavioral, and physiological systems.

As suggested by the quote above, it may be virtually impossible to get through life without experiencing some type of trauma—yet there are major differences in the levels of traumatic experiences; the age at which the trauma occurs and the subsequent impact on individual development; and the resources available to the traumatized person, both psychic and social (Becker-Lausen, Sanders, & Chinsky, 1995; Briere, 1992; Finkelhor & Dziuba-Leatherman, 1994; Herman, 1992).

Only in the latter part of this century has trauma become the focus of widespread scientific inquiry. Since the recognition by psychiatry in 1980 of PTSD as a diagnosis, research has supported the assertion that traumatic experience is a relatively common occurrence. Surveys reveal about one fourth of American adolescents to about three fourths of U.S. adults report extremely stressful experiences; full PTSD for these individuals was estimated to occur in about 10% of adults and about 20% of the youth experiencing trauma (van der Kolk & McFarlane, 1996).

Yet as indicated in the earlier discussion, many youth living with violence are responding to a complicated interplay of victimization, exposure to violence between adult caretakers, and street violence. Furthermore, as Pynoos et al. (1996) point out, earlier investigations of family factors, such as parental psychopathology or substance abuse, have failed to consider the traumatic experiences inherent within these situations, such as finding a depressed parent attempting suicide or cleaning up the vomit of an unconscious, drunken parent. These complex interactions affect measurement and may be one of the reasons child maltreatment and delinquency have failed to be consistently related in research studies.

Key issues related to the traumatic stress response affect how individuals perceive and process the world around them (van der Kolk & McFarlane, 1996): (a) the persistent intrusion of traumatic memories that distract from incoming stimuli in the present; (b) the compulsive exposure to situations similar to the traumatic experience; (c) the avoidance of environmental cues related to trauma-based emotional reactions, with accompanying numbing of emotional responses; (d) loss of ability to modulate responses to general physiological stress; (e) a generalized difficulty with attention and concentration; and (f) shifting defenses and identity diffusion.

Knowledge of the effects of trauma has gradually accumulated throughout this century, ever since Freud first uncovered his patient's memories of incest and then rejected the incest interpretation in favor of the explanation that these were fantasized sexual wishes of the young child toward the parent (Herman, 1992). Clinical work with combat veterans, first from World War I and then from World War II, as well as with concentration camp survivors from World War II, added to the understanding of effects of the experience of extreme circumstances on human beings, and studies of Vietnam War veterans substantially increased awareness of posttraumatic stress symptoms (van der Kolk, Weisaeth, & van der Hart, 1996). Finally, studies of women and children experiencing trauma such as rape, incest, child maltreatment, and kidnapping further broadened the awareness of traumatic experiences.

A framework for treatment of traumatic stress has evolved gradually. A phase-oriented approach to the treatment of traumatized individuals has been described and endorsed by many in the trauma field. Herman (1992) has proposed that recovery moves through three stages: (a) establishing a sense of safety; (b) remembering the trauma and grieving over it ("remembrance and mourning," p. 155); and finally, (c) reconnecting with everyday life. Furthermore, the greater the trauma, the more the individual is expected to move back and forth between stages (e.g., returning to the establishment of safety again and again as traumatic experiences are worked through).

Others have delineated the stages further, yet the three-stage model provides a useful overlay for the more detailed formulations, outlined briefly here based on those proposed by Brown and Fromm (1986) and van der Kolk, McFarlane, and van der Hart (1996). The first phase, often termed stabilization, includes the establishment of a therapeutic alliance, education of the patient regarding the effects of trauma, identification of feelings, and the teaching of coping strategies. During the period of remembering and mourning, traumatic memories and responses are deconditioned, and the cognitive schemes connected with the trauma are restructured. This is the period of integration, which should begin only after stabilization is established, when supportive therapy can provide the client a safe place to gradually uncover and integrate the past experiences into his or her present self-concept. This period provides the foundation for the final stage, that of reconnecting with everyday life. Self-development includes distinguishing appropriate boundaries between self and others, values clarification, exploration of identity issues, and interest in new and previously untried activities to expand the limits and possibilities available to the newly integrated self. Work on establishing secure social relationships, which may include interventions such as assertiveness training and sex therapy, assists the client in a successful passage into this final stage of treatment.

Throughout these phases, and particularly at the beginning of therapy, psychopharmacology may be appropriate to help the client manage symptomatology (Brown & Fromm, 1986). Intense emotionality, including grief, anger, and withdrawal, is an expected reaction to the process of working through and integrating traumatic experiences (van der Kolk, McFarlane, & van der Hart, 1996).

Although the framework for these interventions initially came from work with adults, the interventions subsequently have been found to be useful structures for work with children and adolescents as well (Gil, 1991; James, 1989; Johnson, 1989; Straus, 1994). Use of play and other techniques specific to children and youth substitute for adult methods, but the approach still follows the pattern of safety and stabilization; remembering, grieving, and integrating the experience; and ultimately, moving back into ordinary life. However, treatment of children must take into account the child's developmental level and the resources available to the child at the time of treatment, so that, for example, the entire focus of psychotherapy may be on stabilization only.

Thorough diagnosis and assessment also have been stressed as essential at the beginning of therapy. Numerous assessment devices for diagnosing PTSD are described by Newman, Kaloupek, and Keane (1996), including self-report measures, interviews, and psychophysiological assessments. Although most of these measures were designed for adults, some may be applicable to adolescents. Checklists, such as the Trauma Symptom Inventory (Briere, Elliott, Harris, & Cotman, 1995) and the Trauma Symptom Checklist for Children (Elliott & Briere, 1994), are useful with youth, particularly adolescents in the justice system who may have severe deficits in reading ability. In some cases, interviews and behavioral ratings by others (e.g., parents, teachers) may be the primary source of information about these youth, because of widespread difficulties with reading in this population.

TREATMENT PROGRAMS FOR JUVENILE OFFENDERS

For youth who have committed only minor offenses, some form of diversion program to prevent the development of more serious delinquent behavior is preferable to incarceration, particularly where adolescents who have committed more severe infractions are housed. Preventive approaches are critical, particularly given how ubiquitous violence has become in today's society. Community-based, comprehensive prevention programs that include thorough assessment of local problems, identification of target issues, and selection of a range of interventions for employment by the community, as well as encouraging collaboration among civic groups, juvenile justice, local leaders, and youth themselves, have the best possibility of success (Howell, 1995).

Prevention of gang participation, for example, may be especially crucial for some communities. Three general strategies have been identified by the Office of Juvenile Justice and Delinquency Prevention (OJJDP; Howell, 1995): preventing youth from joining gangs in the first place, channeling gangs into prosocial activities, and crisis intervention or mediation to defuse rival gang conflicts. Risk factors such as community climate favorable to delinquency and the disintegration of neighborhoods must be addressed in these approaches. Prevention efforts need to include the encouragement of prosocial attitudes and skills and the provision of opportunities for relationships with peer and adult role models. Spergel et al. (1994) conducted an assessment of gang prevention and intervention efforts around the country. They concluded that programs that focus on high-risk youth by employing deterrence and rehabilitation approaches are preferable to broad-based prevention efforts.

Prosocial attitudes and skills may be encouraged through various forms of youth service programs. Such programs provide youth with the opportunities to volunteer their time for the benefit of peers or other members of their community. Activities may be quite varied, from tutoring other youth to assisting in programs for young children, elder adults, and homeless, mentally ill, or developmentally delayed individuals. Evaluations of these programs have produced mixed results, with some indicating positive effects for the participating youth and others showing little or no benefit (Allen, Philliber, & Hoggson, 1990; Howell, 1995). However, the research so far has been limited, and more studies are needed before conclusions can be drawn about the efficacy of such programs.

Job training and employment programs are another means used to decrease delinquency by increasing opportunities for involvement in legitimate activities. Studies of such programs have shown that they tend to be carried out on a larger scale than many other types of interventions (e.g., federal programs such as the Job Training Partnership Act), and that their strengths include the ability to successfully reach high-risk youth, to increase employment and earning opportunities, and to increase educational attainment (when education is a component of the program). However, vocational training that is substituted for traditional secondary education has shown few positive effects. Studies of the impact on crime and delinquency have shown discouraging results for job training and employment programs, suggesting that they may be useful as prevention measures by decreasing risk factors and increasing protective factors, but not as effective as a direct intervention for youth crime (Howell, 1995).

Among the treatments identified for children and youth with more serious behavior problems are cognitive-behavioral interventions, such as problem-solving skills training, social skills training, and parent training in child behavior management; family therapy; psychopharmacological approaches; and school or community interventions (American Psychological Association, 1993; Tate et al., 1995).

Although preventive approaches are always preferred, by the time youth are incarcerated, severely dysfunctional behavior has become pervasive throughout their lives. As discussed above in regard to juveniles placed in adult facilities, exposing younger or less experienced offenders to older, more violent, or more established perpetrators makes them highly vulnerable to victimization, as well as more likely to adopt behaviors similar to those around them (American Psychological Association, 1993).

Unfortunately, studies have indicated that about 15% of high-risk youth are responsible for 75% of the violent juvenile offenses committed. These chronic, violent offenders are considered the least receptive to preventive efforts, primarily because they have such a high degree of cumulative risk factors. Early interventions with firm sanctions are considered the best strategy for this group; however, this is not typically what has occurred: Although violent youth behavior tends to peak between ages 16 and 17, arrests peak at ages 18 to 19 (Howell, 1995).

Encouragingly, studies of institutional treatment programs have, in general, shown positive results with regard to recidivism. Behavioral treatment programs appear to be more effective than psychodynamic approaches or life skills programs. Andrews et al. (1990) delineated the essential appropriate correctional services necessary for an institutional program to be the most effective. These services included targeted delivery to those with higher risk factors, behaviorally oriented programs, and matching of treatment to individual needs. Programs not using behavioral interventions were also found to be appropriate when they were designed for a particular crime and were highly structured. Least effective strategies included traditional, nondirective counseling or group counseling where the focus is on communication only, without other interventions, as well as other approaches that were unstructured, loosely structured, or based on ineffective assessment of need. Deterrence programs that attempt to shake up the youth by exposing them to information about criminal penalties or to adults who have experienced them (such as a Scared Straight approach) have also been shown to be ineffective.

Many states have adopted an approach that allows for a graduated program of increasingly severe sanctions, depending on the nature of the offense, the individual's criminal history, and other risk factors relevant to escalating delinquency behavior. The array of services may include any or all of the following, from the least restrictive to the most secure:

1. Mentoring programs are for early intervention with teens in high-risk groups or for low-level juvenile offenses (e.g., truancy).

2. Community *supervision* may be carried out by volunteers trained to work with juveniles at low levels of delinquency, who in turn are monitored by professionals. Community *service* provides short-term, supervised work that may be for the purpose of restitution to victims or on projects for the betterment of the community. Either of these sanctions is designed for minor offenses and allows juveniles to remain at home and within the community.

3. Intermediate sanctions are targeted for violent offenders with the lowest risk factors: juveniles committing serious crimes such as robbery or arson, regardless of risk factors, and those committing less serious crimes, such as vandalism, auto theft, or larceny, who have high levels of risk factors. Intermediate sanctions programs include:

   a. Intensive supervision programs, the least restrictive of intermediate sanctions. The range of these services includes day treatment programs, where youth remain at home but attend special educational, counseling, and recreational services; specialized group homes, where adolescents live in a small residential facility but attend school and pursue other activities within the community; and programs that combine secure residential treatment with day treatment and aftercare services.

   b. Family preservation programs, with intensive, individualized treatment plans addressing systemic issues within the home. Multisystemic therapy, described below, may be a part of these programs.

   c. "Boot camps," wilderness camps, and job training programs that provide discipline, physical challenges, and work training in short-term, residential settings. These programs typically last about 90 days and are followed by aftercare in the community. They may be designed for nonviolent offenders only, such as the About Face program in Memphis, Tennessee, or in some cases, for more serious offenders, such as VisionQuest, a nationwide wilderness program. VisionQuest, which lasts 12 to 15 months, has been shown to reduce recidivism rates for serious juvenile offenders. However, research on the effectiveness of the boot camp approach has been mixed. Strictly punitive programs stressing control have been found to be generally ineffective, whereas those mixing control with treatment produce inconclusive results (Howell, 1995). Recidivism has not been shown to decline after the boot camp experience; however, educational and employment gains have been documented for some programs (Peterson, 1996).

    d. Community-based residential programs, which generally provide 6 months or more of intensive intervention in a restricted setting. Individual, group, and family therapy, combined with behavior modification programs, are usually part of this treatment approach.

4. Programs for the most violent offenders are typically secure, locked facilities where the average stay is about a year. The best of these programs limit the number of residents, provide anger management and conflict resolution, and work to disengage youth from gangs. Initial aftercare may consist of referral to an intermediate sanctions program for continued intervention.

Based on a thorough review of research and assessments of all types of youth programs on a continuum of care, including those representing prevention, diversion, residential, and aftercare services, the OJJDP (Howell, 1995) concluded that the principles associated with effective programs are essentially the same regardless of the stage in which they occur. It is, they suggest, not the stage in which intervention takes place that matters, but rather the program's quality, the intensity of the intervention, the appropriateness of fit with the stage it addresses, and its direction. What successful programs appear to have in common are the ability to address risk factors effectively for individual youth, strengthen those factors that provide protection and enhance resiliency, provide sufficient support and effective supervision, and increase prosocial attitudes by providing youth with a sense of having an increased stake in society.

Because of the multiplicity of risk factors associated with serious, violent offending by youth, multimodal, well-coordinated efforts must be mounted to counteract this behavior pattern. Interventions must address issues within the educational system, family system, peer group, and neighborhood if they are to be effective (American Psychological Association, 1993).

STATE-OF-THE-ART OFFENDER TREATMENT: MULTISYSTEMIC THERAPY

A program of multisystemic therapy (MST) has been developed that provides the sustained, multilevel interventions necessary for effective intervention with young offenders. So far, it is the only treatment that has shown short- and long-term success in reducing antisocial and violent behavior in youth. MST is child-focused and family-centered. By addressing issues multisystemically, MST meets the criteria for intervention at multiple levels that has long been recognized as needed for effective treatment of youthful offenders, and it also provides flexible, individualized, comprehensive services that empower families and communities (Henggeler, 1994).

Based on a social-ecological approach, MST reflects the perspective that family members behave in a context of multiple connections with systems both outside the family and within. Delivery of services within the natural environment of home, school, or community is essential to the effectiveness of interventions, which are designed in collaboration with family members (Henggeler, Schoenwald, & Pickrel, 1995). Interventions are present-centered, targeting factors that have been identified as related to adolescent delinquent behavior, particularly those that are intrapersonal and systemic (Borduin et al., 1995). Sessions are action-oriented and usually occur in the family home or in a community setting. (For a detailed account of the multisystemic approach, its rationale, and the various applications, see Henggeler & Borduin, 1990.)

Borduin et al. (1995) studied 176 juvenile offenders at high risk of recidivism (average prior arrests = 4.2; mean severity of most recent arrest = 8.8 on a scale of increasing severity from 1 to 17, where 8 = assault/battery, 11 = grand larceny, 17 = murder). The group receiving MST was compared to a group that received individual therapy only, using multimethod assessment batteries from multiple sources before and after the intervention. Those receiving MST were more likely to show improvement in key family factors related to antisocial behavior and to show better adjustment among individual family members. A 4-year follow-up analysis of subsequent arrests indicated that those who received MST, compared to those who received only individual therapy, were less likely to be re-arrested and less likely to commit violent offenses. Other studies with this modality have shown equally promising results (Henggeler et al., 1995).

Henggeler et al. (1995) credit the success of MST to four key elements: (a) Factors determined through empirical research to be related to dysfunctional behavior are addressed comprehensively, yet tailored to the individual client; (b) services are delivered to youth and families in their natural settings; (c) therapists are well-trained, well-supported, and monitored for adherence to the treatment approach; and (d) considerable effort is invested to develop, nurture, and maintain positive relationships among the various agencies involved.

INTEGRATION OF MULTISYSTEMIC AND PHASE-ORIENTED TREATMENT APPROACHES

Both MST and phase-oriented therapy for trauma are relatively new and exciting breakthroughs in treatment with a great deal to offer the clinician attempting to intervene with an adolescent during the incarceration period. MST findings suggest the importance of collaborative efforts among systems so that follow-up community treatment may continue after incarceration. Working to bring family members into the setting for systemic work, to the degree that it is possible, also appears to be an extremely important element. Where parents are not available to the youth because of substance abuse, their own incarceration, or because they have simply disappeared from the scene, the clinician should attempt to locate other family members, such as aunts, uncles, cousins, or older siblings, and try to interest them in taking a role in the youth's care.

Although MST has been used with families where child maltreatment and other family violence is occurring (Brunk, Henggeler, & Whelan, 1987; Henggeler & Borduin, 1990), the focus of the MST approach has not been the reduction of traumatic symptoms. We suggest that phase-oriented treatment of trauma should inform any individual work with these youth, who are likely to have experienced traumatic events in their history, particularly those who are from neighborhoods with high levels of community violence. Especially during incarceration, providing a safe space for youth within the therapeutic relationship may help them contain symptoms and also may allow further work to occur once the adolescent is back in the community.

Both treatment approaches stress the importance of thorough assessment at the outset, and this cannot be overemphasized. MST approaches, by including assessment of exposure to violence and other traumatic experiences in the family, as well as in the individual youth, may improve the design of individualized treatment plans. Treatment of traumatic symptoms, particularly dissociation, depression, rage, and psychic numbing, in youth and in family members, may further increase the efficacy of the multisystemic intervention. Likewise, trauma-oriented clinicians may increase the potency of individual treatment of adolescents by working systemically with schools and families.

POLICY IMPLICATIONS

According to a report by the American Bar Association (1993),

> Once sentenced, a growing number of young people are detained in unhealthy and dangerous conditions, and denied necessary services. . . . Today, almost one-half of all incarcerated juveniles are held in overcrowded facilities. . . . Overcrowding is unhealthy and often generates violence among residents and between residents and guards. (pp. 63-64)

The report goes on to note that in addition to overcrowding, juvenile facilities often lack compliance with basic standards for safety, education, health care, and the monitoring of suicidal behavior. In some states, juveniles in need of mental health care are "dumped in correctional facilities" (p. 67) because there are too few psychiatric treatment facilities for adolescents.

Clearly, in this atmosphere, where there is any attempt at treatment, the clinician faces an uphill battle. Consequently, reform of facilities and of the juvenile justice system itself must be a high priority for all who are concerned about the well-being of youth in this country. Task forces from the National Research Council (1993), the American Bar Association (1993), and the American Psychological Association (1993), among others, all conclude that prevention at an earlier age, and short of that, treatment interventions demonstrated to be effective, are far preferable to our current attempt to lock up problem youth. To encourage the public, legislators, and policymakers to invest in prevention and treatment efforts will require all professionals with an interest in children and youth to join efforts, to speak with one voice.

The American Psychological Association and the American Bar Association have begun such a collaboration for children's issues. Although at the present it is focused on divorce and custody issues, the intention of the collaboration is to build a broader coalition for children and families. The two associations cosponsored a conference in April 1997 in Los Angeles that was titled "Children, Divorce and Custody: Lawyers and Psychologists Working Together." An APA task force on APA-ABA relations is actively involved in building a longer term relationship encompassing common concerns.

Convincing the public and policymakers that prevention is cost-effective will be one important place to begin. Tate et al. (1995) note that in 1992, keeping an adolescent in a correctional facility cost about $105.27 per day, compared to the $31.43 per day for multisystemic therapy (about $3,300 per client for 15 weeks of treatment). Likewise, the American Bar Association (1993) pointed out that incarcerating a juvenile costs about $30,000 a year, and foster care to age 18 costs $123,000, which is "more than it costs to attend a first-class boarding school, private college or to support a slot in the Job Corps" (p. vi).

We can make a difference with youth. We have tools that are proven to be effective in reducing recidivism, and we are more knowledgeable about the root causes of delinquency than ever before in our history. But until we work together to change the structure of the juvenile justice system, our treatment of offenders is likely to fall far short of our vision of what is possible.

REFERENCES

Allen, J. P., Philliber, S., & Hoggson, N. (1990). School-based prevention of teenage pregnancy and school drop-out: Process evaluation of the national replication of the Teen Outreach Program. *American Journal of Community Psychology, 18*, 505-524.

American Bar Association. (1993). *America's children at risk: A national agenda for legal action.* A report of the American Bar Association Presidential Working Group on the Unmet Legal Needs of Children and Their Families. Chicago: Author.

American Psychological Association. (1993). *Violence and youth: Psychology's response: Volume I. Summary report of the American Psychological Association Commission on Violence and Youth.* Washington, DC: Author.

American Psychological Association. (1996). *Violence and the family: Report of the American Psychological Association Presidential Task Force on Violence and the Family.* Washington, DC: Author.

Andrews, D. A., Zinger, I., Hoge, R., Bonta, J., Gendrew, P., & Cullen, F. (1990). Does correctional treatment work? A clinically relevant and psychologically informed meta-analysis. *Criminology, 28,* 369-404.

Becker-Lausen, E., Sanders, B., & Chinsky, J. M. (1995). Mediation of abusive childhood experiences: Depression, dissociation, and negative life outcomes. *American Journal of Orthopsychiatry, 65,* 560-573.

Bell, C. C., & Jenkins, E. J. (1991). Traumatic stress and children. *Journal of Health Care for the Poor and Underserved, 2,* 175-185.

Bell, C. C., & Jenkins, E. J. (1993). Community violence and children on Chicago's southside. *Psychiatry Interpersonal and Biological Processes, 56*(1), 46-54.

Bell, C. C., & Jenkins, E. J. (1994). Effects of child abuse and race. *Journal of the National Medical Association, 86,* 165, 232.

Berman, S. L., Kurtines, W. M., Silverman, W. K., & Serafini, L. T. (1996). The impact of exposure to crime and violence on urban youth. *American Journal of Orthopsychiatry, 66,* 329-336.

Borduin, C. M., Mann, B. J., Cone, L., Henggeler, S. W., Fucci, B. R., Blaske, D. M., & Williams, R. A. (1995). Multisystemic treatment of serious juvenile offenders: Long-term prevention of criminality and violence. *Journal of Consulting and Clinical Psychology, 63,* 569-578.

Briere, J. N. (1992). *Child abuse trauma: Theory and treatment of lasting effects.* Newbury Park, CA: Sage.

Briere, J., Elliott, D. M., Harris, K., & Cotman, A. (1995). Trauma Symptom Inventory: Psychometrics and association with childhood and adult victimization in clinical samples. *Journal of Interpersonal Violence, 10,* 387-401.

Brown, D. P., & Fromm, E. (1986). *Hypnotherapy and hypnoanalysis.* London: Lawrence Erlbaum.

Brunk, M., Henggeler, S. W., & Whelan, J. P. (1987). A comparison of multisystemic therapy and parent training in the brief treatment of child abuse and neglect. *Journal of Consulting and Clinical Psychology, 55,* 311-318.

Collins, J. J., & Bailey, S. L. (1990). Traumatic stress disorder and violent behavior. *Journal of Traumatic Stress, 3,* 203-220.

Cornell, D. G. (1993). Juvenile homicide: A growing national problem. *Behavioral Sciences and the Law, 11,* 389-396.

Coudroglou, A. (1996). Violence as a social mutation. *American Journal of Orthopsychiatry, 66,* 323-328.

Duncan, R. D., Kennedy, W. A., & Patrick, C. J. (1995). Four-factor model of recidivism in male juvenile offenders. *Journal of Clinical Child Psychology, 24,* 250-257.

DuRant, R. H., Cadenhead, C., Pendergrast, R. A., Slavens, G., & Linder, C. W. (1994). Factors associated with the use of violence among urban Black adolescents. *American Journal of Public Health, 84,* 612-617.

DuRant, R. H., Pendergrast, R. A., & Cadenhead, C. (1994). Exposure to violence and victimization and fighting behavior by urban Black adolescents. *Journal of Adolescent Health, 15*, 311-318.

Elliott, D. M., & Briere, J. (1994). Forensic sexual abuse evaluations of older children: Disclosures and symptomatology. *Behavioral Sciences and the Law, 12*, 261-277.

Elliott, D. M., Briere, J., McNeil, D., Cox, J., & Bauman, D. (1995, July). *Multivariate impact of sexual molestation, physical abuse and neglect in a forensic sample.* Paper presented at the Fourth International Family Violence Research Conference, Durham, NH.

Finkelhor, D., & Dziuba-Leatherman, J. (1994). Victimization of children. *American Psychologist, 49*, 173-183.

Fitzpatrick, K. M., & Boldizar, J. P. (1993). The prevalence and consequences of exposure to violence among African American youth. *Journal of the American Academy of Child and Adolescent Psychiatry, 32*, 424-430.

Garbarino, J. (1993). Children's response to community violence: What do we know? *Infant Mental Health Journal, 14*(2), 103-115.

Garbarino, J. (1995). *Raising children in a socially toxic environment.* San Francisco: Jossey-Bass.

Gil, E. (1991). *The healing power of play.* New York: Guilford.

Hawes, J. M. (1991). *The children's rights movement: A history of advocacy and protection.* Boston: Twayne.

Henggeler, S. W. (1994). A consensus: Conclusions of the APA task force report on innovative models of mental health services for children, adolescents, and their families. *Journal of Clinical Child Psychology, 23*(Suppl.), 3-6.

Henggeler, S. W., & Borduin, C. M. (1990). *Family therapy and beyond: A multisystemic approach to treating the behavior problems of children and adolescents.* Pacific Grove, CA: Brooks/Cole.

Henggeler, S. W., Schoenwald, S. K., & Pickrel, S. G. (1995). Multisystemic therapy: Bridging the gap between university- and community-based treatment. *Journal of Consulting and Clinical Psychology, 63*, 709-717.

Herman, J. L. (1992). *Trauma and recovery.* New York: Basic Books.

Howell, J. C. (Ed.). (1995). *Guide for implementing the comprehensive strategy for serious, violent, and chronic juvenile offenders.* Washington, DC: U.S. Department of Justice, Office of Juvenile Justice and Delinquency Prevention.

Irwin, J., & Austin, J. (1994). *It's about time: America's imprisonment binge.* Belmont, CA: Wadsworth.

James, B. (1989). *Treating traumatized children.* Lexington, MA: Lexington Books.

Johnson, K. (1989). *Trauma in the lives of children.* Claremont, CA: Hunter House.

Kaplan, M. S., Becker, J. V., & Cunningham-Rathner, J. (1988). Characteristics of parents of adolescent incest perpetrators: Preliminary findings. *Journal of Family Violence, 3*, 183-191.

Keeping every child safe: Curbing the epidemic of violence: Joint hearings before the Subcommittee on Children, Family, Drugs and Alcoholism, of the Committee on Labor and Human Resources, United States Senate, and the Select Committee on Children, Youth, and Families, House of Representatives, 103rd Cong., 1st Sess. 33 (1993).

Kruttschnitt, C., & Dornfeld, M. (1993). Exposure to family violence: A partial explanation for initial and subsequent levels of delinquency? *Criminal Behaviour and Mental Health, 3*(2), 61-75.

Kupers, T. A. (1996). Trauma and its sequelae in male prisoners: Effects of confinement, overcrowding, and diminished services. *American Journal of Orthopsychiatry, 66,* 189-196.

Leiter, J., Myers, K. A., & Zingraff, M. T. (1994). Substantiated and unsubstantiated cases of child maltreatment: Do their consequences differ? *Social Work Research, 18*(2), 67-82.

National Research Council. (1993). *Losing generations: Adolescents in high-risk settings.* Panel on High-Risk Youth, Commission on Behavioral and Social Sciences and Education. Washington, DC: National Academy Press.

Newman, E., Kaloupek, D. G., & Keane, T. M. (1996). Assessment of posttraumatic stress disorder in clinical and research settings. In B. A. van der Kolk, A. C. McFarlane, & L. Weisaeth (Eds.), *Traumatic stress: The effects of overwhelming experience on mind, body, and society* (pp. 242-275). New York: Guilford.

Osofsky, J. D. (1995). The effects of exposure to violence on young children. *American Psychologist, 50,* 782-788.

Osofsky, J. D., Wewers, S., Hann, D. M., & Fick, A. C. (1993). Chronic community violence: What is happening to our children? *Psychiatry Interpersonal and Biological Processes, 56*(1), 36-45.

Peterson, E. (1996, June). *Juvenile boot camps: Lessons learned.* Fact Sheet #36. Washington, DC: U.S. Department of Justice, Office of Juvenile Justice and Delinquency Prevention.

Pierce, L. H., & Pierce, R. L. (1987). Incestuous victimization by juvenile sex offenders. *Journal of Family Violence, 2,* 351-364.

Pynoos, R. S., Steinberg, A. M., & Goenjian, A. (1996). Traumatic stress in childhood and adolescence: Recent developments and current controversies. In B. A. van der Kolk, A. C. McFarlane, & L. Weisaeth (Eds.), *Traumatic stress: The effects of overwhelming experience on mind, body, and society* (pp. 331-358). New York: Guilford.

Rickel, A. U., & Allen, L. (1987). *Preventing maladjustment from infancy through adolescence.* Newbury Park, CA: Sage.

Rickel, A. U., & Becker-Lausen, E. (1995). Intergenerational influences on child outcomes: Implications for prevention and intervention. In B. A. Ryan, G. R. Adams, T. P. Gullotta, R. P. Weissberg, & R. L. Hampton (Eds.), *The family-school connection: Theory, research, and practice.* Thousand Oaks, CA: Sage.

Sanders, B., & Becker-Lausen, E. (1995). The measurement of psychological maltreatment: Early data on the Child Abuse and Trauma scale. *Child Abuse & Neglect, 19,* 315-323.

Schwartz, I. M., Rendon, J. A., & Hsieh, C. M. (1994). Is child maltreatment a leading cause of delinquency? *Child Welfare, 73,* 639-655.

Shakoor, B. H., & Chalmers, D. (1991). Co-victimization of African-American children who witness violence: Effects on cognitive, emotional, and behavioral development. *Journal of the National Medical Association, 83,* 233-238.

Spergel, I. A., Chance, R., Ehrensaft, K., Regulus, T., Kane, C., Laseter, R., Alexander, A., & Oh, S. (1994). *Gang suppression and intervention: Community models: Research summary.* Washington, DC: U.S. Department of Justice, Office of Juvenile Justice and Delinquency Prevention.

Straus, M. (1994). *Violence in the lives of adolescents.* New York: Norton.

Tate, D. C., Reppucci, N. D., & Mulvey, E. P. (1995). Violent juvenile delinquents: Treatment effectiveness and implications for future action. *American Psychologist, 50,* 777-781.

van der Kolk, B. A., & McFarlane, A. C. (1996). The black hole of trauma. In B. A. van der Kolk, A. C. McFarlane, & L. Weisaeth (Eds.), *Traumatic stress: The effects of overwhelming experience on mind, body, and society* (pp. 3-23). New York: Guilford.

van der Kolk, B. A., McFarlane, A. C., & van der Hart, O. (1996). A general approach to treatment of posttraumatic stress disorder. In B. A. van der Kolk, A. C. McFarlane, & L. Weisaeth (Eds.), *Traumatic stress: The effects of overwhelming experience on mind, body, and society* (pp. 417-440). New York: Guilford.

van der Kolk, B. A., McFarlane, A.C., & Weisaeth, L. (1996). History of trauma in psychiatry. In B. A. van der Kolk, A. C. McFarlane, & L. Weisaeth (Eds.), *Traumatic stress: The effects of overwhelming experience on mind, body, and society* (pp. 47-74). New York: Guilford.

Widom, C. (1989a). Does violence beget violence? A critical examination of the literature. *Psychological Bulletin, 106,* 3-28.

Widom, C. (1989b). The cycle of violence. *Science, 244,* 160-166.

Zigler, E., & Gordon, E. W. (Eds.). (1982). *Day care: Scientific and social policy issues.* Boston: Auburn House.

Zigler, E., Taussig, C., & Black, K. (1992). Early childhood intervention: A promising preventative for juvenile delinquency. *American Psychologist, 47,* 997-1006.

Zingraff, M. T., Leiter, J., Myers, K. A., & Johnsen, M. C. (1993). Child maltreatment and youthful problem behavior. *Criminology, 31,* 173-202.

10. Preventing Juvenile Delinquency and Promoting Juvenile Rightency

Martin Bloom

DEFINITION OF TERMS

Juvenile delinquency: First question: What are the terms that you associate with the phrase "juvenile delinquency"? Humm, let's see. That list would include illegal behavior, antisocial behavior, status offenses, acting-out behavior (if it were serious enough), serious problem behavior, truancy, criminal behavior committed by young people, stealing, immoral behavior (at least the kinds that are illegal), serious aggressive behavior, disruptive behavior, behavior involving excessive use of alcohol (depending on the laws of the specific state), any use of illegal drugs, being at risk for untoward behavior of any sort, harassment, persistently bugging or annoying people, conduct disorder, vandalism, destruction of property, attacks on people, academic failure, fire setting, noncompliance, out-of-control (uncontrollable) behavior or incorrigible behavior, being a runaway . . . have I omitted any?

Second question: What are the terms that you associate with the opposite of juvenile delinquency? Hummmmmm, let's see. That list would include nondelinquent, nontruant, nonacting-out, noncriminal, not being a thief, not being disruptive, being drug free or not using drugs, not being incorrigible. . . . However, these "nonterms" are really pale imitations of ideas that one could set as goals for living—or for service programs. It is difficult to think of any formal terms that represent the positive version of which juvenile delinquency represents the negative, except maybe being a good kid, or a nice kid, or a law-abiding child, or a moral or righteous child (not in the religious or political sense, but in the dictionary sense of obeying moral standards). Even when a "positive" term exists, such as "corrigible," its meaning still carries a negative implication—as in "capable of being corrected or reformed," which implies that one has been problematic before.

256

Third question: What have you learned from the responses to the two prior questions? Clearly, society as a whole, and the "helping" or "controlling" professions in particular, have more ways to think about bad behavior than good behavior, more ways to characterize children and youth as pathological or deviant than socially healthy. I would assert that our language appears to influence how we think and act toward children and youth who are at risk. We haven't the technical language to direct our thinking toward young people with potential, with strengths to be actualized, with constructive objectives that can be incorporated into ordinary socialization efforts at home, at school, and in the community.

This is not to deny that young people may be at risk for problem behavior (to say nothing of the adjudicated delinquents and the many more unapprehended youths who have committed antisocial acts without being detected), and that social and physical environmental contexts may facilitate problem behaviors. Rather, it is to make a plea to frame any discussion of "juvenile delinquency" in system terms so as to view the entire situation—strengths and limitations of people, groups, communities, and physical environments—as they may be relevant to the problem at hand, in this case, the prevention of juvenile delinquency and the promotion of its opposite. I will refer to this encompassing analysis as a configural perspective, viewing all of the system components in relation to one another in order to observe the pattern of pushes and pulls resulting in some target behavior.

Juvenile rightency: For the sake of discussion, I propose to use the term *juvenile rightency* to represent the conceptual opposite of juvenile delinquency, that is, a general term pointing to positive social behaviors as the goal of socialization of children and youth, and not merely the absence of negative or antisocial behaviors. The term *delinquency* has been problematic because it has a multitude of definitions and interpretations (see Burchard & Burchard, 1987; McCord & Tremblay, 1992; Quay, 1987). Introducing a new term provides the opportunity to stake out exactly what is intended. Juvenile rightency refers to the range of legal and socially acceptable actions, from the merely adequate (such as being law abiding), to the mid-level desirable (such as getting good grades in school and other age-appropriate behavior), to the highly desirable behaviors (such as constructive, socially valued behaviors like volunteering as a hospital aide) enacted by people younger than state-defined legal adult status. I will amplify on this working definition with reference to its corresponding term, juvenile delinquency. "Societally acceptable actions" refer to actual behaviors and thus are parallel to committed illegal acts whether or not apprehended (for discussion of these definitional factors, see Farrington, 1992). The "societally accepted" part means that the behaviors are socially approved and differentially rewarded depending on their contribution to self and/or society, as suggested by the three-step division mentioned previously.

Some of these positive behaviors are rewarded publicly (as in school graduations), whereas others may result in private or familial commendation (as in eating appropriately). Some positive behaviors may be self-rewarding (like having good friends) and receive little apparent attention or public reward (although they may be carefully noticed and monitored). Each of these socially acceptable actions may involve a range of behaviors. For example, getting passing grades is adequate, getting high grades is more desirable, and attaining the highest grade is most desirable in the typical academic context for its own sake and as a predictor of future behaviors. The phrase indicating age of actor is couched in language that recognizes local and state options in defining who is or is not a "child."

In general, society seeks to socialize its young to become rightents, that is, juveniles who act within the range of legal and socially acceptable norms of behavior to socially desired behaviors. In brief, young people are socialized to act somewhere between acceptable sinners and extraordinary saints. That is, adolescents are supposed to test the limits of healthy independence without violating laws and with fulfilling social expectations and personal potential.

Primary prevention: One can glibly define this term as the *prevention* of untoward predicted outcomes in people or groups at risk; the *protection* of existing states of health and healthy functioning in these people and groups; and the *promotion* of desired states of functioning for these same parties (Bloom, 1996). This is a reasonable definition, but as Albee (1983), Duncan (1994), and Elias (1995) have well argued, primary prevention is often ill-used even by its well-meaning supporters. There are several villains in this piece; let me clarify the full meaning of this definition of primary prevention.

The first problem is what may be termed the *problem bias:* This involves the assumption that we know exactly what will lead to a problematic behavior, and thus all we have to do is inoculate the people involved (to make these people problem-free) or make changes in the environmental agents and contexts (to make these problematic agents or problematic environments problem-free). The underlying orientation is that this view of prevention is all negative; we have to correct the problem, and then prevention will be accomplished. What is lacking is a positive goal to seek as we attempt to reduce the negative factors. Something constructive has to be offered in place of the predicted untoward events. These untoward events tend to be pleasurable and hard to give up, whatever moral arguments are brought to bear (cf. Coates, 1990), so a major part of primary prevention involves introducing something equally or more pleasurable that is also positive and constructive.

The second problem may be termed the *healthy-state bias:* If the wheel isn't squeaky, don't oil it. It is true that we don't want to change healthy functioning for the sake of change, but health and healthy functioning aren't accidental, nor are they created by chance, although it may seem that way to the young and the short-sighted. Nor is health and healthy functioning guaranteed to continue indefinitely. There is a positive dimension in primary prevention that involves being aware of good health and keeping healthy functioning maintained at the same high level (or better), especially as inevitable changes of age and circumstance occur, such as maturational changes or transitions to important new environments like high school (cf. Felner & Adan, 1988).

The third problem may be termed the *poverty of promotive imagination:* We don't have the words or the imagination to construct a positive and constructive agenda for people, groups, communities, and states to establish clear personal and social agendas over the long run. Budgets are annual affairs; recreational plans are seasonal considerations; producing synergy in organizations are piecemeal occasions at best.

Promotion of desired states has been maligned as utopian, that is, out of mind and possibility, worthless and woolly thinking. This is a gross distortion of terms, because long-term actions start, whether we know it or not, in immediate choices; a journey of a thousand miles begins with its first step. If we deny looking at those first steps or the plans for where those steps may be taking us, we fail at a basic contribution that promotion can provide.

Configural or systems perspective on juvenile delinquency and juvenile rightency: Many people write about systems thinking, but few engage in it. As this chapter's survey of prevention programs in juvenile delinquency will show, most projects are focused on one or another component within the whole system of events that influences behavior.

The difficulty is not in describing a systems perspective; it is in putting the pieces together after one has broken them out for careful consideration. The last section of this chapter will offer some attempts at this kind of reconstruction.

Albee (1983) provides the impetus for systemic thinking in primary prevention with his formula on ingredients affecting rates of mental illness. It will be more useful to generalize on his formula as follows, so as to provide an outline for the survey of prevention literature:

The formula is to be read that a target behavior, such as juvenile

	A	B	C	D	E
	Individual Strengths	Primary Groups Strengths	Secondary Groups Strengths	Society/ Culture Strengths	Physical Environment Strengths
Juvenile Delinquency/ =					
Juvenile Rightency	F	G	H	I	J
	Individual Limitations	Primary Groups Limits	Secondary Groups Limits	Society/ Culture Limits	Physical Environment Limitations

delinquency or juvenile rightency, as a general categorical term is some function of a set of strengths (individual, primary group, secondary group, societal/cultural, and physical environmental) as reduced or modified by a set of limitations (individual, primary group, secondary group, societal/cultural, and physical environmental). To achieve juvenile rightency or to prevent juvenile delinquency, we have to consider all of these 10 factors individually and then as a system of interactive components. Not all 10 factors may be applicable, nor will it be feasible to consider all of these factors in any one project, but having the configural perspective will enable planners to make choices that are feasible and potent within a given locale. My hypothesis is that the more nearly that all factors are considered, and those that are relevant are brought within experimental manipulation in a project, the more likely the project is to be successful. (This does not mean that 10 factors are going to be more successful than 2 or 3 factors; it depends on how feasible and potent any given set of factors is in the given situation.)

Each factor can be further explicated, which is useful in program planning. Individual factors may be defined to include the biological/physiological elements; the affective, cognitive, and behavioral components; and some might argue, spiritual or existential components as well. Primary groups include small, intensive, face-to-face groups such as families and peer groups of various sorts, tutor/tutee pairs, or Big Brother/Little Brother pairs. Secondary groups include larger groupings where division of labor occurs to achieve some common objective, such as in factories (not small work units therein) or universities. Society refers to a very large-scale entity having multiple levels between the individual citizen and the ultimate sources of authority and power. Culture (or more usefully in the present context, subculture) refers to a set of common experiences, shared values, language, and lifestyles that provides continuity and familiarity to a group of people.

Given this definitional background, I will summarize some exemplary programs that emphasize one or another of these 10 factors, and in some cases, how they combine factors in successful programs.

REVIEW OF EXEMPLARY PROGRAMS ILLUSTRATING COMPONENTS OF THE CONFIGURAL FRAMEWORK

Studies Emphasizing Individual Strengths Supporting Rightency

Biological/Physiological Components

There are several distinguishable components of "individual strengths" including the biological/physiological, cognitive, affective, and the behavioral. In the following review, I will emphasize here those portions of studies that can be interpreted as indicating individual strengths, even though these same studies may also be used later in the chapter as examining individual limitations.

The biological/physiological includes inborn temperament (Thomas & Chess, 1977), health and wellness (the capacity of infants to master the homeostatic mechanisms of life without special efforts and within normative limits), genetic transmission of structures and functions that enable the person to adapt to life demands, and so on. Of these, very little is known through preventive/promotive programs such as altering genes to produce infants with easy-to-raise temperaments. We have some bases for predicting some untoward conditions (such as Tays-Sacks or sickle cell anemia), but juvenile delinquency (as a complex, socially constructed entity) is not among these. More to the point of this section, neither can we promote the biological bases of rightency, if there are any biological bases. We have engaging scientific hints, such as those based on studies of twins and adoption and cross-fostering studies, that have produced results that "are not inconsistent with" an inherited disposition to behave in a delinquent matter (Trasler, 1987, pp. 193-194), but these have not led to social actions by which to prevent delinquency or promote rightency. On the other hand, the old claims that "certain forms of delinquency may be an expression of genetic abnormalities, is so far without empirical support" (Trasler, 1987, p. 194), which means that we do not have to concern ourselves at this time with changing complex genetic structures, which, in any case, lie far in the future. However, this provides equally unclear instructions for seeking genetic reconstructions for promoting rightency. Whatever else the biological revolution has wrought, it has not had any direct applications for preventing juvenile delinquency or promoting juvenile rightency.

Equally provocative is the research on behavioral inhibition of forbidden behaviors, in which some children may not be physiologically responsive to parental disapproval and thus do not learn how to control their antisocial behavior or psychopathic behavior. Mednick (1979) developed a theory and provided empirical testing of the idea that delinquent behavior is produced by a deficiency in responding to punishment that is meted out by the parent in order to stop a child from performing an antisocial behavior. He and his colleagues did not look at the converse of these findings, that there may be physiological responses that are conducive to rightency. It is probably assumed that if these responses are within normal ranges, then parental socialization will automatically produce rightent behaviors in children. This is an assumption that not only needs study, but, should it be true, we need to know the active ingredients that favor positive socialization outcomes. Mednick's discussions are very complex and have resisted unitary interpretations of given empirical outcomes (cf. Trasler, 1987, p. 207, on hyporesponsivity, or attenuated phasic autonomic nervous system responses). Moreover, even presuming that these theories are fruitful, action programs based on them have not yet been considered in primary prevention, either for preventing limitations from leading to delinquency or promoting strengths leading to rightency. However, it may be possible to imagine disciplinary procedures on the sole basis of reinforcing desired actions rather than punishing undesired ones for children who appear to be insensitive to punishment.

This positive reinforcing type of discipline might be useful for all children, including those who respond within normal ranges of parental censure. The behavior modification admonition "catch 'em being good" might be expanded systematically into a full form for child rearing for both inhibition-deficient and inhibition-sufficient children (cf. Hawkins et al., 1992, p. 147). Thus, although basic knowledge in biology and genetics grows rapidly, there is still an enormous distance between this explosion in information and its translation into primary prevention (Johnson, 1996).

Cognitive Component

Quay (1987, p. 114) summarizes the literature from what I termed the problem bias, that is, one that emphasizes the negative problems. This literature stubbornly shows that youth with conduct problems test about eight IQ points below their peers who do not exhibit these problems. Finer analysis seems to locate most of these differences in the verbal skills rather than performance skills. The more aggressive delinquents appear to score a full standard deviation below that of their nondelinquent peers (Quay, 1987, p. 113). But whether or not this means that less bright kids become delinquent is to go far beyond the causal information in these data. What may be important is the hint about verbal skills as one path that prevention might explore. Let's reinterpret these findings with regard to rightency. Presumably, Quay is reporting that youths who do not show conduct problems, but rather exhibit positive behavior patterns, have "normal" IQ scores. It would be more helpful to know whether those youths who exhibit high levels of positive behaviors have higher than normal IQ scores, especially in verbal aspects. Even though the direction of causation would not be clear, it would provide impetus for promotive training programs in verbal skills as one aspect of delinquency prevention and rightency promotion. The promotion programs that deal with verbal skills, such as Levenstein (1988), Barnett (1993), Shure and Spivak (1988), Gordon (1970), and many others, might then be connected with this overall topic as follows.

High-quality Head Start-type programs, such as the well-known High/Scope (Perry) Preschool Program (Barnett, 1993; Schweinhart & Weikart, 1988) and other early intervention programs like Levenstein's (1988) Mother-Child Home Program (also known as the doll demonstrator project), indicate that it is very possible to improve the IQ scores of service children over those of controls. However, these differences tend to wash out in the early grades probably because of the bleaching effect of a public education that is less stimulating and caring than were the Head Start-like experiences. Yet longitudinal studies that follow these preschoolers into their young adult years suggest cost-effective outcomes, such as percentage ever arrested or charged (as juveniles or adults), number of property or violence arrests, and adult total nonminor arrests. All of these instances favored the preschool group over the nonpreschool group at statistically significant levels (Berrueta-Clement, Schweinhart, Barnett, & Weikart, 1987, p. 230). There are other educational, employment, and parenthood advantages for preschool veterans compared to their control group peers. It is interesting to note an addition to the Piagetian basis for the Perry Preschool program that involved having these young pupils plan what they wanted to do in a given day, implement those plans, and, later, discuss what they have experienced; these involve verbal skills combined with planning and analysis skills. Thus, a reasonably solid piece of evidence for preventing juvenile delinquency and promoting juvenile rightency comes from the Schweinhart and Weikart project. However, it is important to note that the preschool group still had considerable problems—one third had not finished high school; half were not working at age 19; and about one third had been arrested by age 19. Because a program works well statistically with an experimental group does not mean that individual members of that group go free of all problems.

Levenstein's (1988) Mother-Child Home Program (MCHP) approached working with very young children and their mothers (as principle and often sole parent) in a quite different way from Head Start. MCHP was a home-based program centering on stimulating a rich verbal interaction between mother and child. Age-graded toys and books were given to the family in the course of demonstrating how they could be used for mutual enjoyment as it strengthened the child's verbal skills. Results indicated improved IQ scores for the experimental groups, better social-emotional ratings, and stronger positive attitudes toward school. Levenstein and her colleagues did not measure delinquency as an outcome of the MCHP program, but these rightency components are important objectives in their own right. By promoting maternal verbal interactions with the child, long-term positive school performance appears to have been attained, an appropriate objective of juvenile rightency promotion.

Another important cognitive program promoting the strengths of individuals is the Shure and Spivak (1988) studies in interpersonal cognitive problem solving (ICPS). In this carefully crafted series of planned classroom interactions, children were aided to think about alternative solutions to a given problem and the potential consequences of each of those possible solutions. This aids youngsters in the process of how to think, rather than teaching them what to think, and thus provides a fundamental tool to deal with the full range of ordinary life situations. It is just these interpersonal problem-solving skills that institutionalized delinquents are found to lack at adequate levels. Shure and Spivak (1988) and their colleagues started a programmatic series of studies to fill in this cognitive black hole so as to prepare young people to deal effectively with everyday affairs. Results over a wide range of populations suggest that this is an effective program promoting cognitive problem-solving skills. It has also been incorporated into other prevention programs as a discrete module because of the fine manual and training program that these researchers have put together.

Affective Components

The Kauai longitudinal study (Werner, 1987, pp. 28-29; Werner & Smith, 1992) is a particularly fruitful prospective study following a group of people from birth to 32 years of age. I will emphasize here the affective components of this study, even though this is only one of many factors Werner and Smith examined. One part of this study examined children born in highly stressful conditions; these included at least four or more risk factors before the age of 2 that were key predictors of delinquency—including poverty, exposure to perinatal stress, a mother with 8 grades or less of education, and family distress. Some of these individuals did become juvenile delinquents; but there were 72 children (42 females and 30 males) who became juvenile rightents (my term, not Werner's)—young adults with positive social and personal attributes. Werner and her colleagues have identified the (statistically significant) distinguishing protective features between the delinquents and her resilient group (rightents). First, the resilient group contained more firstborns, whose mothers perceived them as "very active," "affectionate," and "easy to deal with" as infants. Differentiating features of resilients versus youths with delinquent records included better verbal ability, a more internal locus of control, higher self-esteem, and higher scores for nurturing and responsible attitudes (for both boys and girls; Werner, 1987, p. 29).

In addition to protective factors cited above—those that promote rightency—Werner also identifies factors that increase vulnerability in children at risk for delinquency. These included the absence of structure in the lives of these children at risk and the absence of strong social bonds. "The lack of emotional support was most devastating to children with a constitutional tendency toward withdrawal and passivity, with low activity levels and irregular feeding or sleeping habits" (Werner, 1987, p. 30).

Werner (1987, pp. 30-31) goes on to note that increased vulnerability was found in children whose mothers were pregnant again before the index child was 2 years old. Mothers rated these children as more difficult to handle in terms of their tempers, eating, and sleeping habits. During childhood, these children who later became delinquents changed schools more often and lost more close friends. Their parents were more often ill (mental and physical illness), and the families exhibited more discord and permanent father absence. By age 18, a greater proportion of delinquent-prone children than resilient children had very low opinions of themselves, as well as an external locus of control (believing that events happened to them beyond their own control).

Reviewing these factors, one gets the general sense of a group of children that suffered many affective blows and losses throughout their lives, events that made it more difficult for these vulnerable children to feel good about themselves or their social world. Werner (1987) notes that among the significant discriminators in infancy between high-risk children who did or did not commit delinquent acts were

characteristics of the caretaking environment critical for attachment and the establishment of a secure bond between the infant and the

primary caretaker. That is, the amount of attention given to the infant
and the quality of the early caretaker/child relationship. (p. 35)

Given these data that indicate, among other individual and social
environmental components, that affective conditions are important
for healthy growth and development, are there any preventive/pro-
motive programs that have used these conceptual ideas in addressing delinquency and rightency? Certainly, there are many programs
that present affective or psychoeducational training. However, in the
literature, these studies are identified as vehicles providing for the
sake of the general development of children, as contrasted with the
goal of providing a specific delinquency prevention or rightency
promotion. By reviewing these studies, I want to make the point that
the self-conscious promotion of correlates of rightency is a positive
contribution for overall human development and, in particular, the
prevention of delinquency.

Booth, Spieker, Barnard, and Morisset (1992) present one program
that emphasizes the affective (among other components) by promoting mother/infant attachment (using the Ainsworth, Blehar, Waters,
& Wall, 1978, classic Strange Situation as a measurement tool). Booth
et al. use two types of intervention with their 147 high-social-risk
women who sought prenatal services from health department clinics.
After pretreatment assessments, women were randomly assigned to
a standard public health model (termed Information/Resource [IR])
that provided information to the client and aided in making her
aware of community resources; or to a mental health (MH) model
that promoted the mother's competencies and the mother/child
relationship skills. It is these relationship skills that I would conceive
to be most relevant to the affective component. Services were individualized and used the therapeutic relationship to assist the mother
to achieve what she (the mother) wanted. This included making
use of the mother's available support systems, fostering decision-
making skills, dealing with situational concerns, increasing the mother's
self-image, and—most relevant for the present discussion—enhancing mother-infant attachment (Booth et al., 1992, pp. 31-32). To do
this, the nurse engaged the mother in various ways of becoming
aware of the fetus and in discussing values, beliefs, and expectations
regarding the infant (cf. Belsky & Benn, 1982). Results suggested that
"less competent mothers had better outcomes in the MH group and
more competent mothers had better outcomes in the IR group"

(Booth et al., 1992, p. 35). Implications of these findings became clearer in follow-up studies when the children were 4 years old. In general, insecurely attached children tended to be successful in getting their goals met but used aggressive techniques to do so; these authors predict that this kind of short-term solution may be related to peer rejection in the future, which is "predictive of subsequent deviance" (Booth et al., 1992, p. 38). Thus, this study suggests that by taking positive actions to increase affective relationships between mother and child, the child will become more securely attached, which will have a ripple effect on other rightent objectives.

Behavioral Components

The bottom line for delinquency or rightency is the behavior of juveniles within the societal and cultural contexts that define these actions as desired or undesired, rewarded or punished (if detected). Michelson (1987, pp. 292-293) presents his behavioral social skills training (BSST) model to address children's antisocial, aggressive, noncompliant behaviors. From this perspective, such children have not learned the necessary skills to function optimally and thus need to be trained in these intra- and interpersonal skills. Michelson (1987) notes that "the primary objective of the BSST program is to train children and adolescents in specific adaptive behaviors related to critical areas in interpersonal functioning" (p. 293)—whatever is needed by a particular child at a given time. To this end, Michelson, Sugai, Wood, and Kazdin (1983) developed and tested a series of 60 modules that have yielded significant outcomes across normal, at-risk, maladjusted, and inpatient populations (Michelson, 1987, p. 294). Simpler skills were trained first, moving progressively to more complex social skills. All of these modules were designed to promote appropriate social behavior using (a) instruction and coaching by the trainer and (b) modeling. The ordinary behavioral repertoire of practice, prompting, feedback, and reinforcement of successful efforts were used. Results support the beneficial effects on BSST on children with marked antisocial behaviors.

However, Michelson notes that combining the behavioral BSST with the cognitive interpersonal cognitive problem solving (ICPS) model (Shure & Spivak, 1988) probably represents the most promising procedure for both prevention and treatment. Michelson (1987) writes:

BSST develops the behavior through repeated practice, feedback, reinforcement, and modeling experiences across a large number of critical interpersonal situations. ICPS is based on the view that social maladjustment results from deficits in several cognitive processes and verbal mediation skills and the control that these processes and skills exert over behavior. (p. 298)

Michelson cites research to support his claim.

As I will discuss later, these cognitive and behavioral components are eminently combinable. Indeed, it is part of the configural approach to construct the most feasible combination possible so as to optimize chances for successful outcomes. Gordon's (1970) parent effectiveness training programs have been shown to be successful on a broad scale with parents seeking to promote effective, no-lose communication skills. Botvin and Tortu (1988) describe a comprehensive life skills training program to prevent substance abuse, whereas Schinke and Gilchrist (1984) offer a different but equally comprehensive approach to life skills training to promote effective development in all adolescents. Danish, Pettipas, and Hale (1993) provide for life skills training through sports, thus capitalizing on this powerful attractant for juveniles.

Token economies are another behavioral method to promote desired behavior by giving the person a token each time he or she performs some desired behavior, on the presumption that doing the reinforced desired actions will become habitual. These tokens can be exchanged for whatever particular reinforcer the client chooses, because what may be reinforcing at one time may not be at another. Elaborate plans are established in which the clients learn to expect so many tokens for a certain behavior, thus adding a cognitive component to the situation. Once made "dependent" on the anticipated reinforcement for desired behaviors, the client needs to be put on a self-reinforcing schedule where he or she provides the (cognitive or affective) reinforcement for doing the "appropriate" behavior. Such token economies usually require a closed institutional environment so that all relevant behavior may be monitored and reinforced as appropriate. Phillips (1968) and his colleagues used token reinforcement procedures in a home-style rehabilitation setting for predelinquent boys; the program was named Achievement Place. Well-trained house parents lived with a small group of youth (ages 10 to 16) who had had repeated contacts with the juvenile authorities

(Quay, 1987, p. 254). The program involved a point system for desired behaviors that was eventually phased out as the youth moved toward leaving the home. Measures on changes during the time the youth were at the home were very positive—improvements were seen for "social behavior, cleanliness, punctuality, school work, conversational skills, and conflict negotiation" (Quay, 1987, p. 254). However, postprogram data were disappointing, because the positive effects appeared not to generalize to youths' behavior in the community. Later variations of this model, now called the Teaching Family Model, had similar disappointing postprogram results, suggesting that the capability of an institutionalized behavior modification program to facilitate generalization of positive behaviors is limited (Quay, 1987, p. 256).

Tharp and Wetzel's (1969) model for behavior modification in natural environments may yet have useful implications for token economies in the homes of ordinary community families. Some kind of clear point-system-superseded-by-learned-behavior-system for rightent behaviors might promote the same kinds of desired behaviors observed in Achievement Place. However, because these would take place in the home—the natural community environment—there would not be the problem of generalization. Probably, good parents everywhere reinforce desired behavior relatively consistently and humanely, thus achieving rightency in the majority of children. The task may be to clarify these natural procedures and to extend them to parents less-well informed and motivated.

Emphasizing Primary Group Strengths Supporting Juvenile Rightency

Let us distinguish two-person groups, such as a tutor and tutee or a Big Brother and his Little Brother, from greater than two-person groups (here termed multiple-person groups), such as the mixed nondelinquent and predelinquent kids combined into groups in the St. Louis study (Feldman, Caplinger, & Wodarski, 1983) or the peer culture development intervention described by Gottfredson and Gottfredson (1992).

Two-Person Groups

One of the oldest delinquency prevention projects was the Cambridge-Somerville study, initiated on the eve of World War II. As

Allport (1951) described the originator's (Richard Cabot) intentions in dealing with difficult and rebellious youths living in problematic circumstances: Such a predelinquent "may conceivably be steered away from a delinquent career and toward useful citizenship if a devoted individual from outside his own family gives him consistent emotional support, friendship, and timely guidance" (quoted in McCord & Tremblay, 1992, p. 198). Two matched pairs of boys were selected based on age (mean age, 10.5 years old); intelligence; physiques; family environments; social environments; and their records indicating delinquency-prone behavior, and then randomly assigned to experimental or control conditions (McCord & Tremblay, 1992, pp. 198-200). From 1939 to 1945, social workers (at least those who did not go into the armed forces) assigned to the boys met about twice a month on the average. Half received academic tutoring, about one third received medical or psychiatric attention, and almost half attended summer camps. Most had participated with their social workers in athletic or craft activities, and the boys' families also asked for help with illness and unemployment. Excellent service records were kept (McCord & Tremblay, 1992, p. 200). The control group may have gotten various kinds of community aid but not as an integrated package provided by the experimental-group social workers, a kind of early counseling and case management.

The negative results came as a surprise, and further analysis suggested that the experimental treatment may itself have been harmful (McCord & Tremblay, 1992, pp. 202-204). Even when the social worker believed he or she had helped the most, or had a very good rapport with the client, still the objective evidence (indexed crime record; died prior to age 35; or received a medical diagnosis as alcoholic, schizophrenic, or manic-depressive) showed negative results. McCord's analysis of these findings may be helpful: Cabot believed that one should compensate for, or seek to undo, the deficits in people's backgrounds who were at high risk for delinquency. The study children had many types of problems with their parents; the social workers attempted to become substitute parents, mainly dealing with fun activities but also providing support where needed. The social workers were generally well liked by their charges—but not enough to get them to model rightent behavior. Also, McCord notes, this attention may have stigmatized the child as being at risk or being inadequate, and that supportive, friendly guidance was not sufficiently strong to counteract the various factors in the child's personality and environment that put him at risk of delinquency. One might add that meeting on the average of two times per month may not have been intense enough to make a significant positive impact. McCord suggests that control theory, which assumes delinquency is the result of failure to develop appropriate attachments to family, school, and the community norms, may also have been a false lead, a point that I will raise again in connection with the work of Hawkins and his colleagues. Long-term follow-ups sustain the initial pattern of untoward findings.

The reason this study is important is that many prevention projects are still conceived in the compensatory model, a kindly and charitable approach that may not address the full range of issues in the high-risk situation, rather than as a guide to promoting rightency behaviors. Also, the control theory may not be an adequate guide to delinquency prevention or rightency promotion. [See other studies with negative results employing related theories and practice methods, e.g., O'Donnell, 1992, on the Buddy System: "This finding meant that the Buddy System was helpful for the 13.2% of the youths with a prior arrest, but harmful for the remaining 86.8%!" (p. 215). One of the points raised in his critical assessment of his own project is the possibility that predelinquent kids met one another and formed negative peer influences outside the counseling or buddy systems. Goldstein and Glick, 1994, develop their model of the prosocial gang from this point. I will return to the later developments of O'Donnell's thinking and the Goldstein & Glick program.]

Another one-to-one program may serve the promotion of rightency more directly. Peer tutors bring together a student in need of some specific kind of help and another student who is somewhat more advanced on that topic, even though the tutor may not be free of problems in other areas. So, when a predelinquent 10-year-old who is just getting by in reading or math is invited to be a tutor to a 7-year-old who is having trouble at the very beginnings of reading or math, then we have a quintessential tutoring paradigm. The results from a variety of studies suggests that the tutee gets some help from the one-to-one tutoring, but, more interestingly, that the tutor him- or herself may derive a number of benefits from this experience (Allen, Philliber, & Hoggson, 1990; Havens & Stolz, 1989; Jason & Rhodes, 1989). One benefit is the extra practice and the thought that goes into preparing to teach the basics, which adds to the tutor's own reading or math skills. Another is the social approval that the tutor gets, unlike the usual aversive experiences he or she receives from authority figures. This may lead to feelings of increased self-worth and the mastery of some academic and interpersonal challenges that serve as the beginnings of other social successes. Both tutor and tutee appear to escape from the stigmatization of adult/child projects, and what may be lacking in accuracy and polish may be compensated for by the enthusiasm and immediacy of the juvenile culture and communications.

However, I could find no specific primary prevention project that used peer tutors to prevent delinquency per se. The objectives of current projects were generally much closer to the immediate academic and personal problems tutees and tutors were experiencing. That is, they were rightency objectives and should be valued both for their own sake and for the hypothesized linkage between these objectives and the long-term goal of good adult citizenship.

Multiple-Person Groups

Feldman (1992) and Feldman et al. (1983) present findings from their St. Louis experiment, briefly described as effective treatment of antisocial youths in prosocial peer groups. It is important to note that only one antisocial youth was placed in a given prosocial group so as to maximize the predicted effect of the transfer of a positive peer culture to the antisocial youth (Feldman, 1992, p. 235). One of the interesting features of this study of youths enrolled in a suburban community center where the random mixing of antisocial and prosocial peer groups took place is that three types of behaviors were studied simultaneously: "prosocial behavior"—any action by a group member that was directed toward completion of a group task; "antisocial behavior"—any action that disrupts, hurts, or annoys other members; and "nonsocial behavior"—any action not directed toward completion of group tasks, but that does not interfere with another member's participation (Feldman, 1992, p. 239). Prosocial behaviors bear a strong resemblance to rightency behaviors, although limited to the group context, and thus are of particular interest to the goal of promoting rightency.

The research design was quite sophisticated, with different group methods of group practice involved and different levels of experience by the group leaders. The overall results may be summarized briefly as follows:

> Boys who were treated by experienced leaders benefited considerably more from the program than boys who were treated by inex-

perienced leaders. . . . By the end of treatment, 96.7% of these boys' observed behaviors was prosocial. . . . In contrast, at the end of treatment merely 2.4% of their behavior was antisocial." (Feldman, 1992, p. 243)

The experienced group leaders were graduate social work students, and the inexperienced leaders were undergraduate students. The particular group method used had little impact on the boys' behavior changes. Problematic boys in mixed groups of boys—both those "referred" for problematic behaviors with those who were "not referred"—showed significant decreases in antisocial behaviors, whereas those in unmixed groups did not (Feldman, 1992, p. 244).

Note that the peer culture development (PCD) intervention described by Gottfredson and Gottfredson (1992, pp. 315-321) involved a half-and-half mix of students in trouble in school and students not in trouble. These 14- to 17-year-olds come together in a for-credit high school class for 15 weeks, examining and confronting antisocial behavior under the guidance of conventional role models. Results suggest no positive effects of this intervention and some indications of adverse effects regarding delinquent behavior and drug use. One obvious implication concerns the proportion of antisocial to prosocial youths and the peer culture evolving from this mix.

Another conceptual-action model was developed by Patterson (1982) and his colleagues at the Oregon Social Learning Center (Dishion, Patterson, & Kavanagh, 1992). Beginning from a behavioral perspective, these theorist-practitioners moved to a coercion model that describes the evolution of antisocial behavior as beginning in the display of trivial aversive behavior that is not countermanded by parents and that grows into a persistent pattern of problem behavior. Parenting skills appear to be inadequate to deal with these early expressions of aggressive or harmful behaviors. Using a sophisticated multimethod and multitrait approach, these researchers carefully defined their concepts in measurable ways and developed a general model of antisocial (and prosocial) behavior—like the delinquent and rightent terms used in this chapter. The focus is on families as the critical variable. (See Geismar & Wood, 1986, for a review of the family variable in connection with juvenile delinquency.) Dishion et al. (1992) also note that a child's antisocial behavior leads to adjustment problems with peers and in school.

Let us consider some of the concepts and methods used by the Patterson group: "Inept parental discipline practices" (Dishion et al.,

1992, p. 257) in interaction with a child's coercive behaviors (a general term for antisocial behaviors) became the focus of attention in home observations; the researchers chose not to use the less objective parent reports of behaviors in these natural environments. Dishion et al. (1992) found that "poor parent discipline practices increase the likelihood of child coercive responses, and high rates of child coercion impedes [a] parent's attempts to provide evenhanded, consistent, and effective discipline" (p. 258).

The research findings were then translated into preventive/promotive practices. These transactions were observed in their moment-to-moment changes such that when parents were aided to make specific changes, there were immediate reductions in the child's coercive responses (Dishion et al., 1992, p. 258).

The Adolescent Transitions Program (ATP) involved 119 at-risk families (with children of a mean age of 12 years) assigned randomly to one of four interventions, which were later collapsed into two groups—family management skills (with either a parents-only or a parents-and-teen focus) and a nonfamily focus (a teens-only or a "self-directed change" approach that approximated a no-treatment control group). It was hypothesized that the family management skills group would perform better than the nonfamily focus group. The 12-week program included parent training on four critical skills: monitoring, prosocial fostering, discipline, and problem solving. Two staff leaders are aided by a parent consultant—a person who completed the course earlier and who models appropriate parenting skills, and who is available both in-session and between-session to aid parents in implementing these skills—a kind of adult-peer tutor.

The teen curriculum involved training for self-monitoring, prosocial goal setting, developing peer friendships that were prosocial, problem-solving skills, and communication skills. The self-directed intervention did not involve weekly group meetings as did the other interventions, but rather the informational materials developed in these other groups were mailed to families on a biweekly basis.

In general, the results support the hypothesis that improvement in child problem behavior is mediated by improvements in parent discipline practices (Dishion et al., 1992, p. 276). These results are especially clear in the school setting (teachers' ratings), which has important significance to future problem behavior. Delinquency is not specifically named, but antisocial behavior and school adjustment problems would be consistent with other predictors of delinquency. Note that Dishion et al. call this a secondary prevention program, probably because 12-year-old participants already have serious problems; presumably, the same kind of program could be adopted for use with younger children. This remains another step for demonstration research. (See a related project using the Patterson model in a Montreal kindergarten system and followed for 6 years, to date, with similar results; Tremblay et al., 1992.)

A different approach was developed by Goldstein and his colleagues over the past quarter century (Goldstein & Glick, 1994), building on the social learning theory by Bandura (1977, 1986). Skills training programs emerged in the 1970s among the dominant psychological methods—the psychodynamics, nondirective, and behavioral models.

> Viewing the helpee more in educational, pedagogic terms rather than as a client in need of therapy, the psychological skills trainer assumed he was dealing with an individual lacking, deficient, or at best weak in the skills necessary for effective and satisfying interpersonal and intrapersonal functioning. (Goldstein & Glick, p. 47)

The approach these authors developed, termed Skillstreaming, was used with various kinds of people locked in violent situations—family disputes, child abuse, and aggressive adolescents.

Skillstreaming has been successful in enhancing a variety of prosocial or rightent skills, such as assertiveness, empathy, negotiation, perspective-taking, and self-control (Goldstein & Glick, 1994, pp. 49-51). It is combined into a larger program, termed aggression replacement training (ART), that has three components: (a) affective (involving an anger management program); (b) cognitive (via Kohlberg's moral education program, which I will discuss later); and (c) behavioral (the Skillstreaming program). I will emphasize this third component here: Skillstreaming involves the modeling of desired behaviors, the role playing of these behaviors, performance feedback, and transfer of learning. Given the weak, generalizing results of other behavioral programs, Goldstein and Glick (1994, pp. 55-56) wisely amplified their transfer of learning training.

The core ART curriculum consists of a 10-week program involving each of the three components each week. For example, the first session involves skillstreaming work on expressing a complaint, moral reasoning with three case situations, and an introduction to anger management. Goldstein and Glick present evidence to suggest that this is a fruitful approach. This includes some beginning data on the all-important generalization of effect, from one gang to other gangs it contacts.

Goldstein and Glick's work is essentially with aggressive gangs, so their approach is closer to treatment than to primary prevention. However, it is likely that the anger management and the moral educational components would be useful for youths in similar social environments—before they are involved with gangs. Skillstreaming would have to be redirected to fit the needs of an at-risk group, but this seems feasible. In short, it seems possible to use the Goldstein and Glick model to promote rightency; this is a hypothesis that requires longitudinal research to testing.

Emphasizing Secondary Group Strengths: Neighborhoods, Communities, Agencies, and Institutions Supporting Juvenile Rightency

Neighborhood schools frequently have been used as points for preventive and promotive activities because they offer the opportunity to influence almost every child in the country. However, schools, teachers, and associated organizations differ greatly in how much beyond the 3 Rs they take into their curricula and how this extra content is delivered. Likewise, other institutions offer a broad opening for primary prevention messages to large numbers of people: Mass media; public agencies at the federal, state, and local levels; religious organizations of many types; some private social welfare agencies; and some entrepreneurial organizations may influence large and/or specialized audiences. This section will review some of these secondary groups for their influence supporting juvenile rightency.

The Seattle Social Development Project (Hawkins et al., 1992, p. 141) involved a 4-year experimental program with teachers and parents of a multiethnic panel of children going from Grades 1 through 4 in eight urban schools. The goal of this project was to reduce childhood risks for delinquency and drug abuse by promoting factors hypothesized by their social development model (Hawkins & Weis, 1985) to protect against both types of behaviors. I would term what this project sought to promote as components of juvenile rightency.

The social development theory conceptualized its goal as attachment and commitment to, and belief in, conventional social units
(family, school, peers, and, by extension, neighborhood, community,
and state). By sequentially forming strong bonds at appropriate
periods in their development, young people will be protected from
engaging in delinquency or drug abuse. I would add that the set of
conventional beliefs, values, and actions they engage constitute components of juvenile rightency.

The experimental program consisted of having teachers in Grades
1 through 4 trained in an instructional package with three major parts
(Hawkins et al., 1992, p. 144-145): (a) proactive classroom teaching,
which involves establishing an environment that is conducive to
learning and appropriate student behavior while minimizing disrup-
tions; (b) interactive teaching, which assumes that all children can
learn if each specified learning objective is mastered before going to
the next; and (c) cooperative learning, which involves the use of small
groups of students as learning partners dealing with a common
problem. This package of interventions reduces academic failure,
early conduct disorders, and peer rejection as risk factors for delinquency and drug use by involving students in rewarding activities
that would bond them to the school and their peers.

Likewise, students were trained in the interpersonal cognitive
problem solving program (Shure & Spivak, 1988), which enhanced
social adjustment through the development of skills in communication, decision making, and conflict resolution (Hawkins et al., 1992,
p. 146). This component sought to reduce early conduct disorders,
peer rejection, and involvement with antisocial others through social
skills that students would find rewarding and that would lead to
bonding with prosocial peers and others. Put positively, it sought to
increase prosocial skills and the group contexts in which these would
be practiced and reinforced—in short, the promotion of components
of rightency.

The third part of the program involved voluntary parent training,
adjusted for the age of the involved children (Hawkins et al., 1992,
pp. 146-147). One part, "Catch 'Em Being Good," consisted of teaching parents to monitor desired and undesired behaviors in their
children along with appropriate reinforcement or moderate aversive
contingencies. Also included were ways to involve children in age-
appropriate roles within the family and more shared time together.
A second part, "How to Help Your Child Succeed in School," sought

to improve parent-child involvement through a positive learning environment at home and through cooperation with the school. Both of these were assumed to increase bonding with the family. Only about half of the parents participated in these voluntary programs.

Results appear generally promising (Hawkins et al., 1992, p. 155). Note that the strategy of this project was not to attack delinquent or drug behavior directly but rather to encourage positive bonding with family and school—what I would term promotion of components of rightency. Indeed, experimental students held the same norms about drug use as did control students, but "they were more strongly bonded to family and school and fewer had initiated either delinquent behavior or alcohol use by fifth grade than controls" (Hawkins et al., 1992, p. 156). I interpret these results to be saying that promoting certain types of rightency was achieved and also resulted in less delinquency.

Kellam's important studies in Chicago/Woodlawn and in Baltimore combine both community epidemiology with life course development (Kellam & Rebok, 1992, p. 162), thereby uniting the mapping of collective risk states with individual developments in order to identify specific antecedents for preventive and promotive programming. For instance, "the Woodlawn studies showed that aggressive behavior of first grade boys was strongly predictive of delinquency and heavy substance use 10 years later" (Kellam & Rebok, 1992, p. 170), whereas the combination of aggressive behavior and shy behavior compounded the antisocial effects. (Shy behavior, by itself, is predictive of later anxiety.) Knowing this, researchers were able to direct particular attention to these combined predictive behaviors. They further discovered the centrality of concentration problems for both aggressiveness and shyness (as well as poor academic achievement). One part of their Baltimore program involved the Good Behavior Game, which involved an entire class in group-contingent behavior management: Good behavior was promoted by rewarding teams; thus, the antisocial behavior of individuals became of concern to the whole group.

Results were generally supportive: "For both males and females, the Good Behavior game had a significant impact on aggressive and shy behavior as rated by teachers. Peer nominations of aggressive behavior by their classmates were also significantly reduced" (Kellam & Rebok, 1992, p. 185). The effects were strongest with the most aggressive children. The authors correctly note that teachers were also the change agents, and so independent observers are being added to evaluate the outcome more objectively.

It is interesting to note that Kellam and Rebok view these positive findings about what I would call improved rightency behaviors as being short-term effects as compared to the long-term goals of reducing delinquency and drug abuse. However, I would suggest that rightency behaviors can involve both short-term objectives and long-term goals, and that a full-formed primary prevention program should take both into account.

In the Hawkins et al. (1992) study, the social development model suggests a sequential building up of rightency effects in which the achievement of bonding in the family makes it potentially easier to achieve bonding in the school, and so on. The accumulative effect of rewarded behavior is likely to persist in new contexts as expectations are raised for constructive social behaviors likewise being reinforced. However, Kellam and Rebok (1992, pp. 186-187) note that crossover effects did not occur in their Baltimore study; that is, between groups having academic achievement training (called "mastery learning") and those having the cooperative behavior training (in the Good Behavior Game), there was little cooperative learning by the former group and little improvement in academic achievement by the latter. This lack of crossover effects argues for the combined use of program components, either sequentially, when the learning of one logically and practically precedes the learning of the other, or simultaneously, when the learning of one will contribute to the learning of the other. It is also possible that the learning of one program might interfere and reduce the effects of the other—or simply be irrelevant to it. Research on these topics is needed.

Gottfredson and Gottfredson (1992) describe three field experiments. One, the unsuccessful peer culture development (PCD) intervention, was mentioned earlier wherein groups made up of equal numbers of delinquent and rightent students were created, seeking to reduce antisocial behavior through positive peer influence. I will now discuss the other two studies dealing with more macro elements, involving changes in social organization.

Positive Action Through Holistic Education (PATHE) involved a comprehensive school improvement program "that simultaneously altered school organization and management and intervened directly with high-risk youths" (Gottfredson & Gottfredson, 1992, p. 312). The former part apparently increased social bonding to the school and reduced disorder, but the latter part did not reduce delinquency or increase learning for high-risk students.

Student Training Through Urban Strategies (STATUS) involved a year-long alternative class for high-risk youths that introduced different social institutions—school, criminal justice system, family, law, and the social contract. Active engagement with these institutions in terms of rules, decision making, rights, and responsibilities was augmented with field visits and speakers—a high-interest and participatory curriculum. STATUS appears to be successful in reducing delinquent behavior, self-reported or official contacts, improved school success experiences, and increased perceived stake in conformity, for the most part. However, students in STATUS did not increase their commitment to future educational goals.

The Gottfredsons seek to sort out the meanings of these findings. One note is that the prediction that increasing social bonding will increase school success, which will in turn decrease delinquency, did not receive support. But discovering which parts of these three projects contained the active ingredients that produced positive results requires us to consider not the ingredient alone but the entire context in which the ingredients appeared. No one answer seems to work with all youths.

Mass media may also be used to send preventive/promotive messages. For example, DeJong and Winsten (1990) report on the use of mass media in the prevention of substance abuse. They note that commercial advertising is designed to bring about new or reinforced attitudes and patterns of purchasing behavior, whereas public health messages seek fundamental changes in listeners, either to start new changes or to encourage changes already underway. They illustrate this theme with the Harvard Alcohol Project launched in 1987, which sought to encourage the use of designated drivers and to promote a fundamental shift in social norms about drinking and driving through prime-time television (i.e., introducing the idea in top-rated show scripts as relevant). Results suggested an increase in use of the designated driver (DeJong & Winsten, 1990, pp. 33-34). They go on to suggest the outlines of a public health approach using the mass media. They do not consider delinquency or prosocial behavior as such, but the implications are provocative.

Would it be possible to use top-rated television shows to promote particular kinds of prosocial behavior by offering desirable alternatives (like the designated driver) within appealing risky situations (as in drinking-and-driving contexts)? This requires that we have a clear picture of the long-term rightency goals. Although there is no constitutional convention at work on these at the moment, I would suggest that Freud's ideas on mental health, expanded by others over time, might do very well for juvenile rightency: To love well, to work well, to play well, and to serve well. Translated to the juvenile sphere, to love well would include the various forms of bonding with family, peers, and particular people or partners. To work well involves performing well in school, in household chores, or in paid or voluntary jobs. To play well involves recreation but also imaginative gaming. To serve well takes the individual into the social realm, where his or her role is seen in the larger sense of giving to others as others had given to him or her. Would these messages "sell"? I would hypothesize that there are some video heros for every generation whose message could include the love/work/play/serve themes as good ways to live in this time and place. Sesame Street provides some of these messages for young children; what remains to be done is to translate these messages into television for older children.

Emphasizing Social/Cultural Strengths Supporting Juvenile Rightency

Davidson and his colleagues (Davidson & Redner, 1988; Davidson, Redner, Amdur, & Mitchell, 1990; Gottschalk, Davidson, Gensheimer, & Mayer, 1987) offer a state-level prevention program for juvenile delinquency: diversion from the juvenile justice system. I interpret these series of studies as being at the societal level because diversion from the ordinary judicial process requires agreement at the state level. This alternative intervention plan emerged because of the ineffectiveness of traditional treatment methods with adjudicated delinquents, their prohibitive expense (institutional treatment of youthful offenders ran more than $40,000 per year in existing crowded facilities), and because of the widespread desire to prevent the problem from occurring (Davidson & Redner, 1988, p. 125).

However, preventing delinquency raises some methodological issues, such as when to intervene most efficaciously without stigmatizing youths with the negative label that may have a self-fulfilling prophecy. Davidson and his colleagues chose the point when a youth was at immediate risk for getting involved with the formal juvenile justice system. Thus, this represents a kind of late prevention program for youths with known high risks; it is not a primary prevention project in the sense that we can promote rightency with youths who have not yet committed serious problems. However, the reality of contemporary life is that this very high-risk group is a cost-effective way of trying to test ideas about preventing recidivism and therefore may also serve as a way of pulling a successful diversion program back to a true primary prevention context.

Likewise, the question of who would work with these youths—professional or nonprofessional—was decided based on cost considerations: Nonprofessionals who had undergone intense (6-week) training would be most cost-effective. The content of the program involved short-term (16 to 18 weeks), intensive efforts (6 to 8 hours per week) based on the social learning model (structured implementation steps; Davidson & Redner, 1988, p. 125).

The actual study involved several phases in which one or another element was varied. In the initial experimental model, two faculty supervised some advanced graduate students who trained undergraduates for the direct contact with youths (average age, 14.3 years) who had been referred to the court for a serious charge. In addition to this model, there were several other comparative interventions: One had a family focus, another had a relationship-therapy focus, a third program was administered within the juvenile court setting, and the fourth was an attention placebo condition. Results on recidivism during the 2 years following the program strongly favored the experimental groups over the control groups. Later phases of the study varied the type of worker and the urban/rural setting, and all proved to support the major effect of diversion over contact with the juvenile justice system.

Now, it is possible to raise the question of diversion programming for youths long before they are referred to the court for serious charges. Davidson and Redner chose not to do this because of the practicalities of funding and the uncertainty of their program effectiveness. They have presented some evidence that suggests that these methods are effective across a variety of contexts, service providers, and locations. It might be appropriate to study an early warning type of diversion program that seeks to promote particular rightency objectives with youths who are beginning to test the borders of their social environment. There are useful ways to test the (social) waters—to grow and develop into one's maturity. We currently leave these to chance; the question the Davidson and Redner project raises is the

broader one of addressing direction toward rightency objectives and
goals.

Various cultures have more or less formal rituals for initiating the
young into maturity. In relatively closed cultural environments, these
folk ways are still quite strong determinants of a child's developing
values. In relatively open cultural settings, these folk ways break
down. Immigrant children tend to take on the local culture, however
hard the parent generation seeks to maintain the old ways. There is
relatively little research on the use of primary prevention to reduce
predictable conflicts as cultures meet. Felner and Adan (1988) describe a transition program as students enter high school. Both social
environments and individuals are targets of preventive changes. The
reported successful outcomes suggest that there may be other ways
to take a proactive stance toward rightency with societal and cultural
groups. Cherry and Redmond (1994) attempted to involve new immigrants in the prevention of alcoholism among youth, who are
facing the conflicting demands of an alcohol-soaked American culture and their parents' nonalcoholic Moslem culture in Afghanistan.
A social marketing technique was used. Unlike a public health approach that seeks behavioral change in all relevant individuals, the
social marketing approach focuses on targeted audiences (market
segmentation). Research on these targeted groups is supposed to
reveal what values are held that may be translated into activities that
would lead people to adopt a particular program. In this particular
case, the issues involved negotiation of having to live in the new
American culture and yet also wanting to maintain traditional values. A balance is sought by all parties involved. I would assert that
this is the development of a set of rightency objectives for this cultural
group in a conflictual context.

Emphasizing Physical Environment Strengths
Supporting Juvenile Rightency

The physical environment has been largely ignored in the delinquency discussion, even though it is recognized that the location of
people in space and time influences behavior. Generally, the physical
environment is blended into sociocultural environments, which
means that we lose some distinctive possibilities. Population density
involves more the perceived sense of crowding than the mere number
of people per square mile (cf. Freedman, 1975; Schorr, 1963).

Gold (1987, p. 62) describes the social ecology of delinquency as the study of the geographic distribution of this type of antisocial behavior. By geographic distribution, he refers to the classic research of Shaw and McKay beginning in the 1920s, where the residences of juvenile offenders were plotted on a map along with their various social characteristics. Gold reminds us that this is the time of highly restrictive immigration laws being enacted and the eugenic fears of the diluting effect of the low-intelligence scores of immigrants. Shaw and McKay's (1942/1969) research found otherwise:

> No racial, national, or nativity group exhibits a uniform, characteristic rate of delinquents in all parts of Chicago. Within the same type of social area, the foreign born and the natives, recent immigrant nationalities, and older immigrants produce very similar rates of delinquents. (p. 4)

Indeed, they found that social areas produced relatively constant rates of delinquents as different people moved in and out of these areas over the course of 50 years. These kinds of demographic facts established the superiority of social over genetic explanations of delinquency and crime (Gold, 1987, p. 67).

The physical environment is overlain with the sociocultural, but its physical characteristics are important considerations. With certain locations come the various degrees of accessibility to needed resources. Certain physical locations are more healthful than others, as Hippocrates noted more than 2,000 years ago, and which John Gaunt (1620-1674) and Thomas Sydenham (1624-1689) expressed in early epidemiological terms. Certain places become preferred because of aesthetic or value reasons.

Taking these ideas about physical environments and human responses into account has led to such professions as city planning and social architecture (building with the needs, abilities, and limitations of human beings in mind). One classic expression of fine architecture and disgraceful social functioning was the public housing unit, Pruitt-Igoe, in St. Louis. Winner of architectural awards, this set of mammoth high rises had narrow corridors, dim lights, and elevators that stopped at alternate floors (all to save money); in addition, it had limited play areas on the concrete "lawns" located at a great distance from sight and sound of parents, as well as none of the old community props to provide a sense of meaning and place. It efficiently stored large numbers of poor people at great distances from the suburban area, but it failed to provide homes. Thus, after a few years of falling into abject disrepair—even the city would not be a good absentee landlord—and social disgrace, it was blown out of existence, a symbol of literal monumental failure (Ittelson, Proshansky, Rivlin, Winkel, & Dempsey, 1974). I believe that the high crime rate in this housing unit also contributed to its downfall. Dark corridors made it hard to protect one's property and self from attack. The lack of accessibility and mobility within the buildings led to "dens of thieves" of all types.

Another set of studies of physical location involves the damage that place (and things that occur in place) does to its occupants. Noise from traffic from nearby freeways is correlated with children's poorer achievement in schools, which has lifelong implications (Monahan & Vaux, 1980). Pollution (such as lead in automobile fumes) affects children living on lower floors of high rises near commuter highways more than it does children living on higher floors. This form of lead poisoning also leads to academic problems as well as physical health concerns ("Is there lead in your water," 1993; Lin-Fu, 1979).

In general, the physical environment alone can be shown to have important effects on human behavior, but especially so in combination with sociocultural symbols placed on these physical events. I have listed mainly detrimental ones because these cause identifiable problems, but it should be equally true that the physical environment can be the basis for stimulation and promotion of health and happiness. The "Garden Cities" movement at the turn of the century was an attempt to obtain the strengths of rural areas—healthy environments, beautiful woods and streams—with the strengths of the urban areas—rich, stimulating cultural possibilities and places of learning. At the same time, these early planned communities tried to avoid the drawbacks of each—the rural isolation and the urban crowds and dirt.

Our New Age thinking tries to transform the existing physical environment into one more compatible with social and personal needs. We set aside large areas as national and state parks for extended vacations. We create greenbelts near cities to recreate our social nature. We built fitness trails, work-out exercise rooms in skyscrapers, and pools in community buildings, all to bring the physical environment and our part in it into closer coordination. But whether any of this is related to the promotion of rightency is doubtful. Wilderness experiences for at-risk youth do not appear to show empirical results in relation to sustained prosocial behavior. We have much to learn in this component of rightency.

Emphasizing Individual Limitations/Weaknesses That Facilitate Juvenile Delinquency

This section of the chapter now takes a more traditional cast, as studies addressing various components of the human ecology are viewed in a pathogenesis perspective. I have already introduced many of these topics in order to discuss rightency; in this section, I will emphasize those that appear to be related to delinquency.

Biological/Physiological Components

Trasler (1987, p. 184) defines biogenetic as related to temperamental, cognitive, and reactive characteristics that are thought to be genetically transmitted, and are governed to some degree by the physiological system in the brain and the autonomous nervous system, that have an effect on behavior and are thought to have the potential to promote or restrain various kinds of delinquent and criminal behavior. Such biological theories now produce bad vibes for many because of early discredited theories such as the view that criminals were degenerates, produced by morally inferior people, which led to eugenic ideas about purifying the races of such atavistic types, and the horrors of the Nazi gas chambers or of Serbian "ethnic cleansing" to carry out these ideas.

However, if we take a deep breath and look at some of the evidence on modern studies of genetics and psychological reaction time, we may find more grounds for understanding the whole picture of delinquency. First, consider twins studies. In these cases, presumably genetically similar or identical people are separated at birth, usually for socioeconomic reasons, and are identified many years later. Then, their psychological and social behaviors may be compared, including their juvenile delinquency or juvenile rightency. Trasler (1987) summarizes the complex research:

> The basic lesson to be drawn from twin studies seems to be that the inter-generational mechanism which predisposes some [monozygotic or identical] twin pairs to high concordance for officially-recorded delinquency is probably mediated both by genetic transmission and by social processes of bonding and interdepen-

dence; there is no known way in which the respective influences of
inherited characteristics and learned social patterns can be disen-
tangled. (p. 189)

Likewise, studies concerning sex chromosome abnormalities as related to crime also have not been supported by evidence (Trasler,
1987, p. 193).

In adoption studies, children are raised by nonbiological parents,
but research attempts to compare the adult criminality of these
children to the criminality of their biological parents. Trasler (1987)
summarized this body of research—a methodological mine field—by
noting that "criminality in biological parents of children adopted
early in their lives was a more reliable predictor of adolescent and
adult criminality than the presence or absence of criminal convictions
in the adoptive or foster parents" (p. 190).

In a different type of biogenetic study, researchers look for physiological differences between delinquents and nondelinquents. Psychologists have found that some people's capacity to respond to
punishment or disapproval is slower or less acute than the average
person's. So, when a child misbehaves and is sent strong disapproval
from the parent, the less responsive child does not pick up the
disapproval and consequently does not learn the internal cues for
stopping certain kinds of (antisocial) behavior. This is a technically
sophisticated literature, and yet the findings are not clear at this time.
"Attempts to demonstrate that delinquents . . . are poor learners, or
are resistant to conditioning, have not been successful" (Trasler, 1987,
p. 206).

Overall, this biological area has produced more inconclusive results than conclusive ones, except in the adoption studies, where we
cannot reject the hypothesis that there may be some genetic connections to delinquency. With all of the other aspects of biology growing
rapidly, we are likely to see a continuation of this research seeking
some genetic connection. But at this time, there is little information
that can guide preventive or promotive research, as reflected in the
current literature.

Intellectual Factors

There have been many studies of intelligence and delinquency, and
yet there are many remaining problems. First, socioeconomic status
(SES) is positively correlated with intelligence, and most delinquents

fall in the lower SES, so that delinquents in general are likely to have lower IQ scores. However, as mentioned earlier, when SES is taken into account, there is still a stubborn eight IQ points between the (lower scoring) delinquent and the (higher scoring) nondelinquent (Quay, 1987, p. 106). Further differentiation in types of intelligence show that most of this difference lies in the area of verbal skill, rather than performance skill, and the aggressive delinquent has an even greater discrepancy with the average nondelinquent (Quay, 1987, p. 113). What these differences mean is another story. Quay (1987, p. 114) speculates that having a lower intelligence is one of many factors that puts a given child at an early disadvantage in the process of life course development. This would include being more vulnerable to poor parenting, poor schooling, and the seductions of antisocial peers—all points of departure for high risk of delinquency.

Temperamental Factors

Thomas and Chess (1977) have identified some general classes of infant responses to the world, which sounds a familiar chord in many parents. One type is called "easy to raise" and is characterized by an openness to new experiences. Another type is called "difficult to raise" and is characterized by being closed to new experiences, even those that are beneficial to their growth and development. Consequently, the temperamentally difficult-to-raise children interact with parents of various degrees of skill and produce a child whose socialization may be bumpy or fully disorganized, with a result of lesser or greater amounts of antisocial behavior.

If these infant temperamental patterns are combined with caretakers who cannot adapt effectively to the infants, then we are likely to find problems. Those mothers who lack a variety of support systems, including being unwed, poor, less educated, and so forth, may be at greater risk of ineffective adaptation to difficult infant adjustment patterns. Werner and Smith (1992) note that unresilient children lack the ability to find an adult, not necessarily a parent, who could supply their developmental needs at crucial times. It may be that temperamental factors contributed to this lack.

Health and Wellness

Researchers are exploring the relationship between child abuse and delinquency, possibly on the supposition that abusers model aggression, which the abused learn and apply in later life. The evidence on the relationship of abuse and delinquency is fuzzy because of methodological problems (Lane & Davis, 1987). In their review of this literature, they offer the following warranted suggestions: (a) Child abuse and neglect are associated with a variety of negative outcomes other than subsequent delinquency, including death; and (b) there is an indication that intervention with *families* of abused or neglected children may prevent the siblings of the maltreated child from becoming abused or neglected, or from committing a juvenile offense, in addition to preventing the recurrence of maltreatment toward the target child and preventing the target child from committing a juvenile offense. These results, however, need to be demonstrated empirically (Lane & Davis, 1987, pp. 135-136).

Attention Deficit Hyperactivity Disorder (ADHD)

Children with significant problems of inattention, impulsivity, and hyperactivity may be diagnosed as having ADHD; about 3% to 10% of the school-age population has this disorder. The imprecision in diagnosis may indicate problems with the concept itself or methods of measurement, or both. The correlates of this condition are also predictors of antisocial behavior: poor tolerance of frustration, noncompliance with authority figures, and difficulty with peers (DePaul & Barkley, 1992, p. 89).

Medication (methylhenidate or MPH) has been shown in many short-term studies to be an effective aid in bringing mother-child interactions into the normal range, as well as reducing problems in the classroom and among peers (DePaul & Barkley, 1992, pp. 96-106). However, other

> long-term follow-up studies . . . have found that protracted use of stimulant medication may not alter the risks for later antisocial behavior, substance abuse, academic failure, or emotional psychopathology *in adolescence*. . . . In fact, in some studies . . . duration of treatment with stimulants is actually negatively related to outcome in that the more treatment subjects received, the more antisocial behaviors displayed at adolescent follow-up. (DePaul & Barkley, 1992, p. 109)

The reasons for this lack of association in long-term connections are unclear; other factors, such as family characteristics, may be involved.

Emphasizing Family/Primary Group Weaknesses/ Limitations Facilitating Juvenile Delinquency

In an interesting analysis—a self-analysis that illustrates an ideal self-correcting basis of science—O'Donnell (1992) described the journey that he and his colleagues made over the course of 20 years, from a simplistic behavioral model to one that led him to hypothesize some social factors that may account for the negative findings of their earlier projects.

Based on the prevailing behavior modification theory of the time (1970)—which assumed that some specific reinforcement increased the probability of a response, whereas extinction reduced or eliminated a response—O'Donnell initiated a Buddy System Project in which at-risk youths (average age, 14 years) were seen by indigenous workers (buddies) who were, in turn, trained and supervised by graduate students and faculty. After building rapport, the buddy would identify problem behaviors that needed change and would institute a modification plan to accomplish this. Results were disappointing with regard to the ultimate variable, delinquency. Experimental youths (who received the buddy intervention) did more poorly than control youths when neither had a prior arrest. (The buddy system did work well with the 13% of youths with a prior arrest.) This finding, and others like it from other studies, suggested that effective work in a specific setting did not generalize to other areas of life.

This recognition led to a (soul) searching review of theory, research, and practice. Starting from a belief in individualized behavior modifiers for particular youths in unique settings, the researchers were gradually won over to the conception of behavior occurring in a social environment with interacting influences—a perspective that social work has held for more than a century. In any case, a new project, the Youth Development Project, was formed that incorporated this perspective. This "is a school-based, social skills training and student-team learning program. . . . Cooperation among the students is required to complete the assignment and receive the individual and group credit" (O'Donnell, 1992, p. 221). The focus is on positive student networks (instead of the kinds of negative associations in the buddy project, where at-risk youths became friends with other at-risk youths, which appears to have led to increased delinquent behavior). In another work, O'Donnell and Tharp (1990) explicate this idea into a more general, behaviorally based community psychology whose key concept is the activity setting. This is defined as

> events in which collaborative interaction, intersubjectivity, and assisted performance occur; they incorporate cognitive and motoric action within the objective features of the setting. . . . The activity setting is not dependent on the experience of any given person, but is the social process common to the participants from which the cognition develops. (O'Donnell & Tharp, 1990, p. 223)

In practical terms, this means the end of attempting to use behavior modification with the individual seen in isolation, because being able to perform some action is only one of many elements to getting that action performed. Likewise, it is not wise to look only at the setting itself without considering the individuals in that setting and related settings. The buddy project tried to change individual (truancy) behavior outside of the activity setting where the behavior would occur (i.e., the classroom). Because the positive changes that happened as an immediate result of the project did not take place in the activity setting where it occurred, the continuation or generalization of that desired behavior was unlikely to occur. In the Youth Development Project, which directly changed classroom structure and individual behavior, this combination of events in the appropriate setting may have contributed to successful results (O'Donnell, 1992, pp. 226-228).

This discussion (of O'Donnell's odyssey) has its parallels in the helping professions at large, in which single sovereign variables give way to multiple variables in complex situations (see also Botvin & Tortu, 1988).

Gordon and Arbuthnot (1987) likewise begin their paper with a selective review of the general lack of effectiveness of individual approaches with delinquents in both community and institutional settings. Group approaches, with both institutionalized and community youth, were effective for some situations but not for others. As researchers began to specify more sharply the targets of intervention that appear to be related to antisocial behaviors, the results look more promising than in earlier studies.

Gordon and Arbuthnot (1987) address research on sociomoral reasoning in youth and particularly delinquents. Following the work of Kohlberg, Arbuthnot and others have provided evidence that "many individuals can experience an advance in moral reasoning stage as a result of structured interventions which typically use guided dilemma discussions . . . to arouse cognitive disequilibrium, combined with exposure to one-stage-higher . . . reasoning" (Gordon & Arbuthnot, 1987, p. 302). Furthermore, they cite evidence that both internal (cognitive) and external (behaviors) show improvement with this sociomoral procedure (Arbuthnot, 1992; Gordon & Arbuthnot, 1987, p. 303).

Gordon and Arbuthnot (1987) also examine outcome research in family interventions in delinquency. First, they consider systems and nonbehavioral family therapy (such as Satir's conjoint family therapy), which show some positive outcomes but have many methodological problems, leaving the reader with some cautious optimism. Second, they discuss social learning approaches to parent training (such as Patterson's Oregon Social Learning Center studies) and find some positive outcomes, including one cost-effective component of a Patterson study (Gordon & Arbuthnot, 1987, p. 309) and some rigorous designs. Closely related is the work of Klein, Alexander and Parsons (1977) using a behavioral-systems family approach, focusing on the entire family as the object of change. Some rigorous research suggests positive outcomes. One interesting point of this preventive program is that the siblings of targeted delinquent youth in the experimental program tend not to get involved with delinquency— an example of primary prevention of a high-risk group.

Overall, there are some rigorous preventive programs that show promise in the delinquency prevention field.

Emphasizing Secondary Group Limitations Facilitating Juvenile Delinquency

Cloward and Ohlin (1960) developed a theory that revolved around opportunity structures, that is, social structures that facilitate the socialization of young people into the normative roles in society. Certain youths (lower class, minority status in particular) are isolated from productive experiences with major institutions (especially employment, but also adequate schooling and support systems). Lacking these normative opportunities, they find substitutes in delinquent gangs that provide socialization into adult roles that are valued in their subculture. These ideas were instrumental to the development of a major federal project, Mobilization for Youth, that, among other things, provided youth with vocational guidance and the opportunity to gain some work experience; the project also tried to make local and state governments more responsive to the needs of low-income people and communities. This and other types of community action programs lost their federal funding, in part because they challenged the powers that be, who did not take well to this effort. Various ideas from these projects surface in other studies to aid institutions and communities in preventing juvenile delinquency.

At the early part of this century, sociologists Clifford Shaw and Henry McKay developed a theory about the origins of juvenile delinquency that revolved around the term *socially disorganized neighborhoods*, where there were neither the resources facilitating positive social goals nor the controls over negative behaviors, resulting in conditions that moved children into antisocial gangs in an attempt to attain what they could not attain in other ways from family or neighborhood or society. Based on extensive empirical studies of rates of delinquency in different zones of the city (Chicago), they developed a preventive strategy:

> Reduction in the volume of delinquency in large cities probably will not occur except as general changes take place which effect improvements in the economic and social conditions surrounding children in those areas in which delinquency rates are relatively high. (Shaw & McKay, 1942/1969, p. 441)

In 1932, Shaw went to the next step to develop the Chicago Area Project, which was an attempt to prevent delinquency by developing neighborhood self-help community groups for inner-city poor who would thereby have some control over their own lives. Different groups developed recreational programs for local youth; community improvements (such as sanitation, education, and health care); and the use of detached workers for local gangs. Lundman (1984, p. 62) writes that Shaw led the Chicago Area effort by going into the targeted communities and rousing local sentiment by accentuating the strengths of these people (as groups) rather than emphasizing their individual limitations. He tried to free people of ethnic and racial stereotypes that paralyzed reform efforts. Shaw was able to galvanize local efforts on their own behalf. However, he performed no evaluation, and we are left with some subjective and biased opinions. Perhaps the best that can be said for the Chicago Area Project is that it showed that poor areas in a large city could mobilize for self-help projects; raise local funds; and be a stable, long-term presence in those neighborhoods.

In other studies, the detached worker idea was tested and found lacking in proof that delinquency could be prevented in this fashion (Miller, 1962). Goldstein and Glick (1994) note that organized efforts to reach out beyond the walls of agencies to befriend at-risk youth has been occurring since the mid-19th century. The general hope is to transform antisocial values to prosocial values—and, it is hoped, behaviors. The detached worker makes contact with youths in a neighborhood by simply being there over a long period of time when his role becomes clear—not cop, not welfare worker, but a kind of social worker helping them in their prosocial activities and controlling their antisocial ones. This involves teaching problem-solving skills and the promotion of prosocial values.

Results from various studies have been uniformly negative (Goldstein & Glick, 1994, p. 31), and even innovators in this area have suggested that the approach not be employed further.

However, Goldstein and Glick (1994) argue that the case is not closed on detached workers because the idea has not been used thoroughly, intensely, or comprehensively with techniques that are efficacious. Their own prosocial gang concept extends the idea of detached workers in new areas, as I discussed earlier under the heading of efforts to promote rightency.

Emphasizing Societal/Cultural Limitations Facilitating Juvenile Delinquency

Although not a primary prevention project, the following program will be useful in understanding how the community and its subcultures are important in juvenile delinquency through attracting and holding members. The Provo Experiment (Empey & Erickson, 1976) emerged from thinking about the role of the community in the development of delinquent behavior. Delinquency was viewed as group behavior of lower-class youths who lacked easy access to the opportunity structure (cf. Cloward & Ohlin, 1960); that is, they lacked access to legitimate means to attain socially approved conventional goals. In a critical assumption, Empey and Erickson thought that if delinquents were exposed to what I would call rightent values (prosocial values), they would become ambivalent about their own delinquent value system. This is like Kohlberg's assumption that higher-level moral reasoning attracts people operating at lower levels.

In the Provo Experiment, serious juvenile offenders were offered an alternative to institutionalization, an intensive group program involving either school or work, and daily group meetings. This group-oriented treatment was based on the assumption that one could challenge the delinquent reward structure by providing realistic alternatives for expressing ambivalent feelings (about a delinquent lifestyle) as well as possibilities for taking on a prosocial lifestyle—even if it involved the drudgery of legitimate employment and ordinary living habits. Through daily guided-group interactions over about 6 months on average, these principles were presented forcefully.

The actual process of these guided-group interactions was like a sensitivity training group where the agenda for talking seemed to emerge from the participants themselves. Actually, a staff person suggested they talk about their delinquent acts, and when participants realized that they could talk about undetected delinquencies, they began being more open with each other (and the staff). As they talked, the delinquents expressed ambivalence about their activities because of the high risks involved (imprisonment). They discovered that what they took to be private ambivalence was, in fact, common among most of the group inside this protected setting. Slowly, some youth began to take leadership roles in helping others see this ambivalence and the risks involved in delinquent behavior.

The work experience was an important component to the project because it was seen to provide a legitimate opportunity structure along with good work habits. At first, adults monitored youths' work behaviors, but this did not work well, and so members began to rotate in the role of foreman (on parks-and-grounds-type city work).

In a quasi-experimental design, Empey and Erickson found that their community-based program was more effective than the state training school in recidivism after 3 to 4 years. However, there was no difference between the community program and probation officers who were acknowledged to have unworkably large caseloads. In several other partial replications of the Provo experiment, either favorable results or no differences emerged between the community-based and the state institutional programs. Because there were considerably lower costs in the community-type projects, they were viewed as the treatment of choice (cf. Kobrin & Klein, 1982).

As Arbuthnot (1992) and Gordon and Arbuthnot (1987) noted, it has been possible to facilitate higher levels of moral reasoning and behavior (based on the Kohlberg model), and so this should suggest a project in which younger or less seriously involved youths receive the sensitivity training about life options before their choices become problematic for them and society.

Emphasizing Physical Environmental Limitations Facilitating Juvenile Delinquency

As mentioned earlier, the epidemiology of juvenile delinquency presents a revealing picture, both for its major emphases—the connection of poor areas and crime, regardless of what sociocultural groups were occupying these areas at a given time—and its minor themes—that there are forms of delinquency in every social class and setting. Attempts to soften the harsh living areas by putting in recreational facilities have not proved to be effective deterrents to juvenile delinquency, and so I would suggest that more attention be given to the sociocultural nature of physical environments in considering causal factors and primary prevention programs.

PUTTING THE PIECES TOGETHER: INTEGRATED VIEWS ON JUVENILE DELINQUENCY AND RIGHTENCY

As readers might have noticed, there are a number of themes that recur among the studies reviewed in this chapter, and it would seem natural to begin with these as the skeleton on which to hang a systemic view of preventing juvenile delinquency and promoting juvenile rightency.

Of individual factors, it would be wise to promote healthy babies who are well-attached to nurturing and consistent parents, given the apparent importance of affective and behavioral data. It seems at this time that biological factors are not easily included in any configural equation on the prevention of juvenile delinquency or the promotion of juvenile rightency. On the other hand, it seems very possible to offer preschool children programs to improve verbal skills, and some basic socializing skills. Likewise, it appears possible to provide school children efficacious programs in cognitive skills, such as interpersonal problem-solving skills that may be applied to a wide range of everyday tasks and challenges.

It should be noted immediately that in offering these individual skills, other people are involved—parents, teachers, and peers, at least. Some of these individual skills can be greatly facilitated by having a trainer (such as a community worker) train the immediate helper (such as a parent). This training not only is useful for the child's benefit, but these helper (or tutor) experiences appear to aid the immediate helper as well. It appears that some parents have not read the training manuals that came with their newborns, and they may need occasional specific training on how to use evenhanded, consistent, and effective methods of disciplining and child rearing. Possibly, all parents could stand to benefit from some review of basics of expected child development along with efficacious ways to facilitate development without tears.

It is quite obvious that all young children need some supportive adult in order to make their way through ordinary life challenges, and if the parents are not available for any psychological or health reason, then research has provided a less obvious observation: that some other adult (a teacher, a member of the clergy, a janitor at the school) may take on that function and so facilitate the resilience of the child. It also appears possible to use other prosocial youths to encourage rightency in target children. Groups appear to be an effective instrument of these normative indoctrinations.

In all of this supportive training, it is necessary to ensure that the children be able to generalize from the specific learning situation to the broad range of community affairs. Generalizing good learning is a critical factor and one that is currently quite weak among delinquency prevention programs.

Sequential bonding to conventional society—family, school, peers, neighborhood, community, cultural group—appears to have payoff, even though it will take directed effort at each new level. The point appears to be to move young children through their developmental years into adult citizen roles without them taking exciting but antisocial by-ways that could result in long, false leads to adulthood. This is easier said than done by any given family, but because it takes a "village to raise a child," we might want to mobilize that sense of community that makes child rearing a shared responsibility. The power of the local barrio or ghetto is to have many friendly eyes following the growth and development of all of their children. Community projects facilitate this sense of wholeness in urban areas where diversity may make it difficult to have one subcultural influence. It appears possible, even in areas relatively poor in social resources and supports, to mobilize residents to get involved with their neighborhood schools and in the community so as to make a difference. Research also suggests that, as children get older, they should be involved in decision making to the extent possible. These involvements tend to take place in alternative settings, but the principle seems applicable to mainstream institutions as well.

The larger world impinges on children and youth through the mass media, and it is now demonstrated that there are many positive and negative influences that come through this multifaceted resource. It is possible to have this mass educational tool serve positive human ends, as well as commercial ones. It may be possible to influence the norms of large groupings in prosocial ways through mass media, supported by small group gatherings for high-risk individuals. However, as more macro elements are brought into view, increasingly complex decision-making processes are necessary to make the laws and the administrative procedures to bring about what we desire. Yet this is the nature of government, and we need to understand its workings in order to use it appropriately for desired social ends.

In a complex society, there may be many versions of "desired social ends" for which negotiation of the social and cultural groups involved will be necessary. It is the nature of representative democracy to enable groups to become involved in these negotiations. But many groups do not become involved, and so, ultimately, a master task of all helping professionals is to raise the consciousness of consumers to their needs and their rights in seeking desired social and personal ends.

This slippery package of delinquency prevention and rightency promotion is far beyond the work of any one helping professional. What appears to be needed, as illustrated in the demonstration projects by Hawkins and his colleagues, is some articulator of factors that both prevent delinquency and promote rightency. Therapists and police-related workers have been given the task of preventing problems; we still need a service category dedicated to planning and coordinating the many factors involved in rightency.

As a summary to this exciting field of ideas and actions, I would like to present a brief review of the findings of the U.S. Department of Justice's *Guide for Implementing the Comprehensive Strategy for Serious, Violent, and Chronic Juvenile Offenders* (Howell, 1995), with particular emphasis on the section written by J. D. Hawkins and his colleagues. In a careful analysis of the evaluated programmatic literature on primary prevention in the delinquency field, these authors report "effective (or proven) interventions" and a group of others identified as "potentially promising program areas," as well as other interventions that "showed no or negative effects on risk and protective factors (pp. 127-128). I will list these three areas and provide some illustrative citations. First, the winners—"well-implemented programs [using] relatively strong research designs and ... thorough and appropriate data analysis" (p. 127). But note the specificity of the program descriptions; what works for kindergarteners may not work for third graders.

Effective (or Proven) Interventions

1. Reductions of class size for kindergarten and first grade (Slavin, 1990a)

2. Continuous-progress instructional strategies (where students proceed through a defined hierarchy of skills and are tested at each level to assess their readiness to advance to the next skill; Slavin & Madden, 1989, p. 64)

3. Cooperative learning (in which students work together on a shared project for which each student has specialized information that needs to be shared with the group in order for the group to attain success; Slavin, 1990b)

4. Tutoring (one-on-one tutoring of a younger child by an older student or adult; Wasik & Slavin, 1994)

5. Computer-assisted instruction (in helping students achieve basic reading and math skills; Slavin & Madden, 1989)

6. Diagnostic and prescriptive pullout programs (see also Wasik & Slavin, 1994)

7. Ability grouping within classes in elementary school (Slavin, 1987)

8. Nongraded elementary schools ("where students are grouped according to their level of academic performance, not their ages"; Gutierrez & Slavin, 1992, p. 334)

9. Classroom behavior management techniques (Kellam, Rebok, Ialongo, & Mayer, 1994)

10. Behavioral monitoring and reinforcement of school attendance, academic progress, and school behavior (Murphy, Hutchison, & Bailey, 1983)

11. Parent training (Kazdin, Siegel, & Bass, 1992)

12. Marital and family therapy (Markman, Renick, Floyd, Stanley, & Clements, 1993)

13. Youth employment and vocational training programs with an intensive educational component (Cave, Bos, Doolittle, & Toussaint, 1993)

The next group of interventions have some evidence for positive program effects but not enough for saying that these are more than potentially promising program areas. Again, note the specificity of the statements, because a program such as mentoring that lacks behavior management techniques has not been proven to be effective. These areas need more rigorously designed research to determine their preventive effectiveness. I will list them all but refer to several illustrative ones (Howell, 1995, p. 129):

Potentially Promising Program Areas

1. Structured playground activities

2. Behavioral consultation for schools

3. Special educational placements for disruptive secondary school students

4. Conflict resolution and violence prevention curricula (Marvel, Moreda, & Cook, 1993)

5. Peer mediation

6. School organization (Comer, 1988)

7. Mentoring relationships that include behavior management techniques

8. After-school recreation

9. Gang prevention curricula (Thompson & Jason, 1988)

10. Gang crisis intervention and mediation

11. Youth services (Allen et al., 1990)

12. Restrictions on the sale, purchase, and transfer of guns (Loftin, McDowall, Wiersema, & Cottey, 1991)

13. Regulations on the place and manner of carrying firearms

14. Metal detectors in schools
15. Intensified motorized patrol
16. Field interrogations (stopping people who appear to be suspicious and asking them about their activities, and sometimes searching them or their cars)
17. Community policing
18. Neighborhood block watch (Lindsay & McGillis, 1986)

Last but not least are the losers, programs whose evaluation showed no or negative effects on risk and protective factors. I will illustrate these with representative citations as well (Howell, 1995, p. 128):

Ineffective Programs

1. Humanistic and developmental instructional strategies (Slavin & Madden, 1989)
2. Teachers' aides (Slavin, 1994)
3. Tracking or between-class ability grouping
4. Nonpromotion of students to the next grade (Holmes & Matthews, 1984)
5. Special educational placements for disruptive, emotionally disturbed, learning-disabled, and/or educable developmentally disabled elementary students (Safer, 1990)
6. Peer counseling (Gottfredson, 1987)
7. Youth employment and vocational training programs without an intensive educational component (Ahlstrom & Havighurst, 1971)

It is not that these are terrible programs that never should have seen the light of day. Each in its own time was an interesting hypothesis, a possibility that needed testing. Each was tested and, given the specific form each demonstration project took, was found lacking. Each enabled us to more toward more effective primary prevention by knowing what not to do as well as knowing what to do. We should continue to read these studies in order to understand our own humane impulses that lead to demonstration projects that may not lead us where we wish to go. But we should also read and further develop the wide array of successful and promising methods for reducing the risks and increasing the protective factors, including the rightency factors, related to antisocial behavior among youth.

REFERENCES

Ahlstrom, W., & Havighurst, R. J. (1971). *400 losers: Delinquent boys in high school.* San Francisco: Jossey-Bass.

Ainsworth, M. D. S., Blehar, M. C., Waters, E., & Wall, S. (1978). *Patterns of attachment.* Hillsdale, NJ: Lawrence Erlbaum.

Albee, G. W. (1983). Psychopathology, prevention, and the just society. *Journal of Primary Prevention, 4,* 5-40.

Allen, J. P., Philliber, S., & Hoggson, N. (1990). School-based prevention of teen-age pregnancy and school dropout: Process evaluation of the national replication of the Teen Outreach Program. *American Journal of Community Psychology, 18,* 505-525.

Allport, G. (1951). Foreword. In E. Powers & H. Witmer (Eds.), *An experiment in prevention of delinquency: The Cambridge-Somerville Youth Study* (pp. i-xxx). New York: Columbia University Press.

Arbuthnot, J. (1992). Sociomoral reasoning in behavior-disordered adolescents: Cognitive and behavior change. In J. McCord & R. Tremblay (Eds.), *Preventing antisocial behavior* (pp. 283-310). New York: Guilford.

Bandura, A. (1977). Self-efficacy: Toward a unifying theory of behavior change. *Psychological Review, 84,* 191-215.

Bandura, A. (1986). *Social foundations of thought and action: A social cognitive theory.* Englewood Cliffs, NJ: Prentice Hall.

Barnett, E. E. (1993). Benefit-cost analysis of preschool education: Findings from a 15-year follow-up. *American Journal of Orthopsychiatry, 63*(4), 500-508.

Belsky, J., & Benn, J. (1982). Beyond bonding: A family-centered approach to enhancing early parent-infant relations. In L. Bond & J. Joffe (Eds.), *Facilitating infant and early development: Primary prevention of psychopathology* (Vol 6, pp. 281-308). Hanover, NH: University Press of New England.

Berrueta-Clement, J. R., Schweinhart, L. J., Barnett, W. S., & Weikart, D. P. (1987). The effects of early educational intervention on crime and delinquency in adolescence and early adulthood. In J. Burchard & S. Burchard (Eds.), *Prevention of delinquent behavior* (pp. 220-240). Newbury Park, CA: Sage.

Bloom, M. (1996). *Primary prevention practices.* Thousand Oaks, CA: Sage.

Booth, C. L., Spieker, S. J., Barnard, K. E., & Morisset, C. E. (1992). Infants at risk: The role of preventive intervention in deflecting a maladaptive developmental trajectory. In J. McCord & R. Tremblay (Eds.), *Preventing antisocial behavior* (pp. 21-42). New York: Guilford.

Botvin, G., & Tortu, S. (1988). Preventing adolescent substance abuse through life skills training. In R. Price, E. Cowen, R. Lorion, & J. Ramos-McKay (Eds.), *14 ounces of prevention* (pp. 98-110). Washington, DC: American Psychological Association.

Burchard, J. D., & Burchard, S. N. (Eds.). (1987). *Prevention of delinquent behavior: Primary prevention of psychopathology* (Vol. 10). Newbury Park, CA: Sage.

Cave, G., Bos, H., Doolittle, F., & Toussaint, C. (1993). *JOBSTART: Final report on a program for school dropouts.* New York: Manpower Demonstration Research Corp.

Cherry, L., & Redmond, S. (1994). A social marketing approach to involving Afgans in community-level alcohol problem prevention. *Journal of Primary Prevention, 14 (4), 289-310.*

Cloward, R. A., & Ohlin, L. E. (1960). *Delinquency and opportunity.* New York: Free Press.

Coates, T. J. (1990). Strategies for modifying sexual behavior for primary and secondary prevention of HIV disease. *Journal of Consulting and Clinical Psychology, 58,* 57-69.

Comer, J. P. (1988). Educating poor minority children. *Scientific American, 259*(5), 42-48.

Danish, S., Pettipas, A., & Hale, B. (1984). Life development intervention for athletes: Life skills through sports. *The Counseling Psychologist, 21,* 352-385.

Davidson, W. S., & Redner, R. (1988). The prevention of juvenile delinquency: Diversion from the juvenile justice system. In R. Price, E. Cowen, R. Lorion, & J. Ramos-McKay (Eds.), *14 ounces of prevention* (pp. 123-138). Washington, DC: American Psychological Association.

Davidson, W. S., II, Redner, R., Amdur, R. L., & Mitchell, C. M. (1990). *Alternative treatments for troubled youth: The case of diversion from the justice system.* New York: Plenum.

DeJong, W., & Winsten, J. A. (1990). The use of mass media in substance abuse prevention. *Health Affairs, 9*(2), 30-46.

DePaul, G. J., & Barkley, R. A. (1992). Social interactions of children with attention deficit hyperactivity disorder: Effects of methylphenidate. In J. McCord & R. Trembley (Eds.), *Preventing antisocial behavior* (pp. 89-116). New York: Guilford.

Dishion, T. J., Patterson, G. R., & Kavanagh, K. A. (1992). An experimental test of the coercion model: Linking theory, measurement, and intervention. In J. McCord & R. Tremblay (Eds.), *Preventing antisocial behavior* (pp. 253-282). New York: Guilford.

Duncan, D. F. (1994). The prevention of primary prevention, 1960-1994: Notes toward a case study. *Journal of Primary Prevention, 15*(1), 73-80.

Elias, M. J. (1995). Primary prevention as health and social competence promotion. *Journal of Primary Prevention, 16*(1), 5-24.

Empey, L. T., & Erickson, M. L. (1976). *The Provo experiment: Evaluating community control of delinquency.* Lexington, MA: Lexington Books.

Farrington, D. P. (1992). The need for longitudinal-experimental research on offending and antisocial behavior. In J. McCord & R. Tremblay (Eds.), *Preventing antisocial behavior* (pp. 353-376). New York: Guilford.

Feldman, R. A. (1992). The St. Louis experiment: Effective treatment of antisocial youths in prosocial peer groups. In J. McCord & R. Tremblay (Eds.), *Preventing antisocial behavior* (pp. 233-252). New York: Guilford.

Feldman, R. A., Caplinger, T. E., & Wodarski, J. S. (1983). *The St. Louis conundrum: The effective treatment of antisocial youths.* Englewood Cliffs, NJ: Prentice Hall.

Felner, R. D., & Adan, A. M. (1988). The school transition environment project: An ecological intervention and evaluation. In R. Price, E. Cowen, R. Lorion, & J. Ramos-McKay (Eds.), *14 ounces of prevention* (pp. 111-122). Washington, DC: American Psychological Association.

Freedman, J. L. (1975). *Crowding and behavior.* New York: Viking.

Geismar, L. L., & Wood, K. M. (1986). *Family and delinquency: Resocializing the young offender.* New York: Human Sciences Press.

Gold, M. (1987). Social ecology. In H. Quay (Ed.), *Handbook of juvenile delinquency* (pp. 62-105). New York: John Wiley.

Goldstein, A. P., & Glick, B. (1994). *The prosocial gang: Implementing aggression replacement training.* Thousand Oaks, CA: Sage.

Gordon, D. A., & Arbuthnot, J. (1987). Individual, group, and family interventions. In H. Quay (Ed.), *Handbook of juvenile delinquency* (pp. 290-324). New York: John Wiley.

Gordon, T. (1970). *Parent effectiveness training.* New York: Wyden.

Gottfredson, D. C., & Gottfredson, G. D. (1992). Theory-guided investigation: Three field experiments. In J. McCord & R. Tremblay (Eds.), *Preventing antisocial behavior* (pp. 311-349). New York: Guilford.

Gottfredson, G. D. (1987). Peer group interventions to reduce the risk of delinquent behavior: A selective review and a new evaluation. *Criminology, 25,* 671-714.

Gottschalk, R., Davidson, W.S., II, Gensheimer, L. K., & Mayer, J. P. (1987). Community-based interventions. In H. Quay (Ed.), *Handbook of juvenile delinquency* (pp. 266-289). New York: John Wiley.

Gutierrez, R., & Slavin, R. E. (1992). Achievement effects of the nongraded elementary school: A best evidence synthesis. *Review of Educational Research, 62,* 333-376.

Havens, G. G., & Stolz, J. W. (1989). Students teaching AIDS to students: Addressing AIDS in the adolescent population. *Public Health Reports, 104*(1), 75-79.

Hawkins, J. D., Catalano, R. F., Morrison, D. M., O'Donnell, J., Abbott, R. D., & Day, L. E. (1992). The Seattle Social Development Project: Effects of the first four years on protective factors and problem behaviors. In J. McCord & R. Tremblay (Eds.), *Preventing antisocial behavior* (pp. 139-161). New York: Guilford.

Hawkins, J. D., & Weis, J. G. (1985). The social development model: An integrative approach to delinquency prevention. *Journal of Primary Prevention, 6*(2), 73-97.

Holmes, C. T., & Matthews, K. M. (1984). The effects of nonpromotion on elementary and junior high school pupils: A meta-analysis. *Review of Educational Research, 54,* 225-236.

Howell, J. D. (Ed.). (1995). *Guide for implementing the comprehensive strategy for serious, violent, and chronic juvenile offenders.* Washington, DC: U.S. Department of Justice, Office of Juvenile Justice and Delinquency Prevention.

Is there lead in your water? (1993, February). *Consumer Report, 58,* 73-78.

Ittelson, W. H., Proshansky, H. M., Rivlin, G. G., Winkel, G. H., & Dempsey, D. (1974). *An introduction to environmental psychology.* New York: Holt, Rinehart & Winston.

Jason, L. A., & Rhodes, J. E. (1989). Children helping children: Implications for prevention. *Journal of Primary Prevention, 9*(4), 203-212.

Johnson, H. (1996, Jan.). Violence and biology: A review of the literature. *Families in Society,* pp. 3-18.

Kazdin, A. E., Siegel, T. C., & Bass, D. (1992). Cognitive problem-solving skills training and parent management training in the treatment of antisocial behavior in children. *Journal of Consulting and Clinical Psychology, 60,* 733-747.

Kellam, S. G., & Rebok, G. W. (1992). Building developmental and etiological theory through epidemiologically based preventive intervention trials. In J. McCord & R. Tremblay (Eds.), *Preventing antisocial behavior* (pp. 162-195). New York: Guilford.

Kellam, S. G., Rebok, G. W., Ialongo, N., & Mayer, L. S. (1994). The course and malleability of aggressive behavior from early first grade into middle school: Results of a developmental epidemiologically-based preventive trial. *Journal of Child Psychology and Psychiatry, 35,* 259-281.

Klein, N. C., Alexander, J. F., & Parsons, B. V. (1977). Impact of family systems intervention on recidivism and sibling delinquency: A model of primary prevention and program evaluation. *Journal of Consulting and Clinical Psychology, 45*(3), 469-474.

Kobrin, S., & Klein, M. W. (1982). *National evaluation of deinstitutionalization of status offender programs: Executive summary.* Washington, DC: U.S. Department of Justice, National Institute for Juvenile Justice and Delinquency Prevention.

Lane, T. W., & Davis, G. E. (1987). Child maltreatment and juvenile delinquency: Does a relationship exist? In J. Burchard & S. Burchard (Eds.), *Prevention of delinquent behavior* (pp. 122-138). Newbury Park, CA: Sage.

Levenstein, P. (1988). *Messages from home: The Mother-Child Home Program and the prevention of school disadvantage.* Columbus: Ohio State University Press.

Lindsay, B., & McGillis, D. (1986). Citywide community crime prevention: An assessment of the Seattle program. In D. P. Rosenbaum (Ed.), *Community crime prevention: Does it work?* (pp. 46-67). Beverly Hills, CA: Sage.

Lin-Fu, J. S. (1979). Lead poisoning in children. *Children Today, 8*(1), 9-14.

Loftin, C., McDowall, D., Wiersema, B., & Cottey, T. J. (1991). Effects of restrictive licensing of handguns on homicide and suicide in the District of Columbia. *New England Journal of Medicine, 325,* 1615-1620.

Lundman, R. J. (1984). *Prevention and control of juvenile delinquency.* New York: Oxford University Press.

Markman, H. J., Renick, M. J., Floyd, F., Stanley, S. M., & Clements, M. (1993). Preventing marital distress through effective communication and conflict management: A 4- and 5-year follow-up. *Journal of Consulting and Clinical Psychology, 47,* 743-749.

Marvel, J., Moreda, I., & Cook, I. (1993). *Developing conflict resolution skills in students: A study of the fighting fair model.* Miami, FL: Peace Education Foundation.

McCord, J., & Tremblay, R. E. (Eds.). (1992). *Preventing antisocial behavior: Interventions from birth through adolescence.* New York: Guilford.

Mednick, S. A. (1979). Biosocial factors and primary prevention of antisocial behavior. In S. A. Mednick & S. G. Shohad (Eds.), *New paths in criminology* (pp. 45-54). Lexington, MA: Lexington Books.

Michelson, L. (1987). Cognitive-behavioral strategies in the prevention and treatment of antisocial disorders in children and adolescents. In J. Burchard & S. Burchard (Eds.), *Prevention of delinquent behavior* (pp. 275-310). Newbury Park, CA: Sage.

Michelson, L., Sugai, D., Wood, R., & Kazdin, A. E. (1983). *Social skills assessment and training with children: An empirically-based handbook.* New York: Plenum.

Miller, W. B. (1962). The impact of a "total comunity" delinquency control project. *Social Problems, 10,* 168-191.

Monahan, J. T., & Vaux, A. (1980). Macroenvironment and community mental health. In P. M. Insel (Ed.), *Environmental variables and the prevention of mental illness.* Lexington, MA: Lexington Books.

Murphy, H. A., Hutchison, J. M., & Bailey, J. S. (1983). Behavioral school psychology goes outdoors: The effect of organized games on playground aggression. *Journal of Applied Behavioral Analysis, 16,* 29-35.

O'Donnell, C. R. (1992). The interplay of theory and practice in delinquency prevention: From behavior modification to activity settings. In J. McCord & R. Tremblay (Eds.), *Preventing antisocial behavior* (pp. 209-232). New York: Guilford.

O'Donnell, C. R., & Tharp, R. (1990). Community intervention guided by theoretical development. In A. S. Bellack, M. Hersen, & A. E. Kazdin (Eds.), *International handbook of behavior modification and therapy* (2nd ed., pp. 251-266). New York: Plenum.

Patterson, G. R. (1982). *Coercive family process.* Eugene, OR: Castalia.

Phillips, E. L. (1968). Achievement Place: Token reinforcement procedures in a home-style rehabilitation setting for "pre-delinquent" boys. *Journal of Applied Behavior Analysis, 1,* 213-223.

Quay, H. C. (Ed.). (1987). *Handbook of juvenile delinquency.* New York: John Wiley.

Safer, D. J. (1990). A school intervention for aggressive adolescents. In L. J. Hertzberg, G. Ostrum, & J. Field (Eds.), *Violent behavior. Vol. 1: Assessment and intervention.* Great Neck, NY: PMA.

Schinke, S. P., & Gilchrist, L. D. (1984). *Life skills counseling with adolescents.* Baltimore: University Park Press.

Schorr, A. (1963). *Slums and social insecurity.* New York: Macmillan.

Schweinhart, L., & Weikart, D. (1988). The High/Scope Perry preschool program. In R. Price, E. Cowen, R. Lorion, & J. Ramos-McKay (Eds.), *14 ounces of prevention* (pp. 53-66). Washington, DC: American Psychological Association.

Shaw, C. R., & McKay, H. D. (1969). *Juvenile delinquency and urban areas* (rev. ed.). Chicago: University of Chicago Press. (Originally published in 1942)

Shure, M. B., & Spivak, G. (1988). Interpersonal cognitive problem-solving. In R. Price, E. Cowen, R. Lorion, & J. Ramos-McKay (Eds.), *14 ounces of prevention* (pp. 69-82). Washington, DC: American Psychological Association.

Slavin, R. E. (1987). Ability grouping and student achievement in elementary school: A best-evidence synthesis. *Review of Educational Research, 57,* 293-336.

Slavin, R. E. (1990a). Class size and student achievement: Is smaller better? *Contemporary Education, 42,* 6-12.

Slavin, R. E. (1990b). *Cooperative learning: Theory, research, and practice.* Englewood Cliffs, NJ: Prentice Hall.

Slavin, R. E. (1994). School and classroom organization in beginning reading: Class size, aides, and instructional groupings. In R. E. Slavin, N. Karweit, & B. Wasik (Eds.), *Preventing early school failure: Research, policy, and practice* (pp. 122-142). Boston: Allyn & Bacon.

Slavin, R. E., & Madden, N. A. (1989). Effective classroom programs for students at risk. In R. E. Slavin, N. Karweit, & N. Madden (Eds.), *Effective programs for students at risk*. Boston: Allyn & Bacon.

Tharp, R. G., & Wetzel, B. J. (1969). *Behavior modification in the natural environment*. New York: Academic Press.

Thomas, A., & Chess, S. (1977). *Temperament and development*. New York: Brunner/Mazel.

Thompson, D. W., & Jason, L. A. (1988). Street gangs and preventive interventions. *Criminal Justice and Behavior, 15,* 323-333.

Trasler, G. (1987). Biogenetic factors. In H. Quay (Ed.), *Handbook of juvenile delinquency* (pp. 184-215). New York: John Wiley.

Tremblay, R. E., Vitaro, F., Bertrand, L., LeBlanc, M., Beauchesne, H., Boileau, H., & David, L. (1992). Parent and child training to prevent early onset of delinquency: The Montreal longitudinal-experimental study. In J. McCord & R. Tremblay (Eds.), *Preventing antisocial behavior* (pp. 117-138). New York: Guilford.

Wasik, B. A., & Slavin, R. E. (1994). Preventing early reading failure with one-to-one tutoring: A review of five programs. In R. E. Slavin, N. Karweit, & B. Wasik (Eds.), *Preventing early school failure: Research, policy, and practice* (pp. 143-174). Boston: Allyn & Bacon.

Werner, E. E. (1987). Vulnerability and resiliency in children at risk for delinquency: A longitudinal study from birth to young adulthood. In J. Burchard & S. Burchard (Eds.), *Prevention of delinquent behavior* (pp. 16-43). Newbury Park, CA: Sage.

Werner, E. E., & Smith, R. S. (1992). *Overcoming the odds: High risk children from birth to adulthood*. Ithaca, NY: Cornell University Press.

Index

About the Editors

Thomas P. Gullotta, MA, MSW, is CEO of Child and Family Agency of Southeastern Connecticut. He currently is the Editor of the *Journal of Primary Prevention*. For Sage Publications, he serves as a general series book editor for *Advances in Adolescent Development* and is the senior book series editor of *Issues in Children's and Families' Lives*. For Plenum, he serves as the series editor for *Prevention in Practice*. In addition, he holds editorial appointments on the *Journal of Early Adolescence, Adolescence,* and the *Journal of Educational and Psychological Consultation*. He serves on the board of the National Mental Health Association and is an adjunct faculty member in the Psychology Department of Eastern Connecticut State University.

Gerald R. Adams is Professor of Family Relations and Human Development at the University of Guelph. His research interests include the study of personality and social development, family-school contexts and individual development, and developmental patterns in identity formation during adolescence and young adulthood. He is a fellow of the American Psychological Association and American Psychological Society. He has editorial assignments with such publications as the *Journal of Adolescent Research, Journal of Adolescence, Journal of Early Adolescence,* and the *Journal of Primary Prevention,* among others. He teaches courses in adolescent development at both the undergraduate and graduate levels at the University of Guelph.

Raymond Montemayor is Associate Professor of Psychology at Ohio State University. His research interests include parent-adolescent relations, especially the study of conflict and stress between parents and adolescents. In addition, he is interested in the effect of peer relations on adolescent social development. He is Associate Editor for the *Journal of Early Adolescence* and is an editorial board member for the *Journal of Adolescent Research*.

About the Contributors

Evvie Becker, PhD, Assistant Professor of Clinical Psychology at the University of Connecticut, was a 1993-1994 Fellow at Harvard University and Boston Children's Hospital, funded by a National Research Service grant for family violence research. Prior to that appointment, she was a 1992-1993 Congressional Science Fellow sponsored by the American Psychological Association (APA), working for U.S. Senator Christopher J. Dodd in his capacity as chairman of the Senate Labor Subcommittee on Children. Dr. Becker is coauthor (with Annette U. Rickel) of the book, *Keeping Children From Harm's Way: The Impact of National Policy on Human Development*, published by APA (1997). She was a 1991-1992 Psychology Fellow in Pediatrics at Harbor-UCLA Medical Center. Dr. Becker serves on the board of directors for the Connecticut Children's Law Center, was a member of APA's ad hoc Committee on Legal and Ethical Issues in the Treatment of Interpersonal Violence, and served on APA's Committee on Legal Issues from 1994 to 1996. Prior to receiving her doctorate (University of Connecticut, 1991), she was a Public Information Officer for the National Aeronautics and Space Administration and received a NASA Special Achievement Award in 1985.

Martin Bloom received his PhD in social psychology from the University of Michigan after obtaining a diploma in social study (social work) from the University of Edinburgh. He has taught in schools of social work most of his career. Among his publications are *Primary Prevention Practice* (1996) and *Primary Prevention: The Possible Science* (1981).

Charles M. Borduin, PhD, is Professor of Psychology at the University of Missouri—Columbia and Director of the Missouri Delinquency Project. He received his doctorate in clinical psychology from the University of Memphis and interned at Rutgers Medical

314

School. His research interests include adolescent violent and sexual offending, family dysfunction, and the development and refinement of a multisystemic treatment approach for serious juvenile offenders. Dr. Borduin has published extensively in the areas of juvenile delinquency and adolescent psychopathology, and he has served as a consultant to numerous state and federal agencies on the reform of children's mental health services.

A. Cattarello, PhD, is an Assistant Professor of Sociology in the Department of Sociology and Anthropology at the University of Wisconsin—Eau Claire. While at the University of Kentucky, Dr. Cattarello served as the study director for the National Institute on Drug Abuse grant to examine the effectiveness of the DARE program in Lexington. She has published in the area of adolescent prevention, HIV, and criminology. Her research interests include communities, crime, women, and HIV.

R. R. Clayton, PhD, has extensive experience in drug and alcohol research, having been principal investigator for the National Institute on Drug Abuse (NIDA)-funded DARE study and the Manhattan Survey of Young Men. He is the principal investigator for the University of Kentucky's NIDA-funded Center for Prevention Research and has served on the NIDA National Advisory Council. Dr. Clayton has also served on the NIDA Resource Development and Training Committee and the Epidemiology and Prevention grant review committee. He currently serves on the Center's grant review committee. Dr. Clayton is also a member of various committees for the National Institute on Drug Abuse and the Center for Substance Abuse Prevention, and he has served on two Institute of Medicine Committees. He is currently a national program director for the Robert Wood Johnson Foundation and the Chair of the Research Network on Tobacco Dependence.

J. Mark Eddy, PhD, is a researcher at the Oregon Prevention Research Center, part of the Oregon Social Learning Center (www.oslc.org) in Eugene, Oregon. His research focuses on the development and refinement of interventions to prevent parent and child problem behaviors. He is particularly interested in the prevention of conduct disorders.

Daniel J. Flannery is Associate Professor of Criminal Justice Studies at Kent State University. His research focuses on developmental psychopathology and youth violence. He serves on the editorial board of several adolescent and family journals. He is coeditor (with C. R. Huff) of the forthcoming book *Youth Violence: Prevention, Intervention and Social Policy* for American Psychiatric Press, and he is principal investigator of a longitudinal study of youth violence prevention funded by the Centers for Disease Control and Prevention.

Robert Googins, M.B.A., LL.B., is Professor of Law at the University of Connecticut where he has taught a course on Dickens and the law for many years. He is the founder and past director of that school's insurance center. He served as insurance commissioner for the State of Connecticut under the Weicker administration. Prior to that position, he was executive vice-president and general counsel for Connecticut Mutual Life Insurance Company. In addition to his teaching responsibilities, he is currently the executive director of the Insurance Marketplace Standards Association in Washington, DC.

Laurie Swanson Gribskov, PhD, is Adjunct Professor with the Institute on Violence and Destructive Behavior in the College of Education at the University of Oregon. She is an elected municipal official and serves as the president of the Eugene City Council. She also chairs the Lane County Public Safety Coordinating Council. Prior to her current position, she was Executive Director of the Southern Willamette Private Industry Council. Her research focuses on public policy implementation and the evolution of youth gangs.

C. Ronald Huff, PhD, is Director and Professor in the School of Public Policy and Management and Director of the Criminal Justice Research Center at The Ohio State University. He has recently completed two major studies of gangs. His ten books include *Gangs in America* (2nd ed.) and *The Gang Intervention Handbook.* He is coeditor (with D. Flannery) of the forthcoming book *Youth Violence: Prevention, Intervention and Social Policy* for American Psychiatric Press.

Pam Jenkins is Associate Professor of Sociology at the University of New Orleans. The focus of her research is behaviors and attitudes related to violence and crime. She is coeditor of *Preventing Violence in America* (1996) and also of *Witnessing for Sociology: Sociologists in the Courts* (1996). In addition, she has published articles in *Social Work, Behavioral Sciences and the Law, Impact Assessment,* and *Journal of Family Issues.*

C. G. Leukefeld, DSW, has published in the areas of drug abuse prevention and intervention research. He served in various capacities at the National Institute on Drug Abuse (NIDA), including the Chief of the Prevention Branch as well as the Deputy Director of the Division of Clinical Research, before coming to the University of Kentucky. Currently, he is the principal investigator for the NIDA-funded Kentucky AIDS Outreach Cooperative Agreement, the Center for Substance Abuse Treatment State Needs Assessment Studies, the NIDA-funded Adolescent Follow Up Study, and for a NIDA Stage I Behavioral Therapy grant. Dr. Leukefeld serves as a consultant to federal agencies and currently is on the NIDA Health Serves grant review committee.

T. K. Logan, PhD, has experience in managing and designing large national evaluations for health-related social programs. Dr. Logan has served as the study director for a national study of nutrition education training and a WIC/Head Start Cooperative Study. She designed and directed a national study of services integration and needs assessment study of pregnant and mothering adolescents for the U.S. Department of Agriculture, Food and Consumer Service. Dr. Logan is currently a postdoctoral scholar at the Center on Drug and Alcohol Research at the University of Kentucky and is the study director for a National Institute on Drug Abuse-funded Adolescent Follow Up Study and for a federally funded study by the Center for Substance Abuse Prevention.

D. Lynam recently received his PhD in clinical psychology from the University of Wisconsin—Madison and is currently Assistant Professor in the Department of Psychology at the University of Kentucky. His research interests include the role of individual difference factors in deviance across the life course. He has published numerous articles on cognitive factors in adolescent delinquency, and his most recent work deals with the early identification of chronic offenders.

Michael Manos is Assistant Professor in the Department of Psychiatry, Case Western Reserve University, University Hospitals of Cleveland. He is also Clinical Director of University Hospital's ADHD program. Dr. Manos received his doctorate in special education and clinical psychology from the University of Arizona. He taught and conducted educational research at the University of Hawaii and was executive director of a school for learning disabled and ADHD children in Honolulu.

C. Martin, PhD, has extensive clinical experience as a child psychiatrist. She is interested in hyperactivity and has practiced and published in this area. She has also studied and published in the area of adolescent impulsivity and substance abuse, as well as conduct disorder and impulsivity. She has a particular interest in biochemical markers and their relationship with substance abuse.

Aleta L. Meyer, PhD, is Assistant Professor of Psychology at Virginia Commonwealth University and Director of Training for the Life Skills Center. She received her PhD in human development and family studies from Penn State. Her specialization is the development, evaluation, and improvement of prevention and health promotion programs for young adolescents.

R. Milich, PhD, has extensive experience as a psychologist in studying children and their transition through early adulthood. His primary research focus is attention deficit and hyperactivity disorder (ADHD), and he has published more than 70 papers and chapters dealing with long-term outcomes, peer relations, attention and comprehension, and classification issues among this population. He is currently Associate Editor of the *Journal of Abnormal Psychology*, the premier journal in the field.

Annette U. Rickel is Professor of Psychology at Wayne State University and a clinical professor in the Department of Psychiatry at Georgetown University Medical Center. Recently, she was a Senior Congressional Fellow and worked on the Health Policy staff of U.S. Senator Donald W. Riegle, Jr. In addition, she served on President Clinton's Task Force for National Health Care Reform and staffed the Mental Health Work Group. She received her PhD from the University of Michigan and is a Fellow and past president of the APA Society for Community Research and Action. Her research has focused on identification and intervention with high-risk populations and has been published in numerous scientific journals as well as several books. Currently, she is working on the development of a training program in managed care for graduating physicians and allied health care professionals that has been funded by the Kellogg Foundation.

Cindy M. Schaeffer, MA, is a doctoral student in the clinical psychology program at the University of Missouri—Columbia. She received her master's degree in clinical psychology from the University of Missouri and her bachelor's degree from the University of Maryland. Her research interests include sibling relations of delinquent adolescents, family dysfunction, and community psychology.

Robert D. Sege is Assistant Professor of Pediatrics at Tufts University School of Medicine and a member of the Division of General Pediatrics at The Floating Hospital for Children at New England Medical Center. He graduated from Yale College, received his PhD in biology from MIT in 1987, and received his MD from Harvard Medical School in 1988. He completed training in pediatrics at the Children's Hospital, Boston, MA in 1991. Dr. Sege is currently the Director of the Pediatric and Adolescent Health Research Center at New England Medical Center and Assistant Chief of the Division of General Pediatrics at The Floating Hospital for Children. His research involves the development of a health care response to adolescent peer violence and its prevention. His research has been supported by a Robert Wood Johnson Generalist Physician Faculty Scholarship award.

Ruth Seydlitz is Associate Professor of Sociology at the University of New Orleans. She is primarily interested in juvenile delinquency and has published studies about this subject in *Youth & Society* and *Sociological Spectrum,* and in Concetta Culliver's book, *Female Criminality: The State of the Art.* She has also completed research concerning the impact of the offshore petroleum industry on

Louisiana communities and the effect of media presentations of hazards and disasters on the public's responses.

Cassandra A. Stanton, MS, is a doctoral student in the child specialty track of the clinical psychology program at Virginia Commonwealth University. Her primary research interests include the etiology, assessment, and treatment of child and adolescent behavior problems. She is currently working on an NCI research grant designed to promote health behaviors in rural youth.

R. Zimmerman, PhD, is Associate Professor in the Department of Behavioral Science. He is currently a coprincipal investigator in the final year of a NIDA-funded epidemiologic and prevention study. Dr. Zimmerman had primary responsibility for gaining consent and tracking subjects over 3 years. He has also been involved in several CDC-funded studies of HIV prevention, education, problem behaviors, and sexually transmitted diseases in adolescents and young adults.